THE LIFE AND MUSIC OF BÉLA BARTÓK

Bartók soon after arrival in New York, c. 1941.

THE LIFE

AND MUSIC OF

BÉLA

BARTÓK

By HALSEY STEVENS

REVISED EDITION

OXFORD UNIVERSITY PRESS

LONDON   OXFORD   NEW YORK

OXFORD UNIVERSITY PRESS

London   Oxford   New York
Glasgow   Toronto   Melbourne   Wellington
Cape Town   Ibadan   Nairobi   Dar es Salaam   Lusaka   Addis Ababa
Delhi   Bombay   Calcutta   Madras   Karachi   Lahore   Dacca
Kuala Lumpur   Singapore   Hong Kong   Tokyo

TO HARRIETT, *my wife,*
this book is gratefully dedicated

THE history of Hungarian music earlier than the sixteenth century must be deduced from its remains in the music of the peasants, and from the comparatively few references to musical practices made by early writers. Unlike the music of western Europe, its roots are predominantly oriental; when one considers the divergent influences that have affected Hungary itself, the character of its indigenous music should occasion no surprise. Closed in by the great semicircle of the Carpathians, which sweep for nearly a thousand miles along Hungary's historic frontiers, and halted in their westward expansion by the successful resistance of the Germans in Austria, the Magyars were long prevented from a normal intercourse with the nations of western and central Europe. The Balkan Peninsula to the south, with its irregular mountain ranges, formed a further barrier; but within the Carpathian Basin, extending from the *Porta Hungarica* at Dévény to the spectacular Iron Gates, where the Danube cuts through the Transylvanian Alps, the Magyars developed a closely integrated state.

Parts of the Carpathian Basin were once incorporated into the Roman Empire. Transdanubia in the west, called *Pannonia* in Latin, was a Roman province, and the Dacian state in the east came under Roman rule during the reign of Trajan; but the Romans were repatriated before the end of the third century after Christ, and the colonies were abandoned. Thereafter came the great migratory waves from Asia: first the Ostrogoths, a Teutonic people, dislodged from the territory north of the Black Sea by the pressure of the Huns; then the Huns themselves, and the Avars, both Turkic peoples, pushed westward after the annihilation of their Asiatic empire by the Chinese; and, to a lesser extent, the Slavic peoples, who infiltrated rather than conquered.

Toward the end of the ninth century the Magyars arrived. Their origin has been traced, chiefly through the Magyar language itself, to a fusion of Finno-Ugric and Turko-Bulgar races before the fifth century of this era. By that time they had already begun their migrations. From the eastern slopes of the Urals they moved to the vicinity of the Sea of Azov in the Caucasus, where from their association with other Turkic peoples they developed into a nomadic but thoroughly disciplined race of conquerors. As a part of the Kazar Empire, which fell under eastern attack in the ninth century, the Magyars were again dislodged. For nearly sixty years they lived in the region between the Dnieper and the Don, and later in the low country above the estuary of the Danube; from here they moved only once more, to settle in the Carpathian-ringed Danube Basin in the winter of 895-6.

Though the wanderings of the Magyars were over, they continued to look in the direction of western Europe until their defeat by the Germans in the battle of Lechfeld, A.D. 955. Thereupon they consolidated their gains and settled down to become a primarily agricultural people. They apparently absorbed the tribes already present in the area, but later immigration, some of it encouraged by István (Saint Stephen), the first king of Hungary, brought in Germans and other minority groups, including Ruthenians, Romanians, Slovenes, and Croats. István, together with his father, Géza, was largely responsible for the Christianization of Hungary, and also for its alliance with western Europe rather than the eastern Orthodox countries.

With the advent of Christianity, remains of the pagan period—literature and music, for example—quickly disappeared; in the plainsong period that followed, few indications of any indigenous music are to be found. In 1241 the Tartars, who under Jenghiz Khan had conquered a territory that reached from China to the Carpathians, pierced the mountain fortress and overran Hungary, as well as Poland to the north and Cumania to the southeast. Crossing into Transdanubia, the Golden Horde left devastation everywhere; but they withdrew from Hungary after a single year, though they remained in control of Russia for another century.

With the extinction of the Árpád dynasty in 1301, the military and economic systems of Hungary were reorganized under the Anjou kings, and foreign ties strengthened. By the end of the fourteenth century the population of Hungary had increased to more than three million, with 49 cities, several hundred towns (mezővárosok), and thousands of villages. It was during this century that the Ottoman

Empire became a threat to Hungary; the Turks invaded Europe, subdued the Serbians, and in so doing undermined the whole Byzantine Empire. The Balkan principalities to the south and southeast of Hungary were developed as buffer states, but could not long delay the advance of the Turks; nor could the temporary victories of János Hunyadi, brilliant as they were, stem the tide. Hunyadi's son Mátyás (Matthias Corvinus) assumed the throne in 1458. Besides building up a powerful empire, he offered the greatest encouragement to science and culture, bringing to Hungary many fine scholars and artists to enrich his library and court. With his death in 1490, his ideals of statesmanship were abandoned, and Hungary entered a period of comparative inactivity which reached its culmination in the summer of 1526, when Lajos II led his pitifully small army into battle against the Turks on the plains of Mohács, only to have his forces wiped out.

Until the very end of the seventeenth century Hungary was occupied by the Turks, and the imprint of that occupation is still felt. Hungarian students, barred from travel to Italy and other countries of western Europe, completed their studies in Krakow and Wittenberg. The folk poetry of the Magyars incorporated Turkish motifs, and their folk music apparently became impregnated with characteristics of Turkish music.

During this whole period, after the introduction of Christianity in the eleventh century, the cultivated music of Hungary was that of western Europe, plainsong and Protestant hymnody leading the way. For centuries the Church armed itself against the infiltration of Hungarian secular music with its pronounced Eastern characteristics, but nevertheless the secular style ultimately colored the music of the Church. There are rather obvious disparities: the monody of all oriental music as opposed to the polyphony of western European music, the modal and pentatonic melodic structure of the Magyar tunes as opposed to the diatonic major-minor system, the melismatic fioritura of the eastern melodies.

That ornamentation was intensified by the fantastic improvisations of the gipsies, who appeared in eastern Europe in the fifteenth century, coming apparently from northwest India, to whose language their own, Romany, is closely related. Nomadic, traveling in small groups, they quickly established themselves in all of Europe, including the British Isles; but it was in Hungary, Romania, and Spain that

they became most firmly entrenched. The relation of the gipsy to
the peasant music of Hungary has been the subject of much investigation. Ferenc Liszt credited the gipsy with having originated the
music of Hungary, and the Magyar with its debasement—conclusions
diametrically opposed to those Bartók, Kodály, and others reached
in this century.

After the Turkish invasion, Hungary was at war for 300 years,
defending itself and all of western Europe against the encroachment
of the Turks, and at the same time trying to ward off the incursions
of the Court of Vienna. These struggles colored a large share of the
music of Hungary. Sir Philip Sidney, who spent some time in Hungary in 1573, wrote in his *Apologie for Poetrie* (c. 1581) that at each
festival and each entertainment he heard songs about the bravery
of earlier heroes. Many references to events of the period are to be
found in the peasant songs collected by Bartók and others in the past
fifty years.

The musical life of the cities was strengthened in the seventeenth
century, with seignorial orchestras and musical ensembles among the
middle classes. The war of Ferenc Rákóczy for Hungarian liberty
gave rise to the Kuruc songs, with their fervent, often savage, patriot-
ism, and the *verbunkos*,[1] whose romantico-heroic style dominated
Hungarian music for a hundred years or more.

No significant native composer arose in Hungary until the nineteenth century. The musical culture of the country was weakened by
the migration of more and more foreign musicians, especially Germans, who were particularly strong in Pozsony, Kassa, and Kolozsvár.
Hungarian musicians wrote in the German style, and the early nineteenth century, characterized by Bihari, Csermák, and Lavotta, was
dilettante in spirit. With the awakening of a national consciousness
as a consequence of the romantic movement, Hungary produced her
first important composer, Ferenc Erkel. But he remained isolated in
his native country, and after the war of independence in 1848-9,
which ended with the exile of the patriot Lajos Kossuth, the future
of Hungarian nationalism, including national art, appeared dim.

The neo-Hungarianism of Erkel, Liszt, Mosonyi, and their contemporaries, founded as it was upon the *verbunkos*-style, did little

---

[1] German *Werbung* = recruiting. The *verbunkos* was a dance performed by
uniformed Hussars with the purpose of attracting young idlers, getting them in-
toxicated, and 'inducting' them into the army.

toward establishing an autochthonous Hungarian school. Most of these accepted as manifestations of an authentic Magyar *melos* the effusions of dilettante composers of the early nineteenth century, as they accepted with equal enthusiasm the distortions of the gipsy fiddlers, brushing off as debased the tunes of the peasants themselves.

Though a native of Hungary, Liszt was by training and inclination a German composer, and when in 1875 the government made him president of the new Academy of Music in Budapest, Erkel being director, the work in composition was given to Robert Volkmann, a German composer who kept aloof from the problems of a specifically Hungarian music although he spent a large part of his life in Hungary. When he died in 1883, the chair of composition passed to another German, Hans Koessler, a pupil of Rheinberger, who lived in Budapest for more than forty years without even learning the Hungarian language.

It was with Koessler that Bartók studied when he went to Budapest, ostensibly to avoid the Germanizing influence of Vienna. Kodály and Dohnányi were also Koessler's pupils. All three began composition strongly influenced by the Germanic tradition; Dohnányi never freed himself from it, but the pronounced nationalism of Bartók and Kodály led them early to seek means of national expression in music, and when they came into contact with Hungarian peasant music, ignored as corrupt by their predecessors, they found in it elements which, once assimilated, were to lead them to the production of an art music as Hungarian as its sources and yet international in its communication.

The literature on Bartók, spotty and incomplete during his lifetime, has burgeoned in the years since his death. To the early books by Nüll and Haraszti have been added biographical studies by Moreux, Geraedts, Lesznaj, Citron, Szegő, and Székely, and especially the exhaustive documentary biography by János Demény. Numerous technical analyses have appeared, among them those of Lendvai, Engelmann, and Uhde. Demény has edited three volumes of Bartók's letters in Hungarian and one in German; several volumes of Bartók's writings on music have been published in various languages. The periodical literature is enormous.

While the majority of Bartók's musico-ethnological works are still

out of print, the Hungarian Academy of Sciences has published five
volumes of an extensive series based upon the folksong research of Bartók and Kodály; and the Slovakian Academy has issued the first of three
volumes of Bartók's Slovakian research. The study of Romanian folk
music is soon to be published.

This book is concerned primarily with Bartók's music, approached
from both the analytical and the critical points of view. The biographical study makes no pretense of exhaustive or definitive treatment; that must come later, when source materials are more readily
available. The material for the biographical section has been derived
mainly from three sources: Bartók's autobiographical sketch (1921),
his letters (both the published volumes and a number of unpublished items), and a detailed account of his childhood and youth,
prepared in 1921-2 by his mother, Paula Voit Bartók, for her grandson. Many of those who knew Bartók, a privilege denied the author,
have filled in details.

The opinion has been expressed [1] that Bartók's letters are lacking
in human interest; that they are so impersonal that no insight can be
gained through them into the character or personality of the writer.
I hold the contrary opinion. The several hundred so far published,
read in chronological order, cannot help but vividly re-create their
author. For that reason the chapters which follow quote generously
from them; if a lack of balance results, it is only because letters from
certain periods are still inaccessible.

In general, the music has been discussed chronologically within
its several categories. It has seemed more appropriate to group the
string quartets in a separate chapter than to interrupt their succession
to consider the other chamber works; and the chapter on the vocal
music has been subdivided into three parts: the original works for
voice and piano; the folksong arrangements for voice and piano;
and the choral works, concluding with the *Cantata profana*. With the
separation of the music from the biographical essay, and with the
division of the music itself into several groups on the basis of media,
there is necessarily some duplication, some retracing of steps, in the
course of the book.

[1] Heinsheimer, Hans W. *Fanfare for Two Pigeons*. Garden City: Doubleday
& Co., Inc., 1952, p. 111.

The chronological table of Bartók's works is as complete as it can be made at present. Since some of Bartók's early manuscripts are still in Hungary, others in the Bartók Archives in New York, it is not yet possible to guarantee complete accuracy. The bibliography is selective.

Grateful acknowledgment is made to all those who have assisted in the preparation of this book. The University of Southern California made available a faculty research grant; Boosey and Hawkes, Bartók's publishers, loaned the scores of several works not now in print. Among those who provided material in one form or another were Péter Bartók, Betty Randolph Bean, Constantin Brăiloiu, Storm Bull, Elizabeth Sprague Coolidge, George Dawson, János Demény, Ernő Dohnányi, Wilhelmine Creel Driver, Isabelle Ebert, Laurent Halleux, Irene Hanna, Ralph Hawkes, George Herzog, Jenő Kerpely, Harrison Kerr, Gyula Kertész, Rudolf Kolisch, Colin Mason, Yehudi Menuhin, Douglas Moore, Paul Pisk, Margit Prahács, Germain Prevost, William Primrose, Feri Roth, A. Adnan Saygun, Tibor Serly, Harold Spivacke, Mr. and Mrs. Zoltán Székely, Joseph Szigeti, Randall Thompson, Margit Varró, Anthony Vazzana, Imre Waldbauer, Bette Weinstock, and Dean Witter; the contributions of these and innumerable others have been of inestimable value. To my dear friend Stephen Deák special thanks are due for his assistance in translation and his instruction in the rudiments of the Hungarian language; I am also deeply indebted to Mrs. Dénes Koromzay, who translated Paula Bartók's account of her son's early life, as well as other source materials.

Among those to whom I am indebted for assistance in the preparation of this edition are Victor Bátor, Trustee of the Bartók Estate; David Clegg, Benjamin Suchoff, Bence Szabolcsi, István Szelényi, and András Szőllősy.

For permission to quote from Bartók's music I am obligated to Boosey and Hawkes; to the Oxford University Press for the excerpts from Bartók's *Hungarian Folk Music* and from Léon Vallas's *Claude Debussy, His Life and Works*; to Henry Holt and Company for an extract from Virgil Thomson's *Music Right and Left*; to Faber and Faber Ltd. and Charles Scribner's Sons for a paragraph from Constant Lambert's *Music Ho! A Study of Music in Decline*; to G. Schirmer, Inc., for a brief quotation from a *Musical Quarterly* article by Milton Babbitt; to *Musical America* for a few lines from an article by Harry Cassin Becker; and to John N. Burk for Bartók's notes on the Concerto for Orchestra, from the Boston Symphony Orchestra programs. My graduate class in the Music of Bartók, at the University of Southern California, was the proving ground for many of the ideas expressed in this book.

Carl A. Rosenthal is responsible for the musical autography, while Gabriel D. Hackett and Ernest Nash supplied many photographs, of which several were chosen as illustrations.

And finally, the dedication of this volume is intended partially to repay my obligation to one who, by her sympathetic understanding and encouragement, has had a very great share in its writing.

THE necessity for a new edition has made it possible to take advantage of ten years of Bartók scholarship since the first publication of this work. Errors have been corrected wherever discovered, translations reconsidered; works previously unknown have been examined and discussed. Since every major work and many smaller ones have been recorded, some of them many times, it has seemed supererogatory to include a Discography, and the reader is referred therefore to the current catalogues of records and tapes. The Bibliography has been extended by the inclusion of the more important studies, but it is manifestly impossible within the scope of this book to include more than a sampling of the many hundreds of items recently published.

H. S.

Inglewood, Calif.
January, 1964

A NOTE ON PRONUNCIATION

HUNGARIAN is one of the Finno-Ugric languages, unrelated to the Italic, Germanic, Celtic, Slavonic, and other Indo-European tongues. Every word is stressed on the first syllable, no matter whether it is long or short; vowels with one (ó) or two (ő) accents are prolonged, those without accents (o, ö) always short. Doubled consonants are doubly pronounced. Each of the characters in the Hungarian alphabet has only one sound; these are approximated in the table below.

a—short, rather like *au* in *caught*
á—long, like *a* in *father*
b—as in *but*
c (cz)—like *ts* in *its*
cs—like *ch* in *church*
d—as in *door*
e—short, between *e* in *let* and *a* in *cap*
é—long, like *a* in *cape*
f—as in *fun*
g—as in *get*
gy—like *d* in *duty*
h—always aspirated except at the end of a word
i—short, nearly like *i* in *it*, or *ee* in *meet*
í—long, like *i* in *police*
j—like *y* in *yes*
k—as in *kite*
l—as in *life*
ly—rather like *y* in *yes*, but slightly liquid
m—as in *met*
n—as in *not*

ny—like *gn* in French *campagne* (almost like *ni* in *onion*)

o—short, like *o* in *poker*

ó—long, like *o* in *nose*

ö—short, like *eu* in French *peu*

ő—long, like *eu* in French *beurre*

p—as in *paper*

r—as in *ring*

s—like *sh* in *shame*

sz—like *s* in *sin*

t—as in *time*

ty—rather like *t* in *virtue*

u—short, like *oo* in *boot*

ú—long, like *oo* in *mood*

ü—short, like *u* in French *nu*

ű—long, like *u* in French *brume*

v—as in *verve*

z—as in *zeal*

zs—like *s* in *pleasure*, *j* in French *jour*

A further note:

According to Hungarian custom, the family name is followed, not preceded, by the baptismal name. This leads to confusion in countries where the reverse prevails. In this book the western order is employed: Béla Bartók, rather than Bartók Béla, which is correct in Hungary. But it is worth mention that in at least one instance—Kodály's *Háry János*—we have accepted the Hungarian order instead of changing it to *János* (or John) *Háry*.

CONTENTS

LIST OF ILLUSTRATIONS

I

BIOGRAPHICAL STUDY

THERE is bitter irony in the fact that not one of the Hungarian towns in which Béla Bartók spent his youth is now within the boundaries of Hungary. The Treaty of Trianon, in June 1920, stripped Hungary of two-thirds of her territory and half of her population, allotting to Romania, Yugoslavia, and Czechoslovakia land that had been Hungarian for more than a thousand years.

To Bartók, whose profoundly nationalistic spirit had been nurtured by his research in Hungarian and related cultures, the dismemberment of his native country came as a deep, personal tragedy. His feelings may be perceived throughout his correspondence and other writing—at the end of his autobiographical sketch, in many of his published articles on musical ethnology—and they are evident as well in much of his later music, in which the undercurrent of psychological pessimism is translated into something more intense, and in which it is occasionally, and for the first time, replaced by a feeling of resignation.

Béla Viktor János Bartók was born in the Torontál district of Hungary, 25 March 1881. The whole district has been absorbed into Romania,[1]* forming the westernmost tip of that country; Nagyszent-

* The notes appear on pages 309 to 322.

3

miklós, which was Bartók's birthplace, is now called Sânmiclăuşul
mare. The town lies just east of the Tisza river, in the great Alföld,
a farming region of much importance. Bartók's father (also named
Béla) was director of a government agricultural school—one of those
training schools, fairly numerous in Hungary, in which modern farming methods are taught by both theory and practice.

The elder Bartók was a man of ability, with many enthusiasms,
music among them. Writing of him in 1921, Bartók described him as
a gifted musician who not only played the piano, and learned to play
the cello so that he might play in a little amateur orchestra, but also
composed dance pieces. He died on 4 August 1888, when the child
was only seven years old; thus it was not primarily through his father's
interests that Béla Bartók was led into music as a career.

In 1921 and 1922, Paula Voit, Bartók's mother, set down for her
grandson an account of the composer's early life; and it is from this [2]
and from Bartók's own autobiographical sketch [3] that knowledge of
this period must be drawn. For the later periods his published correspondence [4] is an inexhaustible source of information.

His childhood was beset by illness, although he had been a
healthy baby. Vaccinated for smallpox at the age of three months,
he suffered for a number of years with a recurrent skin rash, or
eczema, which disappeared during a fever but returned as the fever
subsided. This lasted until he was five years old, and the child hid
from people in embarrassment. Other sickness, including pneumonia,
delayed him in learning to walk, and he was past two years old
before he began to talk. Much earlier, however, he had displayed an
interest in music as his nurse sang to him, and especially as his
mother played the piano. Paula Bartók recalled that at a year and a
half he listened intently to a specific piece, smiling and nodding his
head; the next day he brought her to the piano and shook his head
until she played the right piece. At three he was given a drum, which
he beat in time to his mother's playing; if she changed the rhythm,
he would stop momentarily and then begin again in the new rhythm.
A year later he was playing from memory—with one finger—as many
as forty songs.

Bartók was a serious, quiet child; prevented by the state of his
health from playing with other children, he spent a great deal of
time listening to his mother's songs and stories. A bronchial condition
developed when he was five; a few months later an examination dis-

closed what was diagnosed as a spinal curvature, and the child was subjected to drastic treatment, not being permitted to sit down, taking his meals standing, and when exhausted, allowed only to lie supine on floor or ground—to discover upon consultation with a physician in Budapest that the provincial practitioner's diagnosis had been in error. A 'cold-water cure' at Radegund when he was six was apparently beneficial, and the next year he began school, where he learned readily and enjoyed his work despite the lack of competition, finishing the fourth elementary class with nothing but 'firsts.'

In the meantime his musical training began. His mother tells of the first concert the young Bartók heard—one given by the amateur orchestra in which his father played, led by a gipsy musician with some education. In Nagyszentmiklós a formal concert was quite unknown, but an orchestra was expected to furnish background music as the listeners ate and drank. Béla Bartók went with his parents. As the orchestra began the *Semiramide* overture, he put his silver down and listened intently, asking, 'How can all the others eat when such beautiful music is being played?'

His first piano lesson was given him by his mother on his fifth birthday, 25 March 1886; by his name-day, 23 April, the two were able to play a four-hand piece for his father. Lessons, however, were interrupted because of his illness, and it was not until he was seven that he was found to possess absolute pitch. Shortly thereafter his father died, and in October 1888 the family—which now included a younger sister, Erzsébet (Elza)—began the series of removals that took them to widely separated parts of Hungary before they settled permanently in Pozsony in April 1894.

The first move was simply to another house in Nagyszentmiklós, where Paula Bartók began giving piano lessons to support herself and her children. Béla Bartók began studying again, and made good progress although his mother could not induce him to count rhythms, which he felt instinctively.

The next year they moved to Nagyszőllős, in northern Hungary. Carpatho-Ruthenia, in which the town is located, became in 1920 a part of Czechoslovakia; cast adrift by the Slovakian proclamation of independence in 1939, it is now incorporated into the Soviet Union. There Bartók continued his studies, and began spontaneously to compose. His mother tells how at the age of nine he 'remembered' a tune he had never heard, but because she was resting in the next room, he could not play it for fear of disturbing her. When she awoke, he played it for her, and she wrote it down—a waltz not like any of those he knew. After that he made up many dance tunes, which she notated for him.

Years afterward, Bartók credited the organist and choirmaster Christian Altdörfer, who came to Nagyszőllős from Sopron, with discovering his talent. Altdörfer predicted a brilliant future for him, and his mother took him to Budapest for professional opinion about his capabilities. Károly Aggházy, who had studied with Bruckner, Volkmann, and Liszt, and was then teaching at the conservatory, wanted to take him as a pupil; but Paula Bartók decided against this course, not only because of the financial problem but because she wanted her son to finish the intermediate school at Nagyszőllős first. She had him coached privately in Latin and the next year entered him in the Gymnasium at Nagyvárad, where he lived with his aunt, Emma Voit. He also studied the piano with Ferenc Kersch, a choirmaster and composer, who taught him only superficially, concentrating on brilliant display pieces. At the Gymnasium his progress was unsatisfactory; he was neglected by the teachers for a few of the more promising students, and was on the verge of failure in arithmetic and geography when his mother withdrew him, in April 1892, and took him back to Nagyszőllős.

Paula Bartók had found it necessary to give many extra piano lessons in addition to teaching school in order to pay the expenses of the Gymnasium, and her sister Irma Voit had come to live with her, take care of the house, and look after Bartók's sister Elza. She became a permanent part of the household, and most of Bartók's letters, after he left home, are addressed to his mother and Irma *néni* jointly.

On 1 May 1892, Bartók made his first public appearance as pianist and composer. The occasion was a charity benefit in Nagyszőllős. His program included the Allegro of the Beethoven 'Waldstein' Sonata, opus 53, as well as a piece of his own, *The Danube River*, which described the stream from its source to the Black Sea; his mother had written it down for him. She relates that his success in this first performance was measured not only by the applause, but by the seven bouquets (including one of candy) that he received.

Despite his devotion to music, Bartók as a child was far from one-sided in his development. Having been isolated from other children in his early years, he found it difficult to form friendships with them later on, and he disliked their noisy games and quarrels. They accepted his seriousness, liked his modesty, and benefited from his help with their lessons. He read a great deal, but managed to have time for all the things that interested him—especially natural objects. One summer he acquired silkworms, which he fed carefully, and since at the end of the holiday they had not yet pupated, he packed them carefully with mulberry leaves for the homeward journey, to watch them through their complete cycle. He also collected and mounted insects, an interest that persisted throughout his later life; on his tours he even carried a flask of alcohol in which to preserve whatever insects he came across, and in spite of the language barrier managed to buy pins to mount his specimens in Spain.

Languages held a fascination for him. Hungary under the Habsburgs was, of course, bilingual, and both Magyar and German were necessities; Latin he learned with a tutor, English and French he studied later. In the course of his folksong-collecting he found that he needed both Slovak and Romanian, and so acquired them; he had a few lessons in Italian and Spanish at the time he intended to travel in those countries. And even in his last years he was translating Turkish poems with the aid of a self-compiled Turkish-Hungarian dictionary, though he admitted having difficulties with Turkish in spite of its being considered 'one of the easiest languages, having no irregular verbs, nouns!' [5]

After the Nagyszőllős concert, Paula Bartók took a year's leave of absence and took her family to Pozsony, where she hoped to find another position. This Slovakian city (also called Pressburg, and now Bratislava, in Czechoslovakia) was a somewhat larger place than any of their previous residences, and one with a thriving musical atmosphere.

Located on the Danube between Vienna and Budapest, Pozsony at the end of the nineteenth century was a cosmopolitan town with an admixture of many races. In addition to the busy river trade which gave it commercial importance, it had a long cultural tradition. It had one of the three Hungarian universities in the Middle Ages (1467), with faculties of philosophy, jurisprudence, and theology;

though this, like the universities at Pécs and Óbuda, was short-lived, another was founded in 1777, with faculties of philosophy and juris-prudence, this being transferred to Pécs when Slovakia was severed from Hungary by the Treaty of Trianon.

The sixteenth-century lutanists Hans and Melchior Neusiedler were born in Pozsony; Veit Bach, emigrating from Thuringia, lived there for a time. Mozart visited Pozsony as a youth. In 1785 Count János Erdödy built a theater in his house there, and had Paisiello's *Il re Teodoro* performed to inaugurate it; Italian opera had been played in the city much earlier in the century, by the celebrated Mingotti company.

Pozsony played an important part in the lives of Hungary's most important composers of the nineteenth century: it was as a result of his concert there in 1820 that Ferenc Liszt's meteoric career was launched, through a six-year guarantee of assistance from the local magnates, and it was there also that Ferenc Erkel studied with Beethoven's friend Heinrich Klein.

The particular attraction for the Bartóks, however, was the possi-bility of hearing more music than elsewhere in Hungary, with the exception of Budapest, and of studying both piano and harmony with one of Ferenc Erkel's sons, László, who had settled there in 1870.

But permanent residence in Pozsony was not yet to be possible. Although Bartók's education was free, aside from his lessons with Erkel, and he finished the second class of the Gymnasium well, financial pressure was too great and Paula Bartók had to take a position in Beszterce (Bistriţa) in Transylvania, now a part of Ro-mania. There he could not continue his musical training, since there were no better pianists than he in town. He did, however, find oppor-tunity to play regularly with a young violinist named Schönherr, with whom he went through the standard violin-piano repertory and the concertos. After eight months in Beszterce, Paula Bartók received an appointment to the Pozsony state training school for teachers, and although the school year was about to end, Bartók was permitted to enter the third Gymnasium class, again without tuition. With the aid of another student he concentrated on making up the necessary work, but on the day of graduation he was very late in reaching his home, and his mother had begun to worry. But the boy finally arrived, beaming, with 'excellent' on his certificate, and a prize of fifteen florins for completing the work in so short a period.

Now he could devote himself again to his music, resuming his lessons with László Erkel. Erkel was primarily a pianist and choral conductor, but in the few years he was able to work under his guidance, Bartók acquired a solid grounding in the music of the eighteenth and nineteenth centuries, all the time continuing to compose music of his own. Brahms made the strongest impression upon him; he knew nothing of Wagner beyond *Tannhäuser*, since Pozsony offered no opportunity of hearing the later works. One time a Mr. Róth, who was Paula Bartók's superior at the training school, heard him playing as he went by the house; a cellist himself, he regularly invited Bartók to his home to accompany him and to play chamber music. There, as well as in the home of a family named Rigel, Bartók became acquainted with a good deal of music in the best possible way—through performing it with others. For orchestral concerts and operas he was able to buy inexpensive tickets, and thus acquired an acquaintance with the styles and techniques of his predecessors.

There were opportunities for public performance as well. In a concert celebrating the Hungarian millennium, in 1896, he accompanied a melodrama; in March 1898 he played a rhapsody by Tausig in a concert to celebrate the fiftieth anniversary of the 1848 revolution. Of great importance was his friendship with Ernő Dohnányi, four years his senior and already on the way to recognition as composer and pianist. Dohnányi, a native of Pozsony, was studying there with the cathedral organist, Karl Förstner. Before he was seventeen years old he had written a good deal of chamber music, including the Piano Quintet, opus 1, in C minor, by whose Brahmsian flavor Bartók was deeply impressed.

Shortly after the Bartóks settled in Pozsony, Dohnányi went to Budapest as a student at the Royal Academy of Music; Bartók took his place as organist in the Gymnasium chapel. The Gymnasium always celebrated the name-day of its director; on this occasion in 1897, Bartók played the Spanish Rhapsody of Liszt; the following year, the *Tannhäuser* overture, together with a Piano Quartet of his own, and his orchestration of the Brahms Hungarian Dances was given as well. By this time he was already giving piano lessons, and was paid for accompanying the cellist Biermann; with the money he earned he was able to buy scores for study, among them the *Missa solemnis* of Beethoven.

László Erkel died at the end of 1896, but Bartók continued his work with Hyrtl. Besides the Piano Quartet (1898), he wrote a Piano Sonata (1897), and three songs in German (August 1898).[6] All the early works were suppressed by the composer, but the manuscript of one of the songs, a setting of Heine's *Im wunderschönen Monat Mai*, has been printed in facsimile. Dedicated 'to the Comtesse Matilde von Wenckheim,' the song is a student work, displaying the most conventional melodic and harmonic characteristics, rhythmically so regular as to be monotonous, and prosodically quite lacking in subtlety, with one especially grave fault: the provision of an alternative high B♭, half-note, fortissimo, on the conjunction *und* as climax. It is no worse—and, surprisingly, no better—than might be expected from any moderately talented seventeen-year-old. The really surprising thing is that any young composer, fifty-eight years after Schumann, should have had the temerity to set to music the *Dichterliebe* poems.

With the completion of his course in Pozsony, it became necessary for the Bartóks to look about for a conservatory where the young composer-pianist's talents could be properly nurtured. Vienna was the logical place; so on 8 December 1898, Bartók and his mother went there. He played for the faculty and submitted his compositions, among them the Piano Sonata. Even though he was Hungarian, he was not only admitted but promised free tuition and a scholarship from the Emperor's private fund.

However, Bartók decided to follow Dohnányi to Budapest. The latter had worked at the Royal Academy of Music—an unorthodox procedure—with István Thomán in piano and Hans Koessler in composition. Although he was never a nationalist in his sentiments and, unlike most of his Hungarian contemporaries, always preferred to couch his musical ideas in the lingua franca of western Europe, Dohnányi nevertheless completed his musical education in Budapest, with the exception of a few lessons from Eugen d'Albert in the summer of 1897. At his urging, Bartók made his decision.

In January 1899 he and his mother went to Budapest, where Thomán agreed to admit him without examination, and sent him to Koessler with a note of recommendation. The Bartóks returned from Budapest, the youth's future apparently secure. Then, in February, he became very ill, hemorrhaging slightly, and was immediately put to bed with orders for absolute quiet. Of course it was impossible to continue school, nor could he practise the piano; however, with the aid of one of his school friends, László Tahy, who came to the house to help him with his studies, he was able in June to complete his course. During the summer his mother took him to Eberhard in Carinthia, where at last his health was restored.

By September Bartók was ready to take up his studies in Budapest. He wrote to Professor Thomán on the eighth:

. . . I have already filled out and sent in the entrance application; over one line, however, where it asks whether I have already been examined, I hesitated. Finally—because the blanks must be filled out *accurately*—I wrote that you had examined me in January. I hope there will be no inconvenience over this. . .[7]

When he arrived in Budapest, however, the director of the Academy of Music, Ödön Mihálovich, refused to take him without examination, notwithstanding Thomán's promise of the winter before. Not having played since the preceding February, Bartók was apprehensive about performing for the faculty; nevertheless at Mihálovich's insistence he agreed to play. His mother was admitted to the audition, which took place before the director and three members of the staff: Thomán, Koessler, and Herzfeld. Bartók played a Beethoven sonata, and submitted his own compositions. Mihálovich was enthusiastic, not only admitting him to the second class, but seizing Paula Bartók's hands and congratulating her upon her son's talent. Well content, she found him lodgings and returned to Pozsony.

Bartók began his work with Thomán and Koessler, in piano and composition, and with Ferenc Xaver Szabó in score-reading and orchestration. His lodgings were not too satisfactory; a week after he arrived, he wrote his mother:

Everything would be fine except the piano is miserable. . . Everything rings and buzzes, the pedal squeaks, etc. Besides, I'm always being interrupted; yesterday a captain was there, today two ladies, at the same time I was playing my scales. And then they want me to play something. Yesterday I did, but today I refused, and by and by I shall pound out my exercises there quite freely. As far as I am concerned they may do what they like—why do they always sit there?—and I shall not play at all.[8]

But before he could make much progress, illness struck again. In October his landlady sent for Paula Bartók to come immediately; Bartók was dangerously ill with a bronchial infection. When she consulted with one of the professors at the Academy of Music, he advised her to persuade her son to give up music as a career, since he apparently lacked the constitution to withstand its rigors; he suggested that Bartók study law instead. But Bartók, disconsolate, rejected the idea, and Thomán took it upon himself to explain to the professor that the youth would never be content in any other profession. So upon the advice of a physician, Paula Bartók took her son home and when he had recovered found a place for him in Buda, sending her sister Irma to cook for and to take care of him. Shortly thereafter, Bartók took a room in Pest, in the house with his other aunt, Emma Voit, and Irma Voit went back to Pozsony.

Back at work with high hope, Bartók immersed himself in the music-dramas of Wagner and the orchestral works of Liszt. When he came across the score of *Das Rheingold*, bequeathed to the Academy of Music by Liszt, he found 'very useful things' in it which he had not seen before. The size of the orchestra astonished him, and he listed the instrumentation in a letter to his mother, commenting that while Wagner required thirty lines on some pages, his orchestration teacher, Szabó, employed an orchestra so vast that he was said to use manuscript paper with sixty lines to the page.

Thomán had already given Bartók a copy of *Die Walküre*, and he soon became acquainted with the entire *Ring* trilogy, *Tristan*, and *Die Meistersinger*. But although they did alleviate the Brahmsian influence which had colored his music up to that time, they did not open the new path for which he was searching. Only the virtuosity of Liszt's technique impressed him, not the clues to a new and authentically Hungarian music he might have found there, which later became of great importance to him.

Bartók's own creative work was discouraging. When he brought the sketches of a new quintet to Koessler, the teacher advised him to abandon the work, describing the themes as of little value, and advising Bartók to start a simple song-form instead.

I don't really know what isn't good [he wrote] because he spoke only in generalities, such as that the themes ought to be chosen more carefully, etc. According to this, none of the themes is of any value; but if they are not, I cannot see whether I shall be able to write anything better in, say, a year's time. Why didn't he tell me last January that these pieces are worthless? In my opinion this quintet is in every respect better than the quartet of last year. I thought then that my compositions are generally good, only needing some slight adjustments, mainly as to form. But if they are so bad that nothing can be done about them, of course that is serious. . .[9]

But there were many concerts, opera almost the year round, and opportunities for performance as well. It was the custom of the Hungarian State Opera to turn over two boxes to the students of the Academy of Music; and while for a time the intendant, in pique, discontinued this practice because the students had presented a wreath to a departing prima donna, Bartók was nevertheless able to familiarize himself with the standard operatic repertory. Tickets for concerts were inexpensive and now and then free, Thomán often making it possible for his students to hear important recitals. The pianists who parade through Bartók's letters of his student years include most of the great virtuosi of the period—d'Albert, Emil Sauer (who played 'with such extraordinary color [that the instrument] did not sound like a piano,' and whose mannerisms 'may be . . . what the ladies like'), Teresa Carreño (whose 'force and technique are wonderful [but who] played wrong notes twice'), and especially Dohnányi, who retained Bartók's greatest admiration.

Among the violinists, Jan Kubelik's performance was dazzling; 'he plays harmonics as another person would play ordinary notes.' It is revealing to find Bartók in 1900 writing enthusiastically of Antonio Bazzini's trivial *Hexentanz* as played by Kubelik, even copying an excerpt into his letter. At this period he seems to have been attracted more strongly by technical virtuosity than by profundity or real musical worth. Among chamber groups he reserved his enthusiasm for the Joachim and the Bohemian Quartets, but found the Hubay-Popper Quartet 'not worth writing about.'

Finishing the year with a good record, Bartók went with his mother for the holidays to St. Johann bei Herberstein, in Styria, where he kept up his practice with the use of the schoolmistress's piano; she refused, however, to allow him to study a Liszt sonata for fear of damage to the instrument. The Bartóks also visited Graz, and went on to Radegund, where they climbed Schökkl. On the day before they were to leave, in mid-August, Bartók had a high fever; the physician diagnosed pneumonia, and for a month Paula Bartók watched over her son in the little Carinthian inn. By 15 September they were able to return to Pozsony. One doctor despaired of saving his life; another advised a winter in the Italian Tyrol. Obtaining a leave of absence, Mrs. Bartók took him to Merano, where they stayed from November to early spring. In this ancient resort at last Bartók recovered, gaining ten kilos (more than 22 pounds) in weight. In January, with a rented piano, he was able to work again, and his spirit rose. At the end of this time he returned to the Academy of Music to finish the year, and then spent the summer in the so-called 'Békés Cottage' in Pozsony.

Resuming his studies in September, Bartók received the Liszt stipend of 200 florins, and to extend his resources he gave piano lessons for a small fee, stretching his budget to its limits and in misery when one of his pupils missed a lesson. Later on he taught theory as well; the daughter of a provincial lawyer, a prospective student, embarrassed the youthful musician by receiving him in a revealing red negligée, and unblushingly directing him to hang his coat on a hook already littered with soiled garments.

Gradually he made friends in the musical circles of Budapest. The Arányi family he found interesting because of their relationship to Josef Joachim, and because they resolutely refused to speak German; with his budding nationalism, Bartók felt a kinship with them. The two daughters, Adila and Jelly, were only children when Bartók first knew them; Adila was already studying with Joachim (her great-uncle), but Jelly had not yet begun the violin study that was to lead her to fame.

Bartók began also to frequent the salon of Emma Gruber,[10] who assumed an important role in his life. It was here that he played—at the piano—Dohnányi's early symphony, which required an hour for performance; after supper he played again the first three movements, struggling home to repeat the whole work once more and to find that it was almost memorized. The Adagio he considered 'definitely Hungarian (gipsy-like),' a point of view with which he would have disagreed violently a few years later.

During all this period Bartók devoted himself to the keyboard, abandoning composition entirely for two years. He became known as a pianist of uncommon abilities, and it appeared likely that he would pursue a career as performer. The first public concert of the Academy of Music at which he appeared was on 21 October 1901. The review the next day praised him lavishly:

First Béla Bartók played the Liszt B-minor Sonata with a steely, well-developed technique. This young man has acquired extraordinary strength. A year and a half ago his constitution was so weak that the doctors sent him to Merano lest the cold winter harm him—and now he plays the piano as thunderously as a little Jupiter. In fact, he is *today* the only piano student at the Academy who may follow in Dohnányi's footsteps.[11]

On 14 December he gave his first paid performance, at the Lipót-város Casino. This engagement was through the interest of Professor Gianicelli, and Bartók kept it a secret until he went home at Christmas. Stripping the Christmas tree and distributing the gifts, Paula Bartók came to a tiny coin purse for herself; inside were ten gold pieces—100 florins, the entire fee for Bartók's first professional engagement.

His first public appearance in the Royal Hall, accompanying the violinist Erna Schulz, was on 24 March 1902; Paula Bartók came to Budapest for the occasion. The next December he played a Schumann sonata at the Academy of Music, and the critic of a German-language newspaper wrote: 'The first number disclosed to us a new, extraordinarily strong talent, before whom unquestionably a brilliant career lies.' [12]

All this time Bartók had concentrated on the keyboard, finding it impossible to compose with conviction and satisfaction. Until 1902, there is no record of a completed work since he entered the Academy of Music. Even though he applied himself diligently to a study of the works of the masters, among them Wagner and Liszt (both of whom were then in great favor in Hungary), he found himself confronted by an impasse.

Then, in 1902, came a significant experience.

From this stagnation [he wrote] I was aroused as by a flash of lightning, by the first Budapest performance of *Thus Spake Zarathustra*. . . This work, received with shudders by musicians here, stimulated the greatest enthusiasm in me; at last I saw the way that lay before me. Straightway I threw myself into a study of Strauss's scores, and began again to compose. . .[13]

The new and vital language he found in Strauss acted as a catalyst
for Bartók's own talent. And as Charles III's commission for the
copying of the Velásquez portraits gave impetus to Goya's creative
genius, so the newly discovered Straussian techniques at last freed
Bartók and spurred him on. When he encountered A Hero's Life,
it made such an impression upon him that he arranged it for piano
and played it—from memory—for a group of the professors at the
Academy, who met quarterly to perform their own and other new
music. None of them knew any Strauss, so Thomán proposed that
Bartók be invited to play for them. The performance aroused great
enthusiasm; the director, Mihálovich, embraced him and kept him
for dinner, and even Hubay—in later years strongly anti-Bartókian—
proposed a toast to him. The young musician's happiness that year
was his mother's 'most beautiful Christmas gift.'

During Bartók's last years as a student, the nationalist current in
Hungary, suppressed since the catastrophic uprising of 1848-9, became resurgent. Hungarian scholars were devoting themselves to the
revivification of the older Hungarian culture, to the re-publication
of early Hungarian writers, to the resurrection of the patriotic songs
of the Rákóczy period. Caught up in the restlessness and fever of
the nationalist movement, Bartók became concerned with the problems of a national music.

It must be remembered that in the upper levels, Hungarian musical culture was predominantly Teutonic. Erkel, Liszt, Mosonyi, and
their successors, although trying to invest their music with an authentic Hungarianism, instead veneered it with the tawdriness of
the verbunkos style, while basically it remained western European
in orientation—or, strictly speaking, in occidentation. German musicians or German-trained Hungarians, such as Volkmann, Herzfeld,
Koessler, Thomán, Mihálovich, held the principal musical posts in
Hungary. Although a few Hungarians had begun to tap the vast
reservoir of peasant music—unknown to, or ignored by, the composers themselves in the nineteenth century—their compilations [14]
had little influence upon the serious music of Hungary. Even though
Béla Vikár began in 1898 a fairly systematic investigation of the
peasant music of Hungary, this too escaped recognition by composers
until Bartók and Zoltán Kodály began their research.

But under the dual influence of Strauss and the nationalist fervor,
Bartók began to write again. The year 1902 saw the production of

four songs, to rather naive poems by Lajos Pósa, which were printed
by Ferenc Bárd as Bartók's first published composition, and the Scherzo of a symphony, which was given a performance on 29 February
1904 by the Budapest Philharmonic Society. The Scherzo, unpublished, has not been available for study, but the songs will be discussed later in this book.

The first major work, however, was a vast symphonic poem,
Kossuth (1903)—a Hungarian 'Hero's Life,' whose ten tableaux, pic-
turing events of the 1848-9 war of independence, take as their pro-
tagonist the ardent nationalist and revolutionary leader Lajos Kossuth, under whom Hungary made her abortive bid for freedom from
the Austrian yoke. The subject was naturally one of great appeal
to the young composer, and his letters chronicle its progress over a
considerable period of time. While he was still working on the symphony, he was asked to play parts of it during a musicale at Professor Thomán's, and was twice embraced by his host—once because
of the beauty of the music, and again for the excellence of the performance.

But Koessler was less enthusiastic. When Bartók brought him a
slow movement, he criticized it by saying, 'An adagio must be about
love. But there is no trace of love in this movement, and that is too
bad. Modern composers are generally unable to write adagios, and
therefore should avoid them.' In order to write successful adagios,
he would say, a composer must have undergone 'certain experiences.'

What sort of experiences? [Bartók asked] Very likely of love and all
that is involved: disappointments, raptures, suffering, etc.—Well, I don't
believe experiences have all that influence on the quality of a composition. I have lived through a good many things, and have talent (at least
so they say), and according to such a rule I should be able to write good
adagios. By the way, Koessler doesn't think Dohnányi's adagios above
reproach either. (Neither do I!) [15]

Notwithstanding Koessler's criticism, *Kossuth* was eventually completed, and accepted for performance by the Philharmonic Society.
Before that time, however, Bartók had finished his course at the
Academy of Music, where his final year was filled with activity. In
January 1903 he had played at the Tonkünstlerverein in Vienna, his
program including *A Hero's Life*; there were enthusiastic reviews,
which Paula Bartók carefully filed away. In the spring, Bartók

planned a concert for his native town, Nagyszentmiklós, where there
had never been a formal recital. Although the Bartóks had moved
away fourteen years before, they were well remembered, and the
townspeople turned out in a body. The program was the subject of
much discussion in the weeks before the recital. In addition to songs
by Mme. Ábrányi, this was the final version:

Sonata in F♯ minor, op. 11	Schumann
Nocturne in C♯ minor Etude in C minor Ballade in G minor }	Chopin
Fantasy Study for the Left Hand }	Bartók
Impromptu Etude Valse	Schubert Paganini-Liszt Saint-Saëns
Spanish Rhapsody	Liszt

The visit to Nagyszentmiklós was an altogether happy one, whatever its artistic significance. The hall was filled; Bartók was entertained by the citizenry, and four young girls brought to the house
where he was staying an enormous laurel wreath tied with red ribbon.

Back in Budapest, for the public examination concert, he played
the Spanish Rhapsody again, writing to his mother: 'My success was
brilliant, the applause colossal; they called me back 7 or 8 times.
Professor Herzfeld, Hubay, Mihálovich, all were very well satisfied;
even Szendy too congratulated me, saying that I played very beautifully.' [16]

And in June, a concert of the composition class brought to performance a new Violin Sonata (apparently incomplete, as the second
movement was written later that summer), and the Study for the
Left Hand. The latter was much admired—though in the perspective of half a century it is now rather tiresome—and the critics named
Bartók the most promising young composer of the group.

This was Bartók's last appearance as a student at the Academy
of Music. But he was still far from being a mature artist, though he
had already begun a sort of career as a pianist. Paula Bartók felt that
he should go on to one of the recognized virtuosi for the finishing

touches, and mentioned Emil Sauer in Vienna; this suggestion Bartók disposed of without ceremony:

But mama, how could you think of such a thing—but such a thing (!!!!)—as that I should go to study with *Sauer!!!* with S!z!a!u!e!r!! Well, listen! On Sunday I announced to Professor Thomán that I am going in the summer to Dohnányi, and asked him not to disapprove. And he said, why should he disapprove?—that is to say, he does not disapprove. And after that, and the next day as well, he was even more friendly and cordial than before. However, on Tuesday he told Mrs. Gruber (whom I had already told in private) and added that this hurt him very much; and as for my needs—let me go to Dohnányi; in his opinion it would be without much success. Nevertheless—so he says—he is not angry with me, because I proceeded most respectably.[17]

Despite his disapproval, Thomán offered to give Bartók a letter to Richard Strauss, but hearing rumors that Strauss had accepted an extended American engagement, Bartók feared they could not meet.

The summer of 1903 was spent in Gmunden, in Upper Austria, working with Dohnányi and making plans for the launching of a professional career. Bartók's intention was to work up two complete recital programs, and to that end he spent much time polishing the repertory he had acquired at the Academy of Music rather than learning new works. He mentions in his letters especially the Beethoven Sonata in E minor, opus 90, as well as the Beethoven and Brahms concertos; the 'Emperor' he was to play in Vienna in November, and there was a Berlin recital scheduled for December, while negotiations for other concerts were under way. In addition to the practicing necessary for these engagements, Bartók found time to score *Kossuth* and the Scherzo, both of which were to be played early in 1904, to write a middle movement for his Violin Sonata, and a new Scherzo for piano.[18]

In October he went to Berlin, where he began a systematic effort to widen the circle of his acquaintance among influential musicians. Leopold Godowsky, who had returned to Berlin from a ten-year stay in the United States, welcomed him to his home; there he met Fritz Kreisler and his wife, and played for them and the others a Passacaglia by Dohnányi and his own *Kossuth*, the new Scherzo, and the Study for the Left Hand, 'to general approbation.'[19] He was unsuccessful in reaching Strauss at this time—who had not gone to America after all—but laid plans to meet him through Etelka Freund's elder brother, an intimate of the Strauss circle; and he hoped to meet Busoni through Oskar Kaufmann, to whom he had been introduced by Arthur Halmi.

It is curious to observe Bartók at this period making an effort to play the game of influence—a role which ill suited him, and which he was utterly incapable of maintaining. It is impossible to think of him as devious or scheming; even when he confesses the plot—in his letters—there is something childlike and amiable in it. His inability either to flatter or to arrogate left him at a disadvantage in competition with musicians all too skilful in those accomplishments.

Nevertheless, the season following the study with Dohnányi was promising. There was the Beethoven concerto at the Concertverein in Vienna, on 4 November; in December the recital in the Bechstein-Saal in Berlin, about which Bartók wrote to Professor Thomán:

The very significant Dec. 14 is over: my first real job of clearing accounts in the course of a concert. What I most feared—that my strength might not be equal to it—didn't happen; after the concert I was so little tired that I could have played another program from beginning to end. The Study for the Left Hand went splendidly; the greater part of the public were most impressed by this. The hall was quite 2/3 full. . . Two 'celebrities' were in the audience, Godowsky and Busoni. The latter came to the artist's room after the third part, introduced himself, and congratulated me; he had already heard about me in Manchester, from Richter. My compositions, especially the Fantasy, pleased him very much. I heard the same about the others: he expressed admiration that I, who have such a fine left-hand technique—as he heard in the Study—still played the Chopin C-minor Etude so satisfyingly. . . After the 3rd and 4th parts there were encores (my own composition and the Juon Humoresque). . .[20]

The program for the Berlin *Klavier-Abend* was similar to the one Bartók had played in Nagyszentmiklós: the Schumann and Liszt, the Chopin Nocturne and Etude, a Passacaglia by Dohnányi, and the two Bartók pieces plus the new Scherzo. The critic of the *Vossische Zeitung* wrote with enthusiasm, albeit somewhat tempered:

Béla Bartók, a newly discovered pianist . . . aroused interest; he stood out from his numerous colleagues who, year after year, seek to win public attention. And this means a great deal, because technique and musical skill have nowadays become properties that arouse hardly more admiration than the performance of a skilful dancer or an artistic skater. Bartók is a man who has his own ideas of God and the world; he is a strong personality in himself. His playing has a spiritual undercurrent without which a performance is only a display; and if he succeeds in making his tone production more varied and colorful, we can then class him among the young pianists of whom we have great hopes.

After this there were the performances of the orchestral Scherzo and *Kossuth* in Budapest. The latter was scheduled for the Philharmonic Society concert of 13 January 1904, but an unforeseen incident nearly resulted in the cancellation of the work. To represent the Austrian troops in the 1848 struggle, Bartók had deliberately distorted the Austrian national hymn, *Gott erhalte*, which Haydn had composed and which symbolized to the Hungarian mind the abhorrent yoke of the Habsburgs. During a rehearsal, an Austrian trumpeter refused to play the caricatured hymn, and the journals of Budapest fanned the flames with their comments. But the player reluctantly consented to play the part, and the performance was finally given. All the publicity, of course, had not dampened interest in the new work, and the public cheered its composer, who appeared in festive national costume instead of the conventional formal attire.

A few weeks later, Bartók went to England for a performance of *Kossuth* in Manchester under Hans Richter, appearing at the same time as soloist in the Spanish Rhapsody of Liszt and a set of variations by Robert Volkmann.[22]

This was his first trip outside continental Europe, and every new experience called forth a new response. He described to his mother the condition of the British railway carriages, the details of the voyage across the Channel, the hearth fire in his room. He stayed with the Richters in their pleasant house in Bowdon, Cheshire, and Mrs. Richter sent a gold-bordered card to Paula Bartók to tell her of her son's arrival. Unfortunately no letter has yet come to light in which Bartók mentions the musical aspects of his journey, and for the next year or so the published correspondence is meager. There are records of concerts here and there, plans for concerts, an occasional mention of a new work, but little more.

Three large compositions were completed in 1904: the unpublished

Quintet for piano and strings, the Rhapsody, opus 1, for piano, and
the Scherzo, opus 2, for piano and orchestra.

But the most important event of the year was one which was to
change the whole orientation of his esthetics, to make its impress
upon every subsequent composition. Sometime during 1904, Bartók
made his first notation of Hungarian peasant music, from the singing
of eighteen-year-old Lidi Dósa in Kibéd, Maros-Torda. This chance
discovery brought to the young composer the realization that there
was an autochthonous Magyar music of which he, like most of his
compatriots, was entirely unaware.

Ferenc Liszt, who credited the gipsies with originating Hungarian
music, recognized that their music was exclusively instrumental, and
that such vocal tunes as existed were sung only by Magyars, to
Magyar words.[23] But he identified the folksongs themselves as cor-
ruptions of the instrumental tunes of the gipsies:

> It seems presumable that the Hungarian peasant, whose inferior mu-
> sical organization would render him less conscious of the imperfections
> of his singing, seized upon the melodies which he heard the Bohemians
> [i.e. gipsies] perform, as a sort of windfall. Leading a primitive life undis-
> turbed by any physical agitation, his own voice generally remained suffi-
> ciently fresh for the purpose of singing them; and it is quite natural that
> they should have spread, especially when assimilated with words of his
> own language.
> The existence of songs not appropriated at the same time would thus
> be completely ignored, especially as their gipsy text would confine their
> use to the Ziganes exclusively; so that when, as is probable, they were
> taken over one by one by the instrumentalists (who soon caused their
> purely vocal character to disappear), it was no longer possible for us to
> recognize them under the luxuriance of their new elaboration.

The attitude of Liszt toward the music of the peasants was that
of musicians in general; the peasant tunes were considered crude
perversions of the rather elaborate and fantastic music of the Hungarian gipsy. While music *all'ongherese* was popular with the composers of western Europe long before Liszt, it was the characteristics
of gipsy music rather than of Magyar folk music that these composers
adopted as an exotic element, much as they had adopted as 'Turkish
music' the use of cymbals and other jangling and clashing percussion
in the eighteenth century.[24]

Hungarian songs, as they exist rurally [Liszt wrote] and Hungarian airs, as we hear them executed upon the instruments mentioned above (*furulya*, *tárogató*, *duda*), are both too poor and too incomplete to produce any new artistic result, and cannot yet even pretend to the honor of being universally appreciated, still less to that of being ranked with lyrical works which have already attained to a high degree of repute. But Bohemian [gipsy] instrumental music, as presented and propagated by the Zigane orchestras, is well able to face competition with any other art, whether comparison is made on the score of a bold originality full of the most noble sentiment, or on that of exquisite completion of a form as beautifully inspired as it is happily carried out.

Had he not come quite by chance into contact with Magyar peasant music, Bartók would probably have continued in the neo-Hungarian tradition of Liszt and Erkel, the one molding his ideas in Germanic style, the other leaning toward the Italianate. But once having discovered the existence of a deep layer of native ore beneath the pyrites of gipsy ornamentation, he set out in 1905 to mine it, an undertaking which led him eventually to investigate and classify scientifically the peasant music of Romanians and Slovakians, Walachians, Turks, even the Arabs of North Africa; moreover, to reconsider his whole esthetics, to found a style upon the assimilated essence of peasant music, and to determine the direction of the art music of Hungary for years to come. Bartók made numerous expeditions to the remote parts of Hungary, recording on wax cylinders thousands of peasant tunes. He was joined in these expeditions by Zoltán Kodály, who also recognized the vast significance of the collection, and was also to profit by it for the revivification of his own style; and by many others, including Bartók's own wife, Márta Ziegler, and Emma Gruber, who later married Kodály. After the recording of the tunes came the enormous task of transcribing them, and finally of analyzing and codifying them.

Liszt, who was born seventy years before Bartók, might have been in a better position to discover the authentic Magyar music, which was that much closer to disappearing altogether by the time Bartók, Vikár, Kodály, Lajtha, and others began to search for it at the beginning of the twentieth century. But the conclusions Liszt reached in his unscientific exploration of the field are at the opposite pole from those of Bartók and his colleagues. It is no doubt true that the gipsy musicians were sometimes instrumental in preserving the peasant tunes, but in the process they so distorted them with luxuriant ornamentation that they could scarcely be recognized.

Now, nearly fifty years after Bartók began his work in the field of musical ethnology, research discloses the further degeneration of the peasant music of Hungary.[25] With greater ease of communication, and especially contact with the popular art music of the towns and cities, the old forms of peasant music, like peasant crafts, tend to disappear. Whether the process of obsolescence can be deliberately slowed or arrested, as, for example, by basing school music curricula upon peasant songs, is doubtful; in western countries, including the United States, sporadic attempts to preserve or revive folk arts have been made, but the influence of radio and film music is now too prevalent to permit much hope of widespread success.

Bartók's first publication based upon Hungarian peasant music was the set of Twenty Hungarian Folksongs (December 1906), in which he collaborated with Kodály. From that time on there were numerous folksong settings—for piano, for voice and piano, for two violins, and for chorus. Beginning in 1908, there was a long series of musico-ethnological studies based upon the folksong research. More important than these was the incorporation of elements from the peasant music into his original work: not by a simple borrowing of melodies or motives or a spicing of conventional patterns with evocative modal or rhythmic procedures, but by a detailed examination of the melodic and rhythmic characteristics of the peasant tunes, and by the derivation of harmonies from them,[26] the discovery of the intrinsic nature of Magyar peasant music, and finally its amalgamation with the techniques of art music. It is here that the significance of Bartók's work lies, so far as the listener is concerned; musical anthropology is of little importance to him until it enters the concert hall.

In order to identify the characteristics of Magyar peasant music, it became necessary for Bartók to devise an analytical system. By the time he was ready to publish his research in its definitive form,[27] the system was well ordered. He recognized as peasant music 'all the tunes which endure among the peasant class of any nation, in a more or less wide area and for a more or less long period, and constitute a spontaneous expression of the musical feeling of that class.' The origin of the tunes, whether of known authorship or from the music of another class, he considered unessential. In this connection he made a sharp distinction from the 'popular' or 'national' art music, such as that which furnished the materials for the Hungarian Rhapsodies of Liszt and the Hungarian Dances of Brahms; these are melodies 'from authors who, being musically educated up to a degree, mix in their work the idiosyncrasies of the style of the peasant music of their country with the commonplaces of the higher types of art music.' In America, the songs of Stephen Foster correspond to this category, as do the 'popular' dance tunes of this century.

In tracing the sources of the peasant music of any period, Bartók discovered two opposite tendencies among peasants: the first, to preserve their old traditions and customs without change, and second, to imitate at least the external signs of upper-class culture. These two tendencies are constantly in a state of unstable equilibrium; when the imitative tendency is stronger than the conservative instinct, many cultural elements are borrowed from the upper classes, frequently becoming transformed or varied in the process. Thus new styles of peasant art, homogeneous in themselves, are produced not as the invention of the peasants but as a result of their predisposition to change whatever elements they adopt. Both older and newer styles may exist simultaneously; on the other hand, if the conservative tendency is weak, then the newer style tends gradually to supplant the older, as it has done among the Magyars.

The influence of the peasant music of neighboring peoples is also recognizable in the transformation of some national music: so the Dumy tunes of the Ukrainians gave rise to the old music of the same style among the Romanians of Maramureş, while the new style of the same peoples, strongly influenced by old Hungarian peasant music, is nevertheless quite different from it.

The classification system Bartók employed for the Hungarian peasant songs is a modification of that devised by the Finnish ethnologist Ilmari Krohn. There are four considerations: the number of lines in each tune, the height of the final note (caesura) in each line but the last, the number of syllables to a tune-line, and the compass of the tune. So far as melodic structure is concerned, the earliest tunes are short, consisting of one- or two-bar motives; later there are three- or four-line tunes with a 'definite, rounded-off' form, and finally four-line tunes with a perceptible structural plan. Rhythmically, the earliest tunes are in 'tempo giusto' (unchanging) rhythm, with notes mainly of equal value; 'parlando rubato' tunes, in which the rhythms are adapted to word inflections, come later, and finally the variable 'tempo giusto,' in which rhythmic patterns of the 'parlando rubato' tunes have become solidified, now much more complex than the older 'tempo giusto' but no longer rubato.

Tendencies to short, symmetrically divided, isometric, or isorhythmic, text-lines are more primitive than those to longer, asymmetrically divided, heterorhythmic, or heterometric, lines; a narrow compass is in general more primitive than a wide one; the incomplete or pentatonic scale is more primitive than the complete or heptatonic scale, which is in turn more primitive than a scale with chromatic degrees.

Hungarian peasant music of a number of different categories was discovered in Bartók's research. Among these are marriage and harvest songs of foreign origin; dirges; match-making songs; *regös* (minstrel) songs and children's game-songs different in character from all others; and songs associated with no special occasion, as well as related dance tunes. The music as a whole separates into three main groups: the old style, including songs proper and dance songs in the pentatonic scale with nonarchitectural structures, in both 'parlando rubato' and 'tempo giusto'; the new style, characterized by architecturally rounded forms and heptatonic scales (Dorian, Aeolian, modern major, Mixolydian, occasionally Phrygian and modern minor); and a miscellaneous class of mixed character.

In summarizing the characteristics of Hungarian peasant music, Bartók listed three qualities which he considered typical, differentiating this music from that of any other country: isometric strophe-structure, pentatonic formations, and variable 'tempo giusto' rhythms.

The peasantry of Hungary [he wrote] preserved the idiosyncrasies of old native music, but were not hostile to innovation: hence the birth of the new style which is altogether homogeneous, quite different from that of any other peasant music, typical of the race, and closely connected with the no less typical old style. There is, to my knowledge, no other country in which, of late years, a similarly homogeneous new style has cropped up. And the originality—even the very existence—of this new Hungarian style are all the more astonishing when one considers that so many alien elements had penetrated into Hungary before this style began to take shape. That these alien influences did not seriously interfere with the

national character of Hungarian peasant music at the new stage in its
evolution is the best possible proof of the independence and the creative
power of the Hungarian peasantry.[28]

Although Bartók perceived from the beginning the importance of
the reservoir of Hungarian peasant music and set about collecting
it systematically—taking every possible occasion to spend a week
here, a fortnight there, with the peasants in many parts of Hungary—
the possibilities for use of the materials thus assembled opened up
only gradually before him. It would be a mistake to search for a
pronounced influence of Magyar folksong in the compositions of
1905-6. The First Suite for orchestra, written in Vienna in 1905 and
partially performed there in November of that year by Ferdinand
Loewe in one of the Gesellschaftskonzerte, is almost entirely free
from traces of peasant music, continuing the trends already shown
in the previous works. Apparently under the momentum provided
by it, Bartók began the same year a Second Suite, this one for small
orchestra. The history of music is full of such instances where the
energy required to produce one work frequently carries the composer
through a second of the same type in quick succession. The Fifth
and Sixth Symphonies of Beethoven were created in this way, as
were the Seventh and Eighth; Brahms's Second Symphony followed
close on the heels of the First; the *Academic Festival* and *Tragic*
overtures were twins, as well as the two Sonatas for clarinet and
piano. In Bartók's list there are other examples: the Sonatas for
violin and piano, the two Rhapsodies for the same instruments, the
Third and Fourth Quartets.

With the Second Suite, however, Bartók had completed only the
third movement when he put it aside, to return to it two years later
when his work with peasant music had begun to show the way that
lay before him.

One of the most memorable events of 1905 was his extended visit
to Paris to participate in the competition for the *Prix Rubinstein.*
Since he was entering not only as pianist but as composer, it became
necessary to provide certain scores for consideration. The Rhapsody,
opus 1, of the preceding November, was completely reworked in a
version for piano and orchestra, a rather extensive introduction provided, out of which the motives of the work seem to grow—much
as Brahms prefaced the already completed first movement of his

First Symphony with an introductory adagio with a similar function—
and parts of the remainder rewritten to permit orchestral scoring.
The impersonality of the music is shown by the success of the scoring: although the original was pianistic enough, following the Liszt-
ian tradition, it does no real violence to the textural conception to
arrange it for orchestra.

Besides the Rhapsody, Bartók took with him the other recently
completed works—the Piano Quintet and the Violin Sonata—and
set off to spend several weeks in Paris. The competition took place
in early August; he was unsuccessful in both divisions. The prize in
piano went to Wilhelm Backhaus, who was already teaching at the
Royal College of Music in Manchester. Bartók wrote that he 'really
played beautifully.' But the withholding of the composition prize
was a grievous disappointment.

> The preparation for the Rubinstein Competition gave me so frightfully
> much to do, and all to no purpose! Five people were candidates for the
> composition prize; the works of the other four were below average, mine
> above, but the conservative members of the jury, who subscribed to the
> byword 'the golden mean,' didn't award the prize to anyone at all. . .
> I am furious because the people required so much superfluous work for
> the competition. . .[29]

The entrants, besides Bartók, were Attilio Brugnoli (who later
taught in Parma and Florence, composed 'several works' for the
piano, and became a music critic) and other young composers named
Flament, Weinberg, and Ságody. The jury was heavily weighted
with Russian and French musicians: each of these countries had five
votes, as opposed to three for Germany, one for the Netherlands,
and one for Hungary. Leopold Auer listened to Bartók's Violin
Sonata and said, '*Ja, das ist die neue Schule; wir sind schon zu alt
für so etwas.*' Camille Chevillard, the French conductor, thought it
'*serr interessan*'; Gustav Hollaender, director of Stern's Conservatory
in Berlin, wanted to play the Sonata with Bartók on one of his visits.
But when it came to a vote, the result was discouraging. Bartók out-
lined to his mother the questions put to the jury:

> Should the first prize be given? (Yes, 2; no, 13).
> Should the 2nd prize be given (2000 francs)? (Yes, 5; no, 10).
> If no prizes are given, should we give certificates of merit? (Yes, 10;
> no, 5).

To whom should we give such certificates? (Brugnoli received 10 votes, Bartók 9, Flament 2, Weinberg 1, inasmuch as any juror might name 2 or 3.)

So Brugnoli received the first *mention;* the last 2 don't even get certificates. And I myself will return my (un-) honorary certificate to Auer in St. Petersburg as soon as I get it. . . I may say that Brugnoli's things are completely worthless eclectic conglomerations. The most scandalous thing is that the jury couldn't see how much better my works are.

But the pieces were relatively well played. . . And how they baited me; I almost decided to withdraw. They insisted that the parts of the *Concertstück* [i.e. the Rhapsody] were faulty, the piece was too difficult, and could not be played with so little time for rehearsal. I corrected the parts (there were altogether 10 or 15 errors in them), and after much worry it was finally played rather well, after all.

They declared flatly and decreed that the Quintet could not be learned, since there was not enough time. Fortunately there was the Violin Sonata . . . and we played that. How long it took for us to find a violinist! Finally a young Russian, a pupil of Auer, named [Lev] Zeitlin, rehearsed and played it with me. So I had made the second copy of the Quintet to no purpose. . . And not even the devil glanced at the piano reduction of the *Concertstück,* that took 6 hours of work. Why these empty-headed Petersburg cattle required *this* I really don't know.

The other four composers' things were quite worthless. Brugnoli's were outwardly showy. But Ságody's . . . were so idiotic that it's a wonder the public didn't burst into loud laughter when they were played.[30]

Despite his lack of success in competing for the *Prix Rubinstein,* Bartók profited by his stay in Paris to broaden his outlook in many ways. In his pension (18, Rue Clément-Marot) he was thrown into contact with people of many other countries—'some Spaniards from America, 2 Spaniards from Europe, 5 American English [*sic*], 2 Englishmen, a German, a Frenchman, and recently even a Turk who (he said) lived in polygamy and strongly recommended this state. He has about 5 wives, whose portraits he carried with him in a cleverly divided medallion!! A good scheme.' [31]

Like all tourists, Bartók spent some time in the Louvre and the Musée Luxembourg, jostling through the crowds to see the 'Mona Lisa,' the Raphael madonnas, the beggar boys of Murillo, seeing for the first time in actuality the paintings he had hitherto known only from reproductions. The 'magical color harmony' of the rather sentimental Murillos impressed him strongly; he compared his reaction to his feelings on first hearing *Tristan* and *Zarathustra*, or on first seeing the Stefanskirche in Vienna. At the Luxembourg he saw a large number of impressionist paintings, but did not in this visit become acquainted with impressionist music.

His eyes were open to other beauties as well: the Luxembourg Gardens, the Tuileries, and the Parc Monceau, about which he wrote:

Aimlessly wandering about the Paris avenues, suddenly I stood in a little paradise. The whole garden is perhaps as large as the Erzsébettér in Budapest. Yet only the French are capable of the ingenuity with which, by utilizing nature and art, this tiny spot was so magically fashioned. Under noble trees, amid flowers and shrubs, so many statues are hidden that they would suffice for the preparation of a little spring exhibition. To mention only a few—there are statues of Pailleron, Maupassant, Thomas, and Gounod, important poetical monuments of French art. A tiny pool lies cool in the shade of the trees; along its banks stands a row of brittle, decaying Greek columns, as if they were the ruins of an antique edifice set down here. On a single column creep climbing plants. . .[32]

The less esthetic side of Parisian life also found him an interested observer:

Then there are other things to see, perhaps not in an artistic sense, but otherwise interesting, such as the Moulin Rouge. Young fellows do not write to girls, of course, about such things; but I'll strike the venerated custom a little blow and write that I never saw anywhere in a knot so many butterflies of the night with painted faces. And how friendly these 'elegant' ladies are! One of them even spoke to me, if you please: a little more and she would have kissed me (!) But the watchword should be given before we continue: 'Absolute secrecy!' To stop at this point was not difficult for me, since I then knew not a single syllable of French. (Now I know three or four syllables, and know, for example, that the girls of the Moulin Rouge and their like are called *comme il en faut*. We must thus take care to say *respectable people* instead of *comme il faut* by mistake.)

A cabaret is called *Le néant*. Here instead of tables there are wooden coffins; the walls of the room are black, the decorations are human skeletons or parts of skeletons; the waiters serve in clothing of 'pompe funèbre.' The lighting is such that our lips take on the color of blackberries, our cheeks a waxen yellow, our nails violet (that is, we look like cadavers)—and we may be diverted by such procedures as this: one of the company, wrapped to the neck in a winding-sheet, is placed in a coffin and changed before our eyes into a skeleton. . . (Nothing like it in Szentmiklós?) . . .[33]

Toulouse-Lautrec had died four years earlier, but the Paris he knew was unchanged. To the young Hungarian these glimpses of a new and exotic world were momentarily entertaining, but his roots were too deeply embedded in his native soil to permit him to think of living abroad, even in the Paris that claimed the allegiance of Endre Ady, Hungary's great poet. In the same letter that described the diversions of the Moulin Rouge, Bartók turned his attention to the problem of creating a national Hungarian music. He placed Bach, Beethoven, Schubert, and Wagner, by virtue of the strength of their music, in positions of pre-eminence, to the discredit of all French, Italian, and Slavic music. Liszt he considered as closest to these four, 'but he seldom writes *in Hungarian.*'

Carrying this discussion down to his own music, he referred to the Funeral March from *Kossuth* and concluded:

But a nation cannot appear in the arena with a single four-page piece, were it never so masterly. In short, we are still far from being ready for a start. Work, learn, work, learn, and a third time work and learn: thus we can get somewhere. If we compare the folk music of Hungary with that which I know of other peoples, it far surpasses that in expressiveness and variety. A peasant who could compose melodies like one of those enclosed, if he were lifted out of the peasant class as a child and somewhat educated, might create distinguished, valuable things. Unfortunately, it is seldom that a Hungarian peasant pursues a scholarly career. Our intelligentsia is almost exclusively of foreign derivation—thus the excessively large number of Hungarian gentlemen with foreign names. But only the cultured can comprehend art in the higher sense. And now our gentry lack the capacity; there are exceptions, but as a whole they are unwilling to accept a national art. A real Hungarian music can originate only if there is a real *Hungarian* gentry. Even the Budapest public will have nothing to do with it; we have a haphazardly heterogeneous German-Jewish group, most of them living in Budapest. It's a waste of time trying to educate it in the national spirit—much better to educate the Hungarian provinces. . .[34]

And finally, he looked for a philosophy to compensate for the inequities with which he seemed to be assailed:

Each must strive to soar above all; nothing must touch him; he must be completely independent, completely indifferent. Only thus can he reconcile himself to death and purposelessness. . .

It takes an enormous struggle to soar above everything! . . . It even seems as if sensitivity grows with progress. The child is unhappy if you take away his apple. The adult on a higher level of development is not offended by such trifles, but is it not his enduring misfortune if his ambition is not fulfilled as he desires? Let us climb a step higher! And when one is no longer troubled by ambition, does it not cause one infinite pain that those for whom one has some regard pursue imbecilities and are incapable of climbing higher? And if one has already reached the highest level and experienced neither joy nor sorrow in being able to help or not help people: does not one wish keenly for all humanity to stand upon that level?

Thus in this theory is concealed an apparent contradiction, a thing of impossibility, exactly like something in the theory of the sceptic. The sceptic says, 'One must doubt everything.' 'Thus,' answers his adversary, 'one must doubt that one must doubt.' My mother comforted and encouraged me by saying that I should have a brilliant future.—Yes, but suppose it comes too late? What if the brilliant future leaves me indifferent, as the youth looks unmoved upon the plaything that amused him as a child!!

I shall now make a few observations about the Bible and religion. Let's discuss it together. . .

It's odd that it says in the Bible, *God created mankind,* though it is really the other way around: mankind created God.

It's odd that it says in the Bible, *the body is mortal, the soul immortal,* though the opposite is also true: the body (matter) is eternal, the soul (that is, the form of the body) transitory.

It's odd that the vocation of priest and actor are considered antithetical, when both priest and actor preach the same thing: fables.

I believe this: that in times of religious laxness, mankind is at its most dissolute, while in a time of religious ascendancy, fanatical zealots arise. . .[35]

These were the problems that occupied Bartók's mind in the transitional period between his student years and his attainment of full intellectual and artistic maturity. The questions of religion and philosophy he was to discuss at great length with the violinist Stefi Geyer; [36] in 1907 he professed to have been an atheist for four years. But he felt himself set apart from others, predestined to a lonely existence and reconciled to it. He had few close friends—among them he numbered Thomán and Mrs. Gruber in Budapest, Lajos Dietl and Richard Mandl in Vienna—and searched earnestly for an 'ideal companion,' convinced in advance of the futility of the search, certain that disappointment would follow even if it were successful.

Such anxious searching [he wrote] seems to be incompatible with calm resignation, yet I have almost become accustomed to the thought that it cannot be otherwise . . . We must attain to a level from which everything can be viewed with sober calmness, with complete indifference. It is difficult to acquire this faculty, but once attained, it becomes the greatest triumph we can have over circumstances and ourselves. . . Sometimes I almost feel myself at that height, and then I suddenly fall, to start upward again. This happens over and over. But some day I shall succeed in remaining up there.[37]

BACK from Paris, Bartók buried himself in work. During tne next year he traveled to widely separated areas of Hungary, from Transdanubia in the west to Transylvania in the east, setting down the songs of the peasants. Because of this and his increasingly active concert schedule he completed no original work in 1906.

For several months in the spring he was in Spain and Portugal, part of the time with the thirteen-year-old Hungarian violinist, Ferenc Vecsey. Vecsey's father, like the parents of all prodigies, concentrated on everything that might help his son's career. In Oporto he learned that Saint-Saëns was also there and arranged for the composer to hear the boy play one of his concertos.

I don't remember [Bartók wrote] what the concerto was that he brought 'for performance'—which key or anything, except that the boy played the 2nd (andante) movement at an impossibly slow pace, obviously upon his father's advice. The composer appeared in the hotel room, and we began to play. When we reached the 2nd movement, Saint-Saëns interrupted, saying, 'It's impossible that way'; and, going to the piano, demonstrated the proper andante tempo. With this the otherwise tedious work would at least have been tolerable, according to my way of thinking.

But when Saint-Saëns withdrew, the elder Vecsey burst out, 'Eh, he doesn't know anything about it—he's not a violinist!' [1]

In letters to his mother, Bartók wrote little about the concerts in Madrid, Lisbon, Oporto; these were already less newsworthy than the new sights, sounds, and tastes that he encountered in each new country, each new town. For once his health was good, and he was able to do full justice to all the unfamiliar foods that were placed before him in quantity: 'spinach with oil—imagine!—and a vast number of unknown and unidentifiable dishes . . . What if it were tapeworm omelet, or rat pie!' [2]

Though he wrote no original music during this year, it was not without significance for the future, since late in the year he and Zoltán Kodály published their first collection of folksong arrangements: Twenty Hungarian Folksongs, for voice and piano. Of these songs, ten had been set by each composer. The preface, signed by both composers but written by Kodály, was the subject of much thought; days were spent in framing it to express their intentions clearly and unequivocally. There they distinguished carefully between the two points of view in the publication of folksongs: the one ethnological, its purpose being the scientific comparison of folk material in order to determine its origins and its relationship to its own and other cultures; the other practical, to make folksongs available to the greater public in a form suited to performance. Not all researchers have been guided by such clear-cut aims; collections made ostensibly from the ethnological standpoint have been fitted with accompaniments in publication,[3] while others intended for the general public have been issued with melodies only. Bartók's own publications are of both kinds, but from the beginning he kept them entirely separate, as did Kodály.

In this first publication, however, the concern of the two composers with making the folksongs accessible led them—for the only time, let it be said—to make certain modifications in the tunes themselves, especially in the omission of the ornamentation which plays so idiomatic a part in the performance of the Hungarian peasant. Years afterward, in the preparation of a second edition (1938), they rectified their early error so far as possible, restoring the ornaments in a few of the songs.

The collection met with a favorable reception from a part of the musical public, but in general it was ignored. Dohnányi especially was pleased with it and proposed that they prepare a second volume in which he would collaborate, offering to interest his German publisher in it. But nothing ever came of the plan, and Bartók published no further settings for voice and piano until the Eight Hungarian Folksongs of 1907-17, though he had made numerous transcriptions for piano and for chorus in the meantime.

For his collecting excursions Bartók used an Edison phonograph, enabling him to preserve on wax cylinders every nuance of the performance and later to study the tunes at leisure, notating them from the record, playing them over and over (often at slow speed) to capture each tiny detail. The work sheets of the period, several of which are in the author's collection, show the meticulous accuracy Bartók demanded: the original notation is in black ink, with numerous corrections and variants overwritten in green, modifications in pitch and every fluctuation in rhythm or ornamentation painstakingly indicated. After the notation came the problem of classification according to structure; and as Bartók's horizons expanded he was drawn into comparative ethnology by his investigation of the relationships between Magyar peasant music and that of remote as well as adjacent peoples.

As time went on, Bartók found himself more and more strongly attracted to the peasants, spending as much time as possible with them, learning to know not only their music—which was his primary concern—but their character and their whole way of life. The greatest ingenuity had to be exercised in order to persuade them to sing for him. A long dialogue which he wrote to Stefi Geyer gives an account, perhaps exaggerated, of a conversation between a traveler (himself) and a peasant woman. With much difficulty the traveler persuades the woman to sing, but she persists in singing only the most familiar songs of recent origin instead of the really old ones, which she professes not to recall, directing him repeatedly to friends who perhaps remember others, going over the same ground again and again, until the traveler gives up in despair and moves on to the next place, to go through the same process indefinitely.[4]

Nevertheless Bartók was happiest of all in these surroundings, living most of the time in the open, eating simple peasant food, working out a personal philosophy far from the pressures and distractions of Budapest. But it was impossible for him to spend his entire time in these pursuits; there was the problem of earning a living, and that meant concertizing and teaching.

In the former, Bartók met with a success which, though not spectacular, was nevertheless reassuring. In 1906 Wilhelm Kienzl described him as

A hitherto completely unknown, extremely interesting young artist . . . whose talent aroused my entire attention. That is to say, the manner in which Bartók re-created Bach's Chromatic Fantasy and Fugue was so meaningful and original, without being at all arbitrary, that from the first bar I was won over by the impress of a personal art, which augured well for the works he performed later. And in this I was not disappointed. The pianist fashioned the C♯-minor Nocturne and the G-minor Ballade of Chopin with such spirit and temperament that one could forget the pianist in the musical poet. One felt that the artist had newly experienced the works, and it was this that he allowed the hearer to experience with him. A Scherzo of his own composition, of an individual physiognomy, gave the admirable artist opportunity to exhibit his creative talents.[5]

An interesting sidelight on music criticism of the period is provided by another review:

Yesterday afternoon in the third popular concert of the Grünfeld-Bürger String Quartet, two talented Hungarian composers were heard. The first was Béla Bartók, whose works, in spite of the composer's youth, showed serious worth. In his truly beautiful harmony the ardent national feeling is mingled with classicism. Today they played a piano quintet, in which the composer—who is also an eminent executant—played the piano part. In this work, too, his vigorous Magyar heart speaks, yet at the same time there is a broad knowledge. . . It is a very interesting, sonorous, and penetrating work. The public honored not only the work but the splendid performance with tumultuous applause. By himself, Bartók also played a work of Schubert at the piano, with great warmth and excellent technique.[6]

Bartók might have welcomed such an enthusiastic evaluation—but the critic had written the review without having heard the concert: the Grünfeld-Bürger Quartet could not learn Bartók's quintet, and it was not performed.

In their attempts to establish themselves as composers, both Bartók and Kodály met with rebuff after rebuff in Budapest, and they became increasingly impatient. Despite their hope of revivifying the

concert music of their country, there were times when it seemed a
hopeless task.

With the Hungarian oxen—that is to say, the Hungarian public, [Bar-
tók wrote his mother] I shall not bother any more. Kodály rightly says
that 'pheasant isn't for asses; if we cram them with it, it will make them
sick.' So let's leave these asses alone and take our serious production to
foreign countries. Let those here drown in *The Merry Widow* and *János
Vitéz*—I'll have nothing to do with them. . .[7]

But it was not easy to divorce himself from Hungary. On his concert tours his expenses used up most of his fees, and it was neither
practical nor desirable to take a teaching post abroad. For, notwithstanding his impatience with Hungarians, it was still Hungary that
claimed his spirit. He could have been content nowhere else, and
when opportunity offered, in 1907, he accepted an appointment to
the Academy of Music, succeeding his own teacher, Thomán.

His duties at the Academy were not in the department of composition. From the beginning he resolutely refused to teach young
composers, for fear of impairing his own creative activity. Even in
1940, when he was almost desperately searching for a means of livelihood in the United States and Randall Thompson offered him a
position at the Curtis Institute of Music, which would have maintained the Bartóks in comfort and required only one or two days of
teaching each week, Bartók 'listened . . . like a child and then in
that gentle, almost Franciscan manner, he declined categorically,
saying that he could not and never wanted to teach composition. He
said that to *teach* composition was to imperil his own composing:
it was as though he wanted to keep that side of his nature unspoiled
by any burden of pedagogy.'[8]

The few students who did persuade Bartók in later years to give
them lessons in composition usually found that they were concerned
with notation details, orchestration, and similar elements rather than
the actual creative process. Composers who may legitimately call
themselves Bartók's pupils in composition are almost nonexistent;
on the other hand, there are great numbers of pianists of many nations who studied with him at the Academy of Music. Even after
he transferred his activities from teaching to scientific research, he
agreed to teach at least one promising American pianist who came
to Budapest to work under his guidance, and in his final years in

the United States, burdened with illness and financial cares, he was sought out by his former students whenever they could arrange to be with him for an occasional lesson.

Bartók resented having to teach untalented students, but as his stature grew he was approached by many talented ones, to whose training he devoted the most painstaking efforts. With a magnificent knowledge of European music from the sixteenth century to the twentieth, he brought his students into intimate acquaintance with a wide range of musical literature.

No detail escaped notice [one of his last pupils wrote] from mechanical matters of fingering to the most exquisite particulars of phrasing and tone color and, above all, rhythm. After studying Bach with him and hearing him play the Suites and Partitas, all other Bach playing sounds dull and lifeless to me. . . He was, of course, more at home with some composers than others. I am sure there has been no greater performer of Scarlatti, Bach, Beethoven, Liszt, and Debussy. His Mozart was a bit too fine and aristocratic for our prevailing taste, but probably closer to the late eighteenth-century style than most of the Mozart playing we hear. His Chopin was certainly not sugary enough! But his comments on phrasing [in Chopin] were extremely enlightening, since they were based on a thorough knowledge of Slavic folk music. . . He was perhaps not sentimental enough for Schumann and the 'romantic' Brahms, but in the more classical Brahms—and of course in the Hungarian sections of the Eb Rhapsody, etc.—his playing was superb. . .[9]

Bartók's tenure at the Academy of Music lasted for nearly thirty years. It was interrupted from time to time for his folksong research and his concert tours, and now and then for illness, but it was for much of this time the mainstay of his existence. Kodály had joined the faculty in 1906 and, when Hans Koessler retired in 1908, he became the principal teacher of composition; together Bartók and Kodály exercised the strongest possible influence upon the succeeding generation of Hungarian musicians.

Into Bartók's class soon after his appointment came two sisters, Márta and Herma Ziegler, daughters of a police inspector in Budapest. Károly Ziegler some years before had been a district officer in Pozsony, but the Zieglers and the Bartóks never met there. Márta, the younger sister, was about fourteen years old in 1907, and already showed qualities which Bartók valued highly: alert, well read, musical, and unaffected, she presented a striking contrast to the women

he knew in Pest, and he found his interests and predilections duplicated in hers.

Bartók soon found himself seeking out the hospitality of the Ziegler household, where he found a warmth hitherto missing from his
life since he came to Budapest. Despite the difference in their ages,
it soon became apparent that Márta Ziegler and Bartók were more
than ordinarily attracted to each other. In 1908 he dedicated the
first of a series of compositions to her—*Portrait of a Girl*, in the Seven
Sketches, opus 9. There is simplicity and tenderness in the work, a
suggestion of unrevealed depth, a touch of humor. The first of the
Burlesques, opus 8c, dated November 1908, is also dedicated to her;
it is called *Quarrel*, but the score does not indicate whether it com-
memorates a specific event. A few years later, Márta was to receive
the dedication of Bartók's one opera, *Duke Bluebeard's Castle*, whose
allegorical subject is strangely akin to the composer's own philosophy,
with its fierce rebellion against interference with his inner life.

Stimulated again to composition by the fortunate combination
of circumstances, Bartók returned to the Second Suite (for small
orchestra), which had lain fallow since 1905, and wrote its fourth
and final movement. Between 1 July 1907 and 5 February 1908 he
wrote a violin concerto, part of which was incorporated into the Two
Portraits, opus 5, for orchestra. Other works streamed from his pen:
the Fourteen Bagatelles for piano, opus 6; the First String Quartet,
opus 7; the Ten Easy Pieces; the two Elegies, opus 8b; the first of
the Burlesques; the Seven Sketches; and the four volumes of Hungarian and Slovakian folksong transcriptions called *For Children*.

With the new scores Bartók entered a new phase. The spell of
Strauss began to dissipate, though it was a potent element still for
many years. A re-evaluation of the music of Liszt, which Bartók had
rejected because of its meretricious decoration, gave him an insight
into compositional procedures that were to become important to
him; and he discovered in 1907, through Kodály's interest, the music
of Debussy, in which he found similarities to Hungarian peasant
music. These resemblances he attributed [10] to influences of eastern
European folksong, especially Russian, and it is clear now that
Debussy's music was indeed colored by that of Russia, with which
he first became acquainted during his tenure as pianist for Nadejda
von Meck.

There is a vast difference between Debussy's use of folk elements and that of Bartók. In Debussy they were deliberate exoticisms, entirely foreign to his French heritage. His ear, set almost from the beginning to catch the subtleties of music from distant lands, was charmed by the modal turns in the melodies of the *Five*, as later he and his friends were attracted by the music of the Orient—especially of Java and Annam—at the Exposition Universelle of 1889. Melodic, harmonic, and rhythmic possibilities opened up by these experiences played an important role in the formation of the impressionist style.

Léon Vallas, citing Mussorgsky's influence upon Debussy as one of 'de-Wagnerization,' contrasts the two in terms which might almost characterize the differences between Debussy and Bartók:

[Debussy's] art is made up of fine shading, discreet allusions, vague evocations, subtle impressions, faint outlines and touches. In Mussorgsky, there is no delicate shading; the line is hard and sharp, the coloring brilliant or violent; the contrasts are definite, the musical gesture clear cut. One composer lives in a continual dream; the other in the midst of realities. The music of the former insinuates itself delightfully into the souls of the hearers; it satisfies them, unless it absolutely fails to awaken any tender echoes in their hearts. The music of the latter produces a direct impression, dominant and irresistible, from which there is no escape.[11]

This is not to imply that Bartók's music is ever lacking in subtlety, that it is a harsh, violent, untempered music. But it is almost without exception firm, tangible, even in its most sensitive moments. A few of the scores produced during the period just after Bartók became aware of the procedures of Debussy are soft and—melodically and harmonically—somewhat lacking in solidity, but these represent a very small group. Such works as the first of the Two Pictures, opus 10, and the Four Pieces for orchestra, opus 12, are atypical, with their undigested Debussyisms appearing out of the seeming stylistic chronology of Bartók's works. There are remarkably few reversions in Bartók's music to the characteristics of an earlier period, but these orchestral scores, as well as the Elegies for the piano, demonstrate that the composer had still not attained complete maturity.

In many ways, however, he was ahead of his contemporaries. The piano music of 1908 shows experimentation with bitonality, dissonant counterpoint, chords in intervals other than thirds, somewhat before the works of Stravinsky and Schoenberg in which these devices first came to general notice. But, important as these procedures were in the formation of Bartók's language, all other considerations are relatively insignificant in relation to the influence of the peasant music of Hungary. This music being monodic, it became necessary to derive harmonic materials from it, rather than superimpose harmonies of the Western type upon melodic materials of Eastern origin. With the pentatonic scale, in which the oldest of the peasant tunes are cast, the harmonic possibilities are limited: two triads and their inversions, one seventh-chord (of the second species); all combinations beyond these must embrace major seconds and perfect fourths. Bartók and Kodály came to think of harmonic complexes including these 'dissonant' intervals as satisfyingly consonant, and assigned them unhesitatingly to points of repose—even to final cadences.

Since many of the later modal tunes betray pentatonic characteristics, it was natural to extend the use of the pentatonic harmonies to modal melodies, at the same time expanding the number of possibilities. There is never a question, even in the setting of a folktune, of modal harmonization; the supra-diatonic tones are used freely, chords support melody notes which do not form a part of them, and a system of functional harmony—so important to a Hindemith— never makes its appearance. The office of such a harmony, with its calculated tensions and relaxations, is increasingly supplanted by considerations of rhythm. Rhythmic urgency leads to points of culmination, even though the harmonic combinations become no more rigorous; in contrast, the dissonantal level may remain high while rhythmic manipulation brings about a lessening of potential. It is just such situations that Karl Eschman describes [12] in his discussion of the relativity of cadence, quoting the last few measures of Bartók's Suite, opus 14, whose final 'harmony' includes the notes B♭, C♭, C♯, D, F♭, G♭, A.[13]

Shortly after finishing the Bagatelles, Bartók took them to Busoni, who commented, '*Endlich etwas wirklich neues,*' and gave the young composer a letter of recommendation to Breitkopf and Härtel.[14] But in spite of Busoni's testimonial, the publishers declined to bring out the work, saying that 'your little pieces are too difficult and too modern for the public.' [15] They were, nevertheless, published the next year, together with the Ten Easy Pieces, by Károly Rozsnyai in Budapest, in a beautifully clear, cleanly spaced engraving on paper of excellent quality. The same year Rózsavölgyi issued the First String Quartet; these were the first of Bartók's important compositions to be made available to the public,[16] and for the next two or three years he found the publishers willing allies in the issuance of his music, even though few copies were sold in Hungary. Gradually they became known in other parts of Europe, and both composer and publisher thought it more significant to create a demand abroad than at home.

In addition to his original works and his transcriptions of peasant music, Bartók began the editing of a long series of keyboard music: the Well-tempered Clavier of Bach, music by Couperin and Domenico Scarlatti, Mozart, Haydn, Beethoven, Schubert, Chopin, and a group of piano transcriptions of Italian cembalo and organ works of the seventeenth and eighteenth centuries. Most of these became the standard pedagogical editions in Hungary, and the basis for piano study not only within the Academy of Music but outside it as well.

Although his situation was somewhat bettered by his appointment to the Academy and by the publication of his music, it was still almost impossible to bring his scores to performance. When the Academy opened its new building with a series of concerts, three movements of his Suite, opus 3, were played, but at the end of a very long program, so that many of the audience did not wait to hear it. The following year the Second Suite, opus 4, was scheduled for a hearing by the Philharmonic Society, but it was cancelled at the last moment, 'ostensibly'—Bartók wrote [17]—because of István Kerner's illness. Thanks to Busoni, Bartók received an invitation to conduct the Scherzo of the Second Suite in Berlin, and accepted reluctantly, writing to Etelka Freund, 'I do think it would be better if he would direct!' [18] But Busoni had put out posters advertising the composer as conductor, and the performance took place as scheduled. Afterward Bartók wrote to Thomán:

> After all, it's a great experience to conduct, when the orchestra plays exactly as I intend!
> The effect was like that of the Valse in Pest. Two camps: the one hissing, the other in a storm of thunderous applause—there were 5 curtain calls. Also Oskar Fried was there, and would like to perform the whole Suite. . . . The orchestra is magnificent, everything sounded splendid.[19]

I'm really glad [he wrote to Etelka Freund] that I threw myself into the work—I believe I did it well—at least, everything not only 'came out,' but it sounded brilliant too.[20]

This was a happy interlude, but it unfortunately did not establish a precedent. Especially in Budapest it was still difficult to get a hearing for the later scores, and the First String Quartet, completed in 1909, went unplayed for almost two years. None of the existing quartets was venturesome enough to attempt it, and in 1909 four young string players, personal friends of Bartók and Kodály, decided to take matters into their own hands by forming a new quartet. These were Imre Waldbauer, János Temesváry, Antal Molnár, and Jenő Kerpely —the eldest of them not yet twenty-five, the youngest still less than eighteen. The quartet thus formed retained its identity until 1945, when both Waldbauer and Kerpely came to the United States, though there had been changes in the other chairs.

For many years this was the only outlet Bartók had for his quartets; the Waldbauer-Kerpely quartet played the first two quartets when no other group would touch them, and the Second Quartet by its dedication repays the composer's indebtedness. Waldbauer attributes the formation of the quartet to

. . . the awakening interest of a handful of *avant-garde* musicians, artists, and writers, [which] indicated that the time was ripe for trying the public performance of the new music. Let us not forget that in those days only Schoenberg's *Transfigured Night* was known as new chamber music besides the works of Debussy and Ravel. (We played Schoenberg's I. Quartet in 1911 only in Budapest.) [21]

The first two concerts of the new quartet, given on 17 and 19 March 1910, were devoted to the music of Kodály and Bartók. The photograph commemorating the occasion shows the two composers with the members of the quartet, Bartók and Kerpely in profile as if unaware of the photographer, the others looking straight into the camera. Kodály, with short beard and thatch of wavy hair, has a distinguished air quite at variance with Bartók's appearance; the latter seems mild-mannered, almost childlike, his graying hair unkempt, his slight figure clad in a conspicuously striped suit, with a flowing silk bow knotted at the collar, his piercing eyes concealed by the direction of his gaze. Most of the others, all younger than he by four to eleven years, look older, and their formal dress sets off his deliberate informality.

Bartók's evening included the First String Quartet, the Piano Quintet (1904), in which the composer joined the quartet, and a group of piano pieces, comprising the Bagatelles, the first of the Romanian Dances, opus 8a, and the C♯-minor Fantasy (from the Four Pieces of 1903). Both the old and the new Bartók were thus represented. Not all the music met with approval; the Bagatelles especially provoked adverse comment.

A few months before this, Bartók and Márta Ziegler were married. Jenő Kerpely recounts the curious circumstances of the marriage, somehow typical of Bartók's habitual reserve. Márta, by then around sixteen years old, had come to Bartók's house for a morning lesson, and when it was time for luncheon, he told his mother that 'Márta will stay.' After the meal the lesson went on; presently teacher and pupil went out for a while, returned and continued the lesson until dinner time. When Paula Bartók announced dinner, Bartók again said, 'Márta will stay'—and added, 'She is my wife.'

He kept his marriage a secret, and it became known only when a student inquired for him at his house, to be greeted by the young girl who referred to Professor Bartók as 'my husband.' Even then, he was fiercely resentful that his private life should be the subject of comment by his friends, and became angry when Dohnányi sent him a congratulatory note.

In December 1909 he was in Paris, apparently with his wife.[22] Busoni had given him a letter to Vincent d'Indy and one to Isidor Philipp (who had been for some years professor of piano at the Conservatoire), introducing Bartók as 'the Hungarian composer of various interesting and original compositions, especially for the piano.' [23] From neither of these did he receive much encouragement. D'Indy could discover neither tonality nor form in the third movement of the Second Suite, and dismissed Bartók with the admonition, 'Il faut choisir les thèmes. . .' [24] As for Philipp, who at least was Hungarian born and might have been expected to show more interest, the only thing he offered was to introduce Bartók to several French musicians. Virgil Thomson prints an account, perhaps apocryphal, of their conversation: [25] after Bartók had declined to meet Saint-Saëns (whom he had, of course, encountered several years earlier in Oporto) and Widor, Philipp is said to have asked him whom he did want to know. When Bartók suggested an introduction to Debussy, Philipp said, 'But he is a horrid man; he hates everybody and will certainly be rude to you. Do you want to be insulted by Debussy?' 'Yes,' was Bartók's reply.

This was the period in which Debussy's thoughts were occupied with Poe's *Fall of the House of Usher* and *The Devil in the Belfry*, of which he wanted to make operas. About this time he wrote, 'I am guilty of about ten acts of impoliteness per hour, the exterior world hardly exists for me. It is a delightful frame of mind, but has the disadvantage of being incompatible with the twentieth century.' [26] Apparently no meeting with Bartók was arranged, since it is not mentioned in the latter's correspondence, and he was thus spared the experience of so many 'acts of impoliteness per hour.' The other musicians he met, including the pianist Édouard Risler (whose specialty was the Beethoven sonatas), made vague and lukewarm promises from which Bartók had little hope of benefit. It was still to be many years before he had any conspicuous success in Paris; this must have been particularly disappointing to one whose strong anti-Habsburg feelings led him to seek ties outside the German-speaking countries. Paris especially was a cynosure for Hungarian writers, artists, and musicians, and acceptance there would have provided the stimulus Bartók greatly needed at this point.

In Budapest the new scores were ignored or met with only indifferent success. The works produced from 1909 to 1912 included two Romanian Dances, four Dirges (*Nénies*), the second and third Burlesques, and the *Allegro barbaro* for piano; Two Pictures (*Images*) and Four Pieces for orchestra; and *Duke Bluebeard's Castle*, a one-act opera on a libretto by Béla Balázs. The Four Pieces and the opera remained unperformed for a number of years. Imre Waldbauer played the first of the Two Portraits in 1909, with László Kún conducting the Budapest Symphony—a mild enough work, derived from the First Violin Concerto of 1907-8, but it was anything but successful; and when the Philharmonic Society played the Two Pictures, Bartók fled in dismay from the inadequacies of the performance.

In 1911 the Waldbauer-Kerpely quartet played the First Quartet in Amsterdam, The Hague, Paris, Berlin, and Vienna; but at home both Bartók and Kodály met with apathy or open antagonism from performers and public alike. Realizing that they must create their own outlet for the performance of their music and that of their contemporaries, they founded a society devoted to that purpose: UMZE.[27] Bartók himself played for the first time in Budapest the music of the new French composers, which had up to then been completely disregarded. But the plans for a new orchestra dedicated to the playing of new music did not materialize,[28] the whole enterprise collapsed for lack of interest and support after one or two concerts, and with the rejection of Bartók's opera, *Duke Bluebeard's Castle*, by the jury of a national competition the future looked dark indeed. Having weathered the successive discouragements which had assailed him since he was graduated from the Academy of Music, Bartók could bring himself to struggle no longer, and in 1912 he withdrew from all forms of public musical activity.

While retaining his position at the Academy, he intensified his folk-music research, absenting himself during vacations for collecting trips, covering all parts of Hungary, much of Romania, and in June 1913 traveling to North Africa to study the music of the Arabs around Biskra (Sidi-Okba, Tolga, El-Cantara). During this period, too, he began his extensive musico-ethnographical writings; his articles on Székler and Transdanubian folk ballads, published in *Ethnographia*[29] (1908-9), were to be followed by countless articles in the Hungarian musical and anthropological journals, and presently he expanded his horizons to write for periodicals in Romania, Germany, France, Italy, England, and eventually the United States. His articles are still being translated into numerous languages.

Nor was he content merely to publish the results of his research without pointing out its significance for the future of Hungarian art music. As early as 1911, in an article for the periodical *Aurora*,[30] he took to task certain dilettante musicologists who had written earlier of the 'characteristic properties' of Hungarian music, who 'wanted to define something of which there was still no trace.' He accused them of reversing the natural order of things, in which practice precedes theory, and of accepting the music of Bihari, Lavotta, Csermák, Rózsavölgyi, and Pecsenyánszki, gipsy in origin, as manifestations of a peculiarly Hungarian style; and criticized the 'critics' for their condemnation of music incorporating the modal elements of peasant music, and thus not falling into the major-minor-chromatic system of western Europe.

In later articles Bartók cited folksong influences in the music of earlier, non-Hungarian composers as confirmation of his own theories: for example, the opening theme of the Pastoral Symphony as a folksong of the southern Slavs, which Beethoven might have heard from bagpipers in western Hungary,[31] the chorale-inspired music of Bach, the Polonaises of Chopin, most of the music of Grieg, Smetana, Dvořák, and the Russians, some of that of Brahms and Schumann. Articles were devoted to the purposes and the methods of folksong collecting, and to the art music that resulted from the study and assimilation of folk music. Occasionally (though rarely) a critical review would appear: of Delius's Mass of Life, of Strauss's Elektra, of Kodály's Trio, of Schoenberg's music in Hungary. But these were exceptional, for Bartók had no interest in and little respect for the profession of music criticism, and certainly his own experiences with the critics—who failed as a group to recognize his greatness until it was too late to benefit him—could not have impressed him with their perspicacity.

As his interests led him into the investigation of the music of other ethnic groups, he broadened the scope of his publications, both musical and literary. While Kodály preferred to study only the music of the Magyars, founding his compositional style upon it, Bartók became gradually more international in his viewpoint, allowing himself to become involved in the music of Slovaks and Romanians, not only as a scientific investigator but as a composer also. A considerable number of transcriptions around 1915 were based upon Romanian tunes: the piano Sonatina, the Romanian Folk Dances from Hungary, the Colinde (Romanian Christmas Songs), and some unpublished vocal and choral settings; and besides the second part of For Children there were other compositions, mostly choral, that used Slovakian themes. Bartók reached the conclusion that the richest folk music came from groups whose heritage was impure, groups that had rubbed elbows with other national or racial groups over a considerable period of time. His visit to North Africa confirmed this theory, when he found the music of the Arabs, isolated in the vast reaches of the Sahara, less highly developed and consequently less interesting than that of the Magyars and the surrounding peoples.[32] The avoidance of foreign influences, he concluded, whether deliberate or not, leads to stagnation; enrichment of folk music results from the absorption of such influences.

Bartók took no pains to conceal the derivation of the basic elements of his music, or their dependence on folk music other than Magyar. The third movement of the Suite, opus 14, for piano, and the first and fourth parts of the Dance Suite for orchestra, for example, are openly Arabic in their inspiration, though original in their actual materials; the fifth section of the Dance Suite is as openly Romanian. These resemblances were intentional,[33] but Bartók made no attempt to avoid the force of these and other extra-Magyar influences in his less characteristically folkloristic music. Having accepted the thesis of the beneficial effects of intermingling on a broad scale, it was logical to apply it in a personal way.

So his music, except at the outset, reaps the harvest of his research among the peasants of Hungary and outside. The important role played by the tritone in much of it may perhaps be traced to its use in Romanian and Slovakian peasant music—the latter especially, with its Lydian flavor. Modal considerations also were of some moment in the weakening of the tonic-dominant relation, since the scale-fifth is of less consequence in modal scales than in the major and minor. Nevertheless Bartók's music of whatever period has a homing instinct which relates it to definitely established key centers notwithstanding its avoidance of the traditional harmonic functions. During the period under consideration, it was moving gradually farther from conventional standards of tonality; presently the trajectory was to reach its vertex, in the two Sonatas for violin and piano, and then turn back toward a stronger affirmation of key.

The compositions of the years between 1912 and 1916 are far from numerous. With the reluctance of performers to play his music and of audiences to listen to it, he considered it useless to write, and until the completion of *The Wooden Prince* in the latter year he had produced no large work of any kind since the Four Pieces for orchestra. Instead he became interested in propagandizing for the peasant music of Hungary, in an attempt to impress the broader Hungarian public with its importance. There is a series of letters to Sándor Solymossy, who was secretary of the Magyar Néprajzi Társaság [Hungarian Folk Society] from 1911 to 1914, with plans for a concert and lecture in Budapest, in which he proposed to present peasant performers from Hontmegye, in north Hungary. The preparations were involved, because the peasants could not be depended upon to arrive unless accompanied by someone who could read and write Hungarian; nor could the Society be certain that the performers would not make additional demands at the last moment.

Dr. Győrffy said that the best thing would be for the Society to turn to Alajos Szokoly, the librarian in Hontmegye, with whose help we could get Csuvara, bagpipe and horn player, who is working at the Simek farm for the moment. (That is somewhere between Zalaba and Kis Gyarmat.) The best thing would be to charge some official person to buy a ticket for Csuvara and put him on the train; otherwise his coming would be completely uncertain. The same man could assure Csuvara that we will really give him the fee we promised, and in the same way we should have to bring down the *tekerős* (hurdy-gurdy player) from Szentes. The best thing would be to turn to the museum in Szentes; I don't remember the name of the *tekerős*—in any case we should ask for the best one. Doesn't all this cost too much money? maybe 50 *forint?* Isn't that too much for the Society? [34]

In another letter [35] Bartók indicated that the original plans had been expanded to include four or five people; he offered to give them breakfast and a warm dinner, 'but maybe they will need some bread and bacon for lunch, and that will be at the expense of the Society.' In return for the cost of transportation and subsistence for such a group, he proposed to record as many of their tunes as possible in Budapest.

Again circumstances made it impossible for Bartók to continue with the plans he had made. Having withdrawn from concertizing (and to all practical purposes, from composition as well) in order to devote himself to ethnological research, he was soon to find that avenue almost entirely closed to him. This time it was nothing so personal as opposition from performers and public: it was the tremendous conflict set off by an assassin's bullet in Sarajevo, in June 1914. Plunged unwillingly into war, Hungary nevertheless prosecuted it with all the means at her disposal. Men and supplies in great numbers were put at the disposal of the Central Powers; all of Hungary's energies were focused on the war effort.

Bartók's visit to North Africa in the summer of 1913 had been intended as the first of a number of similar excursions to study the music of the broad ethnic groups whose origins were similar to those of the Magyars, in order to discover so far as possible, by means of persistent cultural traits, the relationships existing between them.

The study of the Hungarian language had provided the most dependable clues to the origins of the Magyars, otherwise shrouded in the darkness of pre-history; but Bartók believed that the music of the Hungarian peasant, scientifically examined in juxtaposition to that of ethnically related peoples, would furnish equally valuable data.

But the African expedition was the last he was to make for many years. With Hungary's frontiers closed by the war, it was possible for him to work only in a restricted area of his own country for the next several years. In the spring of 1914 he and his wife collected many peasant tunes in Maros-Torda; late in the year he was in Hunyad for the same purpose, and the next four years show him working in only a few counties of Hungary. Of course he could study the vast number of tunes phonographed in the preceding years, and a few articles were published (the most important on the music of the Arabs [36]); but the design for a musico-ethnological work of broad scope had perforce to be abandoned.

Restriction was not, however, without its rewards. The impossibility of travel meant that Bartók could spend much more time with his family. His son, also named Béla, had been born in August 1910, and it gave Bartók the greatest pleasure to watch the boy develop, even though he showed no musical aptitude. In the summer of 1915 Bartók collected in Zólyom, writing his mother from Besztercebánya:

I came in to fetch Márta and the boy, who arrive at 12:00, and at 1:30 I go with them to Hédel. I am very glad it could be arranged that way, so that I can show them—especially the child, who hasn't yet seen anything like it—the mountain landscape. . . The landscape is about like that around Eberstein, much more beautiful than Ruprecht! Wonderful pine woods, many nice lanes, and a few quite comfortable ones too. . . I often go, not by the lanes but straight through the woods, where I find a great many insects. (That's my other collection, which also takes much later work.)

There is a mountain here like the Schökli, though somewhat lower, but you have to climb to its peak as there at Radegund. It has a nicely ringing name: Kozi Vrch (goat's back). I should like to take the child up there in some way—maybe on the back of a woman (if not on horseback!). They say that from there there is a quite beautiful view over the Liptó county, where you can see fantastically formed rocky mountains. Today is one of the finest days so far; I hope we'll have nice weather as long as Márta is here.[37]

The same letter provides clues to economic conditions in Hungary at the time:

I'd like to tell you something more about the material situation in Hédel. Well, it's very primitive, and you wouldn't be much satisfied with it. Besides, even if I pay, they don't take care of me for money. That's good in one respect, but it's uncomfortable too, because one is always bound by gratitude and not free enough. Well, that isn't such a bad thing either, because they are very nice people. Food is very simple, as at home: there is no meat, only two dishes for dinner, but as much bread, butter, and milk as you want. It seems that this simplicity doesn't hurt me at all, as I think I have gained a few kilos. It's true that on Sundays when I go to the neighboring villages to collect, the hospitable priests make big dinners in my honor, where there is meat, wine, and white bread enough; and in these cases one eats much more of all these than usual, since one hasn't had them for a long time.

Naturally those excursions are combined with long walking tours through the mountains. I've started taking photographs, too, a painful experience. I forget either this or that, and afterwards I am very sorry for every spoiled picture, as it's very difficult to get those American films. The 36 that I have with me I got only with the special patronage of Emma. Maybe I'll have more practise after a while; it's much more difficult than making phonograph records.[38]

By the end of the summer he had collected some four hundred songs, had eaten his fill of Liptói cheese, smoked cheese, potato *galuska* with cow cheese, black bilberries, and mushrooms, and could settle down to teaching and working on the results of the summer's harvest. But he found that he could not after all abandon composition, and the enforced isolation to which he submitted between 1914 and 1918 set him once more on the creative path. For the rest of his life, he was not to be deflected from it.

The first fruits of the new upsurge of activity—aside from the transcriptions already mentioned—were a ballet, *The Wooden Prince*, a Suite for piano, and the Second String Quartet. The ballet, like *Bluebeard's Castle* based upon a libretto by Béla Balázs, occupied Bartók from 1914 to 1916. And now at last he was again to find favor with the public of Budapest: the production which Egisto Tango directed in May 1917 attained a remarkable success.

Tango, unlike the conductors Bartók had known, was greatly in-

terested in new music. István Kerner, Bartók said,[39] 'never was in
the habit of looking into the score, learning it only in rehearsal'; so
it was a surprise to find that Tango had been studying *The Wooden
Prince* three weeks or more before it even came to rehearsal: 'When
I delivered the score to him on Tuesday, this is what he said: "*Ik
werde eine Woge ganz krank sein vom Studium.*" ' [40]

The conductor demanded thirty rehearsals for the complex new
score, even though at the Opera they had already scheduled Ábrányi's
Don Quixote and Erich Korngold's one-act *Violanta*, 'and God
knows what all besides . . . and now with *Violanta* and everything
else they have removed from the repertory, the Philharmonic concerts
are being prepared without rehearsals . . . Anybody else, with less
ability and self-preparation, would be satisfied with 5 or 6 rehearsals.
The Lord preserve us from this! Tango says he is very glad that he can
conduct a Hungarian work for once, but . . . he should never have
undertaken the other too, but only mine.' [41]

Despite the curiosities of Balázs's libretto, *The Wooden Prince*
was enthusiastically welcomed by both public and critics. Gustáv
Oláh, who was later associated in the production of this and Bartók's
other stage works, felt that the staging of the first version was less
effective than the music and the décor; [42] nevertheless the performance was so successful that the following year Tango at last brought
out *Duke Bluebeard's Castle*.

Before this, however, the Waldbauer-Kerpely quartet had performed Bartók's Second String Quartet, on 3 March 1918; and others
of his works—including the Two Portraits, in which Baré was soloist
and István Strasser conducted the Philharmonic Society—were given
hearings in Budapest. The quartet had occupied Bartók off and on
for two years; it presents for the first time in concentrated form the
results of his folksong study. The second movement has the thrust
and power of the *Allegro barbaro*, even more strongly intensified,
while the movements which enclose it, less rigorous to be sure, owe
their whole existence to the essential elements of Magyar and related
peasant music. *Bluebeard's Castle*, which is full of 'parlando rubato'
melody and otherwise betrays its Hungarian origins, is still highly
colored with French impressionism; it is a Hungarian *Pelléas*, but a
Pelléas none the less. The Second Quartet sublimates the impressionist elements and brings to the fore the more indigenous ones. The
stylistic advances shown in it will be discussed in some detail later

in this book; the whole direction of Bartók's later writing might be deduced from this one work.

Despite the success attained by his dramatic pieces, the Second Quartet was for some time difficult for audiences to accept, though years later it became the most frequently played of Bartók's quartets. It was, incidentally, the first of his music to be recorded (in 1925, by the Amar Quartet,[43] in which Paul Hindemith played the viola) and remained for ten years the only one of his quartets on records.

The upsurge of Bartók's fortunes set in motion by the performances of *The Wooden Prince, Duke Bluebeard's Castle,* and the Second Quartet, led to his twenty-year association with Universal-Edition. From 1919 on, Universal's catalogue underwent a great expansion in the direction of contemporary music, under the supervision of Emil Hertzka (whom Bartók described as 'the Big-Beard from Vienna'[44]); and Bartók's music assumed importance in his plans. In the first few years of the association, more of Bartók's music was issued than the Hungarian publishers had brought out between 1904 and 1918. In the latter year Universal began modestly with several works for piano: the Suite, opus 14, the *Allegro barbaro,* the *Colinde,* the Romanian Dances, together with the Slovak Folksongs for male chorus. In 1920, these smaller pieces apparently having gone well, Universal brought out the Fifteen Hungarian Peasant Songs and the Studies for piano, the Second String Quartet, and the full score of *The Wooden Prince;* in 1921 the Second Suite, opus 4, followed, and the next year *Duke Bluebeard's Castle.* Besides these, Rózsavölgyi had published the Sonatina and the First Suite, opus 3, in 1919; thenceforth until 1938 almost everything Bartók wrote came off Universal's presses with little delay.

In the meantime the war had come to an end, with the defeat of the Central Powers. The dissolution of the Habsburg empire was followed in November 1918 by the revolution which established the short-lived and ineffectual government under Count Mihály Károlyi, who surrendered his powers the next March to the communist dictator Béla Kún. By sheer terrorism the latter maintained his hold for 133 days, and then fled to Vienna when the Romanian army approached. The republic was revoked and Hungary became a monarchy, though with an empty throne; Admiral Miklós Horthy was made regent, and the Guardians of the Crown—the crown sent by

Pope Sylvester II to King István in the year 1000—occupied positions of the highest importance.

Bartók and his family had been living for some years at Rákos-keresztur, an eastern suburb of Budapest. During the communist terror, in May 1919, they fled into Pest 'with six boxes of books and the phonograph cylinders,' but by June the situation was less alarming and they went back to Rákoskeresztur. From there he wrote his mother:

Meanwhile there were plans for the erection of a 'music museum'; Kunffy had already approved the petition, but at the last minute a better solution was offered: to erect within the framework of the present museum an independent music-folklore section. Of this I should be the head; [László] Lajtha would be the assistant, with Márta and another woman as clerks, and besides these a typist and one or two servants. . . For the present, as long as we are living outside, Márta naturally could not take the position, but instead of this took a vacation without pay. It is also possible that the new music section will be located in an already appropriated palace on the Margit-wharf (near the Buda suspension bridge head), on the ground floor of which would be the director's residence as well. In such a case we should move in—that is, we don't know yet what we'll do, because the food situation is still better outside. . . To live in a village is after all preferable to a palace on the shore of the Danube. . .

Besides Reinitz, Dohnányi, Zoltán, and I together are charged with the political music, and as advisers we form a music-directorium (of course as a music authority, not a political). . . . Reinitz has been in Vienna for three weeks, and now it is not known whether he will come back; there has been no news of him at all. Of course great musical reforms are in the making—but because of the uneasy political weather it is impossible to work well and thoroughly enough. It's too bad that Reinitz is absent now; he was one of the few who understood how to impede the illegal and impotent forward rush.[45]

In the meantime Márta Bartók was trying to cope with the steadily deteriorating economic situation:

Although the poor people of Pest struggle not very successfully with famine (which will now probably be less severe within a week or two, when the green vegetables come), we live quite well. Already we have lettuce, and spinach is promised this week. Besides, I've found out how to get things from the peasant (pardon! our comrade field-laborer): with clothing. Thus I bought 60 eggs for a shirt, 30 liters of milk for a pair of stockings; of course I take it in installments.

. . . The republic council has issued white-backed banknotes, which the peasants refuse to accept.[46] (Of course, everyone is paid in this money.) And what is more, they won't accept it in the shops, ostensibly because of lack of change. . . Because of this I have to barter with clothing; money to everyone is just a heap of corn in his bin. We ourselves have 6000 crowns stagnating.[47]

Despite the insecurity of his position and the political and economic turmoil about him, Bartók still found it possible to write. The work completed under these conditions was a pantomime, *The Wonderful Mandarin*, written to a libretto by Menyhért Lengyel. Even as he was completing the scoring, Bartók had doubts about the possibility of performing it, but he could not have foreseen that it would not be staged in Budapest during his lifetime. The score contains some of his most striking music—music with a surpassing vitality, urgent and compelling. Its gravest fault is that it is based upon a plot which could hardly have aroused stronger antagonism had it been deliberately designed for that purpose. One does not think of the nineteen-twenties and -thirties as a period of dramatic austerity, but the *Mandarin* proved too heady a wine for the censors. Although Prague permitted its presentation, it was banned by the Municipal Council of Cologne after a single performance (1925), and in Budapest, when it was scheduled in 1931, official disapproval cancelled the production after the dress rehearsal. Budapest was not ready for realism of this sort. It was finally staged there in 1946, after the composer's death, having been banned again in 1941. So this work, vivid and harsh in both plot and music, did not follow the pattern established by its predecessors; and when, after the communist collapse, neither *The Wooden Prince* nor *Duke Bluebeard's Castle* could be played in Hungary because their librettist, Béla Balázs, was a political exile, Bartók renounced the stage as a vehicle for his music.

In September 1919 Bartók's health was in so precarious a state that he requested a six-month leave of absence from his duties at the Academy of Music. Kodály, at the time deputy director of the Academy, forwarded the petition to the Ministry with a letter [48] recommending its approval. He cited Bartók's long service without his ever having had leave except in case of illness, and in addition to his teaching, mentioned his work as composer, as performing pianist, and as folklore investigator. Kodály added that the problem of placing Bartók's students with other teachers would not be difficult and, although Bartók had not asked for a stipend to see him through the leave, Kodály suggested that he be granted the customary assistance —but later struck out the suggestion in the draft of the letter.

Apparently Bartók was thinking in terms not of a short absence, which such a leave would have made possible, but of an extended residence abroad. In a letter of 23 October 1919,[49] he told his mother that Dohnányi had been granted a year's leave, and that fourteen of the professors at the Academy of Music had thereupon gone on strike. Even though all but two had gone back to work, they were all (including Kodály) awaiting disciplinary action. The chaotic state of Hungary held no assurance for the future:

> It is indeed possible to live here, but to work—that is, to do the work I want to do (folk music study), will not be possible for at least ten years. . . It would be better, for example, to teach in Vienna than Budapest, because there at least there are good musical institutions (orchestras, opera, etc.), which here verge on bankruptcy; they are driving out the best, the outstanding men: Tango, Dohnányi, etc. . . .[50]

Bartók did not feel himself in personal danger, but nevertheless gave serious thought to the possibility of leaving Hungary. Transylvania (by then annexed to Romania), Germany, and Vienna were the places he considered. He sent to Germany with a departing professor the German translations of some of his ethnological work, on Hungarian, Romanian, and Arabian music, in the hope that something could be done in his behalf; but he was most strongly interested in going to Transylvania: 'Outside of Hungary, this is the land I love best.' Egisto Tango had been invited to Romania and Transylvania, and the officer who delivered the invitation from the Romanian Minister of Culture hinted to the conductor that Bartók intended to settle in Transylvania.

Jenő Hubay, who had never been an admirer of Bartók, became director of the Academy of Music in October 1919. Shortly thereafter, Bartók was puzzled by interviews Hubay gave out, declaring that 'I count unconditionally on Dohnányi's and Bartók's support in my great task,' and intimating that he was creating for Bartók a special position, 'so that I might freely and at my own pleasure enrich the musical culture of the homeland.' [51] But the announcements were made without consultation with Bartók, who was thus completely uncertain about his prospects.

You know, of course, that I have long wished to give up teaching and take up something like a museum position; the Hubays know this too, and probably they are thinking of something of the sort. Independent of all this I am forging my own plans, but naturally I shall not leave my position here on any account until there is something considerably more favorable elsewhere. By 'more favorable' I don't mean my own economic status, but the possibilities for working. Because of the wretched circumstances here it is very problematical that, even with the greatest good will toward me, the state should be able to muster up the cost of 600 phonograph cylinders and the expense of collecting. . . This is the greatest difficulty and impediment. For the present I must wait. . .[52]

In the end, Bartók remained in Hungary and kept his position at the Academy of Music. The few published letters from the two years following the one just quoted do not hint at the matter, and it is therefore impossible to trace the reasons for his decision. His friend and librettist, Béla Balázs, who had been active in the short-lived communist regime, had found it necessary to leave Hungary; but Bartók, whose activity during the period had been musical rather than political—even though in an official capacity—could remain.

But as he had surmised in the letter just quoted, it was no longer possible to continue collecting the music of the peasants, at least on such a scale as during the pre-war years; and in that field Bartók's work became one of consolidation, of studying and transcribing materials already recorded, and of preparing for publication the results of that study. During the next fifteen years he was to publish five important ethnological works in book form,[53] besides numerous articles in periodicals; these works form a corpus of the greatest significance in the examination of the Magyar and related peoples.

Musical composition, after the completion of *The Wonderful Mandarin*, was almost at a standstill; the only score dated 1920 is the set of Improvisations on Hungarian Peasant Songs, opus 20, for piano. The interruption of Bartók's activity, the necessity of taking stock, of coming to decisions, led naturally to a reconsideration of what he had already accomplished. On 25 March 1921, Bartók reached his fortieth birthday. The occasion was unmarked in Hun-

gary, but in Vienna the *Musikblätter des Anbruch* published a special
Bartók issue, for which Egon Wellesz contributed an article on the
two string quartets, Kodály one on the children's pieces, and Felix
Petyrek on the piano music. There was also an abridgment of Cecil
Gray's article from *The Sackbut* of the preceding November; and
Bartók himself revised for inclusion the autobiographical sketch
which he had contributed to the *Musikpädagogische Zeitung* in 1918.
The revision consisted chiefly in the addition of three short para-
graphs:

This propitious change [the performance of *The Wooden Prince* and
Duke Bluebeard's Castle] was unfortunately followed by the political and
economic collapse in the autumn of 1918. The consequent confusion of
the next year and a half was by no means conducive to the carrying out
of any serious work.
Likewise the situation today permits no thought of the possibility of
the pursuit of musico-folkloristic work. We can no longer afford this
'extravagance' of our own resources; beyond this, scientific investigation
in the sections detached from Hungary is, for political reasons and on
account of mutual hostility, impossible. Again, travel to distant lands is
out of reach. . .
Moreover, there is nowhere in the world a real interest in this branch
of music-science—possibly it has not that significance which some of its
fanatics have ascribed to it! [54]

The most curious item in the *Sonderheft*, however, was an open
letter to Bartók from the Berlin critic Oscar Bie, charging him with
the responsibility for his own professional obscurity, of 'bending at
the edges' before an important crisis, of withdrawing himself from
contact with those who would further his career. Bie informed Bartók
that Max von Schillings, director of the Prussian State Opera, had
come to see the composer as he was playing his ballet for a friend,
but had gone away after quarreling with the porter who refused him
admittance. He spoke of a possibility of Bartók's providing the music
for the Reinhardt production of *Lysistrata*, and he suggested to Bartók the advisability of 'doing something' in America instead of sitting
at home over his collection of folksongs.

But it is apparent from the tone of the letter that, in spite of his
great admiration for Bartók's music, Bie had seriously misjudged the
man himself. Granted that the artist who is able to put himself
forward may achieve a more rapid success on that account, Bartók

was quite incapable of competing on such grounds. He was not inclined to underestimate the merits of his music, but neither could he bring himself to seize the spotlight in order to further performance of it.

There was little about Bartók as a person to capture the popular fancy. Unprepossessing in appearance, almost painfully shy, he could not have put on the mantle of theatricality even had he wished to do so. His recourse was twofold: to present himself to the public through his music, in which the element of personality is of secondary importance, or through his performance as a pianist, in which the personal element assumes a somewhat greater prominence; both these activities were to be greatly intensified in the years after 1921.

Bie admitted that while Bartók played, it was as if all music lived in him, and the listener was impressed with his strong individuality; but when he ceased playing he retired to the remotest depths of some cavern, from which he could be drawn forth only by force.

Bartók himself knew all this, but could do nothing about it. At the outset of his career he had, in fact, made tentative gestures in that direction, without conspicuous success. There are those who, chameleon-like, by a conscious effort of the will can apparently change personalities to fit the situation; Bartók was not one of these. For him it would have been necessary to change his whole character, not merely the outward manifestations of it, and that he was neither willing nor able to attempt.

T HE 1920's were marked by the resumption and intensification of Bartók's concert career, now deliberately expanded to an international scale. His letters, postmarked London, Paris, Malvern Wells, Aberystwyth, Venice, Palermo, Basle, Philadelphia, Los Angeles, and Seattle, indicate the widening scope of his activity. Thus, in a sense, he carried out Oscar Bie's suggestion, though it is unlikely that it was as a result of Bie's advice. The territorial limits of Hungary had shrunk to a third of her former size; even Pozsony, where Paula Bartók still lived, was in a foreign country, and elaborate formalities had to be complied with whenever Bartók wished to visit her. Though he retained his post at the Academy of Music, the contracted area of Hungary permitted no significant concertizing, and it was natural that he should look to western Europe, and eventually to America, for an audience.

But he did not give up playing in Hungary and neighboring countries. In the provincial towns where he now and then appeared, concerts were sometimes given under enormous difficulties. One which took place in Kassa (Kosice), in Slovakia, was a fantastic comedy of mishaps.[1] Arriving with Imre Waldbauer for a sonata recital, Bartók discovered just before they were to go on stage that they had overlooked the matter of an official permit, which was granted only at the last minute. The makeshift stage was so flimsy that it shook at the slightest motion, and so small that the page-turner had to stand where Bartók's left elbow prodded him. Since there were no stairs, some had to be improvised from a chair and a white-scrubbed kitchen stool. The lights were inadequate, the program inaccurately printed, and whenever the page-turner crossed to turn for Waldbauer, the stage heaved in ground swells. Finally the page-turner knocked the music off the stand and mixed the whole thing up, while the audience burst into laughter.

Such a concert was never given before, [Bartók wrote] but of course the hall was filled, and applause was also plentiful; after all expenses were deducted there was a clear profit of 1400 Czech *kronen,*—and after all it wasn't too bad. . . They still want to arrange another concert here for me—a solo piano recital.[2]

Fortunately such occurrences were not commonplace, and when Bartók made his first post-war visit to England in 1922 he found a warm reception. Armed with a new Sonata for violin and piano— finished in December 1921—he was joined in its performance by Jelly d'Arányi, for whom it was written. Having been isolated so long, he was surprised to find that British audiences knew of him, were eager to hear him and his music. The Arányis arranged a private concert for him in London,[3] which brought him a fee of £30 and was reviewed in *The Times.* Ten days later a public concert was scheduled. In the meantime the newspapers had published interviews, photographs, and other publicity; Bartók was entertained at parties where he met so many musicians, critics, 'and other celebrities' that (he wrote) his head whirled in confusion. Speaking English here, French there, now and then a little German, he managed to make himself understood, and laid a foundation for the understanding of his music. The British critics—Edward J. Dent, Cecil Gray, Philip Heseltine, Henry Leigh—published articles about him in various periodicals; aside from the *Sonderheft Bartók* of the *Musikblätter des Anbruch,* these were almost the first considerations of his music to appear outside Hungary.

From London Bartók went on to Paris, where the Violin Sonata met with a considerable success, which the composer modestly attributed to Arányi's playing. His concert, sponsored by *La Revue musicale* and given at the Théâtre du Vieux Colombier, brought him into contact with Henry Prunières, who, quick to perceive Bartók's stature, not only introduced him to Ravel, Stravinsky, and Szymanowski but also contributed through his published articles to the international celebrity Bartók was now beginning to acquire.

That celebrity was not to make him, during his lifetime, a 'popular' composer. In the 'twenties especially, his music was so uncompromising, so unyielding, that the general public was left far behind, and only the most adventurous could keep pace with him. The two Sonatas for violin and piano (the second was written in 1922, and introduced by Arányi the following May in London) are farther from traditional standards of tonality than anything else Bartók wrote: in the serialization of vertical elements, the avoidance of anything which can indisputably be called a 'key,' the complete independence of the two instruments—which do not even share thematic materials—and the plasticity of melody and form, these Sonatas show Bartók at a stage close to that of the Viennese expressionistic chromaticists. Some years later, when he had already turned in the direction which he pursued for the remainder of his life—that of the reaffirmation of fundamental tonality—Bartók himself admitted the tendencies which might have led him to the employment of the 'technique of composition with twelve tones.' But even these Sonatas, free as they are, he considered as in specific keys: C♯ minor for the first, C major for the second.[4]

In May 1922, *Duke Bluebeard's Castle* and *The Wooden Prince* were produced in Frankfurt; this was the first time any of Bartók's stage works had been performed outside Hungary. Paul Bekker[5] found *Bluebeard's* music 'more thought and felt than formed. It lacks . . . the living scenic countenance, the warm stage-breath; it remains literature. But as such it is . . . not original enough in the first sense to be able to succeed as music. . .' *The Wooden Prince* was more to Bekker's taste, and he excused the inadequacies of the opera on the ground of its earlier composition.

More significant than the performance of the stage works—which did not, after all, betoken their mounting in other European opera houses—was the first International Festival in Salzburg, in August 1922. The opening concert listed Bartók's first Violin Sonata, together with chamber works by Milhaud, Felix Petyrek, and Arthur

Bliss, and songs by Strauss and Joseph Marx. To look through the programs at a distance of some decades is revealing; the sifting process has by now been largely accomplished. Beside composers whose stature was already recognized—Ravel, Busoni, Falla, Stravinsky, Bloch, Schoenberg—and the generation about to achieve prominence —Hindemith, Honegger, Poulenc—appear a great number of composers whose names are now entirely unknown: Fidelio Finke, Ladislav Vycpálek, Paul Schierbeck, Wilhelm Grosz, Guido Bagier. That these last-mentioned and their many fellows disappeared in the ensuing decades is of relatively little importance; they had their chance to be heard, and were only then found wanting. The tendencies demonstrated in the Salzburg chamber-music festival were indeed heterogeneous, but there was no arbitrary predetermination of what specific tendencies would be admitted.

Nevertheless, the composers found themselves bound by purposes and aspirations universal enough to make a more permanent organization desirable. A few days after the first concert, the International Society for Contemporary Music was founded, with Edward J. Dent as its first president; and with sections in many countries the Society was for many years a potent force in the encouragement and dissemination of new music. In 1923 it held its first festival; like its predecessor this was given in Salzburg, and Bartók's second Violin Sonata was on the program of the opening concert. Thereafter he was a frequent contributor to the festivals: the Dance Suite was given in Prague in 1925, the First Piano Concerto in Frankfurt in 1927, the Second in Amsterdam in 1933, one of the Rhapsodies for violin and orchestra in Florence in 1934, the Fifth Quartet in Barcelona in 1936, the Sonata for Two Pianos and Percussion in London in 1938. His relationship with the ISCM was also responsible for the creation of the Sonata for Two Pianos and Percussion, commissioned by the Basle section. And Bartók as pianist took an active part in the performance of his own and other music in the festivals.

The Dance Suite mentioned above was the result of a commission in celebration of the fiftieth anniversary of the merging of Pest, Buda, and Óbuda; similar commissions went to Kodály and Dohnányi, and the resulting works were performed in Budapest in November 1923. The composition of the Dance Suite occupied Bartók during the summer of that year, after he had returned from a concert tour of England and the Netherlands. It was a period of great emotional stress, partly because of the economic status of Paula Bartók, partly because of a drastic change in Bartók's own life.

Paula Bartók, domiciled since the Treaty of Trianon in a foreign country, found her citizenship in question and her pension consequently imperiled. Although she was born in Turčiansky-Svätý-Martin and had lived continuously for thirty years in the territory which was now Czechoslovakia, the Czech authorities were inclined to consider her a Romanian because her husband—who had, of course, died many years before the dismemberment of Hungary—would have been a citizen of Romania. But the Romanians would not accept her as a citizen, since she had not lived in Romanian territory since leaving Beszterce in 1894. To bring about recognition of his mother's Czech citizenship—necessary not only for financial reasons but in order to obtain a passport—Bartók had to appeal to the *Slovenská Matica*, with which society he was negotiating for the publication of his Slovakian folksong collection:

Thus I ask that you write to the Ministry . . . and request a favorable decision in my mother's case, indicating what an invaluable service I am making to Slovakian culture with my work of collecting folksongs. I request strongly that you write very warmly about these services of mine; otherwise it would be ineffectual. I must say that the decision of this case is a matter of life and death. . . I can say that I shall not have a peaceful moment until this wretched affair that harms an innocent widow is favorably decided.[6]

Even more disturbing than his concern for his mother was the crisis in Bartók's personal life. To his class at the Academy of Music had come—as Márta Ziegler had come many years earlier—a young girl, Ditta Pásztory, whose pianistic talents were impressive and whose personal charm was irresistible. For the second time in his life, Bartók found himself drawn to a girl much younger than he. The result was that his marriage became insupportable and was dissolved by divorce. Márta Bartók brought her son to Radvány, in north Hungary, to see his father in August 1923; after they left, Bartók wrote his mother:

Márta and Béla were quite well while they were here; we often took walks together. I myself should have preferred to go on to the forester's house on the mountain, but I remained below so that I might still be with them, and to finish my score. A pity that they could not stay here. In Szőllős Béla will again feel very well and, what is more, Márta also. . . And at such a time, contrast is an important consideration.

I am only today going up to the mountain (the score is already almost completed), where I can still have about five days; on Aug. 20 I go to Pest, where there is still much to be arranged before the end of August, when the marriage ceremony is to be.

I am glad that Márta's letter set you more or less at ease, because it hurt me very much that you were depressed. Of course I completely understand your anxiety. But again you ought to try to resist insofar as possible, since you cannot see the situation clearly. I believe that it will be well thus, it will be better than it has been up to now. Only to Márta it will be far worse; this is the only thing that saddens me. So that I should truly not have asked the sacrifice of her; this I did not know how to do, although the human *raison* should be the commandment. But she persuaded me to this change, and I could not say no; after all, I was not the only one to be considered. Little Béla accepted the situation readily enough—he understood the 'specialness' of the matter. Consequently I hope that you too will gradually become reconciled to it. . .[7]

Late in August Bartók and Ditta Pásztory were married. A few days later he was able to write to his mother:

. . . Ditta is a skilful housewife. In the morning she tidies up, and helps as well with the cooking, at which she is very clever. In the afternoon she does other work, practises the piano, etc. . . . Imagine—my salary is now 600.000 *kronen* a month; this takes care of our household expenses. So far I have the following concert engagements for the winter: on Oct. 23 I play with Waldbauer in Vienna (I get 1,500.000 Austrian *kronen!*); on Dec. 15 I shall be in Paris, where they indeed pay little, but still they promise private engagements as well, so that I can bring something home. I intend to arrange another concert in Szeged also (I played there 2 years ago), but this is still not certain. After that there is the interesting news that *Bluebeard* will be given in Berlin (in the Charlottenburg Opera House), still within the year. Leo Blech will direct. . . Márta is very well, 6 kilos heavier (thanks to Elza); I am really very glad of this. She is in good spirits.—Work at the Academy begins tomorrow: entrance examinations—brrr! I never like them. . .[8]

November brought the first performance of the Dance Suite, together with Dohnányi's Festival Overture and Kodály's *Psalmus hungaricus*. Now for the first time, without in any sense compromis-ing himself by 'writing down,' Bartók had produced a popular success; the Dance Suite was picked up by conductors all over Europe, with as many as fifty performances in Germany in a single year.[9]

Few of Bartók's letters of the next year and a half have yet been published. Henry Cowell tells of meeting him in London in December 1923; both were house guests in the same home, and Cowell, then investigating the possibilities of tone clusters, was playing some of his own music one Sunday morning when Bartók, attracted by the strange sounds, appeared and asked if he might listen. Bartók himself had occasionally piled up adjacent notes in something approaching clusters, but Cowell's development of a tone-cluster 'technique' was quite new to him. 'He immediately arranged for me to play in Paris to his friends, including Roussel, Falla, Ravel, Prunières, and I don't know how many others of some importance . . .' Cowell wrote.[10] 'It was the best thing that ever happened to me.'

Early the next year Bartók wrote to Cowell asking whether the latter would object to his using tone-clusters in his own music; the letter with this modest request has disappeared, but the piano music which Bartók wrote in the next few years shows the effect of his accidental encounter with the young American.

About this time Bartók published three significant works on folk music: *Volksmusik der Rumänen von Maramureş* (in the *Sammelbände für vergleichende Musikwissenschaft*, 1923), *Erdélyi magyarság népdalok* (published in 1923 in Budapest), and *A magyar népdal* (published in 1924 in Budapest, later translated into German and English). The first of these works, completed in Rákoskeresztur in 1918, is a study of material collected in Maramureş between 15 and 27 March 1913, representing 365 songs and instrumental melodies from a collection which had already reached a total of around 3500 tunes. Types represented include the Christmas songs (*colinde*), laments (*bocete*), ballads (*doïne* or *hore*), and dance tunes. The Transylvanian collection, in which Kodály collaborated, is of slighter proportions, with only 150 melodies; but the Hungarian volume of 1924 is somewhat more extensive, with 320 tunes and an exhaustive analysis of the characteristics of Hungarian peasant song.

For the *Dictionary of Modern Music and Musicians*, published in 1924 under the editorship of A. Eaglefield-Hull, Bartók prepared articles on Hungarian folk music, musical instruments, opera, pan-

tomime, and ballet, as well as on Romanian and Slovak folk music; [11]
he contributed brief biographical sketches of numerous Hungarian
musicians (significantly leaving that of Liszt to Calvocoressi); and
he was a member of a committee that met several times under the
general chairmanship of Granville Bantock to write the article on
harmony.[12]

With all of these activities added to his concert schedule and his
duties at the Academy of Music, it is not surprising that Bartók
produced little music. The only work dated 1924 is the *Village
Scenes*, a setting of five Slovak folksongs from the Zólyom district,
for voice and piano, of which three were later transcribed for women's
voices and chamber orchestra at the request of the League of Composers in New York. 1925 brought forth no new composition; but
in 1926, spurred by the necessity of providing new material for his
concert tours, Bartók wrote a large number of works for the piano:
the Sonata, the set of pieces called *Out of Doors*, the Nine Little
Piano Pieces, and the (first) Piano Concerto. And around the same
time he began work on a collection of piano pieces, eventually called
Mikrokosmos, designed to introduce young pianists to the technical
and musical problems of contemporary writing. The first two volumes are dedicated to Bartók's second son, Péter; [13] the later ones—
especially Nos. 5 and 6—make severe demands upon the performer,
and Péter Bartók has said that the set rapidly outgrew his performing
abilities.

The Piano Concerto had its first performance at the ISCM Festival in Frankfurt, 1 July 1927, with Bartók as soloist and Wilhelm
Furtwängler conducting; in Baden-Baden the same month he played
the Sonata for the first time. The new percussive style of the piano
writing aroused some antagonism; several years later, Constant Lambert was still criticizing these works for their 'lack of rapport' between
melodic and harmonic elements:

> . . . the melody becoming definitely simpler, squarer, and more 'folky'
> while the harmonic treatment becomes more cerebral and *outré*. The gap
> between the two becomes such that in some passages . . . the composer
> gives up all attempt to bridge it, merely punctuating each pause in an
> innocent folksong with a resounding, brutal, and discordant crash, an
> effect which, did it not remind one of a sadistic schoolmaster chastising
> some wretched country bumpkin, would verge on the ludicrous. This is an

extreme example, perhaps, but it is obvious that the less consonant harmony becomes, the more artificial is the effect provided by the introduction of folk-type material. . .[14]

Of course the point of view of Bartók, as already expressed in print,[15] is exactly opposed to Lambert's: 'It may sound odd, but . . . the simpler the melody, the more unusual may be its accompanying harmony.' Having come to this decision many years earlier, Bartók saw no reason to alter his logic, attributing to this viewpoint not only his own harmonic treatment, which permitted the greatest possible freedom without utterly destroying the key sense, but also the 'traces of polytonality' in Hungarian art music of the period, as well as in the music of Stravinsky.

Bartók's letters are singularly free from criticism of other composers' music, but a fragment of a letter to his mother, after the ISCM concert at Frankfurt, does mention two works performed on the same program:

I didn't hear the Hauer work [Seventh Suite] very well, only from behind the scenes; by all odds it was the oddest of the things I heard there, but apparently rather monotonous. . . The American work [Henry F. Gilbert's *Dance in Place Congo*] is really *Schmarrn*,[16] really *Biergartenmusik*. In Baden-Baden there were more interesting works. On the 16th there were three concerts; I played in the one at 11 A.M. At 5 P.M., presentation of works written for mechanical piano and mechanical organ; at 9 in the evening, 'Lichtbild' (movie) presentations, of film with music (this is a new invention, which already sounds as well as the better gramophones). After that appeared in succession Schreker (composer), Kerr (critic), and finally Schoenberg. Each spoke of this new invention: of course the sounds were synchronized most precisely with the motion of the lips.[17]

In 1927 Béla Bartók came to the United States. After the summer festivals he had completed his Third String Quartet, and he entered the manuscript in the competition sponsored by the Musical Fund Society of Philadelphia. The only other composition dated 1927 is the set of Three Rondos on Folk Tunes, for piano, of which the first had been written as early as 1916. In November he set out for America, stopping on the way for a solo recital in Stuttgart, playing with orchestra in Munich, and sailing from Cherbourg on the *Columbus* on 11 December. He was scheduled for an extensive

American tour, from New York to Los Angeles, north to Seattle, and back again to New York in a period of less than two months, playing solo recitals, chamber concerts, and appearing with orchestra.

In preparation for his coming, the musical periodicals and the New York papers had carried on an information campaign. *Musical America* published an interview with Bartók, in which he regretted that the state of his health had prevented his coming to America earlier; after inquiring (as all new arrivals must) about American jazz, he was prevailed upon to put into words his 'credo,' and provided the interviewer with a quick survey of his recent works and their tendencies—their adherence to tonality, their avoidance of the objectively impersonal and other 'accepted' musical trends—and affirmed his belief in balance and expressivity.[18]

Bartók made his American debut with the New York Philharmonic Orchestra, under Willem Mengelberg. He had been scheduled to play the Piano Concerto, but because of inadequate rehearsal this was abandoned and the Rhapsody, opus 1, substituted. So the expected violence—a requisite of the explosive 'twenties—was postponed, and with the much blander Rhapsody, already more than twenty years old, Bartók's debut was as a pianist only, not as a composer. Judging by the reception of the Concerto when it was played later in New York under Reiner, it was fortunate that the public could assess Bartók first as a performer without being disturbed by his later compositional style. Olin Downes found the Rhapsody

. . . interesting, but immature and rather old-fashioned . . . comparatively ineffective . . . so free in style it lacks cohesion and concentration, and suffers from an over-richness of material. There are enough good musical ideas to make two Rhapsodies instead of one, and both . . . would be the better for it.

[Bartók] handicapped by an accompaniment far from finished or precise in its accord with the soloist or vivid in the presentation of the orchestral part [showed a] born instinct for the keyboard, with poetry of conception and at times a fury of virtuosity and élan astonishing in a man of his modesty and unostentation.[19]

The American tour, under the sponsorship of *Pro-Musica*, brought him to San Francisco, Los Angeles, Portland, Seattle, Denver, Kansas City, Chicago, and St. Paul, in addition to concerts with orchestra in Cincinnati, Philadelphia, and Boston. Headlines greeting him as a 'Musical Heretic' met his eye in the newspapers, and one western paper announced his arrival in these terms: 'Hungarian Modernist Advances upon Los Angeles to Convince Scoffers . . .' It is hardly surprising that in such circumstances the slight, retiring composer disappointed those who expected a fire-breathing Fafner, and many who might have been genuinely attracted not only by the man but by his music as well may have been turned away by the advance publicity.

Prefacing his recitals with a short lecture in English, on the problems of the contemporary composer in relating his music to the national temperament,[20] he played principally his own music, with an occasional work of Kodály. Even though the piano pieces of the most recent period were in the minority in his programs, still Bartók found audiences and critics puzzled.

That Bartók is a composer of eminence cannot be doubted [one critic wrote].[21] Unfortunately his dramatic, orchestral, and choral . . . works could not be heard. They are his more important utterances [22] . . . The Piano Sonata, written two years ago, was the only larger work, dimensionally speaking, but—Mr. Bartók declining to be a romantic—the virility of moods, use of small intervals, condensed themes, reiteration methods, leave one unconvinced. . . Bartók and his friends speak little of what Beethoven might have called the moral or spiritual content and influence of music. Bartók's music of last night is 'amoral,' beyond good and evil, but hardly of Nietzschean expansiveness. . .

And so in place after place, Bartók's visit made only the faintest of ripples in the musical sea, where it might have set up a turbulence comparable to that of the Pacific beside which he was staying: 'Here I am on the shore of the ocean—that is, I am living in a private wooden house on the ocean beach. The Pacific murmurs and rages noisily, and sometimes at night even shakes my bed. . .' [23]

The size of the United States, the rapid growth of its cities, the unfamiliar food, all were of interest to Bartók. To find that he had travelled a distance equal to that from Madrid to Moscow without leaving the country astonished him; his first acquaintance with an avocado inspired him to a pun:

In Los Angeles I ate 'avocado' (advocate [24]). This is a fruit somewhat like a cucumber in size and color, but quite buttery in texture, so that it can be spread on bread. Its flavor is something like almond, but not so sweet. It has a place in this celebrated fruit salad (green salad + apple + celery + pineapple + raw tomato + mayonnaise).[25]

In an interview published during his tour,[26] Bartók described the tendency of composers of the time to turn toward the musical styles of earlier periods, and his own turning toward the older peasant music of Hungary, as manifestations of a single urge; and he linked these tendencies with the calculated avoidance of the traits of romantic music. His own music of the period, of course, is by no means negativistic. In it are interlinked the characteristics of peasant melody and rhythm and those of early art music, with a consequent simplification of texture and clarification of structure. It is apparent now that Bartók's editing and transcribing of old keyboard music, prompted by pedagogical considerations, helped immeasurably to refine and codify his style.

Back in Budapest, he plunged once more into composition. The year 1928 was one of the most prolific Bartók had ever had; before it ended he had written a Fourth String Quartet—a large and complex work in five movements in an intricately integrated form—as well as two Rhapsodies for violin and piano (the first also available for cello and piano, and both in versions with orchestra), and he had extracted from *The Wonderful Mandarin* an orchestral suite, which was played by the Philharmonic Society in October.

Toward the end of the year, the string quartet competition of the Musical Fund Society of Philadelphia closed, and the first prize of six thousand dollars was divided between Bartók (for the Third Quartet) and Alfredo Casella.[27] The judges were Mengelberg, Reiner, and Stock, together with Dr. Thaddeus Rich, Samuel L. Laciar, and Gilbert R. Combs. Through some error, the first report was that Bartók had received the entire six thousand dollars, and this was printed in the Budapest newspapers.

This looked suspicious to me [he wrote to Frigyes (Fritz) Reiner] and I was somewhat reassured only after your cablegram arrived, it really seemed I had won something. A couple of days later I learned from the newspapers that at least four had won something: how much, it was impossible to dig out from such contradictory news. Consequently I waited patiently until the letter arrived from Philadelphia, with the exact details (and with the check). I can only say how 'well come' this money is; now we can hope for a little freedom, not to mention the *réclame*. You can hardly imagine the sensation this caused here in Pest. Six thousand dollars! From the beginning I told everyone that the amount

could not be so great, but of course in vain; so the public still believes
that I won 6000. I myself had not counted on winning, the affair was
so drawn out; and just a day before the news arrived I sent the *Druck-
vorlage* to Universal-Edition, so that they could give it to the printer. . .[28]

Again there is a hiatus in the available correspondence of Bartók,
preventing a detailed account of the next year or so. In January
1929 he was in the Soviet Union, playing in Moscow, Leningrad,
Odessa, Kharkov, and Kiev; later, in Switzerland, he began a friendship with the young conductor Paul Sacher—a friendship which was
to be maintained for the remainder of his life, and which led, directly or indirectly, to the production of several of his most significant scores. Sacher, twenty-five years younger than Bartók, had
already founded the Basler Kammerorchester, which became an important outlet for new music. By his performances and commissions
he has provided a stimulus for many composers, and the literature
of the chamber orchestra has been immeasurably enriched through
his efforts.

Bartók and Sacher were brought together by an ISCM concert
in Basle, in which the composer was joined by his old friends Stefi
Geyer (now married to the Swiss conductor Walter Schulthess) and
the mezzo-soprano Ilona Durigo, for the performance of his music.
This was the beginning of a long and rewarding relationship. He
returned frequently to Basle to hear his new scores, and wrote for the
Kammerorchester and for the Basle section of the ISCM three of
his best works: the Music for String Instruments, Percussion, and
Celesta (1936), the Sonata for Two Pianos and Percussion (1937),
and the Divertimento for string orchestra (1939).

Sacher's description of Bartók is vivid:

Whoever met Bartók, thinking of the rhythmic strength of his work,
was surprised by his slight, delicate figure. He had the outward appearance of a fine-nerved scholar. Possessed of fanatical will and pitiless
severity, and propelled by an ardent spirit, he affected inaccessibility and
was reservedly polite. His being breathed light and brightness; his eyes
burned with a noble fire. In the flash of his searching glance no falseness
nor obscurity could endure. If in performance an especially hazardous and
refractory passage came off well, he laughed in boyish glee; and when he
was pleased with the successful solution of a problem, he actually beamed.
That meant more than forced compliments, which I never heard from his
mouth. . .[29]

By 1930 there were tangible signs of progress in the acceptance of Bartók's music. As early as 1925, the Amar Quartet had recorded his Second String Quartet for Polydor; and His Master's Voice followed with recordings of several piano works and some of the folksong settings for voice and piano, in which Bartók was joined by Vilma Medgyaszay, Mária Basilides, and Ferenc Székelyhidy. A few other works were recorded in the 1930's, but there was still inadequate representation on records until after the composer's death.

The new compositions of 1929 and 1930 included Twenty Hungarian Folksongs for voice and piano, Four Hungarian Folksongs for mixed chorus, and—most important—the *Cantata profana*, a large choral work with soli and orchestra, based upon Romanian folksong texts. This work, which must be classed among Bartók's finest achievements, had to wait almost four years for performance, and even then it remained for London to bring it out, in a concert of the BBC Symphony and chorus, under the direction of Aylmer Buesst.

In the autumn of 1930 Bartók had been made a Chevalier of the Legion of Honor; [30] his book on *Hungarian Folk Music* was published in England in 1931; his renown in the field of musico-ethnology increased rapidly and he was invited to speak at scientific meetings in western Europe. But in Hungary his fiftieth birthday, like his fortieth, went almost unnoticed. At last *The Wonderful Mandarin* was announced for performance in Budapest. Its setting, a brothel room, was unacceptable to the Hungarian authorities, and the producer, László Márkus, with Bartók's consent changed the scene to a back street, dimly lit; but even this concession did not bring approval, and the performance was officially banned.

There is a long and detailed letter [31] in which Bartók describes the Congress of Humanistic Sciences he attended in Geneva in the summer of 1931. The list of participants included some of the most brilliant names in European arts and letters: Thomas Mann, Paul Valéry, Karel Čapek, Gilbert Murray. The proceedings were multilingual, with translators in readiness to convert each address as soon as it was finished.

I admired these translators most of all. They took notes on the speeches intended for translation, and delivered them fluently and well-nigh extemporaneously. The translator of the German speeches, for example, spoke and gesticulated with an apparent 'deep conviction,' as if he were delivering his own confession of faith: often when he was declaiming he didn't even glance at his notes. This mimicking of the speakers became almost comical, especially when he asserted in one 'speech' exactly the opposite of what his earlier 'speech' had contained. The one impersonation was of the first speaker, the other, of the second who sought to refute him.

Unfortunately the meeting floundered in a morass of parliamentary procedure and protocol, and Bartók felt that little was accomplished. Committee reports, discussion of minor points, emasculated resolutions, took up the time which might have been devoted to more fundamental matters. Bartók was expected to provide the musical stimulus, as the only musician in the assembly.

I explained that I could only propose something the realization of which would cost a great deal of money; they said that was all right. So that evening I drafted something (with regard to phonograph recording), that I read the next day—in German. Also Čapek had a similar proposal that was discussed at the same time. A sub-committee was appointed, and a resolution drafted, which of course was far from the original and served no practical purpose, but for this no money was needed. . .

It was very amusing how one speaker reacted to another. Each one began by saying that he had listened with boundless delight and the greatest of pleasure to the magnificent proposals of his predecessor, his ideas were excellent, only the case is not quite so, a few things need to be altered that make it difficult of realization, and some are incorrect—and finally proved that nothing the previous speaker had said was right. But the main thing is politeness. Of course, after this it is certain that in this committee it will never achieve any result. . .

The social activities of the conference Bartók found pleasant enough,

. . . since I could have communication with people I liked. At supper I sat beside Mrs. Thomas Mann; I also talked a good deal with Thomas Mann. Nini Roll-Anker, the Norwegian author, came to him and gushed over him while she told him how magnificent his book is and how noble his other was. . . I was required to play *Evening with the Széklers* and the *Bear Dance* on the piano, expressly at the wish of the Walach, Oprescu, who had heard me play them before—in Kolozsvár, where he was then a professor.

A dinner at the Hungarian ambassador's called forth acidulous comment on life among diplomatic circles:

[There were] only myself and X., the chargé d'affaires (Hungarian) with his wife (a detestable female). The wife of the ambassador is American, speaks only American, but plays at being Hungarian. Here there were such artfully contrived delicacies that I can hardly remember when I have eaten anything like it. Five or six wine glasses stood in rank and file, all of costly Venetian glass with dolphin feet, just so. To begin the meal a wonderful-tasting cocktail (pálinka), to end—Tokay (naturally indispensable to a Hungarian ambassador). Nevertheless the dinner was not pleasant; for apart from the nasty shrieks of Mrs. X., these polished but sententious diplomats are artificial people, quite unlike artists.

From Geneva Bartók went on to Mondsee, where he had been persuaded to teach in the Austro-American Conservatory, a summer school for students from both countries. Other members of the faculty were the composer Paul Pisk, the Austrian pianist Paul Weingarten, the Polish baritone Theodor Lierhammer, the Roth Quartet, and Josef and Rosina Lhévinne. The sessions were held in the castle of Count Almeida. For some reason the arrangements had been made haphazardly, and Bartók discovered on arrival that most of the students he had been promised had not arrived. Instead of the expected eight, he found only one at the scheduled audition. During the next week two others appeared, and the two women who organized the school also decided to study, so that Bartók was able to write to his mother:

Now I have 3 regular pupils: 1 for piano, not bad; 1 for composition, passable; 1 only for harmony, I suspect—all 3 girls—and the 2 old witches. A sixth wanted to study harmony with me, but didn't even know the scales well, and I said no to that!!

The Viennese Weingarten went back to Vienna, because not even one pupil turned up.—But still everyone says that it's going magnificently this year, but that the school is just beginning to prosper. I don't know how it was possible last year if it was still worse than this. There is a violin teacher from Berlin with only *one pupil!*—I am spending more time with my few pupils, in fact, 8 hours a week. But they pay well: today, with beautiful punctuality, they gave me a check for 496 Austrian shillings, for the week of 8 hours. . .[32]

Because of his distressingly small schedule, Bartók was able to do some other work, among which was the scoring for orchestra of several of his early piano pieces. These, including *Evening with the Széklers* and *Bear Dance* (from the Ten Easy Pieces), A *Bit Drunk* (from the Burlesques), the second of the Four Dirges, and a *Swine-herd's Dance* (from *For Children*), he put together as an orchestral suite called Hungarian Sketches, admitting candidly [33] that it was done 'on account of the money,' and because of the possibility of many performances and broadcasts.

Feri Roth, who was a member of the Mondsee faculty at the same time, recalls that neither he nor Bartók knew how to swim, but were embarrassed about trying to learn when the lake was full of accomplished swimmers. Jokingly, Roth suggested that they make the attempt when the lake was clear, and Bartók carried on the joke by knocking at Roth's door in a downpour and suggesting that now was the time to practice swimming, with everyone else indoors.

At a reception for a visiting dignitary, the faculty were asked to wear their decorations. Bartók put none on, but opened an old-fashioned coin purse and surreptitiously offered Roth the rosette of the Legion of Honor, which he himself declined to wear. When Roth asked him how he happened to carry it in the purse, Bartók told him that his mother had put it there.

These are the last informal glimpses of Bartók to be had for some time. Between 1931 and 1935 there are only two published letters, neither of particular interest. At the beginning of 1932 the Budapest section of the ISCM was inaugurated with a concert 'free from first performances,' [34] the composers represented including Bartók, Jenő Adám, Ferenc Farkas, and Endre Szabó. In 1933, Bartók played his Second Piano Concerto (completed in October 1931) in Frankfurt, and within a few months had performed it in Amsterdam (ISCM Festival), London, Stockholm, Strassburg, Vienna, Winterthur, and Zürich, while Louis Kentner played it in Budapest. The immense vitality of this work, its astonishing bravura, coupled with thematic material of more immediate appeal than the First Concerto, gave Bartók a vehicle of great effectiveness. The *Neue Zürcher Zeitung* described it enthusiastically:

Original forces, hardly existent up to now in European music, break out in the earnest first movement—accompanied exclusively by wind instruments—into an elemental *Allegro barbaro*; but it is controlled force. A world of higher spiritual order, wonderful plasticity and clarity of form, is built in the slow movement from strict alternation of piano-recitative (with kettledrum) and muted string sound. And what deep originality in the shaping of the presto middle section, what abundance of fantasy in the demonic finale! This piano concerto numbers among the most important, the strongest works of new music.[35]

Aside from a number of folksong transcriptions (the Duos for two violins and choral arrangements of Hungarian and Székler songs), there is no further composition between the Second Concerto and the Fifth String Quartet, written in the summer of 1934 on a commission from the Elizabeth Sprague Coolidge Foundation in Washington. The largest of Bartók's quartets, this work parallels outwardly the structure of the Fourth Quartet: there are five movements, of which the first and fifth share materials, as do the second and fourth. But the character of the Fifth Quartet is quite different. It lacks the extreme compression that characterizes the preceding work; its materials take strongly contrasted shapes, and there is an anomalous looseness of form quite at odds with that of the Fourth Quartet. On the other side of the ledger are its more immediate accessibility, its more strongly affirmed key feeling, the intense expressivity of its two slow movements, and the dancelike gaiety of its central scherzo. Played in Washington by the Kolisch Quartet, in April 1935, and at the ISCM Festival in Barcelona the next year by the Hungarian String Quartet, it established a place in the chamber music repertory somewhat more readily than either the Third or the Fourth Quartets—though even up to the present time it is the Second which is more frequently played than any of the others.

In 1935 Bartók completed an extensive series of small works for two- and three-part treble chorus, and a group of three pieces for male chorus, *From Olden Times*. The texts are principally modifications of folksong texts, but the music, though folk-inspired, is original. In 1934 and 1935 Bartók's ethnological studies resulted in two more publications, a pamphlet on the relationship between Hungarian folk music and that of neighboring countries,[36] and a larger volume devoted to the Romanian *colinde* or Christmas songs;[37] material for the latter had been collected between 1909 and 1917, but the preface and introductory study were not completed until May 1935. Even then, publication was made possible only through Bartók's own efforts in securing subscriptions from his friends throughout the world.[38]

In 1935 also, after many years of neglect, *The Wooden Prince* was revived in Budapest, with choreography by Cieplinski and décor by

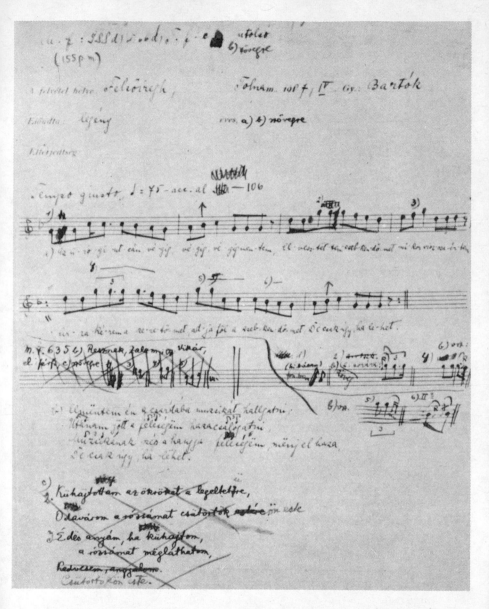

A page of Bartók's folksong-notation, April 1907. Variants and corrections are overwritten in green ink.

Bartók in 1899, Pozsony.

Bartók at home, 1908, with hand-carved Székely peasant furniture.

Collection of G. D. Hackett.

Bartók playing a *nyenyere*, a peasant instrument of the hurdy-gurdy family.

Bartók recording peasant songs in Transylvania, 1910.

Collection of G. D. Hackett.

**Bartók and Kodály with the Waldbauer-Kerpely Quartet, March 1910.
Seated, left to right: Bartók, Antal Molnár, Kodály; standing: János Temesváry, Imre Waldbauer, Jenő Kerpely.**

Bartók in Zoltán Székely's home, October 1925.

Photograph by Mrs. Székely.

Bartók and Ditta Pásztory Bartók, New York, c. 1942-3.

Photograph by Ernest Nash.

Zoltán Fülop and Gustáv Oláh; and the following year *Duke Blue-beard's Castle* was staged, with Oláh's décor and costumes, under the direction of Kálmán Nádasdy. Both were done in abstract, more or less 'cubist' style, certainly inappropriate to the fairy-tale atmosphere of the ballet, and not especially pertinent to the allegorical character of the opera; nevertheless the production of *Duke Bluebeard's Castle* was quite successful, and was taken to the *Maggio Musicale* in Florence in 1938.

Storm Bull, the American pianist, who studied with Bartók from 1933 to 1935, describes him in the late spring of 1935 as being in the best health of any period in which he saw him.[39] Bull had his lessons in Bartók's house in Budapest, Csalán-ut 27. In his studio on the second floor the composer could shut himself away behind two doors—one of them padded [40]—and concentrate on his composition undisturbed. There was a window seat which enabled him to sunbathe as he worked, and frequently Bull would discover him writing there, naked and tanned from head to foot, with the sun beating down upon him.

In 1934 [41] Bartók was, at his request, relieved of his teaching duties at the Academy of Music and became a working member of the Hungarian Academy of Science (Magyar Tudományos Akadémia). Here at last he was able to devote his whole energies to the systematization of the huge collection of folk music which he and Kodály, together with other investigators, had amassed in the course of thirty years. In 1936 his attention was drawn to pamphlets published by two Turkish musicologists, showing the relation of Anatolia to Asia, and to Hungary and other European countries. The authors, A. Adnan Saygun and Mahmud R. Gazamihâl, had written their brochures to correct the error in a Hungarian publication [42] which did not distinguish between the ethnology of Anatolia and that of Arabia and Persia.

Bartók's interest was stimulated, and an opportunity arose to verify some of his hypotheses concerning the origins of Magyar peasant music. The long Turkish occupation of Hungary in the sixteenth and seventeenth centuries naturally left an impress on all strata of Hungarian culture; and hundreds of years before that, east of the Urals and the Caspian Sea, more or less common origins might be postulated. So in an attempt to discover whether actual resemblances existed between the peasant music of the two countries, he wrote to Istanbul with questions about melodic contour in Anatolian folk music. An interchange of letters resulted in his deciding to visit the area, and when a second-class return ticket was sent him, he lost no time in making the trip.

Late in October he reached Istanbul, listened to the records of folk music in the Conservatory library; in Ankara gave three concerts and three lectures on peasant music (in French, German, and Hungarian); and then set out with Saygun and others on a collecting tour in Anatolia. The urban music of Turkey had recently been reorganized along western lines under the guidance of Paul Hindemith, but that of the rural areas had not come under his surveillance. The section chosen for Bartók's investigation lies in the southeastern part of the peninsula, between the Taurus mountains and the Mediterranean, close to the Syrian boundary. It is a section rich in history: at Issus Alexander defeated Darius III; at Tarsus the apostle Paul was born and Cleopatra met Antony; the city of Adana, founded by the Romans, was restored in the eighth century by the great caliph Harun ar-Rashid. But Bartók's interest lay in the nomadic tribes that now populate the area, following a mode of life essentially unchanged for centuries.

Because of illness he worked first in Adana, with singers brought in from near-by villages; but this arrangement was not to his taste, since he felt the best results could be obtained only by living with the peasants in their villages. So after a few days he and Adnan Saygun went out to Mersin, Osmaniye, Cardak, Toprak Kale, and to the camps of the remoter tribes, jouncing over rocky roads and open fields in a primitive horse-drawn cart, carrying the Edison phonograph and wax cylinders on their laps to protect them from damage. There he discovered, to his gratification, peasants singing tunes which were recognizable variants of old Hungarian songs, and set to work recording them, with Saygun transcribing the text as he wrote down the melody. One recording session, involving a sort of oboe (called *zurna*) with a coarse, harsh tone, and a large drum (*davul*), has been described by both Bartók and Saygun: the music was 'almost frightening' in its vehemence, the drummer rattled the window panes and made the flames of the oil lamps leap in cadence, and the penetrating sound of the *zurna* was so deafening that Bartók dropped his writing materials and covered his ears with his hands, thus causing great amusement among the dancing peasants.

The collecting trip was short and, to Bartók, not entirely satisfactory, since he was unable in many instances to discover the sources of the songs and other pertinent data, since he was not permitted to hear women singing, and since he could talk with the peasants only through an interpreter and thus had to sacrifice much of the personal relationship that had been so rewarding in his previous research. But notwithstanding this, he felt that the expedition had succeeded in making certain discoveries: of the ninety melodies collected, twenty were of a similar type, with a descending melodic line related to that of old Hungarian tunes. But the Turkish melodies had charactcristics not found in those of the Hungarian peasants: especially a greater decorative richness, and the predominance of the Dorian mode rather than the pentatonic scale. He could discern no Arabic influence in these melodies; this he considered important in a negative sense.

The results of the trip have not been published, but sixty-six of the melodies collected have been deposited in the Columbia University music library, together with an introductory essay on them, and English translations of the texts. It was apparently these texts that Joseph Szigeti discovered Bartók translating in Mount Sinai Hospital in 1943, with the aid of a self-compiled Turkish-Hungarian dictionary.[43]

Writing in *La Revue musicale* (December 1938) in tribute to Maurice Ravel, Bartók commented that for centuries Hungary suffered both politically and culturally from the proximity of Germany. Even from his earliest years he had a strong aversion to Teutonic influences, refusing to speak German unless absolutely necessary, turning away from German music (though it was through the music of a German—Richard Strauss—that his own creative energies were ultimately to be freed), fiercely resenting the Habsburg domination of Hungary. Now the rising tide of National Socialism, overwhelmingly approved by the German electorate in November 1933, threatened to overrun all of Europe. Step by step the drastic tenets of the party were brought to realization; under the theory of Aryan supremacy the Jews had already been deprived of citizenship, their property confiscated, and their lives subjected to rigorous control

when, in 1937, the Reich Music Chamber demanded an investigation of the 'Aryanism' of Bartók.

Many of the most important musicians of Germany had already
fled—Hindemith, Schoenberg, Toch, and others to the United
States—and Hungary, drawn to the Rome-Berlin axis by its desire
for modification of the Treaty of Trianon, was perilously close to
the German state of mind. But Bartók resolutely demanded that his
own music not be broadcast where it might be heard in Italy or
Germany, notwithstanding the loss of performance fees his decision
entailed. Keeping his music free from political associations was of
primary importance.

During all this period the situation of Hungary became increasingly precarious. For Bartók, 1936 and 1937 were, it is true, rather
productive from the creative standpoint: in the former he wrote the
Music for String Instruments, Percussion, and Celesta, which Paul
Sacher had commissioned for the tenth anniversary of the Basler
Kammerorchester, and he followed it with the Sonata for Two Pianos
and Percussion. In addition to these, he began the Violin Concerto
which Zoltán Székely had commissioned, though this was not to be
completed until the end of 1938.

There were still concert tours outside Hungary as well. In the
early part of 1937 he was in Amsterdam, Brussels, Paris, and London
for concerts and broadcasts, and in Basle for the première of the
Music for String Instruments. There were concerts with Zoltán
Székely, among them a broadcast in Paris, with a flustered announcer
who at first thought Székely was the composer, then confused their
Christian names, making them Zoltán Bartók and Béla Székely, and
finally, after asking them from what country they came, announced
them as Czechs. 'Nobody broke the microphone,' Bartók commented
wryly.[44] In Brussels there was an all-Bartók program with an 'extremely fine orehestra [and] a very skilful conductor'; the program
included the Second Piano Concerto, with the composer as soloist,
the *Village Scenes*, the Second Rhapsody for violin and orchestra,
and the suite from *The Wonderful Mandarin.*

It's quite astonishing how these musicians play at sight [Bartók wrote].[45]
Unfortunately the rehearsal time for this demanding program (1½ hours
of music) was of really scanty proportions; nevertheless, everything came
off quite well, only some tempos were not authentic (and I unfortunately
made some mistakes in the piano concerto!!). . . .

I was greatly delighted with the . . . *Village Scenes* and the Rhapsody, because I had still never been able to hear these two works in a good performance.

In his recitals Bartók had begun playing excerpts from his unpublished *Mikrokosmos,* which by 1937 comprised 153 pieces, ranging from the most elementary to those of considerable difficulty. One of the programs for the concerts with Székely includes twenty-seven of these pieces, in addition to the First Violin Sonata and the Second Rhapsody: after listing the titles, he wrote, 'A program loquacious enough! But at least these many flea-pieces are all "manuscript." ' [46]

The summer of 1937 the Bartóks had planned to spend at Fionnay in French Switzerland, and he had intended to go to Paris to participate in the sessions of the *Comité des Lettres et des Arts* at the end of July. But owing to an attack of bronchitis he had to give up the trip, going instead to Carinthia.

Originally we wanted to go to Italy (the Dolomites); but my hatred towards Italy . . . would have been so unnaturally great that I simply couldn't make up my mind to set foot in that country. This seems like an overstrained and exaggerated point of view, but I want at least in my holiday not to be constantly irritated by Italian aggressiveness. Let me say this, that already the Nazi poison has run through Austria as well, but there perhaps it will not be so ostentatiously displayed.[47]

In May Bartók had undertaken a commission for the Basle section of the ISCM, in celebration of the tenth anniversary of its founding. The work with which he fulfilled his obligation occupied him during July and August: the Sonata for Two Pianos and Percussion. On 16 January 1938, he and Ditta Bartók gave the première in Basle, with Fritz Schiesser and Philipp Rühlig as percussionists. Paul Sacher, whom Bartók had asked to conduct the rehearsals, has described the production of the work:

[Bartók's] impassioned objectivity penetrated everything. He was himself clear to the smallest detail and demanded from everyone the utmost in differentiated precision. Therefore in rehearsals he showed great patience and was never annoyed when the realization of his intentions did not take place without trouble. . . Bartók had summoned me to conduct during rehearsals and eventually at the concert as well. This proved superfluous, however, when the time came, since Bartók and his wife had mastered the two piano parts irreproachably, while the percussionists solved their problems skilfully and to the complete satisfaction of the composer. In these rehearsals Bartók gave proof of his genuine modesty. He undertook with the greatest matter-of-factness all the irksome requirements of the work, and treated both the assisting musicians like colleagues despite his characteristic proud reserve.[48]

To Wilhelmine Creel, Bartók wrote after the concert:

As for the 2 piano & percussion sonata, its world premier has been given in Basle 2 weeks ago. My wife and myself played the 2 pianos—it had a 'tremendous' success. Mrs. Bartók played very well—this was her first public appearance in a foreign country. After that premier I had to go—alone—to Luxembourg, Brussels, Amsterdam, Haag, and London and to accomplish there not very interesting works, only for sake of getting money! [49]

The disaster that Bartók had foreseen was not long delayed. On 16 February 1938, the chancellor of Austria, Kurt Schuschnigg, yielded to inexorable pressure after a conference with Adolf Hitler at Berchtesgaden and admitted five pro-Nazi members to his cabinet. But in an effort to salvage Austrian independence, he announced a plebiscite in the hope of warding off the threatened catastrophe; the result, however, was an ultimatum from Germany, Schuschnigg's involuntary resignation on 11 March, and two days later Hitler entered Vienna at the head of the German troops. *Anschluss*, so long feared, was an actuality.

Bartók now realized that it would be impossible for him to remain long in Hungary with any hope of pursuing his work, with the constant danger of Hungarian capitulation to the 'bandits and assassins.' [50] He began once more to think of emigration as a duty; but as in 1919, it was only with the greatest difficulty that he could face the prospect of living in a foreign country, and now, in his fifty-eighth year, the possibility of having to return to some 'unblessed' work such as teaching to earn his daily bread was entirely repugnant to him.

In such circumstances [he wrote], I should not be able to complete my work. Consequently it is all the same whether I go or stay.—After all, my mother is here: now, in the last years of her life, to abandon her forever —no, this I cannot bring myself to do! What I have written so far refers to Hungary, where, alas, the 'civilized' Christian people are almost entirely devoted to the Nazi system; I am really ashamed that I come from this class.[51]

With the seizure of Austria, the owners and editors of Universal-Edition were turned out, and the AKM (Authors, Composers, and Publishers), which collected performance fees, was entirely 'Nazified.' Kodály and Bartók were both members; together with the German composers they received questionnaires about their ancestry and allegiance, asking, 'Are you of German blood, related race, or non-Aryan?'

Naturally neither I nor Kodály filled it out: our point of view is that such inquisitions are contrary to right and law. (In a way that is too bad, because one could make some good jokes in answering; for example, we might say that we are *not* Aryans—because in the final analysis (as I learn from my lexicon) 'Aryan' means 'Indo-European'; we Magyars, however, are Finno-Ugrics, yes, and what is more, perhaps racially Northern Turks: consequently not at all Indo-European, and therefore non-Aryan. Another question runs thus: 'Where and when were you wounded?' Answer: 'March 11, 12, and 13, 1938, in Vienna!') [52]

These are bitter jokes, which do not conceal the profound spiritual torment that assailed Bartók. Having observed since the preceding November the devious paths to which Hungarian politics had turned, he began to make preparations for what must come. One thing that disturbed him was the possibility of total destruction of his manuscripts, and he arranged to send them to Mrs. Müller-Widmann in Basle for safekeeping, 'naturally without any responsibility; I shall assume all the risk myself.' Carefully he catalogued the manuscripts he sent: the Music for Strings, the original drafts of the Sonata for Two Pianos and Percussion and the *Mikrokosmos*, drafts and fair copies of the Forty-four Duos, the Twenty Hungarian Songs for voice and piano, the Second Rhapsody, the children's choruses.

One ray of light was discernible in the darkness: a few days after the *Anschluss*, Ralph Hawkes, of the British music-publishing firm of Boosey and Hawkes, telephoned Kodály from London to suggest a conference, and the next day flew to Budapest to meet with both Bartók and Kodály.[53] With no further access to Universal-Edition, Bartók was quite willing to contract with Boosey and Hawkes for the publication of his new scores; Kodály was less eager, but later

agreed to the proposal. In June the Bartóks—Béla and Ditta—went
to London to play the Sonata for Two Pianos and Percussion at the
ISCM Festival.

The performance finally went very well; we both played perhaps better and more freely than in Basle; the drummer was about as good as the
one there, but the other [percussionist] was more uncertain than your
Rühlig. In any case we could squeeze out only 6½ hours for rehearsals
here! In Luxembourg [where the Bartóks had played on the way to
England] it was somewhat worse—4 percussionists as well as a conductor
for them, and in spite of this, or more likely because of it, it was less
sure.[54]

In London the final details of the new publishing arrangement
were worked out, and ultimately Boosey and Hawkes acquired publication rights for all of Bartók's music.[55] With a stopover of several
weeks for a holiday at Braunwald in eastern Switzerland, Bartók
returned to Budapest, where in September he completed a commissioned work for Benny Goodman and Szigeti (granting them the
exclusive performance rights for three years), and soon after brought
the Violin Concerto to a close.[56]

War came even closer in those weeks, with Hitler demanding
German occupation of the Sudeten lands by 1 October, and the
British prime minister, Neville Chamberlain, hoping for peace in
'our time,' signed the Munich Pact at the last moment, together
with the French premier, Daladier, accepting the occupation as a
fait accompli.

Bartók had somewhat earlier begun to make plans for leaving
Hungary, despite his great desire to remain with his mother as long
as she lived. To that end he had written to Adnan Saygun to ask
his assistance in finding work in Turkey that would enable him to
carry on the study begun in 1936. Saygun found the way blocked by
a foreign musician in a position of authority over Turkish music,
who could brook no competition; and therefore had to confess to
Bartók that he could not help. A curiously polyglot letter [57] to Mrs.
Zoltán Székely, congratulating her in seven languages on the birth
of her son, speaks of the whole world's drifting into evil, restlessness,
terror, and of the frightening defection of the western countries;
of the necessity of going far from the vicinity of the 'pestilence-ridden

lands'—but where? to Greenland, Tierra del Fuego, the Fiji Islands?
Mrs. Székely suggested that he go to the United States, but
Bartók wrote her:

Your kind and loving letter gave us a kind of emotion not yet experienced: is the situation as bad as you see it? Of course, since March we
are sure there will be a change to worse or to worst which will perhaps
make it impossible to work here and even to live here. But in the country
you mention, would it be possible to do that work which is so very important for me (I mean the scientific work)? I don't think so. If I can
only *végéter* there, then it would be of no use to change *domicile*. I
think it extremely difficult to decide something in that way and really I
am at a loose what to do. In any case, still we must wait for some more
decesive signs of change. Sure, I feel rather incomfortable to live so very
near to the clutches of the nazis or even in the clutches; but to live elsewhere would—it seems at least for the moment—not make things
easier—[58]

But he could not decide to go. As late as 3 June 1939, he wrote
to Sándor Veress in London: 'The information that I am leaving
Hungary is false. But this rumor has been widespread for some time—
many have spoken to me about it.' [59] In the same letter, however,
he announced plans for an American tour: 'Next year in February
or March I am going to the United States for several (5-6) weeks.
There at all events I should like to look around—provided nothing
happens in the meantime to prevent the whole trip.'
Earlier in the spring he had met Székely in Paris to go over the
Violin Concerto, which was scheduled for production in Amsterdam
in April.

We had very good and long rehearsals together—Zoltán and myself
—in Paris, he plays the solo-part of the concerto splendidly indeed. . .
I hope the performance of the concerto will be excellent, what a pity
that I can't be present.[60]

At the end of June Bartók was in Amsterdam and Scheveningen,
and then went to Switzerland, where Paul Sacher had put at his
disposal a chalet at Saanen, in the massif of Gruyère. The German
demands increased; German prestige in central Europe and the
Balkans was in the ascendant; and late in August, events hastened
to a culmination with the signing of a non-aggression pact between

National Socialist Germany and the Soviet Union. Sacher, writing just after Bartók's death, recalled this period:

> As I hastily sought out the composer in a quiet mountain valley . . .
> I found him completely without misgivings for the future, absorbed in his work. The news of the political events which were so cruelly to interfere in his life had not penetrated to him. . .[61]

But Bartók's own letter to his son Béla, dated 18 August, reveals that he was, as always, profoundly aware of what was in prospect:

> The poor peace-loving loyal Swiss are forced to glow with war fever. Their daily papers are full of articles on protection of the country; in the more important passes are defense measures, military preparations. On the Julierpass I myself saw, for example, groups of rocks set into the earth against tanks, and similar nice things. In Holland the situation is the same—even in Scheveningen.—I don't like your wanting to go to Romania; in such uncertain times one should not travel to such an uncertain place. Also the thought constantly disquiets me, whether I can travel home from here, should this or that happen. Luckily I can banish these anxiety-provoked thoughts, if necessary—while I am at work it doesn't disturb me. . . For two weeks I have read no papers; yesterday one fell into my hands. The lack was not at all noticeable—it was as if I had seen an already two weeks old issue. Nothing had happened in the meantime, thank God! [62]

Despite the turmoil that surged about him, Bartók in his Alpine hideaway wrote in only fifteen days one of his gayest, most approachable works, the Divertimento for string orchestra. But the ideal working conditions which had produced this score were not to be permitted him for long. Beginning a Sixth String Quartet, with which he expected to satisfy another commission from Zoltán Székely, he was called back to Hungary after only three and a half weeks by the turn of political events. There, just before Christmas, occurred the death of his mother.

Bartók's loss was heavy. From his earliest years Paula Bartók had played a role of the greatest significance in his life, devoting her whole energy to the development of her son's abilities. In the account of his formative years,[63] written for her grandson, her strong belief in him glows in almost every paragraph, every phrase; and his letters to her, though outwardly impersonal, reveal his warm devotion in the wealth of their detail.

Now that the greatest tie which bound him to Hungary was broken, there was nothing to prevent Bartók's leaving Europe. Szigeti had already gone, playing one of the Bartók Portraits, opus 5, under Mataseles in his farewell appearance in Budapest; [64] and Bartók looked forward to his scheduled American tour, in the hope that something could be discovered that would enable him to settle there, at least until after the war. In the meantime he finished the Sixth Quartet, the last work he was to complete in Hungary; it had become, in a way, a testament, its harsh, discordant *Burletta* and its distorted *Marcia* setting off by contrast the infinite melancholy of the last movement.

April 1940 saw him in Naples, about to leave for New York.

In recent months I have been buried in certain mechanical work, partly in connection with my American tour; finally I fell ill (*not* because of the work, but common influenza), and had to delay the trip. . . I shall arrive in New York on the 11th; on the 13th is my first (and most important) concert, with Szigeti in Washington. If the ship is delayed, it will be too bad for the concert. But this ship was the last possibility; I had to try.[65]

Fortunately there was no delay, and the Coolidge Festival concert went on as scheduled. With Szigeti he played the First Rhapsody and the Second Sonata. The *New York Times* critic,[66] after referring to Bartók as 'the bright adornment of this morning's concert,' found the Rhapsody pleasant but the Sonata incomprehensible—'ideas are drawn out, the themes and rhythms are scrappy, and the least agreeable elements of the violin are singled out for emphasis. There are moments when the composer suggests and maintains a mood, but he breaks off quickly, as if emotion were something to be avoided.' This was only the first indication that Bartók had come too soon; there were many others.

He remained in the United States until 18 May. In the meantime, means were found to enable him to return; Jenő Antal, a member of the Roth Quartet from its founding, conceived the idea of a connection with Columbia University, and a group which included Douglas Moore, Paul Henry Láng, and George Herzog worked out the details. Bartók hoped for something in the nature of folksong research instead of teaching; he had declined an excellent offer from Randall Thompson to teach composition at the Curtis Institute of Music, and there was never any question of his teaching at Columbia, since the Alice M. Ditson Fund, the only source available for a grant, was specifically restricted to nonacademic uses. But a formula was found for using a part of the fund as a research grant, so that Bartók might pursue his own interests in whatever way seemed most appropriate, and he held the appointment as a Visiting Assistant in Music from January 1941 to December 1942, with an honorarium of $3000 a year.

Returning to Hungary to settle his affairs, he wrote to Fritz Reiner on his last day in New York: 'I hope that in October at the latest I may return to the "free" country.' [67] It was by no means easy to make arrangements.

In the first place, both my shoulders developed periarthritis, which had been preparing for about 15 years. My right arm I could for a time not raise at all, so that I could only talk about playing the piano. Now however I am better, but manipulation is tiresome—and still we want to go to America in October. . .[68]

To leave Hungary in wartime, with transportation in confusion and intercourse between certain countries cut off, called for the greatest ingenuity. Visas to enter the United States were readily obtained, transit visas for France and Spain took weeks longer, while there was no certainty that Italian visas would be granted at all. Passage by American cargo ship from Lisbon had been arranged; the itinerary called for travel by train through Milan to Geneva, by bus to Barcelona, and thence by train to Lisbon. Tickets from Geneva to Lisbon had to be purchased by friends in Switzerland, who also provided funds for incidental expenses on the journey.

In October Béla and Ditta Bartók were ready to set out. He made a will, providing that:

My burial is to be the simplest possible. If after my death they want to name a street after me, or to erect a memorial tablet to me in a public place, then my desire is this: as long as what were formerly Oktogon-tér and Körönd in Budapest are named after those men for whom they are at present named [i.e., Hitler and Mussolini], and further, as long as there is in Hungary any square or street, or is to be, named for these two men, then neither square nor street nor public building in Hungary is to be named for me, and no memorial tablet is to be erected in a public place.[69]

On the eighth of October there was a farewell concert, in which Bartók played the Bach A-major Concerto, his wife 'the delightful (and almost unknown) Mozart F-major Concerto [K. 413]—this was her first solo appearance, and she played very beautifully—afterwards we played the Mozart 2-piano Concerto [K. 365], and finally I played from the *Mikrokosmos.*' [70] A few days later they left Hungary, he for the last time. They crossed Italy (he refused to write the name, calling it *Csizma-ország*, 'Boot-country') at night, and in Geneva, thanks to Stefi Geyer, the Müller-Widmanns, and Paul Sacher, found everything taken care of. Bartók wrote to Mrs. Müller-Widmann:

And now here we are with sad hearts and must say farewell to you and your dear ones—for how long, or perhaps forever, who knows—! The farewell is hard, infinitely hard. And this wonderfully beautiful country, your country, perhaps to see it for the last time, and with thoughts of the future that awaits us, and of our friends here. . . Properly speaking, this journey is a leap to uncertainty from certain unbearableness. My condition is not very reassuring; I still think the periarthritis is not completely cured. God knows how much and how long I can work over there.

But we could not do otherwise; the question is not at all, *Muss es sein?*, for *es muss sein*. I thank you and your dear ones for all the beauty, all the love and friendship you have bestowed, and we wish you the best things possible in the future.[71]

Crossing southern France by bus presented few obstacles. They stopped at Grenoble and Montélimar, and overnight at Nîmes, and even though they were told, '*En France il y a la disette*,' they managed to obtain food without *cartes d'alimentation*. But when they reached the Spanish frontier, trouble began to pile up. The bus would go no farther; the customs inspection was to be 'merciless'; the train was about to start, and Bartók had forgotten the Spanish he once knew. At last, by leaving behind 310 kilos of luggage—which was to be returned to them three days later in Badajoz—they were permitted to board the train. But the luggage did not arrive in Badajoz; possibly they might find it in Lisbon, or later in New York. Expecting to have three days in Lisbon, they learned on the train on 19 October that their ship was to leave the following day; they arrived in Lisbon at two in the morning, wandered from hotel to hotel looking for a room, ultimately had a few hours' sleep, and went aboard ship—still without luggage. At that, Bartók felt they were fortunate: Paderewski, eighty years old, had been detained in Spain three weeks.

By midnight on 29 October, after a rough ten-day crossing, having stopped in the Azores and Bermuda on the way, they were in New York Harbor. The next day they disembarked, to begin a new life in a new country.

A few days after their arrival, the New Friends of Music presented the Bartóks in Town Hall, in the Sonata for Two Pianos and Percussion; three weeks later they gave a duo-piano recital there, playing the Mozart Sonata in D (K. 448), Debussy's *En blanc et noir*, four pieces from *Mikrokosmos*, two contrapuncti from *The Art of Fugue*, and the Brahms F-minor Sonata. On 25 November, Columbia University held a special convocation in the rotunda of Low Memorial Library, at which Bartók was awarded an honorary Doctor of Music degree. Degrees were granted at the same time to Dr. Karl T. Compton, president of the Massachusetts Institute of Technology; Sir Cecil Thomas Carr, English barrister; and Dr. Paul Hazard, member of the Académie Française.

This was quite a ceremony [Bartók wrote].[72] As prelude, my measure had to be taken, in yards, feet, and fathoms, the details of my head, shoulder, etc., size to be sent. They dressed all of us in the university toga or cloak; then in pairs we marched solemnly in, amidst the sounding of discreet organ music. The directions were precise: when my name was called, I must stand up; when the chairman addressed me, I must take off the toga; when at last he reached the proper words, I must go up to him, so that he might bestow the diploma; on my back would be hung the pink velvet ribbons of the music degree; then I could go back and sit down. That is the way it happened. Fortunately for us and for the ceremony, we didn't have to speak. . .

In conferring the degree upon Bartók, Nicholas Murray Butler cited him as:

. . . distinguished teacher and master; internationally recognized authority on the folk music of Hungary, Slovakia, Romania, and Arabia [*sic*]; creator through his composition of a musical style universally acknowledged to be one of the great contributions to the twentieth-century literature of music; a truly outstanding artist who has brought high distinction to the spiritual life of his country.[73]

On 1 December Bartók left for a week in Cleveland, where there was a festive evening in the Hungarian colony, 'with gipsy music and *palotás* (!!). Hungarians here, Hungarians there, Hungarians everywhere, but we could not be very glad of this, because the second generation already uses the language only with difficulty.' [74] Returning to New York, the Bartóks moved into a fifth-floor apartment in Forest Hills, twenty minutes from New York by subway, and began the process of acclimatization before the appointment at Columbia took effect. In his letters Bartók describes the 'Americanization' of their living—'crackled-*wheat* (!)' for breakfast, the necessity of learning multitudes of new words (subway stations, names of streets), of becoming acquainted with complex transportation systems (they once spent three hours in the subway, 'traveling hither and thither in the earth; finally, our time waning and our mission incomplete, we shamefacedly slunk home—of course, entirely underground'). Their luggage, which had been taken from them in Spain on 16 October, reached New York only on Christmas Eve.

Before beginning work at Columbia University, Bartók and his wife made a transcontinental tour, playing recitals in St. Louis, Denver, Provo, San Francisco, and Seattle, and returning through Kansas City and Detroit. In some places he found the public better prepared than in 1928 to appreciate his music; in others there was only a perfunctory response. The works programmed were still mainly his own, though they were somewhat more varied than before, through the inclusion of a number of the pieces from the *Mikrokosmos*; in addition Mrs. Bartók joined him in the performance of duo-piano works.

In March he took up his appointment at Columbia. No restrictions were placed upon him in his choice of work, but Dr. Herzog suggested that he might like to investigate the large collection of records—nearly 2500 double-faced discs—made in Yugoslavia in 1934-35 by Milman Parry, professor of classical philology at Harvard University. No systematic study had been made of these materials, since the collector died shortly after his return. The great majority of the discs are devoted to the heroic epic songs of Yugoslavia; here was where Parry's interests lay, since his purpose in making the study was to discover relationships between the Homeric chants of Greece and present-day Balkan 'men's songs.' But among the others there are more than two hundred discs of Serbo-Croatian 'women's songs,' of lyrical character and musically more grateful; and it was this section that Bartók elected to prepare for publication.

Dr. Herzog placed a room at his disposal, and he worked there entirely without supervision; his time was his own. The Archives of Primitive Music (in the Department of Anthropology) duplicated the original discs to prevent damage in the transcribing process, and the Alice M. Ditson Fund made a further grant of $2500 to subsidize the publication of the study, without any claims upon the royalties which would accrue to Bartók.

Near the end of his first year as Visiting Associate in Music, Bartók described his situation in a letter to Zoltán Kodály:

> It was entirely left to me what sort of work I choose to do—I have not to lecture. I chose the transcribing into musical notation of the Parry Collection—I am working now in a wing of the Columbia University, at the phonograph archive of Herzog's. The equipment is excellent. I almost feel as if I were continuing my work at the Hungarian Academy of Science, only in slightly altered conditions. Even the setting resembles its nobility. When I cross the campus in the evening, I feel as if I were passing the historic square of a European city.[75]

Publication of the results of Bartók's study was delayed for several years. Although the preface of his book, *Serbo-Croatian Folk Songs*,[76] is dated February 1943, it was not published until September 1951; another group of notations made during the course of his work have not yet been issued.[77] These latter concern the heroic epic songs in the Parry Collection. Once having begun the study of these materials, Bartók was reluctant to leave it incomplete; in October 1941, as he was planning another trip to the Pacific Coast (for lectures at Palo Alto and Portland, and a conference at the University of Washington), he wrote to Mrs. Creel:

> I prefer to *tell* you than to write about all our good- and mishaps (in fact a great deal of mis-, and tiny bits of good-). My intended letter was to be a very long and un-American letter—complaints and complaints (here one *must* always feel fine and excellent even if dying). The only

bright spot is my work at Columbia University: studying Serbo-Croatian folk-music material from really unique records. . . But—*hélas*—this is only a temporary job and the work probably must remaine unfinished, so even there is mingled a bitter drop.[78]

Realizing that the Columbia appointment could not be made permanent, Bartók cast about for other work. Concert engagements were difficult to obtain; for the 1941-2 season there were in prospect by late autumn only a single concert with orchestra, three duo-piano recitals, and four 'minor engagements' (solo recital or lecture). Bartók's younger son, Péter, had obtained a visitor's visa to come to the United States, but encountered difficulty in securing transit visas 'through the wild-beasts-land. But I don't know,' Bartók wrote, 'if it would not be more advisable for us to go back than for him to come over—that of course is only a vague idea.'[79] In the meantime he was carrying on negotiations with the University of Washington, in case the Columbia appointment were not renewed; in August he wrote to Carl Paige Wood in Seattle that he hoped his appointment would be extended beyond June 1942, in which case he could come to Washington for the year 1943-4.[80] It was not until the spring of 1942 that he was notified of a further extension of the Ditson grant, which assured him of an income until the end of December, and he notified the University of Washington that he would be available at any time thereafter.

Meanwhile the United States itself had been drawn into the war, and communication between Hungary and America was cut off. Bartók, his visitor's visa expiring, was compelled to go to Montreal and re-enter as a non-quota immigrant. Péter Bartók, somewhere between Budapest and New York, was not heard from for weeks, but finally arrived in Lisbon in February 1942. There were a few concerts, among them a two-piano recital in Chicago, about which Bartók wrote Mrs. Creel:

We plaid rather well, and got very bad criticisms. In fact, 1 was good, 1 rather lukewarm, and [a third?] as bad as I never got in my life. Just as if we were the last of the last pianists. So you see your choice of piano-teacher was a very bad one! . . .

And now the bad knews. Our situation is getting daily worse and worse. All I can say is that never in my life since I earn my livelihood (that is from my 20th year) have I been in such a dreadful situation as I will be probably very soon. To say dreadful is probably exaggerated, but not too much. Mrs. Bartók bears this very valiantly: the worse the happenings, the more energetic, confident and optimistic she is. She tries to do some work, teaching for instance. But how to get pupils or a job. . . I am rather pessimistic, I lost all confidence in people, in countries, in everything. Unfortunately, I know much better the circonstances, than Ditta does, so probably I am right in being pessimistic. Do you remember what I said just one year ago: I wonder if it is not too late (concerning war preparations). Now, I am afraid it *is* too late. And I whish only to be wrong in this my feeling. . .

Until know we had . . . two free pianos, a baby grand and an upright. Just today I got the news the upright will be taken from us. Of course we have no money to hire a second piano. So we will have no possibility to study two-piano works. And each month brings a similar blow. I am wondering and asking myself what next? With these dissonant chords, I finish my letter. . .[81]

But Mrs. Bartók added a postscript to the same letter, saying, 'In spite of all the difficulties, I always am thankful for being here and I am thinking how sad it would be for my husband to be in his own country now—'

On 20 April, at the 231st Street subway station in the Bronx, Bartók unexpectedly encountered his son, who had left Budapest four months before. Although he had cabled from Lisbon, the name of his ship had been deleted by the censor. Péter Bartók's arrival was the occasion for a joyful reunion; but other events were far from reassuring. Bartók wrote to Mrs. Creel about his concern for his health,

. . . which is impaired since the beginning of April: since that time I have every day temperature elevation (of about 100°) in the evening, quite regularly and relentlessly! The doctors cann't find out the cause, and as a consequence, cann't even try a treatment. Is not that rather strange? Fortunately, I can do my work; only it may happen for instance this: in Oct. I had a lecture in New York at the Musicological Society. It was aggravated by a dinner and discussions: when I came home, I had 102.[82]

During the whole year he was busy with his work at Columbia University, completing in October the book on Serbo-Croatian folksongs, and also working on a collection of 2500 Romanian melodies he had amassed earlier, for which he provided an introductory study and notes in the hope of eventual publication. These works were written in English—his first work in that tongue. 'All this was a rather tiresome work (and my struggling with the English language) but very interesting indeed.' [83]

At the end of December 1942, the appointment at Columbia was scheduled for termination, since the Ditson Fund could no longer be drawn upon for this purpose. Bartók was notified of this, and was quite naturally concerned, since the amount of the Ditson grant, small though it was, had made it possible for the Bartóks to live in reasonable security, especially when supplemented with occasional fees for concerts and lectures. Of course, such funds as might have accrued in royalties and performance fees in Hungary, together with the payments on his pension, were cut off with the entrance of the United States into the war. And with the constant threat of a physical collapse, there was cause for apprehension.

At Columbia I am 'dismissed' from Jan. 1 on. They seem to have no more money for me. This is annoying because little more than half of the work (connected with the Parry Collection) could be achieved during these 2 years; and I hate incompleteness. If it ever can be continued, Heaven only knows. But from Febr. on, I am invited to Harvard University to give there a certain number of conferences and lectures during the 1st [sic] semester. This gives us a respite until next fall (no possibilities with concertizing or lecturing; we have a 'unique' engagement in Jan. with the New York Philh. Society, but this is a 'family' business, the engagement was made through my friend Fritz Reiner who is guest conductor in some of these concerts. So we are living from half-year to half-year. . .

So, with my books and articles I am gradually advancing to the position of an English writer (I don't mean it seriously, of course); I never had an idea that this will be the end of my career! Otherwise, my career as a composer is as much as finished: the quasi boycott of my works by the leading orchestras continues; no performances either of old works or new ones. It is a shame—not for me of course.[84]

On 21 January 1943, Béla and Ditta Bartók gave the first performance of his Concerto for Two Pianos (the reworked version of the Sonata for Two Pianos and Percussion) in a concert of the New York Philharmonic-Symphony Society. Fritz Reiner conducted. The audience was generally receptive, the critics antagonistic; one [85] went so far as to wish that the concert had stopped at the intermission, so that he would not have had to hear the Concerto. It is curious to find the words 'arid and doctrinaire' applied to this glowing score, especially after the critic has acknowledged its complete sincerity, and admitted that it 'bears [Bartók's] stamp in every measure.'

This was Bartók's last public concert. During the first part of 1943, his health became conspicuously worse. In January and February there was a complete breakdown, with such weakness that he could scarcely walk from one room to another, and a temperature frequently four degrees above normal. He gave three of the scheduled lectures at Harvard, but was completely exhausted by them; and although he had had a continual series of medical examinations, without tangible result,

. . . the Harvard people . . . persuaded me to go through another examination, led by a doctor highly appreciated by them and at their expenses. This had a certain result as an X-ray showed some trouble in the lungs which they believed to be T.B.C. and greeted with cheers and great joy: 'at last we have the real cause.' (I was less joyful at hearing these news.) I went home, was kept in bed during weeks. Then came the ASCAP [86] which got somehow interested in my case and decided to cure me at their expenses (though I am not a member!). They sent me to their doctors who again took me to a hospital. The new X-rays, however, showed a lesser and lesser degree of lung trouble, it appears to be a very slight one indeed, and maybe not a T.B.C. at all! *It does not account for the high temperatures.* So we have the same story again, doctors don't know the real cause of my illness—and, consequently, can't treat and cure it! They are groping about as in a darkness, try desperately to invent the most extraordinary hypotheses. But all that is of no avail.[87]

From April on there were recurrent periods of lower and higher fever; from May, pain in the joints which made walking almost impossible.

The only thing on the credit side is that I gained 9 lb. during Apr. and May (having before the ridiculous weight of 87!). Unfortunately, the terribly oppressing New York heat in June took all my appetite, and I lost again 2 of those precious 9.—So you have a succinct picture of my ailments which makes a tedious and unexhilarating reading!—There is no hope of recovery, and it is out of the question to take anywhere a job.[88]

The summer of 1943 was spent at Saranac Lake, in northern New York, at the expense of ASCAP. Before the Bartóks left the city, Serge Koussevitzky came to Bartók's hospital room to offer him a commission of a thousand dollars from the Koussevitzky Foundation, to write an orchestral work in memory of the late Mrs. Koussevitzky. Unknown to Bartók, the suggestion for the commission had come from Szigeti and Reiner; but the circumstances were concealed from him to prevent interpretation as a form of charity. Bartók was reluctant, even so, to accept, with the prospect of his being unable to fulfill the commission, but Koussevitzky left with him a check for half the amount, the remainder to be paid upon completion of the score, and the Bartóks left for the Adirondacks.

Until mid-August he spent his time reading, finding in the local library such things as Motteux's translation of *Don Quixote*, and being pleased because the seventeenth-century English did not give him 'particular difficulties.' [89] As his recurrent fever abated, he found it possible to work 'practically day and night' on the work commissioned by the Koussevitzky Foundation (which he began on 15 August), and brought the score of the Concerto for Orchestra with him when he came to New York in October to hear—for the first time—a performance of his Violin Concerto. Late in November he met Yehudi Menuhin and heard him play the First Violin Sonata in his New York recital.

He is really a great artist, he played in the same concert Bach's C-major sonata in a grand, classical style. My sonata, too, was excellently done. When there is a real great artist, then the composer's advice and help is not necessary, the performer finds his way quite well, alone. It is alltogether a happy thing that a young artist is interested in contemporary works which draw no public, and likes them, and—performs them *comme il faut.*[90]

Under the sponsorship of ASCAP, Bartók was sent—alone—to Asheville, North Carolina, for the winter of 1943-4, his wife and son remaining in New York. In the meantime, arrangements had been made by Victor Bátor with Columbia University for a resumption of Bartók's appointment there for another six months, with funds partially collected by Joseph Szigeti through solicitation of musical organizations, recording companies, and individuals. But again the details were kept secret from Bartók, who would have felt obliged to decline the appointment as a charity measure. The work was to be done between April and December 1944; Bartók hoped that his Serbo-Croatian study would be published during that period as well.

He had given up hope of being able to publish the Romanian and Turkish materiał, and after the breakdown of negotiations with the New York Public Library, he deposited the manuscripts at Columbia University: 'there they are available to those few persons (very few indeed) who may be interested in them.' [91]

In Asheville, the apparent improvement in his health continued.

At present I feel in the best of health, no fever, my strength has returned, I take fine walks in the woods and mountains—actually I climb the mountain (of course only with due caution). In March my weight was 87 pounds; now it is 105. I grow fat. I bulge. I explode.[92] You will not recognize me.[93]

With his renewed strength—to which he attributed his ability to complete the Koussevitzky commission 'or vice versa'—Bartók wrote during his Asheville sojourn a Sonata for Solo Violin, commissioned by Menuhin and completed on 14 March 1944. This was the last original score he was to finish. In the same winter he also busied himself with arranging and writing out fair copies of 2000 Walachian folksong texts, about which he wrote to Szigeti:

I believe that many interesting things will turn up in this. . . For example, that for the girl it is a much greater misfortune to be jilted than for the boy. This of course we knew before, but now it can be proved in black and white with statistical facts. Further, that girls (or women) are so much more vehement, more wrathful; there are many more texts about girls cursing faithless boys than vice versa. These cursing texts, incidentally, are exceedingly singular: what a Shakespearean fantasy is manifested in them, quite prodigious. Sorry that I can't quote from the Walachian, since you do not understand it. But we Magyars have an abundance of that kind, for example:

> May thirteen apothecary's shelves
> Empty themselves in thee;
> May nine cartloads of hay and straw
> Rot in thy bed;
> May thy towel throw out flames,
> Thy washing water turn to blood.

Or even:

> May God smite thee with bread bought with money,
> With bread bought with money, and a whore for a wife.

Bread bought with money—this the urban Americans would not understand, for doesn't everyone buy his bread? Quite so, but not the small-propertied peasant: he grows the wheat himself, bakes his own bread, and if the frost has struck his crops, then he has to buy his bread with money, but where does he get the money? . . .

And so these are the things that occupy me now—and I await the end of my exile.[94]

Other things occupied him as well. There was so far little progress to show in the European war, and Bartók was depressed to see the entire civilization he had known still in peril of destruction.

But what most worries me is this lagging and slow procedure on the 'battlefields.' There is no end in sight—and the destroying of Europe (people and works of art) continues without respite and mercy. Personally, I do not know how long I can endure the insecurity of this gipsy life. (But for 1944, at least, my living expenses are secured, no worry about that.) And the destiny of poor Hungary, with the Russian danger in the background—the prospects of the future are rather dark.[95]

During all this time he could learn nothing of his family in Hungary—his son Béla and his wife, his sister Elza and her family; nor of the many friends he had left there, the Kodálys and all the rest. Péter Bartók, having passed his regents' examinations in New York, remained there for a time, but in February 1944 enlisted in the United States Navy and was stationed in Panama, after a six months' training course. And the promise of continued improvement in Bartók's health was not fulfilled:

You said in one of your letters that my recovering was a miracle. This is true only with some reservations: it was only a hemisemidemi-miracle. Of course, that lung-infection disappeared as mysteriously as it came. . . There are, however—and almost continuously—some minor troubles which probably never can be completely cured and make a regular job or concertizing etc. impossible for me. So for instance, last April my spleen became rebellious. My Asheville doctor mistook it for a pleuresy. He would have quite gallantly treated me against it, but fortunately I had to come back to New York where the mistake was at once discovered, and my spleen punished by a rude X-ray treatment. Then it appeared there is a disorder in my blood-picture, so they poisoned me with arsenic. Shall I continue? I think better not.

A few weeks ago I said, 'Tell me, doctor, exactly what my ailment is! Choose a nice Latin or Greek word and tell me.' After a moment's hesitation he emitted: 'Polycithemia.' There we are again! Only, 2 years ago this meant too many red corpuscles, and now it means too many white ones.[96]

Even with these difficulties, Bartók felt that he could by exercising care still do some work at home, teaching; but there were only occasional pupils, some who had studied with him in Budapest and came to him for a few lessons when they were in New York: among them were Dorothy Parrish Domonkos and Agnes Butcher. The Bartóks' apartment—at 309 West 57th Street in New York, a few blocks from Carnegie Hall—was too small, but with the shortage of housing they felt fortunate to have found even these two rooms.[97]

In November 1944, Menuhin played the Sonata for Solo Violin in his New York recital. Bartók was present, and was brought to the stage to acknowledge the applause of an audience that filled the hall to overflowing. The critics had little good to say about the work. Olin Downes reported the enthusiasm of the audience, which 'must have been rewarding to Mr. Bartók, who has had his share of the difficulties of the radical innovator';[98] but found the work itself 'a test for the ears, the intelligence, the receptiveness of the most learned listener. . . On initial acquaintance, we take none too kindly to the piece.' But Bartók himself was of another opinion:

It was a wonderful performance. [The Sonata] has 4 movements and lasts *ca.* 20 minutes. I was afraid it is too long; imagine: listen to a single violin during 20 minutes. But it was quite all right, at least for me.[99]

A few days later Bartók was present for another triumph: the first performance of the Concerto for Orchestra, which Koussevitzky and the Boston Symphony played on 1 and 2 December.

We went there for the rehearsals and performances—after having obtained the grudgingly granted permission of my doctor for this trip. It was worth wile, the performance was excellent. Koussevitzky is very enthusiastic about the piece, and says it is 'the best orchestra piece of the last 25 years' (including the works of his idol Shostakovich!).[100]

This, the largest of Bartók's mature orchestral works, was to play a significant role in at last bringing his music to the eminence it now occupies. In 1948-9, American symphony orchestras played Bartók's music more frequently than that of any other composer of the twentieth century except Strauss and Prokofiev. In that season,

American orchestras gave fifty-six performances of eight works by Bartók; there were more performances of Bartók than of such earlier composers as Berlioz, Liszt, Dvořák, Schubert, or Mahler; the level has remained nearly as high in the years since. Side by side with this, and with the cyclical performances of the six string quartets which contributed to the understanding of Bartók's work, came performances of *Duke Bluebeard's Castle, The Wonderful Mandarin,* and the first American performance of the *Cantata profana.* Simultaneously, the demand for his music has led to the recording of almost all the larger works and many of the smaller ones, and the reprinting of most of the out-of-print scores. From being one of the least accessible of twentieth-century composers, Bartók has become one of the best known.

At the end of 1944, Bartók wrote to Mrs. Creel [101] that he was assured of a 'modest living' for the next three years. During that year he had received about $1400 in royalties and performance fees in the United States and Great Britain, as well as some other income; and he had just signed an agreement with Boosey and Hawkes which called for an advance of $1400 annually for the next three years in addition to income from sale and performance. ASCAP was still assuming responsibility for medical expenses.

In December 1944, Ralph Hawkes commissioned a seventh string quartet from Bartók; the following February, at Hawkes's instigation, William Primrose asked him for a viola concerto. Bartók was reluctant to undertake the latter.

He showed no great enthusiasm [Primrose wrote]; [102] rather he seemed doubtful as to the success of such an undertaking on his part. As he was anxious to get some idea of the technical capacity of the viola [as a solo instrument], we arranged that he should attend a performance of the Walton Viola Concerto which I was to give the following week. . . Unfortunately he was too ill to attend this performance, but he listened to it over the air. . .

There was also a commission for a duo-piano concerto for Bartlett and Robertson; from almost complete obscurity, almost complete neglect on the part of performers, Bartók had suddenly become sought after. Had there been time, a whole series of major works was in prospect. But in March he became ill with pneumonia; thanks to recently-developed antibiotics, this was quickly conquered. Yehudi Menuhin invited the Bartóks to spend the summer in California, and Bartók, with his doctor's approval, gladly accepted, planning to leave New York in mid-June. Early in June, however, he had to write to Menuhin:

Regretfully I must tell you that we cannot come to California! I am not feeling very well, and—owing to a variety of things—now my wife has been ill for several weeks and has still not recovered. The whole thing is that we are afraid of such a long journey, which, especially now, would be attended by all kinds of inconvenience. I hardly know how to say how sorry I am. I had so many plans for music in connection with my sojourn there. Now these have turned to naught. . . We must try next winter somewhere to talk about the final form of the Solo Sonata; the matter is not urgent. . .[103]

Instead of California, the Bartóks went back to Saranac Lake. There at last they received news from Hungary. Zoltán and Emma Kodály were well, though they had lost their home and possessions; Bartók's son Béla and his wife, and his sister Elza and her family, had escaped. Both copies of his thirteen years' work of folksong notation had survived, carefully hidden; his own household goods were almost unscathed.[104] But the situation of the country itself was far from reassuring.

More harm—at least spiritually—was done by the extremely bad news about Hungary. Direct news did not arrive. . . But there are regularly reprinted Budapest newspaper (each copy coming probably through the Russian embassy and reprinted in facsimile by a Hungarian language communist newspaper in N. Y.—There we read about Kodály and other musicians, artists, who seem to be (comparatively) well. Dohnányi is a 'war-criminal'! However, so much damage has been done to the country that Heaven knows if and when it can again somehow recover. The Germans were beasts, but the Russians do not seem to be saints, too.[105]

But the summer was not without its rewards. Péter Bartók was discharged from the Navy and returned to the United States in August, stopping in New York and then going on to Saranac Lake to be with his parents. And Bartók found pleasure in the out-of-doors, watching the 'chickmucks'[106] and calculating the number of vibrations per second of the wings of hummingbirds ('My result is about 90 or 100').

During the summer another commission was proffered; Bartók announced it cryptically: 'A turtle wants to order a 5-minute orchestral work from me. . . Only it's too bad that the turtle makes no sound, so that it could be worked into the piece.' [107] This is another instance of Bartók's punning: the 'turtle' was Nat Shilkret (*Schildkröte* is the German word for turtle), and the proposal was that Bartók collaborate in the musical symposium called *Genesis*, which ultimately brought together separate movements by such strange bedfellows as Schoenberg, Stravinsky, Milhaud, Toch, and Shilkret himself. But Bartók could not agree to undertake the composition of such a work for a year,[108] and in addition, because of his commitment to Boosey and Hawkes found participation in the project beset by complications. In the end (Bartók wrote), 'The turtle proved obstinate, he will do nothing at all.' [109]

As for the summer's composition, Bartók divided his waning energies between the Viola Concerto, intended for William Primrose, and a new—and uncommissioned—Piano Concerto. It had been many years since he had worked simultaneously on two major scores; now his desperate activity seems to have been prompted by a realization of the gravity of his illness. On 8 September he wrote to Primrose:

I am very glad to be able to tell you that your Viola Concerto is ready in draft, so that only the score has to be written, which means a purely mechanical work, so to speak. If nothing happens I can be through in 5 or 6 weeks, that is, I can send you a copy of the orchestral score in the second half of October, and a few weeks afterwards a copy (or if you wish more copies) of the piano score.

Many interesting problems arose in composing this work. The orchestration will be rather transparent, more transparent than in the Violin Concerto. Also the sombre, more masculine character of your instrument executed some influence on the general character of the work. The highest note I use is 'A,' but I exploit rather frequently the lower registers. It is conceived in a rather virtuoso style. Most probably some passages will prove to be uncomfortable or unplayable. These we will discuss later, according to your observations.

The Viola Concerto was destined to remain unfinished. When Tibor Serly saw him on the evening of 21 September Bartók was working on the orchestral score of the Third Piano Concerto; Péter Bartók had drawn the measure bars for him, and with the manuscript scattered over his bed he was struggling to fill in the last few measures. Other manuscript pages under a clutter of medicine bottles proved to be the Viola Concerto, the completion of which, Bartók told Serly,[110] was a matter of working out details and scoring. The next day he was taken from the tiny apartment on 57th Street to the West Side Hospital. There, on 26 September, Béla Bartók died.

After the last bar of the Third Piano Concerto, Bartók had written —prematurely—the Hungarian word *vége*, the end. For Bartók the man, this *was* the end: an end such as no man would wish for, in a strange land, far from home, family, friends, all that meant so much to him.

But for Bartók the composer, this was by no means an end. It is callous to say, as some have said, that recognition waited only for his death. Such a point of view implies the half-truth that a great artist creates only for the future, not for his own time. But Bartók created for his own time: the essence of that time is in his music, and there were many who during his life heard it with understanding and keenly perceptive enjoyment. It is tragic that Bartók could not have benefited from the wider acceptance he was able to foresee; when he stood upon the stage of Carnegie Hall on 26 November 1944, acknowledging wave upon wave of applause for a 'difficult' work, and when, a week afterward, he heard the tumultuous reception of his Concerto for Orchestra in Boston, he knew that he had written—and written well—for his own time, and for the future as well. In the years since, with increasing opportunity to know Bartók's music, audiences everywhere have come to realize that here is a colossus among men. And in that sense, there is no longer *vége*, the end, but only *kezdete*, the beginning.

II

THE MUSIC OF BARTÓK

LIKE most of his early work, the piano music written during Bartók's student years was later repudiated by the composer, and the only music of the period which is now accessible is that which had the fortune, good or bad, to be published soon after its composition. There is little reason to suppose that these works, which include the Four Piano Pieces (1903) and the piano transcription of the *Marcia funebre* from the *Kossuth* symphony, are superior to the other compositions of the period or that Bartók valued them more highly. Having been perpetuated in print, they were out of his hands and he could not conveniently withdraw them as he did the scores that remained in manuscript.

Although they were written after Bartók resumed composition under the stimulus of Strauss, neither the Funeral March nor the Four Piano Pieces betray much of that influence. The Study for the Left Hand does open with a rather Straussian arpeggiated melody in octaves, and there are occasional harmonic suggestions here and there, but there is more of Brahms—a Brahms with a limited harmonic palette and a conventional cadence-structure—in the Four Pieces, and both the second Fantasia and the Scherzo owe a great deal to Liszt. Root progressions in thirds are typical of the harmonic

procedures, and Bartók moves from a minor triad to the major triad
on its third, the two together capable of forming the secondary
seventh-chord which plays an important role in his later music,
though he has not yet begun to suspect its possibilities.[1]

Both the Study and the Scherzo adhere closely to the sonata-rondo
in their architecture, while the two Fantasias are somewhat freer. The
second is, to be sure, in a ternary form, but the return is so fancifully
ornamented that it is all but disguised beyond recognition, while
the indicated repetitions further obscure the structure.

These pieces, written at the end of Bartók's studies at the Academy
of Music, are still little more than student efforts. Melodically they
are not very interesting, harmonically there are awkwardnesses and
banalities, and structurally the seams are all too visible. They are
important in that they indicate some of the composer's potentialities,
as well as the state of his musical mind at the launching of his professional career. While he reveals an interest in the technical aspects
of pianoforte playing, and some slight preoccupation with rhythmic
and textural subtleties, all of which were to increase in importance,
it cannot be said that he presents himself in these works as a chal-
lenging creative talent.

The Rhapsody, opus 1, which dates in its original form from
the end of 1904, is a somewhat more convincing work. Since it was
recast for piano and orchestra, in preparation for the *Prix Rubinstein*
competition of the following year, it will be discussed with the
concertos rather than here.

The Rhapsody was the last piano composition of Bartók untouched
by his folklore investigations. Before he wrote again for the instrument, he had collected hundreds of peasant songs from many sections of Hungary, including Transdanubia, the Alföld, and Transylvania. In 1907 he brought back from the Csík district numerous folksongs and, from the village of Tekerőpatak,[2] four tunes played on a
shepherd's pipe (*tilinkó*). Three of the latter provided the basis for
the Three Popular Hungarian Songs [3] of 1907.

These tunes are highly ornamented, with passing-notes, trills, and
acciaccaturas, but Bartók has kept the harmonic support chordal
and extremely simple, with only a hint of contrapuntal treatment.
The chords are chiefly triads and first-species sevenths, with a few
secondary sevenths, especially in the third tune. Bartók returned to
this last for one of the Eight Hungarian Folksongs for voice and

piano (1907-17), one of the extremely few instances in which he used a single folk tune more than once. This is a 'tempo giusto' tune, in contrast to the first two of the set, which are 'parlando rubato'; there is a rustic vigor and forthrightness about it, while the others are more intimate and reflective.

By the time the Fourteen Bagatelles, opus 6, were written, Bartók's expressive vocabulary was beginning to assume its definitive shape. Years later he marked the beginnings of his personal style by these pieces: 'From Opus 6 on,' he wrote to Edwin von der Null,[4] 'I always tried to use the supradiatonic tones with the greatest possible freedom.' The Bagatelles demonstrate many of the devices which later became an integral part of his technique. At least one writer [5] has attributed to the influence of Schoenberg's *Klavierstücke*, opus 11, the 'speculative German rationalism' of the Bagatelles; but they are dated May 1908, while the Schoenberg pieces were not published until the following year, and Bartók apparently did not know them until 1912.

The Bagatelles are almost all short, even laconic, each concerned with a particular problem of contemporary style. The first, *Molto sostenuto*, combines a single-line melody in E major in the right hand with an ostinato scale pattern in the Phrygian mode on C in the left, the bitonal element appearing here before Stravinsky's *Petrushka* or the explorations of Darius Milhaud.[6] The second, *Allegro giocoso*, is a study in major seconds; the third, *Andante*, has a songlike melody in the left hand, the right accompanying with an incessantly rotating five-note figure, G-B-Bb-A-Ab. Number 4 is an arrangement of an old Hungarian folksong which Bartók collected in Felsőiregh, Tolna, in 1907; he has harmonized the tune in alternating lines, first in triads (Aeolian mode), then with added notes forming seventh-chords.

The fifth Bagatelle, *Vivo*, is an arrangement of a Slovak folksong, its melody supported by an ostinato of added-note chords in incessant eighth-notes. The mode is Dorian. The sixth, *Lento*, is a small ternary form with a rather chromatic, freely flowing melody and only the minimum of chordal support: mainly fifths and, in the second section, thirds. The seventh, *Allegretto molto capriccioso*, like the first, has bitonal elements, the left hand chiefly on the black keys at the beginning, the right hand on the white. The whimsical, capricious changes of tempo, together with the downward arpeggiation of the chords, give the piece the air of an improvised dance.

A study in unresolved appoggiaturas, Number 8, is followed by a set of variations entirely in unison. The largest piece of the group is the tenth; it employs various harmonic devices, including bitonality, chords in fourths, ostinatos (some thickened in thirds or minor seconds), and consecutive augmented triads. There are downward arpeggiated chords here also, notated with the wavy line to the right of the chord; later on, Bartók placed the arpeggio sign at the left as customary and added an arrowhead at the bottom, or placed a directional arrow beside the arpeggio sign.[7]

Number 11, *Allegretto molto rubato*, is wayward and capricious. Among its devices are passages in consecutive fourth-chords, and in consecutive sevenths. Number 12, *Rubato*, gives the impression of familiarity with Schoenberg's early piano pieces, in spite of the chronological sequence: its motivic patterns are close to those of the Viennese composer's Opus 11, no. 1. The vibrating repeated A which opens the piece is, however, quite unrelated, stemming from the same impulse which leads in Bartók to the almost limitless repetition of notes in inverted pedals; but here, with its gathering momentum, it has the feeling of some gamelan music, and it is altogether likely that there is a relation, either express or implied, to the music of the cimbalom.

The last two Bagatelles have subtitles: *Elle est morte . . .* and *Valse: Ma mie qui danse. . .* The former has an expressive, elegiac melody supported by two chords only: minor triads on E♭ and A, a tritone apart. The *Valse* is marked presto; it is a somewhat unfeeling, even sardonic piece—a caricature, perhaps, of Poldini—duplicating the second of the Two Portraits for orchestra, which represents the distorted as opposed to the ideal. The distortion goes almost as far as Berlioz's transformation of the *idée fixe* in the Fantastic Symphony, and comes apparently from a similar impulse.

Bartók himself looked upon Nos. 1, 8, 9, 11, and 13 of the Bagatelles as 'experiments.'[8] The set has been taken as proof of Bartók's familiarity with the music of his contemporaries, but it is evident that in these pieces he was writing far in advance of most of them.

The Ten Easy Pieces (1908) are introduced by the same D-F♯-A-C♯ motive which forms the basis of the Two Portraits and, of course, the fourteenth Bagatelle. Since it motivates the dedicatory piece of this set, some extramusical connotation was apparently intended.[9] The Dedication is in addition to the ten pieces, which include a few folksong transcriptions besides the original compositions. Two movements of the group have become very popular: *Evening with the Széklers* (also called *Evening in Transylvania, Evening in the Country*) and *Bear Dance*; both were transcribed in 1931 for inclusion in the orchestral suite called Hungarian Sketches. The former alternates two pentatonic tunes, one parlando, the other a sprightly 'tempo giusto' tune, to arrive at a rondo-like form, while the *Bear Dance* is run through with rapidly repeated single notes, above and below which a rustic dance-tune is blocked out in chords. The *Bear Dance* is by no means an 'easy piece' from the performance standpoint, nor is the *Five-Finger Exercise* that precedes it, the rotating Lydian tetrachords in sixteenth-notes requiring a considerable agility.

But the rest of the set poses no technical problems for the player. Its interest lies in the stylistic development which it marks: together with the Bagatelles these pieces forecast the concentration of idiom which characterizes all of Bartók's later work. Their textures are open, their harmonies simple but fresh, and the original melodies of the set now frequently betray an indebtedness to folklore. In other respects Bartók shows himself open-minded toward the music of his contemporaries; his recent discovery of the music of Debussy is witnessed by the fourth piece, *Sostenuto*, and the seventh, *Dawn*, with their clouded tonalities and their sensitive reticence. The former closes with a whole-tone scale in the bass, but before that it has devoted four measures to the bitonal superposition of the triads of C♯ minor and A minor, while *Dawn* displays in its seventh measure a device which was to be employed so often throughout Bartók's career that it became almost an *Urmotiv:* major thirds moving a minor third up or down, a procedure which effectually cancels tonality.

Of the remainder, the second piece, *Frustration*, takes the tritone as a point of departure, the left-hand ostinato being constructed from two pairs of augmented fourths, the same interval appearing repeatedly in the single-line melody. Of the folksong arrangements, the first is entirely in unison; the *Slovakian Boys' Dance* begins in unison but is presently supplied with a slight harmonic and rhythmic support; while the third, the simplest of all, is dressed in hornlike thirds, fifths, and sixths, with open fifths in the left hand on the offbeats.

In the progress of music in this century the Bagatelles and the Ten Easy Pieces, miniature as they are, assume an importance disproportionate to their length. They are among the earliest works in which the new ways of viewing musical materials resulted in stylistic conviction. Among the several movements of each set there is still disparity, but almost without exception each of the single pieces is stylistically homogeneous. And, taken as a whole, they are more adventurous than the Debussy Preludes or the Schoenberg *Klavierstücke*, opus 11, both of which they antedate.

The first work in which Bartók's folksong research appears in a consistent stylistic codification is the series of piano pieces called *For Children*.[10] These pieces are based on Hungarian and Slovakian folksongs, many of them children's songs or games and therefore at least partly familiar to the young pianists for whom they were intended. The method Bartók has employed in the setting of these tunes is generally to keep the melodies intact, repeating them once or twice with a varied accompaniment, occasionally with episodic material to set them off. The harmonies are usually simple though by no means conventional; the composer is not disposed to superimpose harmonies of western European style upon these eastern songs, but, as he has indicated,[11] tries to devise suitable harmonic support from the characteristic intervals of the melodies themselves, sounding simultaneously intervals traditionally heard in succession. Sevenths may be used as concords, being melodically of equal value with thirds and fifths in pentatonic melodies; chords in fourths may be derived from the frequent melodic fourths in Magyar peasant tunes. By means of procedures such as these, harmonic progression is made meaningful while avoiding the clichés of many folksong settings; and Bartók discovered that the simpler the melody, the more complex might be the harmonization. The unadorned Phrygian melody of No. 34 in the second volume is set to seventh-chords which seem almost to belong to another key, and many instances which border on bitonality might be cited, each entirely acceptable despite the simplicity of the melody.

The value of these pieces lies in their accessibility to young and unprejudiced musicians, who can begin playing them after a minimum of previous study, and will find in them music which retains its interest long after the problems it poses have been successfully resolved. Few of them offer any serious technical difficulties; on the other hand, the musical demands are great.

While the larger number of both Hungarian and Slovakian folk-tunes in this collection are in the major mode, there are many Aeolian, Dorian, and Mixolydian melodies, two pentatonic tunes, one Phrygian, one Lydian, and numerous mixed or indeterminate modal melodies. Use of these pieces at an early stage of musical development would forestall the exclusive reliance upon major and minor modes which so seriously hampers the understanding of con-temporary music, and lay a foundation upon which, augmented by the use of *Mikrokosmos* and other educational music in newer idioms, could be erected a substantial comprehension of the music of this century.

Though most of the settings in *For Children* are harmonic, many have imitative elements and a few, such as the Canon (II:29), are contrapuntal throughout. Number 5 of the second volume is a set of three variations (except for the ninth Bagatelle, Bartók's earliest work of the kind) on an andante theme, with a considerable amount of imitation in the first variation, while the third has a free canon in contrary motion.

Bartók drew upon the collection for his Hungarian Sketches for orchestra (1931), of which the finale is the *Swineherd's Dance* (I:40), with its bagpipe imitations; and others have transcribed sections for violin and piano, among them Tivadar Országh, Joseph Szigeti, and Ede Zathureczky. The educational merits of these pieces are thus made available to the string player, for whom Bartók much later provided the Forty-four Duos.

The two Elegies, which date from the same period as *For Chil-dren*,[12] are the exact antithesis of those pieces. Where the textures in the folksong settings are clear and unencumbered, frequently spare, those of the Elegies bristle with arpeggios, gruppettas, tremolos, bravura chords, and cadenzas. They are virtuoso pieces in every sense, harking back to the Rhapsody, opus 1, rather than looking forward. Bartók himself considered them a retrogression into the romantic style of his early work; but in at least one respect there is a marked advance in the second Elegy: that of structural organization from

limited means. Here the entire movement is derived from a single
five-note motive, not unlike the one that begins the Chopin Sonata
in B minor, opus 58, the fifth note being a tone higher in the Bartók
motive. In the Chopin Sonata the motive is a purely melodic device,
extended by addition without variation or development. An examination of the Bartók Elegy, however, discloses the motive in every
accompanimental figure, in every melodic line, in almost every
chord. Although stylistically these pieces represent a retreat, the
second is architecturally far ahead of Bartók's other scores, pointing
the way to the structural economy which characterizes all his later
work.

In the second Elegy, too, is found a device of which Bartók made
occasional use later: the ad libitum repetition of figurations to suit
the convenience of the performer. In this work the intention is to
provide an even rotation in the accompaniment while the melodic
line is treated quite freely; later on it becomes a purely utilitarian
device, a left-hand pizzicato being employed while the right adjusts
or removes a mute,[13] or a clarinet figure being prolonged while the
violinist changes instruments.[14] Few composers of periods since the
abandonment of the continuo had permitted the performer to
enter into the creative process, though something similar to this
occurs in the Scherzo of Charles Ives's Fourth Symphony.

Harmonically the Elegies show little effect of Bartók's folksong
study, and surprisingly little relationship to the First Quartet. Whole-
tone scale references betray the hand of Debussy, as do their resultant augmented triads, and there are occasional chords in fourths;
but as a rule triads, seventh- and ninth-chords, altered in late romantic fashion, constitute the harmonic mainstay.

Not in the least like the Elegies are the three Burlesques,[15] which
are stylistically in the main stream of Bartók's development. Here
there is no padding of texture, no enrichment of harmonies. Most
of the first, *Quarrel*, is presented in a unison or two-part texture; the
second, *A Bit Drunk*, is largely in parallel triads with acciaccatura-
chords before each; while the pinwheel figures of the third, which
has no title, occasionally suggest a bitonal separation but usually
coalesce into a single line.

All three of the Burlesques are somewhat spiteful, with sharp
clashes of dissonance, harsh and grotesque accents. Suggestions of

the polyrhythmic patterns prevalent later are found in *Quarrel*, two-beat units overlaid on three-beat bars, while the Trio is made up of three-against-four rhythms. The basis of *A Bit Drunk* is a folk-like tune constituted largely of fourths, and played in an unstable rhythm, to which the acciaccatura-chords contribute a further element of inebriety. Their notation is devious: in an apparent attempt to avoid writing accidentals in the principal chords, Bartók notates an auxiliary triad as Eb-F♯-A♯, a sixth-chord as G-A♯-Eb. Despite the meticulous logic of the notation, the procedure makes reading difficult, even unnecessarily so. Yet it is a procedure to which Bartók adheres throughout his career; an extreme example is this from the *Allegro barbaro*, in which sharps and double-sharps are employed in order to notate a melody lying entirely on the white keys: [16]

1. *Allegro barbaro*

The characteristic devices of the third Burlesque include the superimposition upon a six- or seven-note scale of an arpeggiated six-four chord beginning a semitone higher, or the embracing of a five-note scale between the sixth which spans a semitone on either side. Not authentically bitonal, the parts played separately nevertheless establish different keys, and a few bars before the end a grace-note Gb above an Eb-major triad provides a strong major-minor flavor.

The Sketches, opus 9, are somewhat less even in their quality and less homogeneous in their style than the Burlesques. In a sense they are related to the Bagatelles and the Ten Easy Pieces, but they lack the significance of the first and, in some ways, the attractiveness of the second. Bartók seems to have been concerned in these seven pieces less with the development of new means than with the expressive functions of the music. Individual movements or parts of movements show that the earlier works were not adventitious—the series of cadences in the *Portrait of a Girl*,[17] where the same melodic progression is harmonized with four different pairs of triads (D major-G♯ minor, B major-C major, F♯ major-E major, D major-G major); the pseudo-bitonal combinations of *Seesaw;* the tone clusters of the last piece, in which five-note segments of two whole-tone scales are superimposed. The third movement [18] is interesting for the expressive quality of a single motive presented hesitantly and with constant variation, and for the tonally ambiguous progressions of parallel major tenths in the left hand.

But the remaining pieces are of considerably less interest. One of them is a setting of a Romanian folktune; another, in Walachian style, is entirely in unison with the first note of each line sustained as a pedal. The fourth movement is related to the Elegies and the Rhapsody, opus 1, with its widespread arpeggios, its gruppettas, and trills. When Bartók revised the Sketches in 1945, this was the only piece in which he made changes of any importance, and then only in measures 38 and 40, where he carried over the chord preceding the bar-line, instead of changing it on the first beat. His prefatory statement that No. 4 is in C♯ minor and No. 7 in B major was intended to forestall 'those who like to label all music they do not understand as "atonal" music'; the tonality of the former is easily apparent after the first three measures, and the key is definitely re-established at the close; but that of the latter is never closer to B than in the first bar, where it is Mixolydian rather than major, while the pre-eminence of the two whole-tone scales in the last ten measures sets up a pseudo-tonality on A, the lowest note, and B becomes the mode final only because of the corroboration provided by the F♯, there being no perfect fifth above the A.[19]

While the Sketches are rather fragmentary in their thematic construction, the two Romanian Dances of 1909-10 are their exact opposite, broad and sweeping in their design, vigorous in their rhythms. The themes are original but in folk character, and they have the overwhelming vitality of Romanian dance-tunes. The piano style is rugged and percussive except for an occasional moment of relaxation, as in the Trio of the first, its improvisational melody [20] supported by a vibrating current of thirty-second notes.

The material of the Romanian Dances is squarish, that of the first one particularly so, each motive corresponding to a single bar, each bar repeated, and each four-bar group repeated as well. Bartók avoids monotony by shifts of register, by reharmonization, and especially by the irregularity of the episodes that connect one section with another, so that the motive and phrase repetition does not achieve the stultifying effect of similar procedures in the music of Debussy. There is always something new: the repetition is justified by the suspense which fresh treatment can provide. It is this element of suspense, of unpredictability, that much of Debussy's music lacks; once an idea is presented, the listener may be certain that it will immediately be repeated in the same dimensions, and the alternate interest and relaxation make it impossible to perceive the work as a whole.

Tonality in the Romanian Dances is definite throughout. The first is in C minor, the second in G, and they never stray far from these unequivocal keys, no matter how complex the harmonies. Ostinatos and pedals abound, marking a primitive harmonic scheme in which progress is the function chiefly of rhythm, while harmonic fluctuation is rather widely spaced. Naturally there is almost no contrapuntal writing; lines are frequently presented without support, or in octaves, and in other places chords are used for their percussive value only. The intensity of these dances is further emphasized by the violence of their contrasts; Bartók, ordinarily content with a dynamic compass ranging from *pp* to *ff*, here writes *ppp* and *fff* in an effort to expand the expressive range.

There is no such prodigality in the Dirges (or *Nénies*), which recall the subtle expressiveness of the sixth and thirteenth Bagatelles. These four short pieces have a deeply felt pathos with a strongly folk-conditioned style. Their melodies are presented almost entirely in octaves, with a minimum of chordal support; and that minimum eschews all but the simplest harmonic combinations. In the third of the Dirges the accompaniment is in consecutive fifths, both notes generally doubled; in the first and fourth the combinations are largely triadic. It is only at the end of the second that the harmony is enriched: the process is gradual, the melody being first presented in octaves, beginning on C♯; in the second phrase the C♯ is retained throughout, being joined by B♭ for the two succeeding phrases.

Thereafter are added in succession E, F♯, and G♯, and the whole movement is thus harmonized with a single cumulatively revealed ninth-chord.

With the *Allegro barbaro* (1911) Bartók shows for the first time in his music for the piano a complete assimilation of folk elements, a folk-determination of an original work whose autochthony cannot be misread. Its savage energy has its roots in the East; it is an authentically Magyar work, unrelated in its salient details to the pianism of Liszt, and with no trace of the impressionist perfume of French keyboard music, with which Bartók's music had been tinged since 1907. He was never to be free from the influence of Debussy and Ravel, but from this point on it was a sublimated influence, contributing to the development of Bartók's creative personality but almost entirely absorbed within it.

The martellato chords of the *Allegro barbaro* might have degenerated into a machine-like percussion; that they did not evinces the composer's restraint in this otherwise unbridled work. Interruptions of the pounding rhythms (which have suggested to some listeners the trampling hordes of Attila or Jenghiz Khan: why not of the early Magyar?) give the impression of a series of flashbacks to some violent action. The tonal fabric is frequently conceived on two intersecting planes: the opening is Phrygian on F♯, but the melody for the first sixty bars is entirely on the white keys with a strongly pentatonic flavor. As in the second *Burlesque*, the notation disguises the true shape of the music; Bartók seems to have been concerned with the relation of all notes to a single tonality, at the same time writing music which is in essence bitonal.

So far as his piano music is concerned, the *Allegro barbaro* marks Bartók's coming of age. From here on, stylistic progress is direct, without further experimentation, and with no reversion to the idioms of the composer's earlier music. There is economy in the handling of materials, lucidity in textures, compact organization of structures. There is color, too: harmonic elements and keyboard sonorities are exploited with a sureness born of artistic maturity. But, more and more, Bartók recognized the piano for what it is, an instrument of percussion, and turned his creative energies to the production of music in keeping with its nature, music which culminated in the

Sonata, the Concertos, and the Sonata for Two Pianos and Percussion.

There are, however, folksong arrangements and smaller pieces which precede these climactic works. In 1913 Bartók provided eighteen piano pieces at an elementary level for the piano method of Reschofsky; now published as *The First Term at the Piano*, they include a number of simple folksong settings and some easy original pieces, none of any considerable significance. During the period in which he was occupied with the composition of *The Wooden Prince* and the Second Quartet, however, Bartók produced several important works for the piano, including the Sonatina, the Romanian Folk Dances from Hungary, and the Romanian Christmas Songs (*Colinde*); the Fifteen Hungarian Peasant Songs, and the Suite, opus 14. Of these, the Suite is the only one not based upon folk melodies.

Yet even the Suite has in its first movement a strong folk flavor, the dance mood being perhaps inspired by the Romanian tunes with which Bartók had been working intensively; and the third movement, 'allegro molto,' was admittedly influenced by the music of the Arabs of Biskra and vicinity, where Bartók had collected peasant music in June 1913.[21]

But one of the most prominent features of the Suite is its emphasis upon whole-tone passages, both scalar and chordal, and by extension upon the interval of the tritone. The first movement gives the impression of being in a modified B♭ major, but alternates the tonic triad with one on E, a tritone above, while the melodic line includes C, D, E, and F♯ of the whole-tone scale (as well as an auxiliary G♮). A few bars before the end there is a complete whole-tone scale on C which ascends more than three octaves; and with the exception of three G♮'s all the notes of the last eight measures are from one whole-tone scale. The Scherzo which constitutes the second movement is built largely upon broken augmented triads in varying relationships, though for contrast it makes use of minor seconds and major sevenths in occasional passages, both being foreign to the whole-tone system. The rotating ostinato of the third movement generally spans a tritone; its melodic line incessantly repeats a four-note figure which covers a perfect fifth, with the semitone adjacent to each of the outer notes, the alternate notes also forming tritones. Only in the last movement does Bartók relinquish these devices; it is a sustained, sensitive piece in a hesitant rhythm in which iamb and trochee alternate. Its cadence is particularly interesting, providing a sense of finality in spite of the complexity of its chordal structure:

2. *Suite, Op.* 14

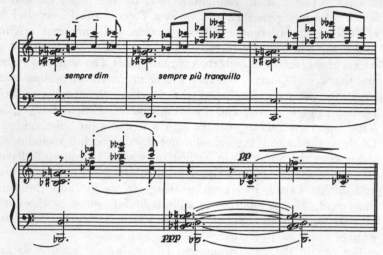

The intensive research in Romanian peasant music which occupied Bartók for several years after 1909 brought into being a small group of piano pieces based on Romanian tunes. Of these, the Romanian Folk Dances from Hungary must certainly be Bartók's most frequently played work, not only in the original version for the piano, but in the numerous transcriptions that have been made: for small orchestra by the composer in 1917,[22] for string orchestra by Arthur Willner, for salon orchestra by Wilke, and especially for violin and piano by Zoltán Székely.

Among the Romanian melodies of the Transylvanian districts, Bartók found both songs and instrumental dance-tunes, the latter being less simple in their form than when accompanied by words. It is from the fiddle-tunes that the Romanian Folk Dances are constructed, following the melodies without change, but with occasionally greater harmonic freedom than in the earlier folksong settings. The seven [23] dances vary greatly in character and in tempo, from the gentle, almost minuet-like *Buciumeana* to the brisk *Poargă românească* and the two brisk energetic closing dances, both called *Mărunţel*. Like the peasant music of Hungary, the dances are almost entirely in 2/4 meter, but the *Buciumeana* is in 3/4 and the *Poargă* alternates between 3/4 and 2/4. The tunes are modal, with augmented seconds in two of them.

Quite different in character are the Romanian Christmas Songs or *Colinde*, of which Bartók transcribed two series of ten each in 1915. Each series is continuous, designed to be played without pause, with each tune merging into the next. As Bartók explains in his *Melodien der Rumänischen Colinde*,[24] these songs, collected between 1909 and 1917, were sung usually by young men, sometimes by girls, who wandered from house to house during the Christmas season. Rhythmically the *Colinde* are consistently less regular than the dance-tunes, even those in 'tempo giusto,' their metrical units varying almost from bar to bar. The plasticity of their rhythms gives these pieces a flexibility quite at odds with the 'tempo giusto' tunes of the Magyars. A few seem to have connections with the rhythms of Bulgarian folk music, with the regular recurrence of irregular groupings: for example, No. 6 of the second series (2/8 + 3/8 +3/8) and No. 9 of the same set (4/8 + 3/8).

One restraint that these rhythmic diversities placed upon Bartók was to prevent him from adopting canonic imitation as a compositional device. There is little imitation of any kind, but only in the final section was he able to write a complete canon, and even here the bar-lines for the two staves do not coincide.[25]

Both the *Colinde* and the Folk Dances have pedagogical value in much the same way as *For Children*. The Sonatina, on the other hand, though it also is based upon Romanian folk dances and presents them practically unchanged, only extending them by means of episodes and, in the third movement, a coda, is somewhat more difficult than the others and is quite suitable for concert performance. The first movement, *Bagpipers*, based upon an *ardeleana* from Hunyad and a dance-tune from Bihar, is in a simple ternary form, with a drone in the first and third sections. The second, *Bear Dance*, is a ponderous, waddling *jocul ursului* from Maramureş; the tune is played through twice, first in the right hand, then in the left, with no added material save the harmonization. In the Finale are again two tunes: a Turkish dance (*măruntel*) from Maros-Torda and a *baba-leuca* from Torontál. Here too there is a drone, the D appearing almost throughout, changing to A for only fifteen measures in the middle of the movement. The primitivistic setting of the entire work preserves the folk quality of the tunes themselves, though the listener is never aware of an arbitrary restriction of resource.

The Sonatina was transcribed for orchestra in 1931, under the title Transylvanian Dances. This was a period in which Bartók provided orchestral versions of a number of early compositions, his attention apparently being directed to them by his work on the Forty-four Duos for two violins, which represented a resumption of his interest in the pedagogical use of folksong settings—and, Bartók himself admitted, the practicality of these simpler orchestral works was also appealing. As has already been indicated, the Hungarian Sketches of the same year comprise orchestral versions of several very early movements; two years later, Bartók took some of the Fifteen Hungarian Peasant Songs of 1914-17 and scored them for orchestra.

The Peasant Songs include both 'parlando rubato' and 'tempo giusto' songs, most of the originals of which are to be found in Bartók's ethnological publications. The majority are of the old style, though there are representatives of both the new style and the mixed class. These fifteen tunes are divided into four groups: Four Old Tunes, Scherzo, Ballad, and Old Dance Tunes. Of these the most interesting from the standpoint of treatment is the Ballad, an old-style Dorian tune in 7/8 which divides in the Bulgarian fashion into groups of the value of two, three, and two eighth-notes.[26] Bartók set the tragic story of Angoli Borbála and her lover [27] in the form of a theme and variations, stating the melody in octaves without other support, repeating it three times while the left hand provides a bass which steps down, bar by bar, in a quasi-chromatic progression embellished by an ascending scale or arpeggio on each of the foundation notes. The color is dark and strong, and the fourth variation, in which the melody is still intact, has a chordal harmonization to provide a climax. The next group of three variations shows considerable melodic modification, and the character is restrained and slightly polyphonic; the last two variations again state the melody in octaves, punctuating its pauses with full, powerful chords of increasing dissonance, until they resolve, sforzandissimo, upon the open fifth with which the Ballad began.

With this group should also be mentioned the Three Hungarian Folk Tunes published in 1942 in the memorial album, *Homage to Paderewski*,[28] which date from the same period as the Fifteen Hungarian Peasant Songs and may have been intended originally for inclusion in that set. The first is an old-style parlando tune, the others 'tempo giusto' tunes in the new style; they are of the same general character as the group published earlier, but lack their distinction. Only in the third of the set, in which there are several transpositions of the tune and an extended motivic coda, is there any departure from simple reharmonization upon repetition; this was scored for orchestra by Tibor Serly as a prelude to his Suite from *Mikrokosmos*.

With these folksong settings Bartók's simple transcription of folk tunes for the piano was almost at an end. Except for a few pieces in *Mikrokosmos*, such further work as he did was not transcription per se but composition with folksongs, as in the Improvisations, opus 20, and, to a lesser extent, the Three Rondos on Folk Tunes.

But the culmination of his original writing for the piano was to follow shortly; it is forecast in the Studies, opus 18, which he wrote in Rákoskeresztur in 1918. These three pieces, obviously not intended to cover the technical demands of the music of this century, nevertheless deal with specific problems in a way which the Études of Chopin, Debussy, Stravinsky, and Prokofiev do not approach. It is true that those of Debussy are nominally designed to assist in the conquering of particular difficulties, including various intervals, chromatic degrees, ornaments, repeated notes, 'composed' arpeggios, and others; and that those of Chopin, though unidentified as to individual purpose, nevertheless appear to have been intended as an exploration of the technical resources of the keyboard. But in neither of these sets is there the purposeful and incisive emphasis that marks the otherwise more limited Studies of Bartók.

Expressively these pieces have a smaller range, while tonally they push the frontiers far beyond those of Bartók's previous piano writing. All of them are concerned to a greater or a lesser degree with the extension and contraction of the pianist's hand. To that purpose the first Study is devoted largely to what may be called a disjunct chromaticism, not unrelated to the octave-displacement that plays so large a part in the twelve-tone technique. A few bars will suffice for illustration:

3. *Studies, Op.* 18

Here the wide stretches between the outer fingers represent the disjointing of a simple chromatic scale-segment; the intervals are ninths and tenths in irregular alternation. There are relevant passages in Schoenberg's early piano music, Opus 11 for example, and the piano parts of Bartók's two Sonatas for violin and piano, not too long after the Studies, will show a similar concern with the displacement of chromatic passages. Constant extension of this kind is extremely tiring to the playing mechanism, and Bartók has recognized this disadvantage by providing frequent relaxation possibilities, passages in which the hand is permitted to contract. The second Study, with its extended arpeggios (which, instead of maintaining the same shape in each octave, make essential changes as they move up or down the keyboard), is devoted especially to considerations of hand contraction, of passing over thumb or fifth finger, while the other hand is occupied with a sustained and expressive melody in three octaves. The third has rapid and rather widespread arpeggiations in the left hand, with capriciously placed chords in the right; incessant metrical changes—2/4, 3/4, 4/4, 5/4, 5/8, 6/8, 7/8, 9/16, 10/16, 11/16—show that Bartók's rhythmic ideas have become as free and untrammeled as those of his harmony and his melody. It is curious to observe that these irregularities persist for only half the piece; thereafter 2/4, 3/4, and, for the last page and a half, 6/8, suffice.

An examination of the cadences of these three Studies will demonstrate the expansion that Bartók's tonal system has undergone:

4. *Studies, Op.* 18

(a)

(b)

(c)

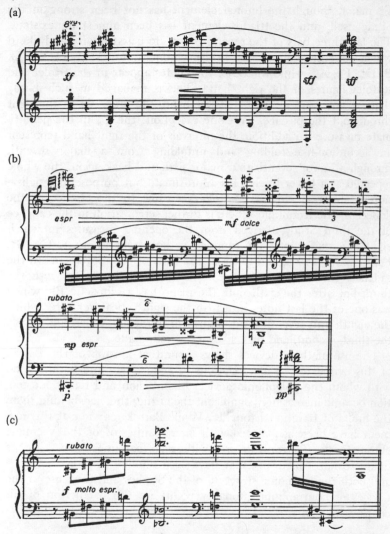

The first ends on the bitonal superposition of triads in G major and
F♯ major, though the bitonal element has not been strong in the
Study itself, and the triadic element has been almost nonexistent.
The last three bars of the second Study are based upon a polychord
which contains eight of the twelve chromatic notes: A, C♯, E, G,
B, D♯, F♯, A♯, while the other four notes appear in the triplet and
sextolet figures of the right hand. This is managed in such a way
that six notes are given to the left hand, the other six to the right
throughout the passage, with one exception: the E♯ in the penultimate measure. In addition, the intervals of the right hand represent
an accordion-like folding and unfolding from a major seventh
through a minor seventh to a major sixth and back again, the whole
repeated at a lower level. This approximate but purposeful serialization is about as close as Bartók ever came to the essence of the
dodecaphonic technique. There is further serialization in the cadence
of the third Study, derived from the opening measures in which
eight chromatic notes are sounded without repetition: A, C♯, B♯,
F♯, G♯, D, F✗, E♯, and taken as the basis of the movement. In the
cadence, these eight notes are again sounded, beginning with the
third; but after the sixth note the piano has a climactic B♭, which
was one of the last notes heard (in the eighth measure), after which
the eighth and seventh notes appear in retrograde order, and finally
the third, second, and first, likewise in retrograde.

The use of these devices shows a spiritual kinship of the Bartók
of this period to the investigations of Schoenberg and his disciples,
with whom the polyphonic devices of inversion and retrograde motion became increasingly significant the farther they left behind them
the limits of traditional tonality. While Bartók may not at this moment have been acquainted with later manifestos of the Viennese
chromaticists, *Pierrot Lunaire*, with such baroque devices as the
double canon cancrizans, may have been familiar to him in score; [29]
and both the harmonic structure of the Studies and their use of the
devices of contrapuntal atonality points up the parallelism of his
course with theirs.

Equally significant in Bartók's development, but for quite different
reasons, are the Improvisations on Hungarian Peasant Songs, opus
20. This is the first work in which the composer, taking authentic
folksongs as a basis, nevertheless treated them as if they were original

themes, not merely providing accompaniments but varying, developing, modifying, turning them this way and that to catch the light
and shadow of his creative will. He recognized three ways in which
folk music might serve as the basis for art music.[30] In the first method,
the composer uses authentic folk melody, unchanged or only slightly
varied, providing it with an accompaniment and possibly with introductory and concluding material. Two subdivisions of this genus are
distinguishable, in one of which the added materials—accompaniment, introductory and concluding phrases—are secondary, while in
the other the melody is secondary, the added materials assuming
greater importance. The second method is one in which the composer uses no authentic folk melody, but invents his own in imitation
of folksong. Bartók admits no essential difference between these two
procedures. The final method is more fundamental: the composer
employs neither folk melodies nor imitations of folk melodies, but
absorbs their essence in such a way that it pervades his music.

The greater part of Bartók's own music, certainly that since 1908,
may be assigned to these categories. In the first are such works as the
folksong settings in the Bagatelles (no. 4), the Ten Easy Pieces
(no. 6), *For Children*, the Romanian Christmas Songs and Folk
Dances, and the Sonatina, while the Improvisations, the Three
Rondos, and many of the Forty-four Duos belong in the second sub-
division of this class. The two Romanian Dances of 1909-10 are outstanding examples of the second category, while the last four Quartets, the Concerto for Orchestra, the Second Violin Concerto, and
most of the other works after 1920 are manifestations of the folk idiom
now entirely assimilated and become an integral and essential part of
the composer's vocabulary.

To answer the criticism which arose from his use of folk materials,
Bartók wrote: [31]

It is a fatal error to attribute so much importance to the subject or theme
of a composition. We know that Shakespeare borrowed the plots of his
plays from many sources; does that prove the infertility of his brain? . . .
Molière . . . not only borrowed the themes for his plays but also . . .
sometimes took over from his source expressions and even whole lines
without change. . . Handel's adaptation of a work by Stradella so far
surpasses the original in beauty that Stradella may be forgotten. . . In
music it is the thematic material which corresponds to the plot of a play,
and in music, as in poetry and painting, it does not matter what themes

we use: it is the form into which we mould them that provides the essence of our work, revealing the knowledge, the creative power, and the individuality of the artist.

On the other hand, Bartók insisted that folksong can become a vital force in the art music of any country only if it is entrusted to the hands of a great creative talent: 'If a composer has no talent it will be useless for him to base his music on folk music or any other music; the result in every case will be worthless.'

In the Improvisations, the folk music of Hungary came into touch with her greatest creative musician, and the result is significant for the direction not only of Bartók himself but of his colleagues as well. The tunes on which these eight pieces are based are genuine peasant songs, some of them from Bartók's collection, from the districts of Tolna, Zala, Szerém, Csík, Udvarhely, and Szílágy.[32]

The first Improvisation differs only slightly from Bartók's earlier folksong treatment, since the melody, in the Dorian mode on C, is repeated three times intact, with a short coda derived from the melody. But the harmonization is somewhat freer than before, the first statement being accompanied only by major seconds, the second by triads of which alternate melody notes form the roots, while the third uses the recurrent D-minor triad as an orientation point and explores from there unrelated triads as accompaniment.

The second, whose melody is partly Mixolydian, partly Dorian on C, has many episodic interruptions, syncopations, and tempo changes, which give it a wayward, capricious character. Its harmonies are composed of clashing seconds and sevenths, as well as polychordal combinations. The 'parlando rubato' melody of the third, as tragic as its text,[33] is set to a nocturnal accompaniment which anticipates *The Night's Music* of the *Out of Doors* suite: a gruppetta embracing two perfect fourths on adjacent notes (C♯ and D), this relationship giving rise to most of the harmonic manifestations of the movement and resulting eventually in a quasi-polytonality of three tonal planes.

The first setting of the fourth tune, *The Wind Blows from the Danube*, a 'tempo giusto' melody in 2/4, is simply a turning ostinato figure in the right hand, its intervals expanded in the second half. The fifth, another 'tempo giusto' tune in an almost pentatonic scale, appears first under an inverted pedal consisting of the minor second

C♯-D, to which is presently added the C♮. Later there are internal pedals and drone fifths, while at the end, as the folk tune is fragmented, the culmination is hastened with a canon in the lower sixth, first at the distance of one bar, then of a half-bar, with percussive chordal clusters as cadence.

The sixth Improvisation is based on a pentatonic tune, stated throughout on the black keys, while the accompaniment is largely on the white, and there is therefore a somewhat bitonal cleavage. Bartók's use of consecutive open ninths, bars 20-22, apparently was stimulated by the melodic structure with its major seconds.

Although the seventh Improvisation, dedicated to the memory of Claude Debussy, was published in the *Tombeau de Claude Debussy*,[34] with works by Dukas, Roussel, Malipiero, Goossens, Schmitt, Stravinsky, Falla, and Satie, it shows no conscious effort to incorporate elements of Debussy's style as a tribute to the *musicien français*, and of course no quotation from Debussy's scores, as is found in the contributions of Dukas (*La plainte, au loin, du faune . . .*) and Falla (*Homenaja*, for guitar). Of the entire group, only Bartók, Stravinsky (with a fragment of the Symphonies for Wind Instruments), Ravel (with a movement of the Sonata for violin and cello), and Satie (with a declamation for voice and piano) were content to pay tribute to Debussy unself-consciously and in their own tongues.

Bartók's contribution is notable for its use of mirror devices in the accompanying parts, patterns being opposed by their own simultaneous inversions. The atmosphere is tenuous, largely by reason of the widespread spacing of the parts, with a bell- or gamelan-like quality quite unlike any of his previous work, though it recurs in the Sonatas for violin and piano, 1921-22, and occasionally thereafter.

For the final Improvisation Bartók took a lusty tune collected in Szílágy by László Lajtha,[35] and gave it an appropriately lusty setting, writing a series of three variations upon it, all of strongly contrasting character, and with proportionately long and fantastic interludes. The first variation invests the melody with triplet gruppettas which lead into the last note of each line; the second is a canon at the tritone, the melody being slightly simplified; and the last is a big, sonorous setting with the melody in three octaves, and dissonant off-beat chords as punctuation, all composed of two tritones a perfect fourth apart. The coda is a continuation and expansion of the last variation.

Between the Improvisations and the works which occupied Bartók in 1926—the Sonata, the First Piano Concerto, *Out of Doors,* and the Nine Little Piano Pieces—no piano music was written; only the two Violin Sonatas, the Dance Suite, and the *Village Scenes* were produced. The period, however, marked the serious beginnings of Bartók's career as an international virtuoso, and it is no doubt because of this career that the year 1926 saw the composition of so much music for the piano after a considerable abstinence. It seems likely that once Bartók began playing in concerts throughout Europe it became necessary for him to equip himself with works for performance,[36] in which he could present himself as composer with music in his most recent style, rather than to have his creative abilities judged on the strength of the Rhapsody, opus 1, and the other early piano pieces.

After the white-hot creative drive of 1926, he was armed with a Concerto for his performances with orchestra, a Sonata to form the major work on his solo recitals, and two groups of shorter pieces to fill in whatever gaps remained. This made it possible to formulate programs which would represent his entire career in retrospect; and an examination of his recital listings from this time on discloses that this procedure is the one he followed. After this time he added to his music for solo piano only the Three Rondos on Folk Tunes, the Petite Suite, and the six volumes of the *Mikrokosmos,* from the last three of which he drew material for his concerts.

As his largest composition for solo piano, the Sonata merits careful study. Technically it makes the greatest demands upon the performer; harmonically it is one of Bartók's least ingratiating works. The piano is now treated percussively throughout; there are no really lyric spots even in the sustained second movement,[37] where the thematic material is as limited in compass as elsewhere in the Sonata. The folklike contours of Bartók's melody are almost entirely sublimated in the first two movements of this work. Instead, the patterns which provide the thematic propulsion are rhythmically activated groups of repeated notes, explosively punctuated by, or statically supported upon, chords in which seconds, sevenths, and ninths, both major and minor, predominate, and which frequently become tone clusters. Although the latter appeared early in Bartók's music, his use of them was intensified after his 1923 meeting with the American composer Henry Cowell.[38]

In spite of the liberation from the use of themes of traditional contour which this work emphasizes, its structure is nevertheless founded upon classical precepts. The first movement is a sonata-allegro with a disproportionately short development group and a full recapitulation; the second is a ternary form with a varied repetition of the first section before the second is heard, and a coda; the last movement combines features of rondo and variations, its strongly folklike theme, in the Mixolydian mode on B, changed almost beyond recognition on its successive returns. It is characteristic of Bartók's creative processes that the closed forms of the classical period serve as vehicles for his most advanced thinking at every period. There is no slavish adherence to preconceived blueprints, but thematic contrast, recognizable development or variation, and return to previous materials—all of which served Mozart, Haydn, and Beethoven admirably as basic structural principles—provide a point of contact between Bartók and his audience, no matter how remote from tradition his harmonic or melodic procedures, which many a devotee of 'free' form might envy.

The machine-like energy of the Bartók Sonata sweeps everything before it. There is no change of pace in the first movement except an increase at the very end. Like the First Piano Concerto it depends in great measure upon the thickening of lines in thirds and octaves, two such streams being frequently opposed in different tonal planes, or one set against a stationary or slightly moving part, the resultant clangor capable of analysis only in contrapuntal terms. It is a polyphony in which the lines consist, not of single notes in succession, but of intervals or even chords in succession. The concept of counterpoint as a combination of individual and independent melodic lines thus undergoes a fundamental expansion: the fabric is now woven not with single fibers but with fibrous strands.

Bartók considered the Sonata as in E major.[39] Through the entire first section there is a persistently recurring A♯ which gives the tonality a Lydian flavor, and both G and G♯ occur indiscriminately. The most important subsidiary, beginning in measure 76, is treated bitonally, the upper line in G♯ minor, the accompaniment devised from the Lydian tetrachord on C. This tritone-emphasis is by no means infrequent in Bartók, especially in his more chromatic phases, but apart from these two points the tritone plays a very minor role in the Sonata, whose materials are largely diatonic and modal. Pedals, ostinatos, reiterated rhythmic figures, act as a cement, still further underlining the primitivistic origins of this music, which is, notwithstanding its stylistic and technical advances, not very remote in esthetics from the *Allegro barbaro* of fifteen years earlier. The martellato is more aggressive, the thrust and power more intense, but in essence the Sonata is an answer to the problems postulated by the earlier work.

The structural relationships of the finale are particularly interesting, since the variational process is not continuous but interrupted, the theme recurring in its original form and key (with only slight deviations) between varied statements which are all in different keys.[40] Bartók at this point adhered closely to the ornamental type of variation, in which the original melody is preserved intact or nearly so, but embellished with unessential notes. Only the first variation represents a simplification of the theme; the chirpings of the third and fourth resemble in certain respects some of the Romanian dance-tunes which Bartók collected a number of years before. The fifth variation returns to the almost pure form of the theme, but with the second motive repeated in rhythmic displacement. The final variation returns to the original key but is greatly broadened with each motive extended; and the coda is close to that of the first movement, with rather Stravinskian 'stamping chords.'

In the five piano pieces of *Out of Doors*, Bartók set himself problems quite different from those of the Sonata. Written between June and August 1926, they represent an excursion into the realm of representational music which had been absent from his piano composition since the Burlesques of 1908-11. For some years previous to this he had been interested in pre-Bachian keyboard music. He had edited for Rozsnyai eighteen pieces by Couperin and a volume of sonatas by Domenico Scarlatti; and in 1926-27 he was occupied with the transcription of Italian keyboard music of the seventeenth and eighteenth centuries: Ciaia, Frescobaldi, Marcello, Rossi, Zipoli. It is impossible not to believe that the *Out of Doors* suite was stimulated by this work, especially by the example of Couperin le Grand.

Yet the techniques employed in the suite, the percussive-repetitive devices, are mainly those which served in the Sonata. The first movement, *With Drums and Pipes*, for example, is rhythmically and melodically very close to the first movement of the Sonata and that of the First Piano Concerto: the 2/4 meter, the pedals and ostinatos, the repeated notes and restricted melodic compass, the heavy martellato, the seconds and ninths, both major and minor, and the toneclusters. The same characteristics are observed in the concluding movement, *The Chase*, with its galloping ostinatos on E, the keynote being F, the whole structure thus anchored to a single note which dominates all but three measures of the piece. The left-hand quintolets require a flexible hand and a wide extension. The piece has an overwhelming energy which persists uninterrupted from beginning to end.

The inner movements offer contrasts. The *Barcarolla* is rather more plastic than the one in the *Mikrokosmos* (III:125, *Boating*), though it has some of the same characteristics, notably melodic progressions in fourths. But it is somewhat more chromatic and more linear, without the bitonal features of the latter. *Musettes* is reduced to vibrant, almost unmelodic sound; the drones are there, and the fantastic ornamentations of primitive wind instruments, but there is almost never a melody.

By far the most striking movement of the suite is *The Night's Music (Musiques nocturnes)*, in which Bartók brought into play his extraordinary sensitivity to the sounds of nature. There had been earlier suggestions in the third of the Improvisations and elsewhere, but here is brought into full flower that remarkable nocturnal music which played so large a part in his writing during the last two decades of his life. This movement is dedicated 'to Ditta,' and from the frequent recurrence of this nocturnal mood, and from its final appearance in the Third Piano Concerto, which was designed for the composer's wife, it is not illogical to postulate an extramusical connotation aside from the merely pictorial.

The techniques here employed to create the atmosphere of the out-of-doors at night include the blurred sounds of pianissimo cluster-chords, each introduced with a gruppetta of three notes, as a background, against which are heard the twitterings, chirpings, and croakings of nocturnal creatures. Presently a folklike tune is heard in a single line, doubled three octaves above; still later a flute melody, in the Dorian mode on C♯, appears, upon which cluster-chords, played with the palm of the hand, impinge; then the two tunes are superimposed, as if heard simultaneously from different directions. Fragments of the flute melody continue to the end, evanescent as the night sounds.

5. *Out of Doors*

In this astonishingly convincing nocturnal excursion Bartók succeeded, as in the many which followed, in devising a music of an intensely personal character which nevertheless re-creates for the listener an atmosphere incapable of misinterpretation. This is not music which requires a program for elucidation; its delicate, sensitive web is a far cry from the excesses of *A Hero's Life*, which had once held Bartók in thrall.

The remaining work from the fruitful year of 1926 is the group of Nine Little Piano Pieces, which are somewhat less even in quality than the *Out of Doors* set. The Four Dialogues are contrapuntal studies in two voices; the first has a few bars with octave doublings, the second some notes sustained, creating a quasi-harmonic texture. They betray less an obligation to Bach, whose Inventions have been considered influential in the formation of their texture, than to the pre-Bachian composers with whose music Bartók had recently been concerned. They are not so much an exploration of tight motivic organization within a polyphonic framework as of freely developed polyphony without regard for imitative considerations. The first of the Dialogues, for example, is canonic throughout, the interval of the canon changing from the lower sixth to the fifth and then the third, while the distance contracts from two beats (in 2/2 meter) to one, and finally to half a beat. The third Dialogue has the rather serpentine chromaticism of the Third and Fourth Quartets and the fugue which opens the Music for String Instruments, Percussion, and Celesta: a chromaticism that modifies an essentially diatonic line without destroying its tonal orientation. The third Dialogue is closer to the Bachian invention-pattern, though the first three statements of the subject, too long to be called a motive, are all in the top voice. The last two statements are in canon at the upper seventh.

The Menuetto is almost a caricature of the minuet style; the Air a setting of a folklike tune in A major, with extended introduction and coda. Two genre-pieces, *Marcia delle bestie* and *Tambourine*, follow; the first is related in character to the *Bear Dances* of the Ten Easy Pieces and the Sonatina, with grotesque, ponderous rhythms and grumbling sonorities, while the second is a brusque, percussive movement which shares with the celebrated *Tambourine* of Rameau only its title. The most extensive of the Nine Little Piano Pieces is its finale, *Preludio, all' ungherese,* in two sections, both of which are based upon the same folklike theme; the first employs dark, tentative harmonies and much imitation, especially free canon, but there is little contrapuntal writing in the Allegro, which transforms the basic theme into a 'tempo giusto' dance-tune with percussive accompaniment.

The first of the Three Rondos on Folk Tunes was written in 1916, the others in 1927; they therefore span the period from *The Wooden Prince* and the Ady songs to the Third Quartet. The first Rondo is stylistically in keeping with the folksong transcriptions of the earlier period; the second and third employ the techniques of the piano music of 1926: the dissonant clashes, the cluster-chords, the martellato rhythms. The structure of the first resembles the folksong treatment in the Sonatina, even that of *Evening with the Széklers,* the separate tunes being presented in alternation with little change except transposition, reharmonization, and occasional motivic extension. The second and third, on the other hand, use the tunes much more freely, as composed themes, subject to fragmentation and development; and the textures are largely contrapuntal where those of the first Rondo were not at all so. The manuscript, in the possession of Mrs. Harold Driver, one of Bartók's last pupils, confirms what he wrote in sending it to her: 'As you will see, I had much trouble with the second Rondo. I wanted first to include a 3rd theme which later proved to be impracticable.'

The Petite Suite consists of transcriptions of six of the Forty-four Duos for two violins.[41] The changes necessary in translating them from string to keyboard terms were principally those of spacing and sonority, but in a few instances more essential changes were made. In the second movement, for example, the offbeat punctuation just before the coda is prolonged for four more beats in the piano version; the third has important reharmonizations and an extra bar at the end; the mirror in the second part of the fifth has its relationship reversed in the repetition; and in the sixth, *Bagpipe,* which combines the two versions in the Duos—the regular drone accompaniment of the first with the acciaccaturas of the variation—one repetition is transposed bodily from A to C♯.

But since the musical problems and their treatment do not vary, the discussion of the Duos, in the chapter on Bartók's miscellaneous chamber music, will suffice for the Petite Suite.

Only one work, then, remains for consideration in this chapter: *Mikrokosmos*. Designed originally for Bartók's son Péter, only the first two volumes, comprising sixty-six of the one hundred fifty-three pieces, were dedicated to him. Péter Bartók has said that the difficulties in the *Mikrokosmos* soon outdistanced his pianistic abilities, but pianists generally may congratulate themselves upon having at their disposal so vast a catalog of contemporary procedures, beginning with the most elementary and proceeding to works of the greatest difficulty, suitable for concert performance.

The value of the *Mikrokosmos* lies not so much in the technical demands it makes upon the player, extensive though they are, as in the acquaintance it provides with the essential characteristics of twentieth-century music. Among harmonic procedures to be found here may be mentioned bitonality (Nos. 70, 86, 105, 125, 142), chords in fourths (131), major and minor seconds (132, 140, 142, 144, 146), cluster-chords (107), and whole-tone scale (136). Contrapuntal devices such as inversion (34), mirror (72, 121, 141), free canon (91) culminate in the two Chromatic Inventions (145 a/b) which may be played either separately or simultaneously, the one being both a melodic and a contrapuntal inversion of the other. Syncopation (133) and irregular rhythms (82, 126, 140) lead to the subtleties of the Six Dances in Bulgarian Rhythms (148-153), dedicated to the British pianist Harriet Cohen.

Many of the pieces are pentatonic or modal, some of them based upon Hungarian folksongs. Others are in arbitrarily devised scales. Some, it is true, are intended to develop facility in specific phases of piano technique—staccato and legato, hand extension and contraction, finger and hand independence. But the musical value of these pieces is much greater than their purely technical value; Bartók himself frequently played extracts from the *Mikrokosmos* in his recitals, and also transcribed seven of them for two pianos, playing and recording them with Ditta Pásztory Bartók. Other transcriptions have been made for string quartet and for orchestra by Tibor Serly.

In comparison with other important twentieth-century composers, Bartók's writing for the piano is far more extensive and more significant. Schoenberg's entire output for the instrument consists of seventeen pieces in five sets, Opera 11, 19, 23, 25, 33, dating from 1908 to 1932. Stravinsky's, discounting the unpublished Sonata (1903-04) and the Study for pianola (1921), includes several works for solo piano, plus two sets of easy duets, and two works for two pianos. Hindemith's, while limited in numbers, does include five sonatas (one for four hands, another for two pianos), besides *Ludus tonalis* (1943), a set of twelve fugal studies interspersed with interludes and enclosed within a prelude and a postlude, one of which is the retrograde inversion of the other. Honegger, Milhaud, and others have occasionally written for the piano, but their most significant contributions are in the realm of the orchestra and the instrumental ensemble, the chorus and the theater.

Of these composers, only Stravinsky was a pianist, and his decision to appear as executant in his own works came when he was already forty years old.[42] Bartók, in contrast, not only had an active career as concertizing pianist but for years earned a livelihood as a teacher of piano. He was therefore in close touch with the medium, and it is no surprise that he left for it a whole repertory, ranging from the simplest of teaching pieces to the most demanding of concert works. It is, however, not as a composer for the piano that he achieved his greatest distinction. Significant as are the piano Sonata, *Out of Doors*, and the last volumes of the *Mikrokosmos*, delightful as are the folksong settings, Bartók reached the apogee of his creative orbit not in these but in the Music for String Instruments, Percussion, and Celesta, the Sonata for Two Pianos and Percussion, the Violin Concerto, the Concerto for Orchestra, and especially the last three Quartets. These are his masterpieces; most of them date from the 1930's and 1940's, a period in which his style was modified from the percussive violence characteristic of the 1920's to a highly organized and mellow polyphony for which the keyboard is ill suited. That Bartók could adapt his piano writing to fit this riper viewpoint is amply demonstrated by the Sonata for Two Pianos and Percussion; but the writing of music for the piano alone apparently ceased because of the limitations of the instrument with regard to the modification of his style. One may regret that there was no second Sonata for solo piano from this period, to incorporate the new textures in a structure appropriate to them.

THE VOCAL MUSIC

IN CONTRAST to his compatriot Zoltán Kodály, Bartók was essentially an instrumental composer, and his comparatively meager list of vocal compositions, though produced throughout his career, is of slighter significance than his work in other fields. Aside from the opera *Duke Bluebeard's Castle,* which must be considered a dramatic rather than a vocal work, there are several published groups of original songs, the *Cantata profana* for double chorus, tenor and baritone soli, and orchestra, and a number of small choral works based upon or inspired by Hungarian folksong. All the rest, whether for solo voice and piano or for chorus, are folksong transcriptions.

The transcriptions, however, are of such variety and such skill that they constitute a whole repertory of vocal music. Three sets for voice and piano represent successive stages in Bartók's attitude toward the handling of folk music: his contribution to the Twenty Hungarian Folksongs (1906), of which the second ten are by Kodály, shows his earliest approach, in which the implications of the folk material are only tentatively realized in the accompaniments; the Eight Hungarian Folksongs (1907-17) display a still uneven but more idiomatic use of folk elements in accompaniment; but it is for the Twenty Hungarian Folksongs (1929) to demonstrate the masterful handling of all the elements of Bartók's technique, by now mature.

The earliest original songs include two sets in German, both of which have remained in manuscript. Of the three dedicated to Countess Matilde von Wenckheim, in August 1898, one has been published in facsimile; [1] it is a setting of Heine's *Im wunderschönen Monat Mai*, done in schoolboy fashion without much regard for the subtleties of prosody, and with the most traditional of accompanimental schemes. The *Liebeslieder* of 1900 were published only in 1963; [2] the five songs *To the Little 'Slovak,'* remain in manuscript.

But in 1902 Bartók set four folklike poems by Lajos Pósa to music in the neo-Hungarian style, and these became his earliest published work. They are, of course, comparatively unimportant items in the catalogue of his music, but they are worth examination because of their chronological position. The first, *Autumn Breeze*, and the third, *There Is No Such Sorrow as Mine*, are slow and melancholy; the others are lively, with humorous texts. Of them all, only the third rises above the commonplace, with some strongly original touches, as in the setting of the last line: 'Oh, my God, how cruel is death' (*Jaj Istenem, de kegyetlen a halál*), with but three notes, D, A♭, E♭, in the melody while the underlying harmony moves from a D-minor triad to a cadence in A♭ major.

The texts of these songs, in a naively folkish style with unsubtle rhymes, could hardly have stimulated the composition of more significant songs, even had Bartók's style advanced beyond a certain neo-Hungarianism. In a later stage of his development he would not have found them worthy of his attention. In a sense it is unfortunate that they were published; but since they are long out of print and there is little likelihood that they will be reprinted by popular demand, they hardly modify the total picture of Bartók's creative production.

According to Dr. János Demény,[4] there was another set of four songs in Hungarian, dating from the same period, the manuscript of which was lost. It may have been of this set that Bartók wrote to his mother, in June 1903:

Mrs. Gruber is rather pleased by the 4 Songs; I am informed by Böske that she esteems them because they were composed by the 'future Magyar Beethoven' (!). Of course I don't know any better *Hungarian songs* than these, but this is not saying much, because there is very little *Hungarian song*.[5]

After these early essays, there are no more original songs until 1916, when Bartók wrote two groups of five songs each. Opus 15 was not published until some years after Bartók's death. The texts are unidentified in the manuscript, and the composer refused to divulge the source of the poems. Though they have been attributed to Béla Balázs, they do not appear in his collected works; the suggestion that at least some of them were written by Bartók is likewise without substantiation. For the songs of Opus 16, Bartók chose poems by the Hungarian symbolist Endre Ady (1877-1919).

Both groups of songs are intense, brilliant, and sensual. They are among the most original works from Bartók's pen: deeply felt, strong, moving, and yet intimate and personal, they challenge both singer and pianist. They have little in common with the impressionist style of *Duke Bluebeard's Castle*, but show marked relationships with the Second String Quartet, in progress at the same time, and especially with *The Wonderful Mandarin* of a few years later.

The accompaniment of *Three Autumn Tears*, for example, with its melancholy waltz measure, calls to mind the first tentative measures of the dance of the girl with the Mandarin; rhythmic, harmonic, and even melodic patterns seem drawn from the same source. The text is in three parallel sections:

> In the autumn noon, in the autumn noon,
> Oh, how hard it is to smile at the girls.
> In the autumn night, in the autumn night,
> Oh, how hard it is to look up at the stars.
> In the autumn night, the autumn noon,
> Oh, how easy—weeping, weeping—to fall down.

Bartók devised harmonic means for emphasizing the three lines. The first has a recurrent pedal B on the first beat of most of the bars, while the second beats are occupied with dissonant chords 'resolving' to less dissonant combinations on the third. These more dissonant second-beat chords always include major seventh or minor second or ninth, and in the second line there is no relaxation on the last beat. The third line begins with an underlining of consonant harmonies, but after a few bars these are changed to a long series of consecutive tritones, which become perfect fourths and fifths in the ninth measure from the end, though sharply dissonant with the vocal line.

The treatment of the melody represents, not a cumulative intensification, but a slackening in the second line, which makes the third even stronger; the contrast of voice and accompaniment provide a counterpoint of means, not merely of melody. Except for the last word of each, the first two verses are set to the same melodic line, the second transposed to a somewhat lower level, the culmination point of each occurring on the verb (*kacagni*—smile, and *fölnézni*—look up); but the melodic contour is altered in the final line to emphasize the words 'oh, how easy.'

A similar prosodic sensitivity is apparent in the other songs of the group. They are all intensely expressive, never taking refuge in an easy 'singability,' nor permitting the accompaniment to serve as a mere convenience. These are ensemble works in the best sense.

Sounds of Autumn is the only one of the Ady songs without erotic overtones. Its pervading melancholy has an element of horror, the swirling mists, the whimpering and throbbing of the wind, the sound of rapping on decaying boards being subtly underscored by the setting. The technical means are simple: fundamentally the accompaniment is constructed almost throughout upon relationships of perfect fourths and tritones, together with consecutive minor ninths. The vocal line is an expressive intensification of spoken inflections, without pretense of melodic expansiveness. As in the entire set, there are constant clashes between the sung note and the harmony, which frequently hint at a bitonal conception, or a deliberate semitonal displacement. The last line shows the procedure in its simplest application:

6. *Five Songs, Op.* 16

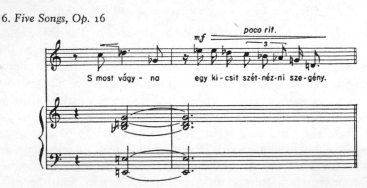

S most vágy - na   egy ki - csit szét - néz - ni sze - gény.

Here the supporting chord E-Bb-D-G is sustained under a phrase which emphasizes Db, Gb, and Eb—though of course the last two notes do belong to the harmony, and all that precedes might be viewed in the function of horizontalized appoggiatura-chord superimposed upon its own resolution. In most instances, however, there is no possibility of such an interpretation.

In *My Bed Calls*, Bartók has accomplished with startling realism the task of wedding sound to text. Ady's poem is a despondent outpouring. The poetic structure, based upon repetition of each half-line, is impossible to parallel in English.

> *Lefekszem. Óh ágyam,*
> *Óh ágyam, tavaly még,*
> *Tavaly még más voltál.*
> *Más voltál: álomhely,*
> *Álomhely, erőkút,*
> *Erőkút, csókcsárda,*
> *Csókcsárda, vidámság,*
> *Vidámság. Mi lettél?*
> *Mi lettél? Koporsó,*
> *Koporsó. . .*

I come to thee. Oh my bed,
Only last year thou shouldst have been otherwise:
Place of sleep—well of strength—inn of kisses, of cheer.
What art thou now?
Coffin, daily clasping more closely. . .

The setting is hesitant in these first lines, with an atmosphere of resignation. The agitation which ensues mounts to a climax in an agony of desire, breaks off, subsides. Then despair turns again to resignation, as the poet heeds the call of his coffin-pallet.

The textual ejaculations might easily have led to a mechanical series of sequences, particularly in the agitato section; but while the spirit is sequential, intervallic changes each time energize the impulse toward culmination. At the same time there is a heightening of the psychological intent. Ady's poem, by the nature of its form, achieves something less than complete conviction. Bartók's music, taking full advantage of the structural idiosyncrasies of the text, is nevertheless able to intensify the meaning without being hampered by the form. The *shape* of the music is freer, more subtle, than that

of the poem itself, yet the two merge in a convincing entity. In this
lies the measure of the composer.

In English, the flavor of *Alone with the Sea* is simultaneously
decadent and embarrassingly naive:

> Seashore—dusk—little hotel room.
> She has gone, I shall never see her more . . .
> A flower is left on the sofa—
> I clasp the worn sofa . . .
> Her perfume floats caressingly about;
> The sea roars below . . .
> I listen to the singing of the wild sea,
> And dream of the worn sofa.
> Here she embraced me, kissed me . . .
> The sea sings and the past sings,
> The sea sings and the past sings.

Bartók's opening phrase, pentatonic, has a curiously banal cast
which makes it difficult to take the song seriously in spite of its
serious treatment. The arpeggiated patterns, apparently intended to
represent the sea, are interrupted too frequently to maintain the
mood; some of the interruptions are stylistically inconsistent as well.

Bitonal procedures, both express and implied, are present throughout much of the song. The triadic harmonies of the left hand in this
passage:

7. *Five Songs, Op.* 16

support a melodic structure which seldom merges with them. In
addition, the ninths in the right hand still further confuse the key
sense. Eight measures later Bartók reduces the piano part to little

more than a succession of major six-four chords, while the voice goes its own way in a melody which has almost no notes in common with them:

8. *Five Songs, Op.* 16

Admirable or ingenious as these procedures may be from the technical standpoint, *Alone with the Sea* falls short of the mark Bartók set with the others of the group.[6] The complexities are inappropriate, intruding between poem and audience. It may be that the shortcomings of the text itself prevented a completely satisfying setting, but in this case it might have been better to err on the side of understatement.

No such criticism can be leveled at the final song, *I Cannot Come to Thee*. It is entirely consistent from beginning to end, bound together not only by its recurrent refrain *Én meghalok* (I am dying) but by the rondo-like use of its musical materials. Those materials are relatively simple, dissonant but unadorned and economical. This is closer in texture to *Three Autumn Tears* than any of the intervening songs, and there is a further parallel in the modifications made in the several repetitions. With a single exception the interludes between the short stanzas are based upon chains of fourths in the right hand, but contour and length fluctuate, and there is occasional amplification of the harmonies as well.

These songs are the best possible demonstration of why Bartók wrote nothing more in the form except for folksong transcriptions. In the direction his style was taking—one which it maintained for many years—the demands it made upon the performer would have been almost incapable of solution in terms of the human voice. The problem of intonation alone, in a tonal concept as harsh as this, would turn away all but the hardiest of singers; and there is a further barrier in the Hungarian language itself, with its peculiarly individual prosody, which does not lend itself to metrical translation into any of the Indo-European languages, and with which non-Hungarian singers are seldom willing to cope. The limitations were too galling; with instruments there was infinitely more freedom to develop his ideas, and consequently after Opus 16 Bartók returned to the solo voice only in the setting of folk material. There is no compromise here, only a recognition of practicality. In his later years, when the ripening of his style might again have permitted the composition of really lyrical songs, he apparently could not—or at least did not—reawaken interest in the problem. Consequently these few songs remain the only available examples of his song-writing after the Germanic and neo-Hungarian songs of his formative period.

Bartók's first published folksong settings are in the Twenty Hungarian Folksongs (*Magyar népdalok*) of 1906, in which the seventh is one of the group he notated from the singing of a Székler servant-girl in 1904. Several of the twenty had been recorded on cylinders by Béla Vikár (Nos. 8, 12, 14, 19, 20); but except for No. 8, Bartók set only tunes he himself had collected, while Kodály set the remaining Vikár songs and six from his own collection.

There is a striking difference in the approach of the two young composers to the task. Kodály adheres rather closely to the harmonic connections of conservative western music, providing in almost every instance a full harmonization without air spaces in the texture, while Bartók devises accompaniments that are much more open, hanging the melody upon an almost motionless interval of a third or a fourth (No. 3a), punctuating on afterbeats (Nos. 5 and 6), and even at this early date avoiding the clichés of traditional diatonic harmony. When a line is repeated he usually repeats the accompaniment literally, but the first song shows the harmonic subtlety of which he was capable in the intensification of the repetition.

Both Bartók and Kodály double the melodic lines in the accompaniments almost without exception, so that they may be played as piano-pieces. After this time, Bartók's folksong settings are treated in the way he would have treated an original song, maintaining an independence between melody and accompaniment without mere duplication.

In 1938, for a revised edition of the collection, Bartók and Kodály restored, so far as possible, the ornaments which had been eliminated from the original publication. Long before the revision they had discovered that the ornamentation is 'an organic appurtenance in the singing of folksong, and could no more be omitted than [that] in the works of Couperin.' [7]

These settings are by no means even in their quality. Six of the ten are 'tempo giusto' tunes, the remainder 'parlando rubato.' No. 3a is beautifully simple, with only the bare essentials of an accompaniment, while No. 8 is overharmonized with dominant sevenths and implied modulations. But in general Bartók's settings do nothing to detract from the melodies themselves—a neutral virtue, to be sure—and in several there is a real and idiomatic enrichment of them through the piano part.

The Nine Romanian Songs for voice and piano, dating from 1915, remain in manuscript, though the piano transcriptions of Romanian material from the same period are among Bartók's best-known works: the Romanian Folk Dances from Hungary, the Romanian Christmas Songs (Colinde), and the Sonatina.

The next set of arrangements for voice and piano is the Eight Hungarian Folksongs of 1907-17, published in 1922. With one exception they are all from the Csík district in Transylvania, source of a vast number of peasant songs of Bartók's own collection. All but two of these tunes are of the old style, half of them pentatonic, the remainder modal.[8] Only three songs are in 'tempo giusto'; the texts vary from the tragic to the ribald.

In general the settings which Bartók provided are simple and lucid. The pentatonic arpeggiations of the first, Black Is the Earth, recall the cimbalom style, as do the rolled chords of the sixth, They're Mending the Great Forest Highway. Harmonies drawn from the pentatonic scale are prevalent: only two triads are available, and the two combine to form a seventh-chord which is treated as consonant. These harmonies are employed not only in accompaniment of purely pentatonic tunes but in modal ones as well, becoming functional within the mode. The seventh-chord, for example, may be erected

on the final of the Aeolian, Phrygian, or Dorian mode, while in the
Mixolydian and the modern major its upper note may be taken as
the final. By no means does Bartók restrict his harmonies, even those
which accompany pentatonic melodies, to these chords; taking them
as basic, he feels free to depart chromatically or diatonically at any
point; to provide chords embodying notes foreign to the mode, or
even (No. 5, measures 10-11) to superimpose upon the mode—in this
case the pentatonic on E—a triad totally foreign to it, side-slipping
chromatically to a tonic harmony at the change of bar. For a moment
the combination is taken as bitonal, and it is only with the resolution that both left-hand chords are understood as nonfunctional.

The fifth song, *If I Climb Yonder Hill*, is based upon the
same tune as the last of the Three Folksongs from the Csík District;
here the sung melody alternates with the ornamented *tilinkó* version.
A comparison of the two settings shows a vastly different concept of
the function of accompaniment. In the piano piece Bartók is still
thinking in terms of traditional harmonic motion; even though he
uses many seventh-chords, they are linked in the customary fashion,
retaining common tones, and the important notes of the melody form
a part of the harmonic structure. In the later version, however, the
accompanying chords no longer follow conventional procedures; they
are largely consecutive six-fours and independent of the melody notes,
which are frequently totally opposed to the harmonic combinations
below them.

The progressive unfolding of the accompaniment in the seventh
song, *Up to Now My Work Was Plowing in the Spring*, in which the
bass descends scalewise from middle C to G♭ an octave and a tritone
lower, dropping to C♭, C, and rising to the final, F, contrasts with
the generally more stable lines of the others. The sensitive rhythms
of more than one accompaniment underline the subtle stresses of the
texts, long vowels in internal syllables being marked with chord
changes, even though the principal stress in all Hungarian words is
upon the first syllable, which is always placed in positions of rhythmic
prominence.

The set of eight songs is so satisfying as a group that it would be
a mistake to extract from it a smaller number for performance.
Superficially one might suppose that a certain tonal monotony would
result from the setting of five of the eight in the same key,[9] but that
is not the case; there is a considerable variety in the character of the

accompaniments, and with the rather violent tonal displacement of the third song, *Wives, Let Me Be One of Your Company*, it does not matter that the next three songs return to the original keynote. The sequence is convincing, and there is admirable contrast in mood.

Two versions of the *Village Scenes* exist: the first for voice and piano (1924), the second, including only three of the five songs, for four or eight women's voices and chamber orchestra (transcribed in 1926 for the League of Composers in New York). These are Slovakian folksongs from the Zólyom district in northern Hungary, which had provided tunes for two sets of choruses some years before.

The *Village Scenes* have been compared [10] to *The Wedding* of Stravinsky, but it must be observed that the only point of resemblance is that each has to do with a peasant wedding. Stravinsky's work is a highly complex score, the vocal elements reduced to a rhythmic chanting within a very limited compass, the instrumental elements entrusted to an orchestra of four pianos and percussion. Bartók's, on the other hand, is unpretentious, preserving the Slovak tunes intact, presenting them as a sequence related only by their common origin and in the picture of peasant life they give. Nevertheless there is a far greater freedom of treatment in these songs than he had permitted himself in the previous folksong transcriptions.

The tunes themselves are quite unlike those of Hungarian provenance, lacking the rhythmic emphasis which results from the characteristic accentuations of the Magyar language, and falling entirely within the Lydian and Mixolydian modes. Occasional transpositions mark a departure from Bartók's earlier folksong settings; original episodic material is added, even in the vocal line; and the piano is not limited to an accompanying function but collaborates with the voice in the best ensemble tradition.

The separate movements of the set—one hesitates to use the term 'cycle' to describe such a compilation of folksongs—are of varying moods. *Haymaking, At the Bride's,* and *Cradle Song* are parlando and somewhat restrained; *Wedding Song* and *Youths' Dance* spirited. In two of the scenes two folksongs alternate: this combination of separate tunes had not previously occurred in Bartók's folksong transcriptions for voice and piano, nor did he resort to it again, except in the choral settings of folk material.[11]

The Twenty Hungarian Folksongs of 1929, for voice and piano, are Bartók's last published work for the medium. Lying chronologically between the Fourth String Quartet and the *Cantata profana*, they represent the period of greatest maturity, in which both style and technique are preponderantly intuitive. Neither listener nor analyst, confronted with the works of this period, finds them 'thought out,' though structurally they may be exceedingly complex.[12] The harmonic basis of these twenty songs is largely dissonant, with numerous seconds and sevenths, some apparent polytonality, and here and there —as in the *Székely 'Friss'* (no. 6), percussive cluster-chords which hark back to the Piano Sonata and the First Piano Concerto of three years earlier. But all these elements are handled with such dexterity that they never come to the foreground, obscuring the folk tune. The choice of tunes for setting is also partly responsible; many of those in the set are less strongly tonal than those, for example, in the Eight Hungarian Folksongs of 1907-17, and there are mixed modes which justify (if justification be needed) the chromaticism of the accompaniments.

A glance at the first song of the group, *In Prison*, shows clearly the derivation of the entire accompaniment from the pentatonic ostinato of the first two stanzas. The tune itself is Dorian, transposed to E, but the harmonization uses neither the second nor the sixth scale-step. The third stanza becomes ostensibly bitonal, the right hand being limited to an octave E recurrently ornamented with the adjacent D, while the left hand has a five-note pattern on the black keys, later expanding to include A♮ as well as A♯. The E pedal is retained throughout the fifth stanza, but the mode based upon it is hybrid: E, D♯, C♯, B♯, A♯, (A♮), G, F♯, while the melody remains within its original mode, creating clashes between D, B, and A and the corresponding sharped notes of the accompaniment. For the final stanza the accompaniment returns to its pentatonisms, with some added notes. The cadence chord, sounding over a low E, includes the seventh-chord A-C-E-G plus an extraneous D♯.

The entire setting, then, represents a cumulative increase in tension which parallels the heightening emotion of the text through the fourth stanza, relaxing again in the last stanza with the expressed feeling of mingled resignation and hope. In this sense the setting greatly enhances the textual emphasis, in a way which the tune, repeated without change, can never do. *In Prison* has become, for practical purposes, a through-composed art song, even though a single four-line tune, untransposed (but rhythmically varied) in its repetitions, constitutes the entire melodic material.

It would be possible to go through the entire group, song by song, analyzing by what consummate means Bartók underlined and intensified the textual content of each while retaining the original peasant tune unchanged, or only slightly altered.[13] Even though stanzas are transposed, sometimes frequently within a single song, and there are occasional fragmented repetitions, there is no further freedom in their treatment. Except for the advance in the accompaniments themselves, the Twenty are closer in point of view to the Eight Hungarian Folksongs of 1907-17 than to the *Village Scenes*; but that advance makes a vast difference in the impact of the songs.

They are grouped in four categories: *Songs of Sadness, Dance Songs, Miscellaneous Songs,* and *New Songs.* Naturally the first consists of parlando songs of the old style, affording an opportunity for piano writing of an improvisational sort. Bartók identifies himself with the song now, instead of preserving the detachment, the reluctance to pit accompaniment against melody in anything like equal terms, which is so clearly demonstrated in the Eight Hungarian Folksongs. This is true as well of most of the songs in the succeeding groups: the piano part *supports* less than it *complements.* Frequent dissonant clashes between voice and piano must be viewed in the light of their individual horizontal motion. The sonorities are seldom, except in ostinato passages, harmonic in conception, while in the earlier set they were almost exclusively so.

Like the Five Songs, opus 16, the Twenty Hungarian Folksongs demand a certain virtuosity from the pianist. It must be remembered that Bartók was only three years removed from the First Piano Concerto, the Piano Sonata, and the *Out of Doors* suite; and his demands upon the performer in the song accompaniments reflect the influence of these solo works of 1926. Frequently percussive, often requiring unusual adaptability in hand-position or fingering, always demanding the full resources of modern pianism, they are not to be performed by the casual accompanist.

Bartók's last folksong setting for voice and piano, available so far only in facsimile,[14] is a Ukrainian tune, *The Husband's Grief,* written in February 1945. Illegible in places, it apparently adds little to the body of his work in this category, but it does disclose slight modifications of the melody itself in the successive repetitions—modifications which Bartók had not hitherto allowed himself. The first three measures are based upon the triad C-E-G; in the second stanza, C becomes B, while in the third it is C♯. Thus the harmonic basis is likewise varied, and what would have been a pure C major is permitted a suspense-building tonal freedom. A somewhat similar freedom, though limited because of the medium, is displayed in the variant of this tune in No. 24 of the Forty-four Duos for two violins.

It was 1912 before Bartók turned his hand to the choral transcription of peasant songs; he did not write an original choral work until the *Cantata profana* in 1930, and he completed his choral composition five years later with thirty short original choruses after old folk- and art-song texts. These works, with the exception of the *Cantata profana*, are not of first-rank importance in the total picture of his output, but neither are they without significance.

Choral literature in a convincing contemporary style is not plentiful. Most composers, reluctant to limit themselves to a style which they feel the general state of choral singing imposes, are unwilling to study the problem with open minds, to discover what may reasonably be expected of a choral group today. Obviously the chorus—especially the amateur chorus—cannot be treated with the freedom of the orchestra, nor does it have a similarly wide range of capabilities. But within its own frame, there is an adaptability to contemporary expression which makes it a subtle and flexible medium for the composer who will approach it understandingly, with a sensitive ear to its unique virtues.

This Bartók did, in both his original work and his settings of peasant music for various choral combinations. In even his earliest choral work, the Four Old Hungarian Folksongs for unaccompanied male chorus (1912), he uses harmonies of somewhat dissonant character; but the individual lines are so logical that it is not difficult to attain the desired sonority. This is the fundamental secret of Bartók's choral writing, as it is of the chorale harmonizations of Bach: the predominance of horizontal motion over vertical harmony.

Of the Four Old Hungarian Folksongs, designed to be sung in succession without pause, the first two come from Csík, the source of so much of Bartók's folk material; the third is from Komárom, the fourth from Fejér (Transdanubia). The texts are unrelated, and contrast is strong from movement to movement. The melody is generally in the first tenor, unchanged upon repetition, and there are no modulations; the last piece does present its melody once in a canon at the octave,[15] between second basses and first tenors, and at the end there is an original coda based upon fragments of the tune.

The first song is a 'parlando rubato' tune of an almost pentatonic character:

> Long ago I told you, sorrowful turtledove,
> Not to put your nest in the road,
> For many travel the highway:
> On your nest they will trample.

Since the tune is bare of ornamentation, Bartók was able to compress it within the limits of a more or less conventional barring without doing violence to its flexibility. The remainder are all 'tempo giusto' tunes, with the pace increasing in each one. One is the song of a braggart, another a nonsense song about the plants in 'My sister-in-law's garden,' the text defying translation; while the final song offers a bit of peasant wisdom:

> Farm-boy, load the cart well;
> Second-crop thorns will prick your palm:
> The more your palm is pricked,
> The better you'll load your cart!

Vocally these pieces are by no means difficult. The compass of each part is well within the customary limits, and the only unconventional treatment of the voice is in the glissandos of the last song. There is little thematic or motivic imitation in the lower voices; the procedures are harmonic, with the exceptions noted above, but the vocal lines are all singable and possess a melodic logic throughout. Since the rhythms are not at all complex, and the vowel sounds coincide in all four voices, these pieces are quite readily brought to the point of performance and, once they are reissued, should find a place in the repertory of many male choruses.

The Two Romanian Folksongs for women's chorus (1915) have not been published; they came in the year of Bartók's most intensive occupation with Romanian materials.

From 1917 date two sets of Slovak Folksongs, one for unaccompanied male chorus, the other for mixed chorus and piano.[16] The

former are soldiers' songs of varying moods. Since the tunes themselves are vastly different from the Hungarian materials of the previous choral settings, it is natural that the settings should differ as
well. Rhythmically they are more primitive than the Hungarian
songs, with only eighth- and quarter-notes except at phrase-ends; the
scales are modal, the first and fourth (the tunes identical) being
Lydian, the second Aeolian with one raised seventh degree, the fifth
Mixolydian. The third, whose provenance was Pozsony (all the others
coming from Zólyom), is in a curiously ambiguous mode which
sounds like G major ending on the supertonic: A is actually the final
—but Bartók harmonizes it consistently with a D-major triad, and
puts numerous C♯'s into the setting elsewhere.

In general, however, the harmonizations of these songs are not
especially adventurous. The first song, parlando, is hung upon an
almost motionless pedal G, with which is combined in long notes a
third, a passing second, or even a sustained seventh; but the melody
is in the first tenor throughout, and always doubled rhythmically in
another voice. The text reads:

> Hey, my dear, kind comrades,
> Give me your attention:
> Such a grievous war
> I'll tell you about.
> In the town of Lublin
> A monstrous great war broke out;
> The sun grew dark,
> Blood flowed like water.
> Crimson blood flooded
> Our faithful eyes—
> God in heaven, help us!

In the second version of this melody (No. 4), the supporting voices
are divided to provide triads and even an occasional secondary
seventh-chord; the first lines are doubled in the two outer voices,
the harmony enclosed within them.

> If I should fall, carry me to Zólyom;
> In the sad graveyard bury me there,
> In the sad graveyard, close by the gate;
> If my sweetheart comes out, let her cease weeping.
> 'Who went so much to her, now the earth covers him;
> Who so often held her in his arms, here his body crumbles.'

The second song, *If I Must Go to the War*, is of slighter musical interest, though chorally effective. The third has already been mentioned; its text deals with the conscription of soldiers to fight in Russia:

> Come, comrade, come, we are going to war;
> Thus said the king: we shall be soldiers . . .
> In Russia the fields are green:
> Our forefathers are lying there.

This, like its predecessor, is harmonized almost note-against-note; but in the final song Bartók for the first time makes use of the imitative possibilities inherent in the choral style. The harmonization, however, takes little advantage of the modality of the tune, and in consequence the over-all tonal impression is one of C, ending on the dominant. A B♭ just preceding the cadence helps prevent a total lapse into C major. The text is the only cheerful one in the group:

> 'Here, sweetheart, are a hundred florins: put them in your pocket;
> When I come back from battle they will be yours.'
> 'What is your money worth to me? Money to me is nothing;
> You cannot pay for my embraces.'
> 'If I can't give you money, then go with me—
> Soon you'll wash your clothes with me in the Danube waters.'

The Four Slovak Songs for mixed voices and piano offer a strong contrast to the soldiers' songs of the preceding group. The treatment indicates the possibility of their having been set earlier;[17] in general they are handled simply, harmonized note-against-note or even presented in unison for long stretches. The tunes themselves all have a strong tritone flavor, but they are otherwise of varied character.[18] The first, a dialogue between a mother and the daughter she gave to a wicked husband in a foreign land, is in 3/4 meter, B♭ minor ending on the dominant—at least to Western ears. Its waltzlike rhythm is more Teutonic than Bartókian, but the accompaniment is fairly unsentimental in spite of the text:

> Thus the mother gave her daughter to a husband
> In a foreign country,
> Telling her, charging her
> Never to return.
> 'I'll turn into a blackbird
> And thus fly to my mother;

I'll sit on a rose stalk in her garden
And thus wait for her.'
Her mother looks out—'Strange is this bird,
How very sad she sounds;
Fly down, blackbird,
From my rose bush.'
'To an evil husband, dear mother, you gave me,
In a foreign country;
Sorry is the lot
Of one who has a wicked mate!'

By altering two notes just before the last cadence, Bartók emphasizes the bitterness of the line.

The hay-making song which follows is in a subtly irregular meter: five measures of 5/8, one of 3/8, and cadencing in 3/4. The rhythmic structure permits an antiphonal use of chorus and accompaniment in the first stanza and a choral division in the second. The last two songs are in dance rhythms, the first a jeering song:

Eating, drinking, are your only delight,
And going to the dance.
The pleating of a petticoat
Was never to your taste. . .

The other is founded on a drone bass to represent the pipes:

Let the bagpipe sound now,
For the dance waits every pair;
Sound it merrily, skilfully:
Let it set the feet a-dancing. . .
While he lived, this was a goat,
Skittish, fond of dancing;
Let him not caper now,
Lest he break his legs asunder.

Endre Szervánsky has transcribed the accompaniment of these pieces for orchestra. The first two are more or less orchestral in scope as they stand; in the last two, however, the piano does little more than mark the rhythm, and to transfer this function to the orchestra is perhaps supererogatory. In the original version the Slovak Folksongs are effective enough; both sets well repay the effort expended on them.

The Four Hungarian Folksongs for unaccompanied mixed chorus
are dated May 1930. There are really five songs in this group, since
the fourth includes two separate tunes, while the text of one has been
compiled from three other songs.[19] Three of these tunes were collected in Bartók's earliest expeditions (1906-07); they come from
Transdanubia and Transylvania, at opposite ends of Hungary. All are
handled with great contrapuntal ease. The 'parlando rubato' of *The
Prisoner* and *The Rover* is highly ornate, with melismatic embellish-
ment of inner lines; the other two, both 'tempo giusto' tunes, are
treated somewhat more simply, but even here the texture is entirely
polyphonic. There is frequent division of the chorus into eight parts,
and this, together with the rhythmic plasticity and the contrapuntal
intricacy of the settings, makes performance as difficult as in any of
Bartók's choral work. Yet the handling of the voices is accomplished
with the greatest sensitivity and dexterity.

The tragic dialogue of *The Prisoner* with his mother is heightened
by Bartók's omission of the last two stanzas of the folksong, in which
the condemned man complains that it would be 'a pity indeed if my
beautiful curly hair were scattered to the winds . . . for six gray
horses and the beautiful saddles that go with them.' The immutabil-
ity of the thief's sentence needs no explanation or extenuation. *The
Rover* also has sections of its text omitted; the profound melancholy
that pervades the song is sufficient in itself, without the self-pity that
certain stanzas express. The metrical transcription of the unmetrical
tune is accomplished with the least possible violence to its plasticity;
a comparison of the first few bars with the version Bartók notated in
the field demonstrates how close to the essence of the 'parlando
rubato' it comes.

The third song, *The Marriageable Girl*, has parallels in the folk
literature of many peoples, including the Germans, Slovaks, and
Romanians: the daughter who objects successively to the suitors
her mother offers her—farmhand, swineherd, cowherd, tinker—and
takes the last one, in this case a shepherd, since 'he who watches
his flock will be a good educator for his wife.' Such a song is the
British *Whistle, Daughter, Whistle*, in which the unwilling girl protests that she cannot whistle (for a cow, a sheep, et cetera), but succeeds when she is offered a man.[20]

The published version [21] has German and English translations
which scarcely approximate the Hungarian text, but the complete

version may be found in Bartók's *Hungarian Folk Music*. For the purposes of the setting Bartók has omitted three of the five stanzas, and has adapted for dialogue certain other lines and added a few ejaculations. The setting is brilliant and emphatic, and somewhat more diatonic than the first two.

The final song, called *Liebeslied* and *Love Song* in the German and English versions, but simply *Dal* in Hungarian, is a curious composite of two tunes in A-B-A form, with the text of the first made up of stanzas from three separate songs, each one from a different district of Hungary. This first tune Bartók notated in 7/8 meter in 1907 (4/8 plus 3/8), but in the choral version he has adjusted the rhythm to fit a 2/4 bar throughout. Another variant collected at the same time (HFM 54a) is in 2/4, but its melody differs in many particulars from this.

The second of the songs in this composite is unrelated to any of those that provided the materials for the first and third parts; it is not even remotely a 'love song,' since it represents a simple statement that the singer's horse has lost its shoes and the blacksmith can fix it up. Rhythmically it is one of the most interesting of the group, with its 8/8 meter divided irregularly into units of two and three eighths, but not in a consistent 'Bulgarian' pattern. A literal recapitulation of the first song, with a caudal extension, rounds out the piece.

Bartók's last choral transcriptions of folk material are the Székely Songs of 1932, for unaccompanied male chorus. These were ostensibly designed to be sung as a group; there are six movements, of which the fifth is a partial, reflective restatement of the third. But Bartók indicates in a footnote that they may be performed in a variety of sequences, omitting one or more movements: a gesture to practicality.

While they are set contrapuntally, these songs are much simpler in their expressive content than many of the earlier transcriptions. Except for the first song, which is in as many as six parts, Bartók uses only four undivided parts; the last five may as easily be sung by a quartet as a chorus. The counterpoint runs to parallel motion in thirds and sixths, frequently in full six-four chords. Stanzas are transposed, and there are occasional episodic extensions, but in general the settings, while effective in performance, show no innovations.

The first two are slow parlando tunes, the others 'tempo giusto.'

The three stanzas of the last song are set in successively higher keys, returning in a rather extended coda to the original:

'Do a dance, priest:
I'll give you a hundred florins.'
'I'll not dance,
    Don't know how—
        It's unseemly,
            Not allowed,
That a priest should dance.'

'Do a dance, priest:
Six fine oxen I'll give you.'
'I'll not dance,
    Don't know how—
        It's unseemly,
            Not allowed,
That a priest should dance.'

'Do a dance, priest:
A comely bride I'll give you.'
'Dance I shall,
    I know how—
        Seemly quite,
            It's allowed,
That a priest should dance.'

Although they are not especially demanding except in compass (the tessitura of the tenor lines is generally high, with many A's, several A♯'s, and two B's), they represent an idiomatic use of male voices, and in many places are richly resonant, with opportunity for a wide range of dynamic contrast. They are well within the capabilities of a good male chorus and, once they are available in translation, should attain numerous performances in English-speaking countries.

Two sets of short original works—*From Olden Times*, for three-part male chorus, and Twenty-seven Choruses, for two- and three-part children's or women's chorus, both dated 1935—together with the *Cantata profana*, conclude the list of Bartók's choral composition.

From Olden Times, a 'peasant cantata' based upon modified folk- and art-song texts, presents the miseries and joys of peasant life in a triptych, a short and dancelike movement between two much larger parlando movements. The texts of the first and third are contradictory:

    i. No one's more unhappy than the peasant,
       For his wretchedness is greater than the sea!
       Never any rest, night and day he must be afoot . . .
       His dolman tattered, he is taken as a pauper;
       He must content himself with a little bread and a few leeks . . .
       If he errs, he is thrown into jail, where he gets nothing to eat or
         drink . . .
       Judge, priest, tradesman, shopkeeper, innkeeper, plague him in-
         cessantly;
       Excuse is vain, so long as they find blood in him . . .

   iii. No one's happier than the peasant . . .
       If there were no peasant, we should have no bread;
       If he did not plow, all of us would starve:
       Roman emperors would take up the plow,
       Valuing it more highly than their empires . . .
       On a fine morning the plowman turns his plow,
       Cuts, carves, guides the blade in the field;
       With hope, with care he plows the field,
       Harvests the ripe wheat with joy . . .
       The peasant makes everything himself,
       Tools, dwelling, decorates his apparel,
       Music he learns not from books . . .
       No one has a finer life than the peasant!

The musical style of this work stems directly from peasant music, but it is peasant music purified and tempered by the refiner's fire. The shadow of the *Cantata profana* falls upon every page, though it was hardly to be seen in the Székely Songs. At times the words are freely, almost tonelessly, chanted; at others there are madrigalisms—fanfares for the Roman emperors, cavernous open fifths for the jail—but at all times there is profound conviction. Rhythmically these pieces appear complex, because of the composer's concern for paralleling the vowel quantity in the music, and since the prosody of the Hungarian language is so individual, it would be almost impossible to translate this work idiomatically into another language. But it is eminently singable in its own tongue.

So also are the Twenty-seven Choruses for treble voices, whose most salient characteristic is their imitative polyphony. Bartók first heard them in Budapest, 7 May 1937, in a concert during the course of which he also played excerpts from the *Mikrokosmos*. 'I can never forget my impression of how fresh, how joyful the youngsters sounded,' he wrote.[22] 'In the sound production of these children from the suburban schools there is a naturalness that still recalls the unspoiled singing of the peasants.' Several years later, after he had come to America, the prospect of hearing several of these choruses sung by 450 children with the Philadelphia Orchestra accompanying, at the May Festival of the University of Michigan, gave him the keenest pleasure.[23]

The texts of these pieces are largely from peasant songs, but modified, combined, and amplified. The sentiments expressed are therefore those common to Hungarian peasant music, but the settings are original, drawing upon folk resources but with no idea of producing synthetic folksongs. The larger part have the melodic characteristics of children's songs, and the main interest lies in the contrapuntal interweaving of the two or three lines in freely imitative or canonic textures. Most of them are diatonic, though the linearity of the writing frequently results in a tang of unusual dissonance, and there are here and there modulations startling in their abruptness. One or two, like the canon *I'm Dying for Csurgó*, comprise more sophisticated materials of a fairly advanced chromaticism; Sándor Veress holds [24] that from this piece future musicologists would be able to reconstruct the music of our time, much as the Reading Rota has provided information as to the state of music of its period.[25] Though such a claim is obviously excessive, there is much of the essential Bartók in passages of this kind:

9. *Twenty-Seven Choruses*

But these are exceptional procedures in the Twenty-seven Choruses.
Most of them are well within the capabilities of the amateur chorus,
and when they have been made available in English (a few have
already been translated, unfortunately with some rhythmic changes
to suit the English prosody) they should find numerous performances.
Although Bartók divided them into two groups—nineteen for children's voices, eight for women—there is no reason why the whole set
should not be done by any treble choir.

For several of these choruses (Nos. 1, 2, 7, 10, 11, 12) Bartók also
provided accompaniments for small orchestra. The two versions differ
somewhat in the choral parts, especially in the *Legénycsúfoló (Boy's
Jeering Song)*, where a number of measures were added. The composer's intention was that the pieces be performed either with orchestra or entirely without accompaniment—never with piano, but that
intention has not been scrupulously observed. The piano may be
useful for rehearsal purposes, but it adds nothing desirable in performance.

Bartók's most important vocal work is the *Cantata profana*, completed in Budapest on 8 September 1930. Based upon Romanian
folksong texts, it requires for performance a double mixed chorus,
tenor and baritone soloists, and a large orchestra.

The legend, as it appears in the *Cantata profana*, concerns a father
who had nine sons, whom he taught no trade, neither plowing nor
horse raising nor cattle raising, but only to hunt in the mountains.
On a fateful day the nine sons, pursuing the tracks of a great stag,
lost their way and were themselves changed into nine stags.

The father, concerned at their absence, took his musket and followed them into the mountains; their tracks led to a cool spring, where he saw nine great stags. Dropping to one knee, he would have fired upon them, but the largest stag spoke to him: 'Dear little father, do not fire upon us, or we shall take you upon our antlers and hurl you from mountain to mountain, from cliff to cliff, and crush you upon a moss-grown rock, so that you will be ground to little pieces.' The father besought them thus: 'Oh my dear sons, come quickly home to your little mother; she awaits you with longing, the torches lighted, the table laid, the beakers filled. . . The beakers are full of wine, she is full of tears.'

But the largest stag, the eldest son, answered, 'Our dear little father, go home now to our dear mother, but we shall not go with you: for our antlers cannot go through doors, only through mountains; our bodies cannot go about clad in shirts, but only among green foliage; our hoofs cannot walk upon the hearth's ashes, only upon dry leaves; our mouths cannot drink from beakers, only from cool springs.'

Bartók divided the *Cantata profana* into three sections; in the first the sons are changed into enchanted stags; the second deals with the meeting between the father and his sons; and in the third, the chorus recapitulates the tale. Such allegory as exists in the work is capable of interpretation in terms of the composer's ardent desire for freedom, not only personal and artistic freedom for himself, but freedom for his native country as well. How far such an interpretation is valid can hardly be determined here; analytically the work must stand upon its own merits, as demonstrated in its content.[26]

These merits are very great. The writing for both voices and orchestra is not only skilful and intricate, but psychologically and esthetically convincing. Some of the best pages Bartók ever wrote are contained within this score; its dramatic intensity is gripping. The vocal lines are closely related to those of peasant songs, in both contour and rhythm, but the folkloric elements have been so completely amalgamated with the techniques of art music that there is never a hint of disparity in their use. The two choruses are employed with the greatest flexibility, now combined, now separate, and again irregularly divided, always with the most discriminating regard for horizontal lines, which are so rationally conceived that vertical sonori-

ties which look almost incapable of attainment—choral intonation
being far from orchestral precision—are achieved through melodic
logic. Such passages as the 'perpetual round' illustrated below, with
the imitation occurring at the interval of a single beat, common
enough in instrumental writing, are rarely encountered in the chorus;
the simultaneous combinations include six or seven different notes,
here the entire Phrygian scale of the passage:

10. *Cantata profana*

To bring off the round with accurate intonation is by no means so
difficult as it appears, since in the two bars which precede the excerpt
each pair of voices is brought in successively in melodic lines of such
straightforwardness that the problem resolves itself. So, too, with a
later passage, in which a cluster of seven notes is built up by opening
out in successive measures the original three-note cluster:

11. *Cantata profana*

These are both at moments of strong dramatic impact; in the first, the father is taking aim at the enchanted stags, not knowing they are his own sons; in the second, the chorus is commenting in hushed tones on the stags' refusal to return to their home. In less impassioned moments both sonorities and textures are relaxed; the simple mirror in thirds and triads which recounts the nine sons' discovery and pursuit of the great stag, and the prelude to the father's plea to the sons to come back with him, couched in a canon in thirds, are typical:

12. *Cantata profana*

(a)

(b)

The first section of the cantata is given over, after the moody orchestral introduction, to choral narration; the account of the hunt is a vigorous fugal exposition, presented entirely over a rhythmic ostinato in the strings, its fourths forming a primitive foundation for the cumulative excitement of the hunting fugue itself:

13. *Cantata profana*

The chorus continues its narrative role through the first part of the second section, a winding chromatic figure (related to the hunting fugue) representing the wandering of the father in search of his sons. Once he finds the stags, the two solo voices carry the work forward, the tenor, as the eldest son, with increasing agitation, in a tremendous parlando line which sweeps gradually to a high C, spanning almost two octaves. Again the fugue subject is expanded as the father makes his passionate plea to the sons to return home; at the end of the section there is a duet between father and son, the agitation subsiding, so that the final section is tranquil almost throughout, as if the listener were reflecting upon the tale he has heard.

The form of the *Cantata profana* is architectonic. Its three main divisions are subdivided into smaller musical forms—canon, fugue, aria, cadenza—but with intricate interrelationships which weld them into a homogeneous whole. In this respect there is a superficial resemblance to Alban Berg's *Wozzeck*, where the larger form of the opera is dependent upon a number of rounded and recognizable forms within it. Ferenc Ottó traces in the *Cantata profana* relationships from the standpoint of melody, harmony, and rhythm, to plainsong and the music of Palestrina, Bach, Mozart, Liszt, and Debussy.[27] But the work is so completely identified with the style of the mature Bartók, in which folk- and art-motivation are inextricably intermingled, that it is superfluous to call up its remote sources. Its first performance in 1934 brought unenthusiastic criticism: '. . . the chorus has to tell its tale in an interjaculatory style with the orchestra hampering them rather than elucidating the disrupted texture . . . it hardly seemed to be satisfactory choral music.' [28] But the passage of years and the growth of Bartók's stature might well change the color of criticism; what seemed fragmentary and eruptive in the 1930's might sound logical and idiomatic today. The *Cantata profana* is without question one of its author's most significant works—but one that is likely to remain infrequently performed.

THERE is no better way to approach the music of Béla Bartók, and certainly no better way of understanding the processes of growth that his music underwent, than through the string quartets. This was the only form which held Bartók's attention from his student days to the very end of his life: his first quartet,[1] later suppressed, was written (according to Kodály) in 1899, when he was eighteen years old; and in December 1944, less than a year before his death, he was planning to write a new quartet,[2] of which only a few motives were sketched. Between are the six quartets which mark not only successive culmination points in Bartók's career, but also in a sense the culmination of twentieth-century activity in the form.

Present-day composers are in general farther from the Haydn-Mozart-Beethoven tradition in the string quartet than their distance in time and ideology would lead one to suspect. The nineteenth-century emphasis upon the expansive, the unrestrained, played havoc with the chamber-music forms. Few of the Romantics made significant contributions to the literature of the quartet, and with most of those who did write for the medium there is often a feeling of unwilling restriction: the limitations chafe, the sonorities threaten to burst their bounds and overflow into the orchestra. Even Brahms, whose restraint is frequently admirable, was not entirely happy in writing for the string quartet, and the Clarinet Quintet, opus 115, in which there is greater opportunity for contrast in timbre, is more convincing as a chamber work than the three string quartets he allowed to survive.

Recent composers have written numerous quartets: Hindemith's six (seven if a suppressed student quartet is included) and Milhaud's eighteen come to mind. But one has the feeling that most of these were gathered unripe, and in quality they can hardly be mentioned in the same breath with Haydn and Beethoven and Mozart. Neither of these series demonstrates the growth process; nor do the four quartets of Schoenberg, their widely divergent character resulting from their chronological separation.

So far in this century, Bartók's quartets alone display progressive growth, and all six are worthy of being placed beside those of the Viennese masters. In succession they range from the somewhat indirect to the entirely direct; they make use of techniques borrowed from here and there as well as techniques completely new, and in the process they remain the personal, intense expression of one man, who if he had written nothing else would still be reckoned among the handful of significant composers of our time.

The contrapuntal freedom characteristic of Bartók's treatment of the string quartet, the extreme plasticity with which the individual lines turn, shift, combine, and oppose, is already present in the First Quartet, opus 7. The significance of the contrapuntal approach can hardly be overestimated. Each player is considered as an individual, with his own strand of the fabric; this autonomy brings about a textural richness comparable to the last quartets of Beethoven— a richness largely lacking in the nineteenth-century quartet of Mendelssohn, Schubert, Schumann, or Brahms, whatever its other merits.

Bartók's polyphony, from which he weaves a canonic, fugal, or freely imitative tissue, is subject to no arbitrary restrictions. Canons are not undeviatingly maintained if changes will sharpen their impress; a fugue subject, once chosen, may be modified in shape or proportion on almost every restatement; and there is no limit set upon the relationships that arise through free imitation.

The six quartets graphically illuminate Bartók's attitude toward tonality. While he himself apparently considered certain works as in specific major or minor keys,[3] the tonalities of even the First

Quartet are handled so freely that one is justified only in saying that they are 'on'—not 'in'—this or that tonality. So the First and Second Quartets are on A, the Third on C♯, the Fourth on C, the Fifth on B♭, and the Sixth on D. By this it is understood that these keynotes serve as orientation points: that the music is organized around them, modally or chromatically, freely fluctuating, using the keynotes as points of departure and points of repose, affecting modulation from and back to them.

To describe the First Quartet as in A minor is to ignore the tonal functions implicit in the minor mode. The first movement opens with an indeterminate tonality, and closes on a minor third, A♭-C♭, which might—if Bartók's meticulous notational procedure were disregarded—be interpreted as the third and the fifth of the E-major triad, and therefore as dominant-representative in A major/minor. The second movement ends on a B-major triad; in the third movement the recurrent pedal E's stand for the dominant, but the chromaticism of the facture seldom confirms the key. At the very end the pedal becomes B♭, merging into a whole-tone scale on B♭, and the last four measures are built from three notes only: A-B-E, all of which occur in the cadence chords. The work is firmly grounded, conveying an impression of tonal stability, of beginning in one place and moving meaningfully in the direction of another; but there are only fleeting resemblances to the minor mode.

The chromaticism of the First Quartet is of a variety that is not generally encountered in the other five. It may be considered an auxiliary chromaticism, while that of the later quartets is fundamental. This statement is, of course, too sweeping in its implications: there are examples throughout of both types; but the distinction between the styles lies in the shifting of the emphasis. In the First Quartet there is seldom a direct approach to a melody note: instead, Bartók moves to a note just above or just below the one apparently aimed for, and only then slips into the note intended. The appoggiatura style results in the quartet's slight Wagnerian feeling, to which Bartók later took exception.[4]

The First Quartet demonstrates the rhythmic vitality which remains typical; even in the opening Lento the rhythms are alive in every bar, and they become cumulatively more active through the later sections. Coming as it did after Bartók's first intensive work with Hungarian peasant music, it is not by any means surprising that the quartet shows the result of that study. The traces are as yet only slight. There has not been time to assimilate all the implications of the peasant melodies; the intervallic structure and the rhythmic characteristics of the peasant tunes have not been sublimated into the mature folkloric idiom of the later works. There are stylistic discrepancies: the recently experienced music of Debussy contributes whole-tone touches at variance with the scalar forms of the preceding works, while the uncharacteristic parallel thirds indicate that the shadow of Brahms is not too far in the background.

Less apparent to the casual ear are the structural relationships between the various parts of the quartet. Each of Bartók's quartets demonstrates the composer's preoccupation with problems of architecture, and the integration of the several movements of each work is achieved in different ways. Characteristic throughout is the motivic work—the construction of entire movements or of entire works from minute musical fragments, constantly varied, extended, transformed. The simplest application of the motivic technique in the solution of formal problems lies in the cyclic method of Franck, one or two thematic patterns giving rise to the entire material of a large symphonic or chamber work. In the Franckian school there is little more than an ingenuous application of the method, successive movements being built from thematic variants, the resultant structure being static rather than dynamic.

With Bartók the opposite is true. His motives, frequently of two or three notes only, are in a continuous state of regeneration. They grow organically; they proliferate; the evolutionary process is kinetic. No doubt many motivic manipulations which seem carefully calculated were brought about intuitively: the line between reason and intuition is never sharply defined, but the compact thematic logic cannot be denied.

The process of integration in the First Quartet is a simple one. One motive, of four notes only, which seems first to appear in the opening bars of the second movement,[5] generates the principal theme of the finale; and a study of the entire work discloses that the motive has already been predicted in the appoggiatura-patterns of the first movement. The difference between this method and that of Franck is that in the Bartók Quartet the motivic material is evolved gradually, not presented as a *fait accompli*. It is apparent that when Bartók began the quartet its course was not predetermined: the func-

tional possibilities latent in the melodic successions of the Lento are
not immediately realized; they reveal themselves only as the work
progresses.

The harmonic idiom of the First Quartet poses analytical problems, most of which are resolved by horizontal rather than vertical
consideration. Protagonists of the 'technique of composition with
twelve tones' make much [6] of the fact that within the first three
measures Bartók sets forth all twelve notes of the duodecuple scale.
This seems a relatively unimportant observation when one considers
that it is also true of the Second Quartet (measures two to five), the
Third (measures two to five), and the Fourth (measures one to three),
and that in none of these four quartets is the pattern thereafter employed in serial or dodecaphonic fashion. For that matter, the subject of Bach's *Musical Offering* contains in a single line eleven of
the twelve notes, with very little repetition. Liszt's *Faust Symphony*
has a theme that includes all twelve notes, without repetition.
While Bartók much later believed that his stylistic development
would lead him to the use of the twelve-tone technique,[7] he never
wrote a twelve-tone work, nor one actually atonal; and although
some scores of the 1920's are relatively far from accepted standards
of tonality, even these have a basis in tonality.

The opening of the First Quartet is somewhat in the style of a
double canon, the intertwining contrapuntal lines of the violins
establishing the slow pace which prevails throughout the movement.
The viola and violoncello enter later with the same material, while
the violins continue with free contrapuntal lines; the canonic imitation is continued, however, for three measures only, and the materials are then freely expanded, much use being made of the falling
sixth with which each of the four instruments began.

The impassioned, improvisational melody of the viola, which constitutes the central section of the movement, looks backward to the
orchestral Suites, rather than ahead. Like most of the motives of the
quartet, it is filled with appoggiaturas, the whole line consisting of
a series of 'Mannheim sighs.' Before the return of the first-section
materials there is a curiously Ravelian passage in consecutive six-four
and sixth-chords; but since it precedes *Mother Goose*, which it somewhat resembles, there can be a question only of coincidence, not of
influence.

The double bar at the end of the first movement is a purely arbitrary device, since the last notes of the viola and violoncello, three chromatically ascending thirds, are immediately seized upon to effect the transition to the Allegretto. This is a sonata-like movement with a greatly compressed and otherwise modified recapitulation. The first thematic complex is worked out mainly upon two short motives: one already mentioned, of four notes, presented as a rhythmic ostinato, over which the second, of three notes (a descending succession, A-G$\sharp$-D$\sharp$), is manipulated. A subsidiary complex [8] provides a waltz-like theme in the inner lines, with another ostinato in the outer parts.

The first two movements have surprisingly little in common with most of Bartók's later work. Both the harmonic and the structural concepts are still essentially romantic, in spite of the motivic work which has its roots in classical procedures. There is an improvisational character at variance with its palpable order. The finale is somewhat more compact, and in many ways more Bartókian. It is here, for the first time in the quartet, that any considerable folk-element is perceptible. The rubato of the cello, in the concerted cadenza which serves as introduction, and the dance rhythms of the Allegro vivace itself, the melodic emphasis upon fourths, the percussive repetition of single notes, the twisting ornamentation of the fugato subject—all these seem folk-inspired. The repeated E's with which the movement begins represent a characteristically Bartókian procedure, rhythmic inverted or internal pedals such as this, amplifications of classical practice, being of frequent occurrence. It may be observed in something like its classical application at the recapitulation,[9] where for forty measures the first violin has only eighth-note E's plus a few auxiliary D$\sharp$'s and F's. The classical use of pedals in approaching cadence or coda established a clash, frequently bitonal, which emphasized even more strongly the final resolution, and this is essentially what happens here.

The basic motive, extended to six notes and furnished with a choriambic prolongation, becomes the principal theme of the movement. That prolongation gives rise to some folklike developments (at nos. 12 and 13, for example), and to the greater part of the coda. One other motive of importance appears in the twentieth measure, an outgrowth of the chromatic auxiliaries just preceding; it consists of a descending minor second (in this instance repeated twice) followed by a descending minor third. The succession is so frequent in Bartók's music of all periods that it may be considered an *Urmotiv*. Here it is presented in minor triads and a seventh-chord, and repeated with slight variation; almost immediately the whole pattern is inverted, establishing a precedent to which Bartók will return again and again in his later music—the 'allegro vivace' of the Concerto for Orchestra and the chorale in the Third Piano Concerto still exemplify the procedure, and there are innumerable examples in the intervening years.

In the course of development the basic motive of the quartet, reduced to eighth-notes and provided with a winding triplet extension, becomes the subject of a rather scherzando fugal section.[10] The subject is exposed to the accompaniment of pizzicato chords in the cello, forming dominant-tonic cadences in D♭ and A, a succession of consecutive triads, and then a series of wilfully resolved dominant sevenths in A which persist in moving to A♭ minor. In spite of its tonal ambivalence, the subject is answered tonally as if it were in D♭ major throughout. The fugal exposition is followed by a stretto on the head motive and one complete statement of the subject, leading to the recapitulation. The treatment of the fugue subject is atypical; it retains its shape throughout, without the progressive modification which later becomes a Bartókian characteristic.

Structurally the First Quartet is less satisfying than those that follow. Bartók himself in later years criticized its lack of economy,[11] and it is apparent that it lacks the close-knit integration of some later works. Stylistically, of course, it is representative of Bartók's idiom in transition from the early Strauss- and Liszt-inspired neo-Hungarianisms to the highly personal style that resulted from the assimilation of the influences of Hungarian peasant music and of Bartók's contemporaries. Its melodic superabundance is overpowering; before it other considerations—harmonic, tonal, architectural—are swept ruthlessly aside.

The over-all character of the Second Quartet is somewhat more rarefied than that of the First, though this may be due partially to the difference in mood rather than the stylistic changes it demonstrates: whereas the First represents a gradual increase of activity from the restraint of the Lento to the abandon of the finale, the Second is restrained in both its first and third movements, and assumes a peasant vigor only in its central Allegro. But there are changes much more profound than one of mere mood. The harmonic idiom shows a remarkable advance over that of the First Quartet; the character of the chromaticism has been largely transmuted—instead of appoggiaturas and other chromatic by-tones the style tends toward 'false relations,' simultaneous major-minor elements, parallelism in such dissonant intervals as tritones, sevenths, and ninths, and some apparent bitonality or polytonality.

This latter province is generally considered to have been explored by Stravinsky (in *Petrushka*) and Milhaud; but as early as 1908, in the Bagatelles for piano, Bartók was combining two separate keys or modes. Milhaud was then only sixteen years old, and *Petrushka* was not yet written. Bartók never made multiple tonality more than one of many means, but he did not hesitate to use it whenever it offered the most convincing solution for his problem. The final cadence of the First Violin Sonata, in three separate keys, is an example, as is the second theme of the Piano Sonata; and there are a number of instances in *Mikrokosmos* and elsewhere.

In the Second Quartet, such a passage as this [12] must be considered essentially bitonal, though it is not pursued very far:

14. *Quartet No. 2*

In the first four measures of the excerpt, the A-major pizzicato of the cello supports the A minor (or Aeolian) of the violins; in the two that follow, the chords are in D major, the viola in D minor. After the fermata, the motive is taken up in overlapping imitation: the first violin in C minor, the second in A♭ minor, the first in E minor, the viola presumably in G♯ (major or minor—the passage does not permit exact identification), and the cello in the Lydian mode on B.

Faced with a new musical work, the analyst is tempted to pour it into a preconstituted mold, a sort of Procrustean bed which the music is compelled by drastic means to fit. The term sonata-allegro is applied indiscriminately to the most diversiform structures. It is true that the first movement of the Second Quartet resembles in certain respects the traditional sonata-movement; but it would be a mistake thus to label it, considering the analytical problem at an end. The traditional sonata-allegro is made up ordinarily of full-fledged 'themes,' stated in their definitive form and fragmented and recombined in the working-out or development section before they are restated. In the Second Quartet of Bartók there are no 'themes': there are only motives, and the process of development is continuous from beginning to end.

Almost everything that appears in the first movement is present in the opening measures:

15. *Quartet No. 2*

The first five notes of the first violin—two ascending fourths, a falling minor second, and a falling fourth, together with the pulsating inner voices, give rise to most of the manifestations of the entire movement. In the eighteen measures that follow, for example, this motive is the only structural element. Its intervals are progressively pulled apart, its rhythmic relationships transformed, until presently it becomes only a series of octave G's, unrecognizable as the same motive except as it has been observed in the process of transmutation. In the next section [13] the first three notes span an octave instead of a seventh, and the descent is one of an augmented fifth; but it is the same motive, giving rise to another figure, the triplet in the second violin, which in turn becomes functional.

An apparently new motive, broader in its character, is found in the proper place for a subsidiary theme; based on the augmented triad A-C♯-E♯, it may be construed as a compression of the opening motive:

16. *Quartet No. 2*

Whether the derivation is reasoned or intuitive is of little moment here. There are innumerable examples, in the music of Bartók, of just such deliberate thematic manipulations—those, for instance, which permit the third movement of the Violin Concerto to duplicate the first, and the episodes in the rondo-finale of the Second Piano Concerto to recall in rhythmic distortion the motives of the first Allegro. Superficially Bartók's music may be considered 'constructivistic' or 'formalistic'; but such a label makes no allowance for what has been called 'the relationships embodied in successive phases of musical growth.' [14]

The formation of another thematic idea may be seen in a simple progression of three notes, A-B-C, ascending, and immediately descending in another octave.[15] This is an outgrowth of the triplet figure previously mentioned; through the next three pages it is the dominant element, eventually flowering into what may be considered a closing 'theme.' Its purest manifestation, however, does not come until just before the end of the movement, where, in the bitonal passage quoted above, it assumes through a process of refinement a simple, folklike quality.

The developmental process is intensified through the central part of the movement, with the harmonic elements similarly heightened. The minor seconds of the opening have a tentative sound, softened by the pedal B♭ in the violoncello; they soon expand to consecutive thirds, and thereby increase the euphony. Later, in moments of stress, the harshest of intervals—consecutive tritones and even sevenths—color the fabric. In one passage [16] Bartók opposes two streams of parallel sevenths in a mirrorlike procedure. These are color devices rather than harmonic: such duplication does not increase the number of parts, and they are not treated as chordal elements. The writing is still horizontal. The culmination of this intervallic parallelism comes, of course, in the 'Giuoco delle coppie' of the Concerto for Orchestra, where successive sections are made up of parallel sixths, thirds, sevenths, fifths, and seconds, and the final cadence telescopes all these intervals into a single chord.

The tritone plays an important part in the Second Quartet, especially in the last two movements. The second, Allegro molto capriccioso, is a series of dancelike sections, much in the manner of the later Dance Suite, but without the ritornel which sets off each section of that work from the succeeding one. No such device is needed in this movement, since its overwhelming rhythmic energy sweeps everything before it, and its few returns to previously heard material provide adequate guideposts.

One of the most characteristic aspects of the movement, and one which it shares with many such movements in Bartók, is the way in which section after section is suspended upon a single tone, repeated in even eighth-note patterns. Here, after the short introduction, it is D, repeated in the second violin more than one hundred fifty times; then, after a momentary interruption, the D's are resumed, together with the adjacent E's, for seventy-nine more repetitions. A's and E's form the basis of the next section; the D's, with auxiliaries, presently return [17] and continue for nearly three pages. By such drastic means—possibly related to the drones of primitive instruments—a tonal level is established which no chromaticism, no matter how remote, can dislodge.

To strengthen resonance, many such passages employ open strings together with stopped strings; obviously the device anchors the musical conception to certain locations in which C, G, D, A, and E may serve as foundation. By making use of the open strings in this way, Bartók is able to build up savage sonorities which still remain within the bounds of chamber music. Such procedures, as well as the long glissandos found in this movement, are even more frequent in the later quartets.

The first three notes of the movement, F-B-F, give rise to the predominant thematic idea, which is, however, in rocking minor thirds rather than in tritones. But the opening motive is important in its own right, since it recurs to set off some of the later sections of the movement. The biting minor second in measure seven is also important as a guidepost, the two tones appearing successively rather than together as in the first movement.

By a rather free recurrence of the materials of the movement Bartók conveys the impression, if not the actual structural plan, of a rondo. The most unpromising of motivic ideas are gradually drawn out into convincing lines—the three-note motive D-F-F♯, for example (the retrograde form of the *Urmotiv* mentioned above), arising from the rocking thirds, itself gives rise to a fairly wide-ranging melody.[18] In the shimmering Prestissimo which occupies the last half-dozen pages of the score, the same thematic pattern is changed from 2/4 to 6/8 and covers an even greater compass. The last twenty-four measures are constructed almost exclusively from the *Urmotiv* F♯-F-D, and the close is in unison on the rocking minor thirds.

The third movement, Lento, is structurally chain-like, one section following another without much apparent thematic connection. But there are unifying devices throughout, so that the movement gives the impression of a set of variations. The minor second plays a great part here, as does the tritone; both are present in the first two measures. One of the most important guideposts is the interval progression which appears in viola and violoncello at the end of the first section:

17. *Quartet No. 2*

Its derivation from the basic motive of the first movement is clear to the eye, if not to the ear. The pattern appears many times through the course of the finale, almost always untransposed, though occasionally extended. It serves as an orientation point, toward which each section tends and upon which each resolves.

Both melodic and harmonic fourths abound. The third section, 'lento assai,' [19] begins with a four-note chord in fourths, treated as two lines, moving out and back in mirror fashion. On the last page, where the same rhythmic pattern recurs, these are expanded to five- and six-note chords in fourths. The tonal ambiguity of the superposed fourths is carried out in other places by the use of major thirds moving up a minor third, either disguising the tonality or creating a simultaneous major-minor feeling.

The moods of the three movements of the Second Quartet may be summed up in the words lyrical—dynamic—reflective. Its economy results in music of the utmost concentration, and nowhere more so than in the final Lento. While Bartók's style was still in transition to the works of the middle and late 1920's, the Second Quartet is, in its own terms, entirely consistent. The most pronounced contrast in the series of quartets comes between the First and the Second; from here on, though Bartók never closed his mind to new procedures, the primary advance lay in the consolidation of his gains. Most of the new elements in the later works are present, in germinal form, in the pages of the Second Quartet.

In the ten years that separate this from the Third, Bartók had reached a point farther from traditional tonality than he had ever before explored. These few years, marked by such works as *The Wonderful Mandarin*, the two Sonatas for violin and piano (to be considered in the next chapter), the Piano Sonata, the First Piano Concerto, and culminating in the Third and Fourth Quartets, represent the apogee of Bartók's orbit; from this point he swings back to the solid ground of definable tonalities, milder tonal combinations, and the principles of classical form.

The Third Quartet is both the shortest and the most intense of Bartók's works in the form. Its position as the least-played of the Bartók quartets results not only from its demands upon the technique and understanding of the performer but from the extreme concentration of its idiom. Here Bartók's motivic technique is seen approaching its highest point. For practical purposes there are only two or three separate motives in the work; all the rest constitutes manipulation of these few.

In one continuous movement, the Third Quartet is divided into four sections of varying character, marked 'Prima parte,' 'Seconda parte,' 'Ricapitulazione della prima parte,' and Coda, this last reusing materials from the second part. Here for the first time are to be perceived elements of the arch-form which was to condition so much of Bartók's architecture for so many years: the first and third sections sharing materials, and acting as piers of the arch of which the second section is the keystone.[20] This pattern was expanded in the Fourth and Fifth Quartets, and the procedure is followed in the Second Piano Concerto and especially in the Violin Concerto.

For analytical purposes the first section may almost be reduced to a single omnipresent motive: an ascending fourth followed by a falling minor third. It is first encountered in the sixth measure, in the first violin, slightly embellished with a free D♯ which interrupts the G-C-A pattern. The ensuing passage, coming after a few introductory bars, is a rather curious one, since it comprises a canon with many unessential notes in the leading voice, imitated, without the unessential notes, in the lower third at the distance of one measure. As has already been observed, Bartók's attitude toward the devices of polyphony is always extremely liberal; his fugue subjects, instead of remaining constant in line and proportion, exemplify a continuous

process of growth, or perhaps of reconsideration, as they are woven
into the polyphonic texture, and he never hesitates to change an
essentially canonic passage if by so doing it may be made more convincing.

This canonic 'theme' is heard in a simpler, almost folklike version
toward the end of the first part: [21]

18. *Quartet No. 3*

The long, expansive line is made up almost exclusively of the basic
three-note motive, occurring in different permutations, sometimes
extended or otherwise varied, but always recognizable. The only
other important motive, a two-note figure consisting of a thirty-
second-note followed a semitone away by a double-dotted eighth,
appears for the first time over a canonic ostinato in muted viola and
violoncello—each with the basic motive a tritone apart, creating a
vague, nocturnal background for the glassy twitterings of the violins,
in a passage of the 'night music' type so prevalent in Bartók's music
from this period on.[22]

Structurally the first part of the Third Quartet may be considered
a continuous development, with elements of the sectional forms—
the feeling of digression [23] and of return thereafter.[24] But these elements are of little importance in comparison to the constant regeneration from a single cell which is apparent in every measure. The
'recapitulation' is by no means exact: it is, rather, a summary or
précis of the first part, in which ten or twelve measures will be represented by two or three. It is a psychological return, not a physical
one; the atmosphere is more attenuated, the mood more restrained.

Restraint is the more pronounced after the second part, with its
vigorous rhythms and its use of coloristic devices—brittle ponticello
passages, clattering 'col legno,' together with all the glissandos and

pizzicatos. Coupled with these color-devices is a polyphonic texture depending in large measure upon canons of all kinds, and a form which comprises a set of variations upon a short theme in consecutive triads.

The initial statement of the variation theme is made by the violoncello, pizzicato;[25] the sixteenth-note passage that follows in the first violin is only a foretaste of an auxiliary melodic line which is to be superimposed upon the triad-theme and itself varied. Its melodic contour is quite similar to that of the triad-passage:

19. *Quartet No. 3*

and later manipulations serve to intermingle the two almost inextricably. The culmination of the part is in a deft fugato[26] on a subject derived from the variation theme (or themes):

20. *Quartet No. 3*

The auxiliary countersubject is closely allied. The exposition is worked out in the customary order, on A, E, A, and E, with entrances at progressively shorter intervals, creating a feeling of stretto before the materials are completely exposed. But there is an actual stretto in the three lower voices,[27] followed by another on the inverted subject. At the height of the activity, and while the incessant sixteenth-notes continue to outline the fugue subject in an extended form, the variation theme itself returns in the violoncello, pizzicato as before, and is imitated canonically by the first violin; [28] there is a return to the more moderate motion of the earlier sections and a dissolution to a unison F in viola and cello, at which point the 'recapitulation' begins.

There are only three pages here, and the last nine pages are devoted to the coda, based entirely upon the materials of the second part. The canons here become more complex: at one point [29] the two violins are in canon a semitone and a single eighth-note apart. At the very end the quartet has percussive chords built up in superposed fifths, moving chromatically apart in the penultimate measure, and returning to one last violent multiple-stopped chord.

The basic economy of the Third Quartet is typical of many of the scores that follow it. Having determined by this time the direction of his future development, Bartók had come to an intensification of the motivic work which had always been a part of his technique; but the archlike treatment of form was something quite new for him. During the decade that followed, it was to be his most important structural tenet.

The Fourth Quartet of Bartók marks the summit of his constructive genius. Superficially it has many of the characteristics of the Fifth Quartet, written six years later, but these resemblances are mainly architectural, while stylistically the Fourth Quartet is closer to the Third, which preceded it by a single year. The rigors of its logic are matched by the extreme concentration of its idiom. It is a quartet almost without themes, with only motives and their development. This is particularly true of the first and fifth movements, both of which employ the same motivic patterns; the second and fourth also share materials, and only the third, which is couched in the 'night music' terms so frequent in Bartók's later works, is permitted the luxury of individual materials. Even here the movement is ternary, so that its two outer parts parallel the outer movements of the quartet, and its central portion, with its fantastic chirpings and twitterings, becomes by virtue of its position the kernel of the whole work.

Leaving aside for a moment all but structural considerations, it becomes apparent that a single motive, employed in both chromatic

and diatonic versions, is of fundamental importance in the first and
last movements. This basic motive, when first heard in the seventh
measure, is a simple rhythmic succession of semitones, moving up
from B to D♭ and back down to B♭. On the following page it is
inverted and cadences in a cluster-chord; then it assumes its diatonic
form, expanded intervallically and extended by repetition of a fragment; this passage, which serves as subsidiary 'theme,' presents its
materials in a sort of free perpetual canon or round. Further transformation occurs throughout the movement, and at the beginning
of the finale the motive is cast in a dancelike rhythmic pattern, utilizing the diatonic form, which is itself immediately inverted, and then
pulled apart intervallically so that the newly assumed rhythm becomes the recognizable element. These changes are tabulated in the
example below:

21. *Quartet No. 4*

The relationship between the last motive and the first would be impossible to discover without the intermediate steps. It is because Bartók always permits the listener to share his thought processes, rather than leaping from a basic motive to its ultimate mutation, that his music is logically convincing. The basic motive of the Fourth Quartet returns in its original shape halfway through the last movement, and from then on plays a prominent part in the organization of the close; but it never seems a deliberate bringing-back for purposes of reference. It is as though the work has come full circle: the composer has shown with what ingenuity the minimum of thematic material can produce, through the most recondite manipulations, a work of astonishing coherence, and then, with a flick of the wand, has brought Cinderella back from the ball and returned her to her original condition. The metaphor is perhaps not quite apt: Bartók's Cinderella-motive is not unprepossessing in its final manifestations; the end of the quartet, in which it alone is heard, is tense and dramatic.

In the second and fourth movements there are two 'themes' only; the transformation is not a cumulative one as in the outer movements, but a simple variational procedure, as the following example demonstrates:

22. *Quartet No. 4*

(a)

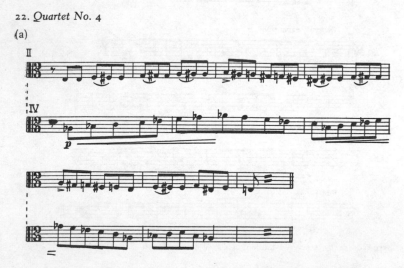

(b)

The two movements are twin scherzos, the second prestissimo and muted throughout, the fourth entirely pizzicato. Though both are based upon the same two thematic ideas, it would be possible to know the quartet rather well and still overlook their identicalness. The first is the chromatic line of the viola and cello at the beginning of the second movement, ascending from E to B and returning to E. The chromatic ascent and descent appear to be an expansion of the basic motive of the first and fifth movements, which follows the same direction but with a much more limited compass and far fewer notes.[30] The resemblance may, of course, be casual, but is worth pointing out. In the fourth movement the theme is in the viola; here it is diatonic instead of chromatic, and consequently covers an octave instead of a fifth, but a comparison of the two lines makes it obvious that Bartók was dealing with two versions of a single pattern.

The second thematic idea is a motive of changing-notes around a single note, imitated immediately in canon a whole-tone higher. The same process takes place in the fourth movement, the canon being at the ninth. The basic structure of the two movements is also parallel, the sectional relationships not quite as close as those of the corresponding movements in the Fifth Quartet, but nevertheless clearly variational.

As the keystone of the quartet, the third movement incorporates in its contrasting sections two particularly Bartókian moods. The sustained chords of the first section, at first non vibrato, then coming suddenly to life with the vibrato, serve as foundation for a long, rhapsodic, Magyar melody in the cello. This line, freely improvisational, bears a generic resemblance to many others in Bartók, and all of them seem related in conception to the pastoral melancholy of the *tárogató*, a Hungarian woodwind instrument somewhat like a straight wooden saxophone, originally with a double reed but in this century reconstructed with a single-reed mouthpiece. These '*tárogató* melodies,' as they are encountered in Bartók's music, have a quiet, rather static, but nevertheless florid character, the principal notes being surrounded with chromatic embellishments.

The profound expressiveness of this rhapsodic section is succeeded by the birdlike sounds of the Trio. Always sensitive to the sights and sounds of nature, Bartók reverted time after time to music of this character, and although its derivation is clear, whatever programmatic significance it may have is sublimated by the musical demands of the composer's psychology. The night sounds, interrupted by the melancholy *tárogató* melody, return to close the movement.

The Fourth Quartet makes very great technical demands upon the players. Bartók began by writing well within the limits of conventional string technique, contenting himself at first with the production of tone in the traditional ways: arco and pizzicato, with an occasional venture into the realm of the ponticello. By the time the Fourth Quartet appeared he had greatly expanded these means. He demands several types of pizzicato: the usual method is augmented by a percussive type which requires that the string rebound from the fingerboard, giving a 'snap' to the sound; by a brush pizzicato, by 'pizzicato sul ponticello,' 'pizzicato glissando,' and others. The glissandi demanded of the player cover a wide range, and are much more numerous than in the Third Quartet. The alternation between vibrato and non vibrato has already been cited; in the finale the dry rattle of the 'col legno' chords is grotesque and almost macabre.

The multiple stops required frequently demand extraordinary solutions. Many times Bartók will indicate the stopping of a low string in a fairly high position, leaving the string above open, and consequently sounding a lower pitch than that of the lower string; the discrepancy in string length produces a strange, tense sonority.

The harmonic idiom of the Fourth Quartet can hardly be called harmonic at all. The coincidence of sounds at any point is so completely dependent upon the horizontal motion of the voices that it seems illogical to analyze them vertically. Such a passage as that in measures 71-72 of the second movement,[31] in which all the chromatic semitones between G and C♯ are sounded simultaneously, cannot be considered a cluster since each of the seven notes is arrived at through the most logical of melodic progressions in the preceding bars; the piling-up of adjacent notes is therefore a contrapuntal, not a harmonic, procedure. The emphasis throughout the quartet is polyphonic, and there are innumerable canons, but curiously, in spite of its tremendous contrapuntal energy, there is in this quartet no fugue or fugato—only the canons and a vast amount of freely imitative writing. A thorough analysis of the polyphonic methods in the work would be a Herculean task, but almost every note could be accounted for.

The Fourth Quartet comes close to being, if it does not actually represent, Bartók's greatest and most profound achievement. It is by no means easy to understand; it requires the most active sort of listening, and the passive listener is likely to find his head whirling in a welter of exciting but confusing sound. But once its arcana are discovered, there are few works of this century so meaningful or so rewarding.

Between the Fourth Quartet in 1928 and the Fifth in 1934, Bartók produced only two major works, the *Cantata profana* and the Second Piano Concerto. In 1934 came a commission for a new quartet, from the Elizabeth Sprague Coolidge Foundation, to which so many contemporary chamber works owe their existence. The score of Bartók's Fifth Quartet indicates the speed with which he fulfilled the commission: it is dated 6 August to 6 September 1934—only a month between its inception and its completion. Such another burst of creative activity brought forth the Divertimento for string orchestra in only two weeks (1939), while the Concerto for Orchestra, Bartók's largest orchestral work, was written in seven (1943).

In what might be considered such haste, there might have been an inclination to slight the composition, to leave loose ends here and there. In actuality, the Fifth Quartet is almost as economical as the Fourth, which it resembles in structural plan. The problems of musical form, unlike those of the graphic and plastic arts which are fixed in time, are principally those of relating the sound-materials to those which have been heard and those which are to come. The attributes of unity, variety, balance, all are perceptible only by an act of will. The understanding of the shape of music is not attained by relaxing and allowing the sounds to flow through one like electricity through a wire. Such a procedure may provide a pleasant tingle now and then by momentary combinations of sound, but the meaning of the music, as expressed in the interrelationship of its parts, is irrevocably lost.

Thus it is necessary, for a valid appreciation of a musical work, to become aware of what is happening in it at every moment. Fortunately, most compositions are not so complex that their basic structure is excessively difficult to perceive. From movement to movement, the Bartók quartets offer no really serious listening problem, but the interrelationships of the movements, so vital to the conception, is likely to be overlooked because of their temporal separation. Yet, once perceived, these relationships make the structure meaningful as a whole, which is infinitely greater than the sum of its individual parts.

The architectural principles which guided the composition of the Fourth Quartet are even more pronounced in the Fifth. There are again five movements: Allegro, Adagio molto, Scherzo alla bulgarese, Andante, and Allegro vivace. As the headings indicate, the three inner movements reverse the pace of those in the Fourth Quartet, with a scherzo replacing the Lento. The two slow movements, quite different in mood, are structurally almost identical. The opening sections are similar, the similarity being perhaps more apparent to the eye than to the ear, and the remainder corresponds, section by section, so that the fourth movement may be considered a variation on the second. To a certain extent this is true also of the first and fifth movements, though these are not so nearly alike in their sectional plans: only the materials—the themes or motives—are shared.

The first and last movements center around B♭, which may be taken as the key of the quartet. So long as no attempt is made to identify the mode (major, minor, or any other), the analysis is valid, but it must be understood that the tonality is extremely free. On the first page, for example, the key of B♭ contains both D and D♭, both E and E♭; this is not unusual in certain Asiatic scales, which, while not completely chromatic, contain more notes to the octave than Western heptatonic scales. Bartók's Second Violin Sonata (1922) and other works show the use of augmented scales, in which what might casually be considered chromatic inflections are actually an integral part of the mode.

The first three and a half bars of the quartet establish the tonality in the simplest possible way: by repeating in rhythmic patterns the

keynote, B♭. It is not until the middle of the fourth bar that a theme
appears, in viola and cello, taking its departure from the repeated B♭'s
and imitated canonically by the violins a few bars later. But the idea
closes on a unison (bar 13), and a section follows which is difficult
to explain in a work otherwise so compact: the material which appears between letters A and B in the score, tentative in character,
never returns. It is as if Bartók were not yet aware of the potentialities of his energetic opening theme, and were searching for some
continuation which he does not really find until bar 25, with the
cross-rhythms of the transitional theme. Here, although the 4/4 meter
is retained without deviation, the metrical groups are set off by dotted
bars, the violins really having two measures of 6/8 followed by one
of 5/8 and other irregular divisions; cello and viola start in the same
way, but a quarter-note later, so that there is in effect a rhythmic
canon at this point. The tonal center has shifted to C, and at this
level the first theme makes another violent outburst before the second, 'meno mosso, dolce,' appears. The contrast is pronounced, but
the theme itself is an augmentation and expansion of the sixteenth-
note quintole of the first theme and its continuation. With the development of this pattern the exposition closes:

23. *Quartet No. 5*

There is by no means the tight thematic relationship in this quartet which is found in the Fourth. There everything came from one
six-note motive; almost nothing else is present in the first and last
movements. In the Fifth Quartet, however, besides the two separate
aspects of the thematic material, in the guise of first and second
themes, there is also a transitional theme of marked individuality,
whose pulsating rhythms will be employed in the course of develop-

ment, and there is as well the comparatively irrelevant material which follows the initial statement of the first theme.

But, possibly because of the separability of its materials, this movement is more readily comprehensible than the corresponding movement of the Fourth Quartet, and it parallels, or predicts, the arch-form of the quartet as a whole. The development group begins by establishing E as a center, and the function of the E in the first theme, as quasi-dominant, becomes apparent, the Bb-E relation emphasizing the tritone which is important in much of Bartók's music. The sectional development first fragments and combines in energetic and strident patterns the three principal motives of the first theme; later [32] the pulsations of the transitional theme recur, giving a Bulgarian cast to the rhythm, and over it the quintole motive of the first theme is treated expansively in octaves.

The recapitulation is reversed, to emphasize the arch-form of the movement (and, by extension, of the quartet). Not only that, but the thematic materials are inverted as well.[33] By the time the first theme is reached, the original tonality has been attained through a gradual upward progression by whole tones, and at this level the coda begins, with a modification of the quintole motive. The hammered-out Bb's reach their culmination, and in the last three measures the coda motive returns, alternately rectus and inversus, and finally both simultaneously, mirror-wise, closing in to a Bb unison.

The introductory measures of the finale, up to the double-bar, act as a sort of orientation point—a bench mark from which the rest of the movement may be surveyed. They are contrived from a simple tetrachord motive, apparently related to the coda motive of the first movement, alternately ascending and descending, and eventuating on Bb in the thirteenth bar. At this point the main theme of the movement begins with repeated E's in the violins; it soon becomes apparent that this is only a free inversion of the first-movement theme. The tetrachord motive recurs from time to time, frequently expanded to include five notes and to span a tritone. The texture is predominantly canonic, and the materials, being largely scale-line, invert with great ease.

The device which begins in bar 183 is characteristically Bartókian: a minor second is progressively enclosed within a minor third, a perfect fourth, and a perfect fifth, and, changing to a major sixth, encloses the whole complex. It is as if the original interval had turned itself inside out. The process is repeated at a higher level, and, with alternating sevenths and a general pause, the stage is set for a new theme, which comes out of the falling sevenths and nearly merges its identity with the principal theme.[34] Imitation and inversion are redoubled; the tetrachord motive provides a transition to a fast fugato [35] on the first theme, accompanied by 'col legno' rhythms. The fugal entries are successively on E, B♭, E, and B♭, once more emphasizing the basic tonal centers of the quartet and, in accordance with its plan, in inverse order. Underneath, in the cello, the same two notes form a drone bass. The fugato is marked *oscuro*, and its hushed scurrying remains below the mezzo-forte level throughout.

The recapitulation, like that of the first movement, is in reverse order. The second theme [36] is only suggested in its original form and then, in a capricious, wayward setting, the falling seventh, now glissando, assumes the function of the whole theme. A few bars later it becomes a rather sardonic polka, yielding again to the tetrachord 'bench mark' and thereafter to the first theme. Here the material is compressed and the movement hurries on toward a close.

But its progress is interrupted by a curious happening. The tetrachord motive, which had spanned progressively a perfect fourth and a tritone, is now stretched out to cover a perfect fifth; it is thus transmuted into a naive, even banal tune in A major, with the viola providing an Alberti bass and the first violin plucking tonic and dominant triads.[37] The extreme relaxation of the harmonic idiom is almost shocking. But over this childishly simple passage the first violin superimposes the same tune, modified, in B♭, and the coda rushes in, stretto-fashion, to close on the keynote.

The second and fourth movements, as already indicated, are simply variants of one plan. Both ternary in form, the second has D as its tonal center, the fourth G: spanning the principal tonality by a third on either side. There are no themes, but only fragmentary motives, combined to form a sectional structure. The introductory sections of the movements correspond, the one in trills and gruppettas, the other pizzicato and pizzicato glissando. The first section of the second movement (at A) presents hesitant phrases in the violin over sustained chords; in the fourth, the chords are rhythmically repeated, *jeté*, the melodic motives given to the cello. The B and C sections of both are related to the 'night music' of the Fourth Quartet and other works; in the second movement the open G-string tremolo of the second violin is ornamented with delicate pizzicato glissandos and sliding scale-segments, and gradually out of this hazy, mystical sound arises a songlike melody. Its own first three notes, inverted, become the basis for the imitative passages in the ensuing section, reaching a climax and then broadening and diminishing to a restatement of the first section, which is repeated in shortened form, the hesitant phrases of the first violin now reduced to single notes. At the end the introductory trills recur, and the movement dies away with the cello's quasi-glissando scale.

The introductory section of the fourth movement is somewhat longer, but from the A section on there is an exact correspondence with the second movement. In the middle section the songlike theme of the second movement is expressively ornamented; toward its close a tiny figure evolves which is present throughout the rest of the movement: the rising minor third of measure 60, sometimes returning to its starting point, but more often not. (A similar figure occurs in the second movement of the Viola Concerto, measure 30, piangendo, with the same sort of chromatic accompanying passages.) The restatement of the first section (at D) is scarcely recognizable; only at the very end, with the rhythmically repeated chords, is the identity made apparent; then the cello's ascending pizzicato-glissando chords bring the movement to a close.

The central movement of the Fifth Quartet is a scherzo with trio, its tonal center C♯ and its scale more or less Dorian. Its character is placid at the outset despite the dance-spirit of its Bulgarian rhythms. These rhythms occur frequently in the music of Bartók; their principal distinction is the division of the measure into asymmetrical groupings, which nevertheless recur regularly.[38] The last six pieces in *Mikrokosmos* are dances in Bulgarian rhythms, as are also Nos. 113 and 115; the Trio of the third movement of *Contrasts* is in a Bulgarian rhythm, with a signature of $\frac{8+5}{8}$. The Concerto for Orchestra is strongly conditioned by Bulgarian rhythms, especially in the first and fourth movements. Here in the Scherzo of the Fifth Quartet the signature is $\frac{4+2+3}{8}$, changing in the Trio to $\frac{3+2+2+3}{8}$. These metrical combinations seem complex to Western ears at first hearing, but, handled as simply as they are, the complicated metrical groupings soon acquire an altogether natural feeling.

The Trio has a ten-note ostinato in the muted violin, while beneath it the viola plays an unassuming folklike tune in a choriambic rhythm, which, like the 'night music' of the Fourth Quartet, serves as the nucleus of the whole work. The 'da capo' of the Scherzo is, of course, a variation upon the original rather than a literal restatement. In its course the metrical groupings, even with the indicated asymmetric measure, no longer fit the bar; although there are several changes of meter, the groups still overflow into the adjacent measures.

Bartók's Sixth Quartet was begun in Saanen, Switzerland, in August 1939, just after the completion of the Divertimento. On 18 August he wrote to his son Béla:

Somehow I feel like an old-time musician summoned as the guest of a Maecenas. As you know, I am the guest of the Sachers here, who look after everything—from a distance. . . As to excursions, I can of course not start anything in spite of the kindness of the weather: I must work. And especially for Sacher: commission—something for string orchestra; even this makes my situation like that of the old musician. Luckily the work went well; in 15 days I have already turned out a work about 25 minutes long; just yesterday I finished it. Now I must satisfy another commission: a string quartet for Z. Székely (for the 'New Hungarian Quartet'). Since 1934 I have worked almost exclusively upon commissions! . . .[39]

But the Sixth Quartet thus begun was completed only in November, after Bartók's return to Budapest; and it was dedicated to the Kolisch Quartet, who gave the first performance in New York in January 1941. In the meantime Bartók had left Europe and was out of touch with Székely and the Hungarian Quartet; the dedication seems to have arisen from propinquity, and in gratitude for the performance of the earlier quartets by the Kolisch group.[40]

The four movements of the quartet are bound together by a recurrent introductory theme which appears unsupported in the viola before the first movement, and returns in successive two- and three-part settings before the second and third, as well as providing the principal material of the finale. This theme, marked *mesto* (a term which it shares with the lassú of the Rhapsody, opus 1), is introspective, even melancholy, contrasting strongly with the moods of the first three movements. Bartók could hardly have known that with the completion of the Sixth Quartet he would never again write a new work in his native country, but it is almost as if with this restrained but ardent theme, cumulatively unveiling the spirit of the last movement, he were bidding a deliberate farewell to Hungary. Even the Marcia and the Burletta which form the inner movements of the quartet have an undercurrent of resignation.

The arch-form which had provided the basis for the three preceding quartets, as well as the Second Piano Concerto and the Violin Concerto, is no longer adhered to; while there are thematic inter-references in the Sixth Quartet and the succeeding works, in essence they are far removed from the closed forms of their predecessors. The first movement proper, beginning after the solo viola theme, is a sonata-form close to the classical plan, but with no superfluous material in the shape of bridges or episodes, whose functions are fulfilled with motivic material. There are, properly speaking, only two 'themes' in the movement, the first appearing at the Vivace (two motives only, one of three notes, the other of six, closely related), the second, of folklike contour, at measure 81.

24. Quartet No. 6

The first theme is seen in the process of evolution beginning in the fourteenth bar of the movement: three notes, G-A♭-E♭, in the cello are reversed and transposed to A-D-C♯, repeated, and extended with another motive, C-E-F-G-F♯-A, whose last three notes are so close to the first motive that they may be considered a mere variant. These ten tentative, rather improvisatory measures, closing on a chord in fourths with a fermata, lead directly to the principal tempo of the movement and the presentation of the first thematic complex, measures 24-80, in which these two microscopic motives provide the entire material. They are seen in typical Bartókian manifestations: inverted, fragmented, the fragments augmented and simultaneously combined with the nearly complete theme in its original values. Always it is the intervallic structure of the theme that is changed: while the rhythmic pattern is preserved, almost any interval relationship will be accepted as thematic.

The choriambic rhythm of the second theme—a trochee followed by an iamb—is reversed in the third measure, the trochee following the iamb in an antispastus; both rhythms are characteristic of Hungarian folk music, and this refusal to be bound by rigid, predetermined patterns contributes to the flexibility of all Bartók's music. It applies not only to rhythms but also to imitative textures in such traditionally inflexible procedures as canon and fugue.

The relationship of the motives of the closing group, measure 99, to the first one in the introductory theme may be accidental; many of Bartók's motives have generic resemblances of such strength that one hesitates to insist that *this* was derived from *that*. They may both be coincidental manifestations of entirely separate impulses: to make a decision on this point is quite unnecessary. The closing group is continued with modified references to both the first and the second themes (measures 109, 111). It is enlightening to discover how readily the ear accepts a simple three-note scale (measure 111) as representing the second theme, or a turning chromatic succession (measures 109, 113, 117) as standing for the first.

All these procedures are really both variational and developmental, but there is an actual development-group, where (measure 158, pesante) the restatement of the tentative, evolutionary measures of the opening gives the impression of a new beginning, exactly in the tradition of the classical sonata: a new beginning which immediately gives rise to all sorts of complexities readily perceptible to the eye, but of little importance to the ear. The logic of the construction cannot fail to make itself felt; the details which contribute to that logic may frequently be overlooked. So, for example, at measure 166, the ear is aware of the prolongation of the first theme in viola and cello, but probably not aware that simultaneously its first four notes are being presented in an inverse retrograde form in the violins. Again, the ostinato passage which begins in measure 180 perhaps does not make itself felt as a variant of the first part of the main theme, and

the subsequent imitative treatment of the remainder of the theme
may seem mere fragmentation; but it becomes apparent upon examination that both parts of the theme are present simultaneously, the
first introducing and serving as support for the second.

The expansibility of Bartók's themes is demonstrated convincingly
in the measures after 197. Here, in the cello, the first theme, originally
nine notes in length, is stretched out to cover twenty-one before it
fulfills its function, and instead of an octave it now spans almost two.
This extended version is immediately reversed (with modifications),
and itself treated imitatively throughout the next section.

In the recapitulatory process (measure 287) Bartók no longer presents his themes in reverse order but adheres to the classsical procedure: first theme, severely truncated; second theme, transposed;
closing theme, also transposed to what appears to be the dominant.
Then at measure 363 the subdominant—traditional key for codas—
is reached, and the movement comes to a close with references to
the first theme, relaxing to lento. The key is, of course, D major.

Again the introductory theme appears, this time in the cello, with
the other instruments duplicating a single contrapuntal part in three
octaves. After a slight prolongation the second violin pronounces a
new motive, D♯-F♯-A-G♯, just before the double bar, and this becomes the point of departure for the Marcia. The motive is strikingly
similar to the Verbunkos of Contrasts, written the year before, but
the working-out of the idea is quite different. There is an erratic,
rhapsodic Trio, with its melody high in the cello, accompanied by
tremolos and strummed pizzicato chords, and concluding with a
quasi-cadenza for all four instruments. The return is greatly modified; canonic imitation with the first violin in harmonics gives an
eerie sound to the first part; there is some inversion of materials,
some doubling in consecutive ninths. The cadence is indeterminate,
the violins holding G♯ two octaves apart, and the pizzicato chords
underneath representing a dominant-ninth chord on B. The clue to
this harmonic structure may be found in the passage which immediately precedes it: the basic motive being there expanded by thirds
to extend from D♯ to E a ninth above—all this an amplification of
the two superimposed thirds of the motive itself.

With the introduction to the third movement, the signature-theme
is expanded to a three-part setting, the viola entering in the tenth

measure to duplicate the first violin in the lower octave. The passage now begins on B♭, whereas it was first presented on G♯ and then on E♭, and there is a further expansion in the line by means of sequential repetition of its opening motive. This time there is no transition: the quartet plunges abruptly into a grotesque, sardonic Burletta, which brings forth a whole arsenal of technical devices from Bartók's storehouse, including some that have not been used in any of the preceding quartets. It is a movement of violent contrasts, rather ponderous humor, and (in the Trio) a momentary tenderness.

On the first page of the Burletta Bartók directs that one of the violins is to play a quarter-tone flat, the unflatted tones appearing simultaneously in the other violin, and both played with a slow upward glissando. The 'wrong notes' are reminiscent of those which Mozart wrote in his sextet called A Musical Joke (K. 522); this is a musical joke of a similar species—the entire movement with the exception of the central portion is in the same character. But even with its deliberate and somewhat coarse humor, the organization of the tonal materials is no less complete than in more serious movements.

Like the Marcia, the Burletta also has a Trio; in it are suggestions of both the important motives of the first movement, the first in a modified retrograde form, the second extended to fill a 9/8 bar. This section is lyrical and tender; with the resumption of the original tempo the Burletta is recapitulated, mostly in trenchant pizzicati. In the coda, which is once more bowed, the 9/8 motive from the Trio is touched upon three times, but its tender mood is brusquely broken off each time, the movement ending with a series of repeated notes, all down-bows 'au talon,' and the flick of a pizzicato chord.

The humor of both the Marcia and the Burletta has a bitter taste. There is no gentleness in their irony, only—and especially in the Burletta—a cutting, savage satire. Set off by the melancholy introductory theme, they illumine its grief without dispelling it. And the fourth movement, in which that theme is called upon for almost all the material, is pervaded by despair. Over it might be written: Lasciate ogni speranza voi ch'entrate.

Yet despite the encompassing gloom, twice there are glimpses of clearer skies in reflective recollection of the first-movement motives. Nowhere in all Bartók's other music is there a movement so restrained and at the same time with such a powerful impact. It is as if this music had always existed, requiring only to be drawn up from the collective unconscious of mankind, not to be composed.

Some writers have considered Bartók's six quartets as roughly forming an arch. But such an analysis implies a reversal of direction midway, the last three retracing the way of the first three; that view must be regarded as superficial. Obviously there are resemblances between the Third and Fourth Quartets; written only a year apart, they naturally are more closely related than the others, and, coming at the height of Bartók's most dissonant style and his most intensive motivic organization, they are set off from the rest. But to discover such resemblances between the Second and Fifth, or the First and Sixth, is to overlook the directness of the route from each one to the next.

The First Quartet is distinguished from the others by the character of its chromaticism and by its relative freedom from folkloric considerations. The Second stands alone because of its structure, which does not resemble that of the Fifth in the slightest degree, nor is their character at all similar. The Fifth, on the other hand, is the logical successor of the Fourth, its formal plan being almost identical, its style slightly less chromatic, in keeping with the direction of Bartók's development in the nineteen-thirties. By the time of the Sixth, that style has reached its ultimate condition. The thematic interrelations which play a part here are not those of the archlike forms, but neither are they the almost adventitious ones of the First Quartet. If there is any resemblance in this to an earlier quartet, it is in the slow finale, which is to the casual ear somewhat like that of the Second Quartet, all the others having allegros and ending fortissimo. But this too is merely coincidental, and the functions of the two movements are explicitly dissimilar.

The first two quartets were for many years the only ones generally played, and they still are the most frequently heard. Through the efforts of a very few quartets, including the Waldbauer-Kerpely, the Kolisch, and the Pro Arte, the others were brought to performance in Bartók's lifetime; but it is only since his death that American audiences, at least, have had an opportunity to become well acquainted with them. Cycles of all six, played in Los Angeles and elsewhere by the Hungarian Quartet, in New York by the Juilliard

Quartet, in Buenos Aires by the Végh Quartet, have encouraged others to take them up, and it is no longer unusual to find the late quartets programmed by the lesser ensembles. And audiences, who once asked of a contemporary quartet only that it be cheerful, uncomplicated, and short, have found that the profundity and vigor of the Bartók quartets match convincingly the last quartets of Haydn and Beethoven, and that they belong with these as the most significant materializations of the form.

T HE remainder of Bartók's chamber music is in several categories, but with the exception of two late works it is entirely for string instruments with or without piano. While he was still a student at Pozsony he had written a piano quartet which was played there in 1898, to celebrate the name day of the director of the Gymnasium; the following year in Budapest he was working on a quintet, but it is not clear whether this was ever completed, Koessler advising him to abandon it because of its inadequacies. A sonata for violin and piano was played in Vienna by Rudolf Fitzner, having first been heard in a concert of student compositions in Budapest on 8 June 1903, and the following year Bartók wrote a piano quintet, which he played in Vienna in November 1904, with the Prill Quartet.

All these works remained in manuscript, and Bartók cautioned the friends to whom he gave manuscript copies that they were not to be performed or published. The Quintet, however, he himself played for several years, and in June 1905 was preparing it for publication; what happened to prevent its appearance is problematical.

With the Violin Sonata and the Piano Quintet, Bartók begins the catalogue of his works, in the autobiographical sketch of 1921, and with them his preparatory period comes to an end. They are similar in style to the other works of the period: *Kossuth*, the First Suite for orchestra, and the Four Piano Pieces. It was only with the First String Quartet, opus 7, that Bartók's individual genius appeared in the chamber-music field.

Of the other chamber works, aside from the quartets, the earliest are the two Sonatas for violin and piano, dated 1921 and 1922. They are followed in 1928 by the two Rhapsodies for violin and piano, both of which are transcribed for violin and orchestra; the first one is also available for cello and piano.[1] The Forty-four Duos for two violins, the Sonata for Two Pianos and Percussion, *Contrasts*, for violin, clarinet, and piano, and the Sonata for Solo Violin complete the list. With the exception of *Contrasts* and the Sonata for Two Pianos and Percussion, all these works make use of traditional media. Bartók found the most usual instrumentation—violin and piano, and the string quartet—entirely adequate for his ideas; there is no paralleling of his interest in unusual sonorities by a similar interest in uncommon instrumental combinations, at least so far as his chamber music is concerned. But his textural treatment in these works is far from conventional, as can be seen from examination of the Sonatas for violin and piano, which he wrote for Jelly d'Arányi.

These Sonatas share with the Piano Sonata, the First Piano Concerto, and the Third and Fourth Quartets certain characteristics presumably conditioned by Bartók's acquaintance with the music of Schoenberg and Stravinsky. But while the later works are formally and texturally somewhat restrained, displaying many neoclassical aspects, the Violin Sonatas are outwardly so free as almost to convey the impression of improvisation, while their fabric is rich and highly colored. The first, especially, with its reliance upon cimbalom and gamelan effects,[2] combines primitivistic elements with a tonal web of extreme sophistication.

Bartók considered the First Sonata as in C♯ minor, the Second as in C major. As in most of his mature scores, key-designations must be considered only as points of reference and of final cadence, while the terms 'major' and 'minor' are hardly useful in identifying tonalities as complex as these. To take the First Sonata as an example: the first three notes of the piano part describe the tonic triad of C♯ minor, it is true, but these cimbalom-like arpeggios cloud the tonality with seven other notes, and the entrance of the violin is on C♮. The movement closes on a minor third, A-C, in the violin, with the piano playing successively Bb, Db, E, F, G, Ab. The Adagio begins with a long unaccompanied violin solo centering largely upon A, and ends with C♯ in the bass, C♮ in the violin (confirming the relationship at the opening of the first movement), but with the addition of F♯, A, and E♯ to the cadential complex. The finale, after its introductory measures, does establish C♯ as a pedal, but the chords founded upon it are arbitrary 'triad' formations comprising a perfect fifth plus a superposed tritone, the one in the left hand taking C♯ as root, that in the right, F♯. At the same time the violin line is in a more or less modal scale which may be viewed as the Locrian on B, with C♯ instead of C♮. The final cadence is even more ambiguous: the piano left hand plays a C♯ minor triad in open position, the right hand one in C♯ major, and the violin one in E major. The whole complex may be analyzed vertically as C♯ major/minor with an added seventh; but the spacing necessitates the perception of the 'chord' on three planes.

Unlike the duo-sonatas of the standard repertory, the violin and piano effect almost no interchange of material in these two Sonatas. It is as if the players were engaged upon different works simultaneously: works which correspond in length and structure and complement each other at every point, but share no themes or motives. The First Sonata has a vast scope, with passionate, sweeping lines in both instruments alternating with relaxed and tranquil passages, and concluding with an energetic dance movement of pronounced Magyar character. The Second is somewhat more economical but no less expressive; compressed into two movements instead of three, its extreme concentration is even greater than that of the Third Quartet, and the materials of both parts are closely related.

Bartók himself preferred the Second Sonata to the First, performing it far more often in concert and on broadcasts with Arányi, Waldbauer, Szigeti, and Székely. His objection to the First was apparently to the first movement, and he would have preferred to play only the last two.

The melodic materials of the First Sonata, especially those of the first and second movements, show striking similarities to certain procedures of Schoenberg which were to result in the 'technique of composition with twelve tones.' The serialization of vertical elements is of frequent occurrence here; repetition of notes at close range is generally avoided, and there are successions in which all twelve notes are pronounced almost entirely without duplication.[3] Another Schoenbergian characteristic is the octave-displacement technique, by means of which successive notes of a melody are placed in different octaves, a procedure quite at variance with the close-coupled line of songlike melody. In this connection, a passage from Bartók's *Hungarian Folk Music* is of interest, not necessarily as having influenced the composer in his adoption of the device, but as possible partial justification of it:

Another remarkable practice—one might almost say, a malpractice—should be mentioned. It is so common nowadays in the performance of new-style tunes that experienced collectors take hardly any notice of it; but it may perplex tiros so much that they will be unable to recognize the real melodic pattern. It is connected with the steadily growing compass of tunes: . . . it is not always easy for the singer to select a pitch which will enable him to intone with equal ease all the low and all the high notes. Hungarian peasants do not devote much care to selecting a suitable pitch, but they simplify difficulties in proportion as they occur: whenever a note is too high or too low for them, they transpose it by an octave, regardless of design and rhythmic conditions. This they will do *ad libitum*, perhaps several times in the course of one tune. Hence at times the most peculiar leaps of a seventh occur. . . In the course of time this practice has become so usual that many peasants resort to changes of octaves without being driven by need.[4]

Both of Bartók's Violin Sonatas have examples of octave-displacement, of which the following is typical:[5]

25. *Second Violin Sonata*

The device is not resorted to indiscriminately; in the First Sonata it gives the distinctive shape to the waltz-like second member of the principal thematic complex, and is thereafter used, with very few exceptions, only for reference to that member. The Second Sonata makes even less use of the procedure, demonstrating again that avoidance of excess which characterizes Bartók's music of all periods.

The period of the Violin Sonatas is one in which the folkloric basis of Bartók's music is less apparent than at any other time in his career. The modality of these works is so all-inclusive that the occurrence of the characteristic intervals of Magyar folksong is almost completely disguised. The intervals themselves are omnipresent; but they are seldom organized in groups or patterns that suggest a Hungarian origin, and consequently these sonatas are probably more 'international' in outward appearance than anything else Bartók ever wrote. Nevertheless their more dancelike sections—the finale of the First, much of the last movement of the Second—have a typically Magyar élan in their unmistakably folklike rhythms.

Bar-by-bar analysis of these impassioned works serves little purpose in conveying an understanding of them. Formally the First Sonata is the more conventional, if that word may be applied to a work which resembles nothing so much as a spontaneous outpouring, without apparent regard for the dioristic details of the traditional forms. The first movement is indeed recognizable as a 'sonata form'—which is to say, its materials are exposed, developed, recapitulated. But in contrast to scores like the Fourth Quartet its organization seems imprecise, even though a single four-note motive (first heard in the eighth measure) is frequently encountered thereafter and plays an especially important part in the development. With the exception of this motive, the materials are merely varied upon their reappearance; they do not grow organically, and consequently they violate the fundamental ethos of the sonata idea.

The second movement, basically a large ternary form, is more readily accessible. The proportions of its three sections show a meticulous exactitude:

A	B	A
a-b-a'-b'	c-d-c'-d'	a-b-a'-b'

Of these, a is presented as a single unaccompanied line in the violin; it has an almost indefinable resemblance to the first theme of the previous movement. At its close, the piano enters with three triads, the first major, the others minor; then it underscores b with groups of consecutive minor triads, ascending along the line of the Lydian tetrachord. Following this, a' is again unaccompanied; the cadential chords are now a minor and two majors, and the parallel triads of *b′* are all major. So by the simplest of means Bartók changes the whole complexion of the repetition. The middle section is more intense, the texture of the violin part enriched in double-stopped minor ninths and seconds and major sevenths; but its outward shape is identical. In the recapitulation the solo materials (*a* and *a′*) are greatly varied, and the remainder compressed, but without obscuring their shape; a brief reference to *c* closes the movement.

Little need be said about the rondo-finale, one of those 'moto perpetuo' dances that came so readily to Bartók's hand. It is, of course, spirited and strenuous, a movement of explosive contrast, of primitivistic fire. For the first fifty-seven measures the violin plays entirely on the G-string, against the piano's percussive rhythmic chords shot through intermittently with flashing arpeggios. Curiously, in contrast to the sonata-form first movement, which was almost totally lacking in developmental procedures, this rondo movement makes great use of them. Fragmentation, recombination, augmentation, inversion, all are used at will; and in this movement at last the two instruments are permitted occasionally to share materials. The close is a maelstrom of sound, from which the three tonalities of the cadence emerge and, combining, clarify the harmonic procedures of the whole work.

Those procedures are often bitonal, at times because of the mirroring of a passage by its simultaneous inversion, at others through less arbitrary means. The tritone emphasis is extraordinary; the constant presence of this interval in both horizontal and vertical functions lends a particular pungency to the work. Yet there are relaxations, such as the consecutive triads of the Adagio, which relieve what might otherwise prove an insupportable pressure. There is little writing which can be considered contrapuntal. By the reinforcement of lines with extra notes, basically polyphonic lines dissolve into harmonies, and their individual direction is obscured.

Bartók in this work is completely cognizant of the sonorous resources of both string and keyboard. Especially in the piano writing he discovers the essential crasis of the instrument; even in the Improvisations of the preceding year he had scarcely approached it. And in breadth and scope, only the Second String Quartet—of his purely instrumental works—had previously attained its level.

The Second Sonata, in contrast to the First, is terse, compact, its first movement fundamentally no more than a sonatina-form, but much more highly organized than its predecessor. Its themes are motivically rich, and the keen ear detects a relationship of detail which plays little part in the earlier sonata. The interrelationship of the materials of the two movements brings about an integration superficially somewhat like that of the Berg Violin Concerto, but achieved without recourse to the twelve-tone technique.

There is nothing arbitrary or artificial about this organization. Essentially there is but one movement: the separation is one of convenience only, no more apparent in performance than the division between the first two movements of the First Quartet. In spirit, however, the parts are related as lassú and friss of the *verbunkos* style, the first being quite parlando in its character, with fanciful ornamentation, the second 'tempo giusto,' a succession of dancelike sections in varying moods. The melodic plasticity and harmonic pungency of the work bear little resemblance to the Rhapsodies of 1928, but in outward form all three, as well as the later *Contrasts*, betray a common ancestry.

Like the First Sonata, the Second displays a stronger interest in sonority than in harmonic progression. It depends in large measure upon the harshest intervallic combinations: minor ninths and tritones abound, the second movement has pages of note-clusters, of hammered-out polychords, of consecutive chords-in-fourths against rapid scales in other tonal planes. It is a mistake to examine these combinations vertically without observing their horizontal function, which always predominates. Except when it is involved in a pure accompanimental pattern, the piano—like the violin—is treated as an independent melodic part, harmonically thickened perhaps, but nevertheless conceived in terms of contrapuntal, not harmonic, progression.

The rondo-like form of the second movement provides opportunity for ingenious variation of the thematic materials upon their several returns, and for episodic reference to the themes of the preceding movement. Since the first theme of the finale has already been predicted in the earlier pages of the Sonata, the whole movement is a natural outgrowth of its predecessor, supplying in a certain sense the proving-ground for the materials previously left undeveloped. When the final climax brings back in the violin the opening theme of the Sonata, fortissimo, but diminishing to close in the rarefied atmosphere of a pure C-major triad, it is as if the listener has come full circle: all the implications have been realized, and it needs but this reminder to summon up remembrance of things past.

In both the Sonatas the piano part, intricate as it is, is overshadowed by the violin, which has the leading role in all but a very few measures. The province of the piano is to underline, to intensify with penetrating comment, to elucidate. In so doing it achieves an ensemble with the violin unlike that in any other sonata: without sharing materials, without any pretense of alternation or equalization in the working out of themes, the two instruments merge in a totality quite unaffected by the disparity of its parts. There is no interweaving, there is only welding. As a result, these two works stand entirely apart from all others in the form; Bartók himself, having solved the exceedingly delicate problem he had set himself, did not return to it in any later work, and it is unlikely that another composer will ever be tempted to venture in these paths.

Although he had from the beginning of his tenure at the Academy of Music been aware of the necessity of providing pedagogical materials for the piano, and had written a large number of works for that purpose, it was not until 1931 that Bartók turned his attention to the needs of other instruments. The 44 Duos for two violins fulfill a function similar to that of *For Children* and the Ten Easy Pieces, in providing folk-based material of no great difficulty for teaching purposes; but they have the additional advantage of a highly developed harmonic and contrapuntal technique, so that they are more definitely contemporary in sound. The melodies themselves are treated with greater freedom, fragmented and developed, rather than left intact, and in this respect they have something in common with the Improvisations on Hungarian Peasant Songs.

Bartók's expanding interest in the folk music of other countries is indicated by some of the titles of the Duos: Slovakian Song, Hungarian Song, Walachian Song, Ruthenian Dance, Romanian Whirling Dance, Serbian Dance, Arabian Dance. Numbers 16 and 24 are of Ukrainian origin, though not so indicated; the latter is a variant of the tune which Bartók set for voice and piano for Pál Kecskeméti in February 1945.[6] Others are game or play songs, children's songs, and folksongs and dances of various types.

In writing for the violins, even after the technical feats of the

Fourth Quartet, Bartók by no means provides a concentration of difficulties. There are few double-stops, and practically all have one open string; one movement (No. 43) is entirely pizzicato, but otherwise there is little use of the device, and only one instance (No. 42) of the strong pizzicato which rebounds from the fingerboard. There are no harmonics, either natural or artificial. Bowings and phrasings are hardly unusual.

But the musical problems are somewhat greater. Matters of intonation in sharply dissonant clashes, numerous bitonal passages (Nos. 11, 33, 34), polyrhythmic canons (No. 33), canons at unconventional intervals such as the tritone—these and kindred subtleties are created to sharpen the player's ear, leaving the niceties of violin technique to be acquired by more traditional means. The two volumes are arranged roughly in order of difficulty, but there is not the compass of the *Mikrokosmos,* and the more rigorous demands of the last few do not follow uninterruptedly upon the earlier pieces of the set.

Several times in the course of these pieces Bartók writes different key signatures for the two instruments, as he did years before in the Bagatelles, and more recently in the Second Rhapsody. Now and then the signature is unconventional, as, for example, two flats on B and D (No. 11); here, of course, the usual signature of B♭ minor could have been used, but with the melody consisting of three notes only—B♭, C, and D♭—Bartók would have considered it pleonastic to notate the useless flats on E, A, and G.

The Duos are occasionally played in recital.[7] This necessitates rearrangement for reasons of contrast in both character and key. With the double-stops in almost every instance riveted to the open strings (E, A, D, G), there is some unavoidable monotony in the pieces which require them; besides, the published order, leading from the simple to the more complex, is by no means the most convincing way of presenting them. Two possibilities present themselves: to choose from the forty-four a smaller number to form an effective group, or else to intersperse the more elementary pieces among the later ones. Either way, they are a valued addition to a very limited repertory.

The Sonata for Two Pianos and Percussion, written on commission for the Basle section of the International Society for Contemporary Music in 1937, marks a further ripening of Bartók's style after the dissonant explorations of the 1920's. Its moods vary from the brooding suspense of the introduction to the dance-like gaiety of the finale; between, there are clangorous, percussive sections, an energetic fugue, and in the Lento the evocative nocturnal sounds characteristic of the later scores. Its almost unprecedented dynamism establishes the Sonata as one of Bartók's most significant works.

Bartók later scored the Sonata for orchestra, as a Concerto for Two Pianos, first played in New York on 4 January 1943. But in its original form it remains complete and convincing. Besides the pianos, the required instruments include three kettledrums, xylophone, two side drums (one without snares), cymbals, suspended cymbal, bass drum, triangle, and tam-tam. The orchestral version adds to these the woodwinds in pairs, four horns, two trumpets, three trombones, celesta, and strings, the piano parts being slightly modified, especially in climactic passages where the weight of the orchestra is called upon.

The three movements of the Sonata show an outward inequality in duration; of the twenty-four minutes required for performance, the first movement takes half, while the other two divide the remainder fairly evenly (five and a half minutes for one, six and a half for the other). Yet in performance no formal disparity is apparent. The reason may perhaps be sought in the thematic wealth of the first movement and its continual regeneration, so that it conveys less the impression of a highly organized closed form than of an uninterrupted outpouring.

But the organization is not only complete but complex.[8] Its basic tonality is C, with a strong tritone emphasis which gives F♯ a place of prominence. This may be seen at the very beginning, with the kettledrum roll and the introductory motive in the piano:

26. *Sonata for Two Pianos and Percussion*

as well as in the quasi-Lydian theme of the finale. The semitone relationships of the motive illustrated are significant; itself spanning a tritone, it encloses seven chromatic notes, and in the fifth measure, where it is prolonged to nine (D and C♯ being added), the canonic imitation at the tritone supplies the other three. A few measures later, doubled in sixths, it is again imitated canonically a tritone away; the inversion (measure 12) is doubled in thirds and likewise imitated, and in the following bar, with the beginning of the acceleration, the doubling is in the tritone in each part.

The motive serves far more than an introductory function: it is an integral part of the movement, even though there are three other themes of major importance. The first of these shares the barbaric abandon of certain earlier works; the perversely reluctant rhythms of the second suggest a Bulgarian ancestry; the third, with its horn-like upward-leaping sixths, has an out-of-doors character. Yet all three are demonstrably superimposed upon the spine of the introductory motive:

27. *Sonata for Two Pianos and Percussion*

(a)

To maintain that the divisional similarities shown above were deliberate would be to overlook the subconscious disciplines which long before this time were deeply ingrained in Bartók. He would have been the first to deny the intention,[9] but he could hardly have disproved the fact. Time after time in his later scores, apparently adventitious resemblances of this kind may be observed, testifying to the composer's complete absorption of his materials. The result, of course, is a structural integration possibly even more complete than Bartók intended.

We are told [10] that he almost never worked on two major scores simultaneously; had he done so, this might have brought about an undesirable cross-reference of materials from one to the other. Occasionally such cross-references do occur between successive works, as in *Contrasts* and the Sixth Quartet; and here it is as if Bartók were reluctant to relinquish his materials without having extracted from them their ultimate essence.

But these are identifiable motives re-used, while the citations from the Sonata for Two Pianos and Percussion display subtler psychological relationships, imperceptible to the casual ear. They are here and there brought to the fore: in the course of development, an ostinato on the introductory motive supplies the foundation for the working out of motive *b* (measures 195-216; inverted, measures 232-261); in the recapitulation the semitone-patterns of *a* are set upon the inversion of *c* (measures 292-300). But in these and other instances there is no merging of the materials; each motive retains its own identity, and it is the differences between them—not the similarities—that are emphasized.

Some of the textural characteristics of the movement have already been touched upon: the parallelism which enriches the sonorities, sometimes in minor sixths, perfect fourths and fifths, or tritones, sometimes in full triads, even in seven-note chords-in-fourths (measures 184-185); the many canonic passages; the ostinatos; the fugal development of motive *d* (beginning at measure 332). The function of the battery in this movement is chiefly one of emphasis, of underlining; only rarely is attention focused upon it. In the remaining movements, however, it assumes a soloistic function, and the xylophone especially, as the only really melodic instrument of the group, is entrusted with passages of thematic importance.

The Lento, in contrast to the complex sonata-form plan of the first movement, is a small but affective ternary form with coda. The opening is a simple drawing in line, with the utmost economy of resource; it is only with the nocturnal sounds of the second section (measures 28-65) that Bartók dips into his palette for the most glittering colors, mixing them with a sure hand. Bell-like sonorities provide a background for a nervously chattering quintole motive; later a slow-moving chromatic melody is invested with savory harmonies which border on clusters, the whole imitated more or less canonically, while the chattering, now subdued, continues in the drums. In returning to the opening theme, Bartók fills in his sketch, at first blurring the outlines with misty scales and double-note glissandos on both black and white keys, then finally bringing his figures into the round with harmonic vesture. The quintole motive has the last word, in the abrupt crescendo of the coda.

With the third movement we are on familiar ground. Here again is the jaunty dance movement in 2/4 meter, with the folklike tunes, the abrupt theme-changes, the pronounced contrast of weight and sonority. The principal theme, given at last to the xylophone, is in C, the mode embracing both F♯ and B♭, and presently with E♭, A♭, D♭, and C♭—the black keys as a unit serving as a species of appoggiatura to the original mode. The scale thus augmented therefore includes eleven of the twelve chromatic notes (lacking only F♮), but its character is nevertheless diatonic.

The resemblance between this theme and the first of the Beethoven Contradances can hardly fail to strike the ear:

28. *Sonata for Two Pianos and Percussion*

The bucolic quality of the Bartók theme is no accident. It gives rise to much of the movement by fission, a fragment of the original—sometimes only the first two notes, frequently four to six—breaking off and assuming a new shape. Both the original and the new forms are subjected to canonic imitation, rectus and inversus, in as many as eight parts (measures 159-170); and they are interspersed, rondo-like, with episodic themes of varying character.

But if a label is to be affixed to the movement, it must be considered a sonata-allegro in the character of a rondo; the developmental process is all-important, and the recapitulation is distinct if somewhat disguised. The main theme may be considered to have three members, beginning respectively at measures 4, 28, and 44; the subsidiary itself is the undulating sixteenth-note theme at measure 103, and the first theme is touched upon once more, just before the development (m. 133). The main theme offers most of the developmental material, and is strikingly transformed at the recapitulation (m. 248), with its second note changed to C♯, the tritone thus shifting its location but thereby emphasizing its structural importance.

The close is astonishingly simple. The Coda (m. 350) develops still further the opening motive of the main theme, in a progressively more hesitant fashion, with a persistent but interrupted rhythm in the side drum, steadily diminishing. The pianos alternate statements of the motive, in a descending Lydian tetrachord (E♭, D♭, B, A), the last mirrored in full but staccato and pianissimo chords, the spaces widening—finally two chords, a quasi-dominant on G, a triad on C—the drum and cymbal (played with the fingernail on the edge) continue for a few bars, run down, stop.

The combination of piano sonority with percussion instruments had for some years interested Bartók, as the First and Second Piano Concertos demonstrate. In those two works the possibilities could be explored only casually; it remained for the Sonata for Two Pianos and Percussion to serve as a proving ground, or rather, a proof, for his theories. As in so many other works, once he had exhaustively explored the field it apparently held no further interest for him: in the Third Piano Concerto the percussion plays an exceedingly minor role. So the Sonata remains a unique work, not only in Bartók's catalogue, but in the entire field of music. The outraged cries it once aroused have long since subsided, and it has been admitted to the small group of genuine masterpieces produced in this century, accepted as one of the most significant works of its creator. Because of the difficulties of performance it is unlikely to find a frequent place in concert programs, but it will amply repay both performers and audience for the effort expended on it.

Benny Goodman's commission for a work from Bartók brought about the inclusion, for the first and only time, of a wind instrument in one of his chamber scores. In this respect his catalogue is peculiarly incomplete. The Wind Quintet, opus 26, and the Serenade, opus 24, of Schoenberg, the Octet and numerous other works of Stravinsky, the Wind Quintet, Septet, and many other ensembles of Hindemith, all testify to the interest of these composers in chamber music for instruments other than strings. Most composers of this century have used wind instruments for variety in their chamber compositions, or have at least written works for solo wind instruments with piano; but Bartók had reached the age of fifty-seven without once having interested himself in the ensemble capabilities of the winds. Had it not been for a commission, he would very likely never have concerned himself with one of them.

Having accepted the assignment, however, he set about fulfilling it in characteristic fashion. The strings he was accustomed to treating as a homogeneous group; with five quartets behind him, they offered no problem in that respect. But since the 1904 Quintet for piano and strings, he had combined the piano only with individual string instruments, in the two Sonatas and the Rhapsodies, apparently having reached the conclusion that no real ensemble is possible between instruments of such pronounced differences in tone production. To add still another type of instrument—the clarinet—meant that there would be even less possibility of blending their sonorities; consequently he approached the problem from the opposite side: playing up the disparities, the *Contrasts* which gave the work its name.

Goodman had expressed the hope that the commissioned work would fit on two sides of a twelve-inch gramophone record, but Bartók found that his materials required more expansive treatment. Designed originally as a Rhapsody in two movements—Verbunkos (Recruiting Dance), and Sebes (Fast), corresponding to the lassú and friss of the csárdás style—it was extended by the inclusion of a slow interlude, Pihenő (Rest), and requires almost sixteen minutes for performance.

The style of *Contrasts* is distinguished by its excessive dependence, both harmonically and melodically, upon the interval of the tritone. It is present in almost every formation, with a resultant heterophony that frequently suggests a relationship to the music of Indonesia. Such passages as these are clearly gamelan-like:

29. *Contrasts*

(a)

(b)

Bartók's interest in gamelan music is further evidenced by No. 109 of the *Mikrokosmos, From the Island of Bali,* which may well have served as a study for the first of the excerpts above:

30. *Mikrokosmos*

The piano is otherwise given bell-like ringing sounds, ostinatos, trills, glissandos, and sliding chromatic progressions which enable it to fulfill an important function without assuming the prominence in the ensemble which its percussive clangor would normally create. With his customary modesty Bartók, designing the work for himself as pianist in collaboration with Goodman and Szigeti, allowed his colleagues the most brilliant parts, while the keyboard is relegated to a secondary—or tertiary—role, much of the time that of accompaniment. Only infrequently is it permitted the luxury of a thematic passage, and often it is used merely for punctuation and rhythmic underlining.

The other instruments, on the contrary, are exploited to the utmost. The violin reaps the harvest of Bartók's long exploration of string techniques—multiple stops, simultaneous bowed and pizzicato notes, glissandos, and all the rest—and adds a new one, scordatura, which does not appear in any other of his scores. At the beginning of the Sebes the violin is tuned to G♯-D-A-E♭, instead of the customary tuning in fifths, making possible two tritones on the open strings. The practice of unusual tunings for the string instruments is rare in music after the eighteenth century, but Mahler, Stravinsky, Berg, and Kodály had preceded Bartók in the twentieth-century use of the device, and some few composers since have called for occasional mistunings, usually to extend the low range by a tone or a semitone, seldom as an essential feature of the string technique. *Contrasts* uses the scordatura for only thirty bars, after which the performer is directed to 'take another violin, tuned as usual,' for the remainder of the movement.

As for the clarinet, the first two movements and the Trio of the third call for the instrument in A, while the one in B♭ is specified for the remainder of the finale.[11] Most of the idiomatic possibilities are explored: characteristic melodic passages for each register, rapid arpeggios and scales, trills and tremolos, varieties of articulation, shifts of register, extremes of dynamics. Long familiarity with the capabilities of the wind instruments in their orchestral functions had made Bartók peculiarly sensitive to their soloistic endowments, so that in the aptness of his writing for them there is really little difference between clarinet and violin. They share the duties and the rewards of the composition quite evenly. The statement of themes is alternated between them; in the manipulation of them now one, now the other, is given the spotlight. The clarinet has a cadenza in the Verbunkos, the violin one in the Sebes. Around them the piano provides the frame which intensifies the landscape without calling attention to itself. It is particularly in the unobtrusiveness of the piano part that Bartók's success lies: it seldom competes with the other instruments, whose qualities come nearer to combining with each other, but nevertheless it never attempts to adopt a manner foreign to itself for the sake of a uniformity of sound. That being unattainable, the piano remains an instrument of percussion, the clarinet a blown air-column, the violin a set of bowed and plucked strings with a resonator; and it is only by a deft manipulation of relative weight that the illusion of ensemble is reached.

Between the slow dance and the fast one that constitute the outer movements, the relaxation of the Pihenő has been felicitously compared to the concentric circles which spread out from the point at which a pebble is dropped into the water. The languid phrases of the violin and clarinet, opposing each other mirrorwise, are marked by faint ripples in the piano. Presently the undulation is intensified and then subsides, while the piano follows with gamelan passages. At the close the piano itself plays the mirrored phrase of the opening, now doubled in thirds and even more watery in sound.

The themes of both the Marcia and the Burletta of the Sixth Quartet are found in essence in *Contrasts:* the first in the Verbunkos, the second in the Sebes:

31. *Contrasts* and *Quartet No. 6*

(a)

Contrasts:

Contrasts, copyright 1942 by Hawkes & Son (London) Ltd. *Quartet No. 6,* copyright 1941 by Hawkes & Son (London) Ltd.

The effect, however, is vastly different because of the differences in texture and sonority. The imitative counterpoint of the Marcia plays only a small part in the Verbunkos; the Sebes lacks the harsh pomposity of the Burletta, and comes closer to the 'tempo giusto' dance-type movement which forms so many of Bartók's finales, but the two are similar in form, both having a central Trio with contrasting meter and mood: in the case of the Sebes a dance in Bulgarian rhythm $\left(\dfrac{8+5}{8}, \text{ actually } \dfrac{3+2+3+2+3}{8}\right)$ in the Aeolian mode, later changing to Lydian. The chromatic side-slipping in tritones which occurs halfway through the section, with the whole-tone scale-clusters still later, has an odd resemblance to the drowning scene in *Wozzeck,* reduced to chamber-music terms.

With the resumption of the original tempo, the dance boils along to its conclusion, piling brilliance upon brilliance. The problem of key is solved at the end with a cadence in B♭; with the first movement in A, and the second beginning and ending ambiguously (its final chord is B-D♯-F♯-A), the tonal organization seems tenuous in comparison with the majority of Bartók's larger works. Nevertheless, with so much modulation and so many passages which are only vaguely tonal to the ear, it is doubtful that many listeners are disturbed by an ending a semitone—and more than a quarter of an hour—away from the beginning.

Contrasts was followed by only two more chamber works: the Sixth Quartet and, in 1944, the Sonata for Solo Violin commissioned by Yehudi Menuhin. The Sonata is one of Bartók's most demanding works so far as performance problems are concerned, and one of the least accessible to the general listener. In this respect it differs strikingly from the other works of Bartók's last years. Part of this inaccessibility is due to the limitations of the medium: the lack of a low compass to provide tonal balance and proportion, the impossibility of sounding simultaneously more than two tones (except in pizzicato) upon the instrument, and the resultant necessity of breaking triple- and quadruple-stops.

But instrumental limitations have never prevented composers from exacting from the performer the ultimate in technical possibilities. The Bartók Sonata is no exception. Its problems are enormous, some of them almost incapable of musical solution; and there are places in which Bartók seems to have found the restrictions galling, where the musical conception seems on the verge of bursting its bonds. In this connection it is revealing to find that, although he did not play the instrument, Bartók nevertheless conducted personal experiments with the violin to discover new possibilities in technique.

The four movements of the Sonata are marked respectively Tempo di ciaccona, Fuga, Melodia, and Presto. It should be observed that Bartók indicated only the pace of the first movement, not its form, by labeling it 'in chaconne tempo.' This is not a chaconne, as certain writers have maintained, but a sonata-form movement in the character of a chaconne. Its main divisions are identified by the appearance of the broad multiple-stopped motive which opens the movement; of the 150 measures of the piece, 52 may be considered exposition, 38 development, 47 recapitulation, and the last 14 coda. The movement is firmly grounded in G, minor at first, closing in major, but treated with extreme chromatic freedom. Intervallically it leans heavily upon seconds, fourths, and sevenths, and thereby shows the derivation of its idiom from Magyar folk music. The relationship is further borne out by certain rhythmic patterns as well.[12] Extremes of range are employed throughout, as well as strong dynamic contrasts. Bartók exploits the open strings, both arco and pizzicato, as is his custom, for purposes of sonority. And there are many examples of the rhythmic repetition of a single note, both with and without an occasional auxiliary, which have formed a part of the composer's technique almost from the beginning of his career.

The fugue is much freer in its form than that, for example, in the G-minor solo Sonata of Bach. Bartók's might almost be called a fugal fantasy, since there are long stretches in which the fugue subject does not appear at all. The subject is characteristic of Bartók: chromatic, of limited compass (B to F♯), its motives separated by rests which become progressively shorter as the subject gathers momentum. The constant modification of the subject, even in the course of its exposition, is another Bartókian characteristic; only the first answer is exact, and the variational process sets in immediately thereafter. The spacing of the motives of the subject is, of course, particularly useful in separating the 'parts' when all are to be played on a single instrument. This has been described as a three-voice fugue, but it is apparent that the exposition, at least, is in four voices, with entries successively in C, G, C, and G—the traditional order, though nothing else is traditional in this fugue.

The exposition is followed by a rather long episode in which no thematic elements are discernible, and there is another extended episode later, leading to a section in which both rectus and inversus forms of the subject appear as a canon 'in motu contrario' (measures 62-75). With the anacrusis to measure 77 the subject appears in triple-stopped chords, interrupted by sixteenth-note scale segments in the "fourth voice.' This is the last complete statement; the remainder of the fugue is concerned with episodic material and motivic fragments of the subject, the first two notes of which (C-E♭) serve as cadence.

The Melodia, with its long-breathed chromatic line, exemplifies the variation technique which is always strong in Bartók's music. Its form is a simple A-B-A, but the ingenuity with which the third section is varied marks a high point in Bartók's handling of the technique. Something of the kind may be observed in the out-and-out theme and variations of the Violin Concerto; and as early as the Second Suite, opus 4, for orchestra, the use of variational patterns contributes largely to structural development.

The melodic line of the A section has numerous Bartókian characteristics: the expected seconds and fourths, the presence of certain *Urmotiven*, the constant chromatic inflection which nevertheless does not negate the sense of tonality. Each of its long, curving phrases terminates in a sort of motto, designated to be played more quietly than the surrounding passages, often wholly or partially in harmonics. The *B* section is chiefly in double- and triple-stops, with inner or lower trills. The melody has a folklike simplicity which is disguised by its setting. This middle section is marked 'con sordino'; in a letter to Menuhin, however, Bartók suggested performance of the whole movement with the mute, and asked about the possibility of playing it entirely without mute.

The relation of the final section to the first must be seen to be completely understood: the ear, although convinced, is unlikely to follow the astonishing subtleties of the modifications without an intimate acquaintance with the thematic material, and the eye takes in the picture much more readily at first. Measures 49-62 correspond exactly to measures 1-16; the essential notes—in fact, almost all the notes—of the original melody are present in the variation, but surrounded with embellishments which transform their functions:

32. *Sonata for Solo Violin*

The finale, a rondo in the character of a scherzo, is by all odds the least problematic of the movements of this Sonata. The first section is related in mood to the Prestissimo con sordino movement of the Fourth Quartet; the second is a folklike tune in the Phrygian mode, with the feeling of hemiola, an alternating 3/4-3/8 pattern being notated throughout in 3/8. The remaining digression (measures 270-311) employs a simple, songlike theme which is immediately inverted, and its fragments used imitatively for a few measures. Elements of all three themes are combined in the coda.

And so, with a work for the most limited medium of any with which he had concerned himself, Bartók bade farewell to the chamber music which occupies so large and so important a part of his catalogue. Only eighteen months of life remained to him, and the two large works he attempted after this were left incomplete at his death.

He was able to hear Menuhin play the Sonata in New York on 26 November 1944. But the Seventh Quartet, which Ralph Hawkes commissioned a few days later, was destined never to be written. A few notes, apparently intended for this purpose, exist: that is all. Nevertheless, in the chamber works he left, the world of music received an ample heritage. Others of his contemporaries surpassed him in actual number of works; some of them provided a more varied fare, with scores for less usual media, especially wind instruments; but in the first half of the twentieth century no other composer made so impressive a contribution to the field. As a group, the quartets are the most significant works in the form since Beethoven; add to them the violin sonatas, including the one for solo violin, *Contrasts*, and the Sonata for Two Pianos and Percussion—and for good measure the Rhapsodies for violin and piano as well as the Duos for two violins—and it becomes apparent that here is a body of music of first importance, unapproached by any other composer of Bartók's time. When the history of music in this century is finally written, these scores alone will ensure their composer a position of enduring significance.

THE CONCERTOS

BARTÓK'S first work in the concerto mold was not originally intended as a concerto at all. The Rhapsody, opus 1, was written for solo piano, and later rewritten for piano and orchestra in preparation for his Paris visit in 1905 to compete for the *Prix Rubinstein*. Dated November 1904, the original differs in certain respects from the version with orchestra, chiefly in the addition of a rather extended introduction, as well as in the amplification of several internal passages in order to provide balance.

The Violin Concerto (1907-08) was neither played nor published during Bartók's life, but he transferred the first movement bodily to the Two Portraits. After this it was nearly twenty years before Bartók returned to the concerto as a form, and then (1926) apparently because he required a vehicle for his concert appearances with orchestra. The First Piano Concerto has much in common with the Piano Sonata of the same year, both in materials and in treatment. The Second Piano Concerto (1930-31) is a bravura piece almost without parallel in the literature, but it is already milder and less percussive than the first, while the Third Piano Concerto, completed, except for seventeen bars, at the composer's death, shares the mellowness of all the last-period works. To these must be added the Concerto for Two Pianos and Orchestra, the almost unperformed reworking of the Sonata for Two Pianos and Percussion of 1937.

The two Rhapsodies (1928) for violin and orchestra are, properly speaking, not concertos at all, but they are included here because they also are written for solo instrument with orchestra. The Violin Concerto (1937-38) was the result of a commission from Zoltán Székely, while the Viola Concerto, left in a confused sketch at Bartók's death and completed by Tibor Serly (who also filled in the last bars of the Third Piano Concerto), was commissioned by William Primrose. A projected concerto for two pianos, commissioned by the duo-pianists Bartlett and Robertson, was never written.

The Concerto for Orchestra (1943) is a concerto only in the sense that it treats the orchestral instruments in a virtuosic-soloistic manner; discussion of this work thus belongs properly in the next chapter.

There are, then, ten concerted works for solo instrument with orchestra, including the Scherzo, opus 2, together with one for two pianos and orchestra. The number exceeds that of Bartók's string quartets, as well as the concerted works of any other important composer of his time. But it is not possible to trace within them, as within the quartets, his entire development as a composer; nor do they occupy, as a group, a place of comparable significance in the catalogue of his works. The dates of their composition indicate the reasons for the seeming discontinuity of their styles. The Rhapsody, opus 1, antedates Bartók's folksong research; the First Piano Concerto comes at the height of his percussive, martellato period; the violin Rhapsodies, being founded on folk materials, are in a different category from the others; while all the rest, with the possible exception of the transitional Second Piano Concerto, date from his harvest years and represent his ripest style.

At this point the Viola Concerto cannot be properly evaluated, since it was completed by another hand. No matter how skilful the reconstruction, it must be admitted that no one but the composer himself could have decided exactly how it was to be done; and for that reason there will always be reluctance to accept the Viola Concerto as an authentic work of Bartók.

The fullest realization of the Rhapsody, opus 1, is the cyclical setting for piano and orchestra. It has, however, been published in several versions: the lassú alone for piano solo; the so-called 'première version,' comprising the lassú and the friss for piano solo, but without the amplifications of the orchestral version; and a reduction of the orchestral version for two pianos. In all but the first of these the transition between the two parts is effected without pause, through the tentative statement of the first motive of the friss; in place of this, the printed version of the lassú alone has a short coda added. The implications of the form are left unrealized in the single movement, while in the 'première version' the formal balance is less satisfactory than in the orchestral setting, with its long introduction. Since the theme of the lassú is brought back in its most grandiose breadth at the close of the friss, this preface, in the character of a series of false starts interrupted by cadenza-like passages in the piano, is entirely necessary.

The Rhapsody abounds in invention, both melodic and harmonic. Its pages are black with notes, in contrast to those of the later works, where values shorter than sixteenths are rarely encountered: here—in the lassú—thirty-seconds and sixty-fourths are usual, and even the five balkens of one-hundred-twenty-eighths are fairly frequent. It is a virtuoso work in the grand tradition, parallel in structure to the Rhapsodies of Liszt but more compact. The lassú and the friss share thematic material in such a way that they are organically related, not merely contrasted. The development of thematic motives is much more extensive than in the two later Rhapsodies for violin and piano, though it does not destroy the air of passionate improvisation typical of the form. Bartók could not have brought himself to the writing of a pot-pourri: integration must be accomplished by musical means and upon musical grounds.

So the themes of the friss are forecast in the lassú, and those of the lassú are transformed in the friss, so that the two are firmly interlocked, and with the return of the Adagio in the last pages of the score, the Rhapsody acquires a unity entirely absent from its predecessors.

The recasting of the work in orchestral garb was done without serious detriment to the musical content. In general the orchestra accompanies, though occasionally in the friss it is given a fairly extended tutti: the exposition of the first theme is repeated by the orchestra, and other sections are divided between the two forces. Little was added in the scoring. In some places the piano part was thinned out to permit the use of the orchestra in a subsidiary function, and in a very few, new imitative material was written. But it is the piano which carries the greater burden, the orchestra which provides the setting. Little or no effort to equalize the forces may be observed: the scoring was motivated by Bartók's desire to provide himself a vehicle for pianistic virtuosity, and to minimize its brilliance would have been antithetical to this desire. Much later, the first two Piano Concertos, also written for his own performance, likewise focus attention upon the pianist, though the orchestra in both of these fulfills a more significant function than in the Rhapsody. The Third Piano Concerto, which Bartók knew he would never play, concentrates less upon bravura qualities and more upon purely musical values; and there are in it passages in which the orchestra absorbs the piano, instead of serving as its foil. The Rhapsody permits no such assimilation of the solo instrument.

As for the themes themselves, they are possibly less Hungarian than Teutonic—neo-Hungarian. While they obviously take their departure from the gipsy modifications of Hungarian popular art tunes, they are composed in the full knowledge of the musical procedures of western Europe—which is to say, those of Germany of the nineteenth century. They are tonal, not modal; they make extensive use of appoggiaturas, especially in the ornamentation; frequent augmented seconds appear.

The harmonic vocabulary is still traditional, its chromaticism being typified by chords of the diminished seventh and of the augmented sixth. Yet there are harmonic changes so abrupt as to be fresh in sound even after nearly fifty years, motion from triad to unexpected triad, mirrored passages, passing clashes, unforeseen modulations, all of which testify to the transformation in store for Bartók's style. All it needed was a fuse to set it off; and that was provided almost simultaneously with the composition of the Rhapsody, in the discovery of the vast storehouse of peasant melody totally ignored by Bartók's predecessors.

But since more than twenty years were to pass before he brought before the public another concerted work, the stages by which the peasant idiom became amalgamated with the Western techniques in which he had been trained must be observed in other works. By the time the First Piano Concerto was produced, the assimilative process had been completed.

The First Violin Concerto displays an intermediate stage. It is included neither in Kodály's list of 1921[1] nor in the catalogue by Denijs Dille (1939) with Bartók's corrections.[2] The score was given to Stefi Geyer, and remained unplayed until after her death. With minor modifications, the first of the Concerto's two movements became the first of the Two Portraits.[3] The Concerto was begun in Jászberény, 1 July 1907, and completed in Budapest in February of the following year. One of the unsolved puzzles of Bartók's music is the significance of a melody that appears toward the end of the second movement, placed between quotation marks and dated 'Jászberény 1907 jun 28' —a conventional tune on the natural overtone series, which might be played by primitive brass instruments. What it is, and why Bartók quoted it in the Concerto he began three days after, may never be determined. The effect is as startling as that of the interpolation in A major—the same key—toward the end of the Fifth Quartet.

The solo line is full of appoggiaturas and chromatic passing-notes; the double-stops are mainly in thirds and sixths; the style does not eschew chords of the diminished seventh. The romantic character of the movement is indicated by the composer's explicit, if polyglot, instructions in a few manuscript pages preserved by Imre Waldbauer: *con molto sentimento, tout à fait désolé, un peu entêté, mit verhaltener Leidenschaft, ellankadva, immer flüchtig.* Most of these indications do not appear in the published score.

Edwin von der Null, preparing his study of Bartók's piano music, received from the composer this reply to his question:

Why do I make so little use of counterpoint? I was inclined to answer you: because my beak grew that way [*weil mir der Schnabel so gewachsen ist*]. But since this is no answer, I shall attempt to clarify the situation:

1. In any case this is its character in performance; 2. In my youth my ideal of beauty was not so much the art of Bach or of Mozart as that of

Beethoven. Recently it has changed somewhat: in recent years I have
considerably occupied myself with music before Bach, and I believe that
traces of this are to be noticed in the Piano Concerto and the Nine Little
Piano Pieces.[4]

Bartók's interest in pre-Bachian composers resulted in his editions
of Couperin and Scarlatti, and his transcriptions of works by Ciaia,
Frescobaldi, Marcello, Rossi, and Zipoli. The diatonicism and contrapuntal clarity of these composers no doubt affected the First Piano
Concerto, but its other qualities are of twentieth-century origin.
The percussiveness of its idiom, quite like that of the Piano Sonata
produced the same year, is not inordinately harsh in spite of frequent use of minor seconds and ninths, and major sevenths; these
have a coloristic function and the ear does not insist upon inter-
preting them harmonically. This is true also of the tone clusters
which play an important role in much of the Concerto.

Contrapuntally there are few intricacies: usually no more than
two lines, each of which is frequently expanded into a harmonic
texture, doubled in thirds or sixths, with or without octaves. The
most involved contrapuntal writing is that in the Adagio, where the
woodwinds play in four different keys simultaneously, the piano accompanying with an ostinato which begins with opposed parallel
major sevenths in left and right hands, filling in the intervals gradually until clusters of ten to twelve notes are sounded.

The thematic material of the Concerto is quite fragmentary. After
a New York performance in 1928, one critic [5] wrote:

There were broken bits of themes hammered out on the piano and
answered by equally angry blasts of wind instruments. The only sustained
motive is that of bitterness, and the sum total is unmitigated ugliness.

It is true that the materials lack complexity, but the continuity of
the work is nonetheless apparent. Its élan, like that of the Sonata,
carries everything before it. The conception of the piano as an instrument of percussion, which it unquestionably is, frees it from the
necessity of ornamentation which has previously characterized it,
and pits it against the orchestra in something like equal terms. Again,
Bartók's orchestral treatment is likewise liberated from its coloristic
function and turns in the direction of linear clarification and rhyth-

mic compulsion. The Concerto is a study in chiaroscuro, as opposed to the opulent palette of the earlier orchestral works.

Bartók described the Concerto as 'in E minor.' As in the works which surround it, its key is merely a point of departure, and it is treated with the greatest of freedom. The first movement begins with a double pedal on B and A, and ends on an E-F♯-B-E chord; the finale begins with an ostinato strongly centered on E and B and ends on the same two notes, without a third.

In spite of the nature of its materials, the structure of the first movement corresponds to the classical sonata-allegro. The first section, 'allegro moderato,' serves as introduction, but contains a thematic motive which recurs in the course of development. The A of the pedal becomes more insistent and at the allegro it is prolonged into the principal theme of the movement. Its basic motives are by no means so readily discovered as those in the Second Concerto, this work being somewhat less economical and its architecture less compactly integrated.

The first thematic complex is in two parts, the second member appearing at rehearsal no. 7. Urgent and martellato throughout, it gives way finally to a transitional passage which makes use of a rhythmically constituted scale in the Locrian mode, imitated in contrary motion, and a second thematic group—a four-note motive arpeggiated in octaves—over a triple pedal (E-F♯-B) in the strings and horns (no. 12). The polyrhythms of the continuing section complete the exposition.

Now the development is begun with the principal theme, all the elements cited, however, being brought into play sooner or later. There are stylistic discrepancies: the extreme diatonicism of one part contrasting with the chromatic complexities of another; the contrapuntal passages played off against impressionistic successions of six-four chords. There is inexorable rhythmic pressure throughout; the eighth-note is king, as in the Piano Sonata, and notwithstanding the frequent change of meter from 2/4 to 3/4 to 5/8 there is little feeling of rhythmic plasticity—only of motoristic drive.

The recapitulation begins with the first theme transposed down a fifth, from A to D, and the rest of the materials are restated in approximately the original order, though with great modification. Practically all the section between nos. 37 and 39, for example, is doubled in minor seconds and ninths, providing a sharper *Klang*.

Where the second theme was initially in 2/4, it is now shot through
with bars of other lengths, and its rhythms become correspondingly
irregular. But there is no cessation of activity until the very last
chord.

Bartók here demands of the player the utmost in technical fluency.
In particular there are many unusually wide and awkward leaps to
negotiate, as well as clusters of tones over wide stretches. There are
problems which seem almost incapable of solution—this, for example,
in which the thumb of each hand is required to play a black and a
white key simultaneously:

33. *First Piano Concerto*

Copyright 1927 by Universal-Edition; assigned to Hawkes & Son (London) Ltd.

Rather surprisingly, between nos. 47 and 50, Bartók uses a key
signature of six sharps in the piano; he also employs one of five and
one of four sharps in the third movement. This is apparently the
last time in a large work that such a signature is found; in abandoning the limitations of signatures upon tonal freedom he was somewhat later than Schoenberg, who had written his last key signature
nearly twenty years earlier. Most of Bartók's major works for some
years previous to the Concerto had avoided signatures, and the recurrence here, curious as it is, emphasizes the composer's new orientation toward the reaffirmation of tonality. That he did not find it
necessary in the works which followed to specify such signatures is
an indication that he found means within the hyperchromatic style
of such works as the Fourth String Quartet to establish tonality without the restrictions of a key signature.

The second movement may be considered in some respects a pre-
cursor of the Sonata for Two Pianos and Percussion, in that throughout much of its length the piano duets with the battery. The percussion is designed for three players in addition to the kettledrums.
In a prefatory note, Bartók meticulously instructs the performers in

the methods of producing the sounds he wants; for example: with the handle of one side-drum stick on the edge of the suspended cymbal while the other is fastened to the leather hanger of the cymbal so that its tip touches the cymbal; with two side-drum sticks, beginning at the edge of the drumhead, gradually moving to the center, and then back again to the rim; with the handle of the side-drum sticks on the dome of the suspended cymbal. All the percussion instruments, including kettledrums, bass drum, two side drums (one with and one without snares), triangle, and four cymbals, are to be placed directly behind the piano.

The principal motive of the Andante is a group of three eighth-note seconds followed by a chord in fourths. Presented by the piano in its lowest sonorities, the passage is supported by kettledrum, two side drums, and suspended cymbal to mark the rhythm. The movement is ternary in form, the remainder of the A part being devoted to a rather long-breathed polyphonic section for the piano, in which there is a foretaste of the polytonality of the Trio. The opening motive in seconds, now expanded to sevenths, recurs, and leads imperceptibly to the ostinato mentioned above, over which the wind instruments weave a contrapuntal web in their separate keys: Aeolian on A (clarinet, English horn, oboe), Dorian on C♯ (bassoon), implied Dorian or Mixolydian on B♭ (bass clarinet), implied Aeolian or Dorian on C (English horn). The ostinato of the piano is progressively thickened to clusters, and then thinned down to its original sevenths:

34. *First Piano Concerto*

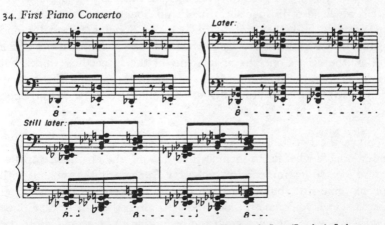

The return of the first part is greatly modified; the coda, at first with the Trio theme, then with the initial motive of the first part, leads by way of a sixteen-measure allegro interlude to the finale, where a motor-like ostinato of more than fifty bars serves as the foundation for the first theme. A second member (which resembles in certain aspects the principal theme of the first movement) and another similar motive are treated contrapuntally. Other motives, more or less closely related to those already heard, constitute the basis of the remainder of the working-out.

Bartók's themes in this work lack the distinctness which makes the analysis of most of his music rather simple. Here the scalar motives are so much alike that it is often difficult to determine exactly which one he is using. This does not necessarily militate against structural logic—it merely makes it more difficult to perceive that logic. The classical composers, dealing with two contrasting themes in their sonata-forms, one 'masculine,' the other 'feminine,' concocted no such problems for their listeners, but in consequence they encountered greater difficulties in structural integration, in homogenizing rather disparate elements.

Bartók's First Concerto is unquestionably homogeneous, even though diatonic and chromatic elements are utilized almost at random. Its immense vitality, at white heat throughout, welds its disparities into a complete amalgam. It is by no means a relaxing or a 'pleasant' piece: sharp and brittle, making full use of the martellato style which also distinguishes the Piano Sonata, it eschews the expressiveness and the profundities of the Sonatas for violin and piano. These qualities are again present in the string quartets which follow the First Concerto, as in many of the succeeding works, but they are found only in limited quantities in the Second Piano Concerto (1930-31), indicating the strong influence of medium upon style.

Since the two Rhapsodies of 1928 exist in several versions, it is questionable whether to include them among the chamber works or those for solo instrument and orchestra. Apparently the versions with piano came first; but the nature of the keyboard writing is rather like a sketch for orchestration, and it is altogether likely that these two pieces were intended from the beginning to be scored. Both are based upon folk materials,[6] both are fantastically ornamented but somewhat more stylized than the 1904 Rhapsody for piano, though like that they are both divided into the conventional lassú and friss; and stylistically they may be considered—the second especially—as the immediate predecessors of *Contrasts*, even though that work was written ten years later.

The First Rhapsody exists in three published versions: for violin and piano, for cello and piano, and for violin and orchestra. Jenő Kerpely played the cello version in one of the all-Bartók concerts in Budapest; Imre Waldbauer wrote [7] that 'As a result of this perform- ance we all came to the conclusion that the work is more suitable for the violin.' Kerpely, however, recalled that Waldbauer seemed to know the violin version before he himself saw the work. Bartók provided two endings for the friss, one of which recalls the main theme of the lassú and results in a closed form, the other intended for use if the friss were played separately. In actual practice it is the second which is usually used, even though it leaves the final cadence in the key of E, the lassú being in G. It was the latter form that Bartók himself always played.

A study of the manuscripts discloses that he was not satisfied with the original versions of the Rhapsodies, but revised them several times, the Second even after publication. In this work the revisions affected principally the friss, tightening it structurally by the omis- sion of more than forty measures and the compression of others, and making it more brilliant by the rewriting of some solo passages and the rescoring of parts of the accompaniment. The First Rhapsody is dedicated to Szigeti, the Second to Székely; the latter is the more striking of the two, using fresher materials and handling them with greater freedom.

Both are scored for a modest orchestra, with the woodwinds in pairs, two horns, two trumpets, a single trombone, tuba, and strings. The Second Rhapsody adds to this small group a collection of percussion instruments, harp, celesta, and piano; the First, how- ever, omits all these and uses the cimbalom, that dulcimer-like Hun- garian instrument used for centuries exclusively by gipsies. The cimbalom made its appearance in Hungarian art music rather late; a damper pedal was added in 1874 and its capabilities thereby in- creased. While the cimbalom played a part in formulating the textures of Bartók's music, he did not require the actual instrument in any other score. Its use in the First Rhapsody was prompted by the desire to achieve what Waldbauer calls 'a certain gipsy-band sound'; but even though an alternative part is provided for the piano, for occasions when the cimbalom is not available, its presence in the score has proved a deterrent to the performance of the work.

More than any other concerted work of Bartók, with the possible exception of the first of the Portraits, opus 5, the Rhapsodies are solo works with orchestral accompaniment. The problem of balancing the respective quantities is of lesser importance than, for example, in the Violin Concerto; the orchestra provides support and an occasional episode, but there are no tuttis of more than a few bars, there is no orchestral exposition of themes.

The lassú of the First Rhapsody is divided into three sections, opening with a heavy-rhythmed tune in a modified Lydian mode (both the major and the minor third being used). The second section, quieter and more flexible, makes use of the short-long rhythms prevalent in Hungarian music, and at the end the first tune returns, with a four-bar coda on the second theme.

The friss is quite moderate at the beginning, with a tune in E major, curiously close to the Shaker hymn that Aaron Copland years later discovered for the variations in his *Appalachian Spring*. A second section (rehearsal no. 6) is more capricious; here the functions of the two parts are reversed in the versions for violin and cello: where the violin is given the melody, the cello has the accompaniment. From this point on, the tempo increases steadily (the metronome mark for the quarter-note moves up from 100 to 120, 152, 160, 168, and finally to 200), breaking off abruptly and resuming the pace and the theme of the lassú, to end with a cadenza. The alternative ending for the second part does not reach the vivacissimo ($\downarrow$ = 200); instead, it reverses the acceleration and brings back the E-major theme (which never recurred in the first version) at a very moderate pace in A major, closing then with a fairly brisk coda.

The lassú of the First Rhapsody is full of a rather pompous humor; the friss offers not only contrasts of tempo but of character as well, ranging from the gentle quality of the opening to the rugged strength of certain later portions. Throughout both sections of the Rhapsody there are the drones of the *duda,* the tinkling of the cimbalom, under-lining the exaggerations of the solo instrument. The latter is given a part of virtuosic brilliance: multiple stops, elaborate passages in har-monics, rough accents, tender legatos, passages of great rapidity, complex bowings and phrasings.

Most of these qualities are found as well in the Second Rhapsody. In addition, both thematically and texturally this is more adventur-ous than the First. To take the first theme of the friss as an example:

35. *Rhapsody No. 2*

the frequent major sevenths, together with the mordents, give the passage a crude, primitive sound that is nowhere approached in the First Rhapsody; later sections of the movement use a Lydian scale with a flatted seventh,[8] imparting a distinctive flavor to the materials. The lassú shows some characteristics of the chromatic fioritura of which Bartók frequently made use, but which is entirely absent from the First Rhapsody.

The lassú of the Second Rhapsody has five sections in the form of a rondo, whose theme is elaborately ornamented with acciaccaturas and gruppettas; in it the augmented second makes one of its few late appearances in Bartók's music. The key is D minor in the first section; when the rondo theme returns it is in the same key but superim-posed upon harmonies that suggest the key of C♯; the final return, disguised by an overlapping with an episodic theme, combines the original tonality with that of G major. It is thus apparent that the Second Rhapsody is more closely related to the works which preceded it, in particular to the Piano Sonata and the First Piano Concerto, than is its companion. The connection is further pointed up by the successions of six-four chords in the friss, by the alternation of rather chromatic with entirely diatonic passages, by the cluster-trills (no. 14), and other procedures. The First Rhapsody is in certain respects back-

ward-looking; the Second looks only forward, employing in a work
outwardly conventional, in content as well as form, the newest techniques and the freest manipulation. The Rhapsodies are thus only
fraternal, not identical, twins.

Like the Fourth and Fifth String Quartets which enclose it
chronologically, the Second Piano Concerto shows an archlike variational treatment, the materials of the first movement recurring in the
finale. But the overall character of the Concerto is much different.
It is extremely active in the two outer movements, with comparatively
few bars of relaxation. The solo piano in the first movement is busy
in all but twenty-three measures; the orchestral strings, however, are
entirely omitted. In its incessant bustle and busy-ness the movement
recalls the Bach concertos, and certain procedures within the movement have other Bachian proclivities.

There is great thematic economy. For practical purposes the themes
of the movement may be reduced to three motives in the first group,
two in a transitional section, and one in the subsidiary group.

36. *Second Piano Concerto*

Copyright 1933 by Universal-Edition; assigned to Hawkes & Son (London) Ltd.

The motives of the first theme-complex are presented in close juxtaposition, *a* appearing in the first bar, *b* in the fourth, and *c* in the
fifth. The first thirty-two bars are made up exclusively of these three
motives treated in contrapuntal and developmental fashion. Two new

motives make their appearance in a transitional section of considerable size (32-57), its dimensions and the fact that it leads, not to a new theme, but to a repetition of elements of the first theme, suggesting that it may have been intended as the second part of a ternary form, the whole doing duty as first thematic complex.

Just before the real second theme, motive d, is heard, fragments of the first theme are tossed about imitatively at intervals of descending fifths, which prove in the ensuing section (as in the Adagio) to be of functional importance, chords in fifths being manipulated as melodic streams. The second theme also appears in fifth-chords, tranquillo, right and left hands arpeggiating in opposite directions and the chord motion appearing in approximate mirror.

Development is entirely polyphonic, the piano having passages of enormous bravura throughout. The section from bar 155 on has a very Bachian sound; immediately thereafter fragments of motive a, inverted for the first time, lead to the recapitulation, in which the basic elements are presented in the original order but entirely inverted, while the transition to the cadenza is effected by means of a stretto on the retrograde inversion of motive a:

37. *Second Piano Concerto*

The second is a 'portmanteau' movement, comprising elements of adagio and scherzo, the whole forming a ternary structure, the restrained, tentative, slow sections surrounding a Presto in which the piano has a breathless succession of scales, tremolos, and tone-clusters that persist for more than two hundred bars. The Adagio itself is separated into alternating sections, the consecutive and mirrored fifth-chord 'chorale' of the strings being set off against parlando improvisational passages in the piano, accompanied only by percussion —a more functional treatment, however, than Beethoven's kettledrum-piano duet in the E-flat Concerto, opus 73. From the technical standpoint, the climactic middle section culminates in rapid pianissimo tone-cluster trills played with both hands flat, spanning all the notes within the octave; the pages in which these passages are included, together with certain parts of the *Cantata profana*, constitute what may be considered Bartók's most advanced use of the cluster technique. The effect of this section is nocturnal—another excursion into the realm of 'night music.'

The concluding Adagio is somewhat shorter than the first, but it shows an almost parallel structure. The piano motive, still accompanied by the drums, is somewhat varied; but as at first, the repetition is inverted. The cadence is ostensibly in C minor, preceded by a segment of the E-major scale.

Although the finale begins with a totally new theme—related in its note-repetitions, its limited compass, and its percussive quality, to the spirit of the First Piano Concerto—the majority of its materials are from the first movement, rhythmically transformed. Bartók does not go so far here as in the Violin Concerto in the duplication of structure as well as materials; and since his thematic manipulation amounts frequently to the complete disguising of the themes, it may be questioned whether the structural logic so apparent to the eye is borne out in performance—at least to the listener who has not first analyzed. So long as the rhythms are preserved, the ear readily accepts other changes without confusion, but when the rhythms are disguised, recognition is far more difficult.

The finale of the Second Piano Concerto is an elaborate rondo form, in which the episodic sections are derived by transformation from motives of the first movement. The form may be diagrammed thus:

Introduction - *A* - *B* - *A* - *C* - *A* - *D* - *A* - Coda
          (new (motives   (motives   (motive
          theme) *b* & *a*)   *c* & *a*)   *d*)

—a seven-part form. The transitions which occur are also based upon materials from the first movement, and the coda as well, so that new materials play a comparatively small role in the finale.

Analysis of all the methods of motivic variation and theme derivation is obviously impossible within the limits of this chapter, but one illustration will provide an intimation of Bartók's attitude:

38. *Second Piano Concerto*

This is a transitional passage (bars 195-206), based upon a new motive derived, as the illustration shows, from the inversion of a transitional motive and the inverse retrograde of motive *a*; the latter is printed upside down to make the relationship more apparent. The new motive is handled imitatively in stretto quite as if it were of major thematic importance.

The polyphonic element is, as a matter of fact, exceedingly strong throughout much of the Concerto. Strettos and fugatos abound, as in all Bartók's music of this period. The harmonic basis is, however, rather less adventurous than in either the Fourth or the Fifth Quartet, certainly much less than in the fugue of the Music for String Instruments, Percussion, and Celesta. Diatonic modes prevail: G major in the first and last movements, while the chromaticism of the Adagio and its parallelism in chords of equal interval enhance but seldom obscure the basic tonality of C.

The Concerto therefore represents a transitional point, lying stylistically between the scores of the 1920's and the harvest of Bartók's final decade. No one can deny its heterogeneities; but it marks indisputably the direction of the composer's path.

Like the Rhapsodies of 1928, the Sonata for Two Pianos and Percussion does not fall readily into any of the standard categories. Even

though Bartók rescored it as a Concerto for Two Pianos and Orchestra, it has seemed most logical to include it with the chamber music,
since it is almost exclusively performed in its original form.

All that need be added here is the composer's explanation of the
rescoring:

> It seemed advisable, for certain technical reasons, to add orchestral
> accompaniment to the work, though, as a matter of fact, it gives only
> color to certain portions of the work. The two-piano and percussion parts
> remain practically unchanged, except for some of the climactic parts
> which are now taken over from the two pianos as tuttis by the orchestra.[9]

The orchestral version employs the normal large orchestra: woodwinds in threes, four horns, two trumpets, three trombones, celesta,
and strings, in addition to the keyboard and percussion resources of
the original.

When Zoltán Székely commissioned Bartók to write a Violin
Concerto for him, Bartók suggested that he compose a large work in
variation-form instead. The suggestion did not meet with Székely's
approval, and he insisted that the work must be a bona fide concerto
in three movements. Bartók acquiesced, and completed the Concerto
on the last day of December 1938; Székely played it the following
April in Amsterdam under Mengelberg. Székely was delighted with
the work, even when Bartók pointed out that, while ostensibly writing a true concerto, he had—as a little private joke—satisfied himself
by making it the variation work he had originally proposed.

Not only is the inner movement in the form of theme and variations, but all the materials of the first movement turn up in varied
guise in the finale, so that the latter itself stands as a variation of the
first movement. As has been demonstrated in earlier chapters, although Bartók had not previously written a large set of variations—
there are small ones in *For Children*, the Fifteen Hungarian Peasant
Songs, and the *Mikrokosmos*—the variational spirit had always been
strong in his music, and the arch-forms of the 1920's and 1930's are
motivated by it. So it was natural that Bartók should have wanted to
crown his efforts in this direction with such a work as the Violin
Concerto; and it is characteristic that in it he so completely carried
through his ideas that he was never afterward impelled to write a
variation-form.[10]

Bartók never heard Székely play the Violin Concerto, though he did work with him on it, in Paris, before the first performance. It was October 1943 before he heard a performance; afterward he wrote:

> I was most happy that there is nothing wrong with the scoring; nothing needs to be changed, even though orchestral 'accompaniment' of the violin is a very delicate business. The critics, of course—they ran true to form, although they wrote a bit more favorably than usual. I wouldn't even mention them but for this brutishness of one of them: he doesn't believe that this work will ever *displace* the Beeth. Mendel. Brahms concerti. How is it possible to write such an idiotic thing: what fool fit for the madhouse would want to displace these works with his own? Had the critic written that he does not believe that the work compares with these, or something like that, then it would have been all right. . .[11]

There can be little doubt by this time that the Bartók Violin Concerto is indeed one of a very small handful worthy of being placed beside those of Beethoven, Mendelssohn, and Brahms. Although it is a virtuoso piece, and one of almost unprecedented difficulty, its musical organization has been accomplished so completely and convincingly that the essential weakness of the solo concerto—the disparity in *quantity* between the solo and the orchestra—never commands attention. It is a full-bodied, virile work, original in form and content; concentrated, economical, and intense.

The correspondence between the two exterior movements goes much further than the simple re-use of materials: the architecture is duplicated almost section by section. Both are large sonata-form movements, with two main thematic groups and a number of pertinent associates. Both open with a significant introductory motive, somewhat different in appearance but upon examination revealing their unanimity:

39. *Violin Concerto*

The principal theme in both is the same, rhythmically transformed and varied, four bars of the original being represented by eight of the variant:

40. *Violin Concerto*

The relation of both to the introductory motive is apparent, of course, as is the dependence of all three upon the intervallic relations characteristic of Magyar peasant melody.[12]

The similarity between the second members of these main themes is less obvious. The first has a somewhat heroic cast at the beginning, while the other is biting and perverse, but both are wide-ranging, made up largely of arpeggios, and in the return to the first member both movements present their themes in canon—one in the lower seventh, the other in the upper fifth.

The transitional themes are twins in every respect save rhythm:

41. *Violin Concerto*

and so also are the themes of the subsidiary sections that follow. The most important aspect of the latter, however, is that they are based upon a chromatic series comprising all twelve tones. There is no question here of a twelve-tone 'technique': Bartók had long since given up whatever ideas he once had concerning Schoenbergian dodecaphonism as a compositional procedure for him. Nevertheless the first phrase, in the solo, includes all twelve tones, each used once; the next phrase, in the orchestral strings, again includes the twelve tones but, significantly, in a slightly different order:

42. *Violin Concerto*

Antal Molnár's article in *A Zene*, in which he discusses the Violin Concerto,[13] brings up the rhythmic resemblances between the two principal themes of the first movement. Bartók took occasion to clear up the matter in a letter to Molnár:

I differ with you on this point: the rhythms of the main and secondary themes are indeed similar, but this constitutes no real relationship, or at most a rhythmic relationship. Properly speaking, measures 73-75 = 76-78 = 79-81 = 82-84. Now, if we investigate the shape of measures 76-78 and 82-84, we find nothing in common between them and the main theme. Measure 96 < secondary theme.[14]

It is thus apparent that Bartók considered the fact of the *presence* of the twelve tones in each phrase as constituting its thematic identity: a point of view in diametric opposition to that of the school of Schoenberg, where the *order* of the tones is all-important. Only Alban Berg treated his *Grundgestalt* with comparable freedom; and even he would not in his later works have written a movement only fragmentarily row-inspired.

The reasons for the presence of this dodecaphonic material in an otherwise very tonal work remain obscure. It is unlike Bartók to have written it, as some maintain, to show the twelve-tone group that their techniques may be turned to tonal purposes; that possibility they had already recognized and deliberately avoided. It is more believable that it is the fruit of one of those accesses of perverse satire that crop out occasionally in his music: the banal sing-song in the last movement of the Fifth String Quartet, the out-of-tune glissandos in the Burletta of the Sixth, the Shostakovich parody in the Concerto for Orchestra. Credence is lent to the hypothesis by the whinnying sounds with which the orchestra greets the passage (measures 92-95) on its first hearing, and the blatant disrespect which follows the sixteenth-note version—for the flutter-tongue in the trombones can hardly be otherwise construed.[15]

Apparently discouraged by the orchestral opposition, the solo begins the development with a long cantilena derived from the introductory motive, and an upward-spiralling triplet figure, 'molto tranquillo.' Especially noteworthy in the development group is the inversion of the main theme over a diaphanous accompaniment of harp, celesta, and strings (measures 194-203). The recapitulation is much condensed to allow for a full cadenza, which begins with a rotating quarter-tone passage in the violin, one of the only two places where Bartók made use of microtones.

Since the structure of the third movement parallels that of the first, it requires little additional comment except to point out that the twelve-tone theme, as shown in the excerpt above, is now embellished with some notes repeated within the course of the phrase, and that there is almost no resemblance between the solo phrase and the orchestral phrase that follows it. It may be significant that no orchestral comment greets the passage in this movement, though in the first it brought forth grotesqueries on each entrance.

Two closes are provided, one with brilliant opportunities for solo display, the other omitting the solo altogether. This was the original version; the ending was rewritten at Székely's suggestion, to allow the work to end 'like a concerto, not a symphony.' Bartók himself, after listening again to some of the great violin concertos of the nineteenth century, agreed that it was a mistake not to give the soloist the final spotlight; nevertheless, both endings are published in the score.

The 'parlando rubato' theme of the Andante is centered on G in contrast to the B of the movements which surround it. But it is a G with a strongly Lydian flavor, notwithstanding its chromatic modifications. Calm, tender, and perhaps a little naive, it is admirably suited to variation treatment of a more usual character, each of the six sections which follow paralleling its structure throughout. The whole movement is scored with extreme delicacy; of the brass, only the horns are used, and even these have a relatively low tessitura. The percussion, on the other hand, plays an important role, though a subdued one. The kettledrums are treated as a melodic instrument in the first variation:

43. *Violin Concerto*

while in the fifth and sixth there are significant parts for side drum, kettledrum, and triangle.

The variations may be briefly summarized as follows: (1) theme elaborated by the solo, as kettledrums and pizzicato double-basses provide the minimum of support; (2) phrases of the theme, somewhat extended in span, alternate with rapidly turning figures in the harp, as woodwinds and divided violins, tremolando, accompany; (3) rough double-stops 'au talon,' with economical support from horns, woodwinds, and kettledrums; (4) simplified version in low strings as the solo plays rhapsodic trills and scales; toward the end the theme appears in multiple canon, the solo violin being followed by violas, cellos, and double-basses; (5) theme treated in scherzo fashion by the solo, with ejaculations from woodwinds, harp, triangle, and side drum; (6) at the beginning a fantastically embellished version in the solo, while the orchestral strings have a simpler version in a three-part canon, pizzicato; later the solo line again becomes lyrical, and the supporting canonic voices are increased to four and then five. The repetition of the theme after the sixth variation is an octave higher than at first; halfway through, the violin is joined by three solo violas in imitation, and the movement closes in an exceedingly tenuous atmosphere, into which the finale intrudes with its brusque introductory motive in unison strings.

Cold analysis of such a work as the Violin Concerto can convey no suggestion of its radiant warmth. The full-bodied themes, the amplitude of their setting, the harmonic color, are intensified by the orchestration. The Viola Concerto, sketched seven years later, was to have had a somewhat more transparent score; but that was necessitated by the character of the instrument itself, and, as has been seen, in the Violin Concerto Bartók was entirely satisfied with the balance between the solo violin and the orchestra.

The serenity of the Third Piano Concerto is remarkable among Bartók's larger works. Reasons have been advanced in explanation, none especially pertinent to this study since they are all either physical or psychological and, while understanding is possible, proof is not. Had Bartók lived to complete a series of works, conclusions about the genesis of their characteristics might with validity have been drawn; but now, if a decision is to be made, it must be upon the basis of this work plus the Viola Concerto, which was left no more than a torso.

Whatever the reasons—and it has nowhere been the intention in this book to examine Bartók's work from the standpoint of its motivations, physical, psychological, or otherwise—his progressive trend toward both structural and tonal lucidity is exemplified throughout the Third Piano Concerto. In both texture and orchestration there is extreme clarity, sometimes to the point of tenuousness. The first theme, a highly ornamented, songlike melody, apparently influenced by the Romanian *doïna*, is presented in pure form, doubled in single notes two octaves apart in the piano, with the minimum of accompaniment in second violins and violas. The rest of the movement is treated with the same reticence—or tenderness. The martellato quality of the First Piano Concerto is entirely absent, and the immense vitality of the Second has been refined almost to the vanishing point.

The other movements have more striking qualities: the Adagio religioso, with its rather naive chorale embracing a Trio in the 'night music' idiom; and the energetic concluding rondo, which contains some of Bartók's most spontaneous fugal writing. The Trio is based upon actual bird-calls which Bartók had notated in Asheville, North Carolina, in 1944; it may not be merely coincidental that this work, apparently intended for Ditta Pásztory Bartók, reverts to the mood of the *Out of Doors* movement dedicated to her nearly twenty years earlier.

The textural simplicity of the first movement is enhanced by the unusual writing for the piano, which is treated much of the time as a single-line melodic instrument. Right and left hands more often than not have identical parts in single notes, or move in parallel thirds and octaves. Even in passages written somewhat more thickly, the elements of duplication and parallelism are almost continuously present; and at the recapitulation, where the first theme is fitted with a counterpoint (in the same rhythm), both lines are doubled so that there is still no independence of hands. The same principle carries over to the orchestration as well, it being almost totally devoid of polyphony, with frequent doubling. The scoring is modest in other ways: the trumpets are used in hardly a dozen of the movement's 187 bars, the trombone in but two.

Tonally the first movement, like most of the Concerto, is unambiguous. It opens and closes in E, fluctuating from the major to suggestions of Mixolydian and Lydian modes, but always firmly anchored to E and B. It is only with the entrance of the first violins in the eighteenth measure that the key shifts, in a series of dominant-tonic progressions that lead progressively to G, C, F, and D♭ before they debouch in the secondary theme, or thematic complex. This, unlike the first, has several faces, but they are shown only briefly before the development sets in. Here the first theme becomes lyrical and straightforward, its rather nervous rhythms now smoothed out into a more flowing line. The second is touched upon for a few bars, and yields to a full-fledged recapitulation, in the course of which the strings attempt a fugato on the first theme, with the successive entries becoming shorter and more closely spaced, the fourth presenting only the first four notes and then slipping over into a part of the second theme (measures 136-143). After the subsidiary section has been restated, the movement takes but a few bars to disappear, solo flute and solo piano providing the cadence.

Despite its delicacy, the second movement embraces a good deal of contrast. The word *religioso* appears here for the first time in Bartók's music, but it must not be taken as indicating a religious intention. It simply describes the character of the first theme, whose phrases, in chorale style, alternate with very quiet cadential extensions in the strings. The shimmer of string trills in clusters provides a tremulous background for the night sounds of the Trio, scored with the utmost fragility for woodwinds and xylophone, muted trumpets and horns, the piano at first with brittle birdlike motives, then with blurred thirty-second-note runs which merge with the murmur of the string tremolos. In the final section, the chorale is given to the woodwinds, the piano accompanying with an invention-like two-part polyphony, at the cadential points interpolating short cadenzas. The last bars are given to the piano alone; it gives promise of closing in the key of C where it began, and the strings once more prolong the cadence, but at the last moment the piano turns mildly though unexpectedly to an E-major triad.

The feel of the finale, a 3/8 Allegro vivace, is not unlike that of the first movement of the Concerto for Orchestra, though without its metrical irregularity. The characteristic rhythm of the first theme, an iamb followed by a trochee, recurs in rondo fashion, set off by fugal episodes in which, despite the conclusions of certain writers, there is no trace of compromise or concession. These passages may be lucid to the ear, but there is no lessening of Bartók's contrapuntal skill: the inversions, the close strettos, the mirrors and other canons, the free polyphony, show the composer in complete command of his faculties.

If the Third Piano Concerto is to be considered weaker than the first two, it must be because of the extreme refinement of its idiom. Lacking the harshness of the First Concerto, the bravura of the Second, it is nonetheless an authentically Bartókian work—the last one from his pen. It is unlikely that Bartók would have deliberately simplified his speech to insure immediate acceptance of this work, when he had refused throughout his entire life to compromise himself or his music. He might have found it easier had he been willing to take the middle way; that course he rejected from the beginning. The Third Concerto is nowhere atavistic. Whatever its faults, the composer cannot be said to have turned back over the way he had come—the composer of the Rhapsody of 1904 could have written it only after his techniques had matured through all the intervening works.

Tibor Serly's task in reconstructing the Viola Concerto from the confused sketches that Bartók left at his death placed upon him a very great responsibility. He has recounted [16] how difficult that task was: although Bartók considered the Concerto complete, needing only the 'purely mechanical work' of orchestration with the possibility of slight reconsideration here and there on the grounds of playability, the draft was notated on odd bits of manuscript paper in such a way that the intended sequence was by no means apparent. Earlier sketches appeared on some of the same pages; there were no page numbers nor movement indications, and, most discouraging of all, Bartók wrote over passages instead of erasing them, with the result that parts of the score were almost illegible.

The printed score bears the notation, 'Prepared for publication from the composer's original manuscript' by Serly. This is obviously an understatement; in all fairness to Serly he must be credited with not only the editing but the orchestration and, in fact, the reconstruction of the Concerto. Although it had been commissioned by William Primrose, because of 'apparently insurmountable difficulties' with the Bartók estate he had given up hope of receiving it when, in January 1949, Ernest Ansermet told him that the Concerto was being rewritten for violoncello. Through the efforts of Ralph Hawkes, who assured him that 'morally' the work was his, Primrose had the score in his hands in the early summer of 1949, and gave the first performance in Minneapolis the following December with Antal Doráti conducting.

Primrose considers the Viola Concerto 'a sensitive and inspired work and a real contribution to the literature of the viola.' [17] It would be pleasant to record that it is Bartók's crowning achievement; it is, unfortunately, nothing of the kind. This is written with full realization of the divided responsibility which brought it about; how close Serly came to the composer's intention is a question which can never be answered. Even with access to the original sketches it is impossible to draw more than tentative conclusions.

The first movement, Moderato, is a fairly conventional sonata-form structure, throughout much of which there is little Bartókian distinction, though Bartókian devices are everywhere to be observed. Both thematic facture and working-out seem perfunctory. Certain sections are like caricatures of pages written more strikingly elsewhere: the twisting triplet passage, measures 41-50, is a distant relative of similar lines in the Second Piano Concerto and the Violin Concerto, but without their vitality and conviction.[18] Even the canonic writing, so largely entrusted with the elements of suspense and culmination in Bartók's music, becomes dry and somewhat scholastic here. The architectural integration, always before so carefully calculated, is incomplete, and such thematic interreferences as occur seem extrinsic.[19]

The second movement, an Adagio religioso like that of the Third Piano Concerto, lacks the distinctiveness of its counterpart. A simple ternary form, it encloses within two extremely tenuous sections, in which the solo is provided with only the barest essentials of an accompaniment, an agitated outburst in which both the piangendo motive of the viola and the supporting thirty-second-note scales seem borrowed from the Fifth String Quartet,[20] where they were much more effectively employed.

The attenuation of the first and second movements of the Viola Concerto is pronounced, but whether the extremely sparing instrumentation which Serly has provided, taking his cue from Bartók's statement that 'the orchestration will be rather transparent,' is responsible for more than a slight overemphasis on this rarefaction is another unanswerable question.

The three movements of the Concerto are connected by interludes, the first in the style of a cadenza (though there is also a cadenza before the reprise), the second with energetic fourth-chords over a waddling quasi-ostinato in sevenths and fourths. Despite this device the movements appear disconnected. The signature theme of the Sixth String Quartet accomplishes its purpose economically and convincingly, introducing the first three movements in successive one-, two-, and three-voice settings, and culminating in a finale for which it supplies most of the material. The interludes of the Viola Concerto, on the other hand, have no cumulative function, and their use appears arbitrary rather than purposeful.

It is only in the finale that one feels a trace of authenticity. It is a fast dance-movement in the flavor of many of Bartók's last movements, with a character of 'moto perpetuo,' folk-inspired. Its themes are lively and rhythmic; and here at last Serly has let the orchestra be heard. The Trio is a bagpipe-tune remotely related to the main theme of the first movement. The only really serious fault of the movement is its extreme brevity: the four and a half minutes it occupies leave an impression of truncation, and one would gladly have it continued for as long again, since it is by far the shortest of the three.

The defects of the Viola Concerto—aside from any inadequacies that may have resulted from its completion by another hand—no doubt betray the painful circumstances of its composition. Ill for several years, unable for two of them to undertake any concerts or lectures which would have alleviated his financial worries, Bartók worked on the last two concertos simultaneously, but left the Viola Concerto in sketch while he completed, save for the last few bars, the Third Piano Concerto apparently intended as a legacy for his wife. It is natural, therefore, that the latter work, upon which he lavished the last few ounces of his strength, should be the more convincing.

But the concerto in which he attained the most complete synthesis from the standpoints of medium, style, and structure, is the one for the violin. In recognizing this the very real merits of the others need not be disparaged; nevertheless the fact remains that Bartók's greatest success with the concerto is not to be found in the three he wrote for his own instrument, but in one for an instrument he did not play at all.

BARTÓK began his creative career full of high hope for the future. His symphonic poem *Kossuth*, written when he was but twenty-two years old, not only was greeted with acclaim in Budapest but also brought about his first visit to England when it was played by Hans Richter in Manchester early in 1904. The First Suite for large orchestra achieved success when Ferdinand Loewe conducted the first three movements in Vienna late the following year. With these performances behind him, it would be easy to imagine that Bartók was on his way to the production of a long list of orchestral scores, and that his fame would soon spread throughout Europe and the New World.

Nothing of the kind happened. The First Suite was followed by a second, in 1907; during the next five years Bartók produced three more orchestral works: Two Portraits (1908), Two Pictures (1910), and Four Pieces (1912). In all the remainder of his life—thirty-three years—he wrote only two more works for full orchestra, both on commission: the Dance Suite in 1923 and the Concerto for Orchestra twenty years later. A few transcriptions of his piano arrangements of folk material were made during this period, and two important scores making use of smaller resources mark the 1930's: the Music for String

Instruments, Percussion, and Celesta, and the Divertimento for string orchestra. That is all.

In the chronology of his orchestral works may be seen Bartók's progressive discouragement over the possibility of performance of his music in large forms. With the success of *Kossuth* and the First Suite as stimulus, he began the Second Suite in 1905, but interrupted its composition for intensive work in the newly discovered music of the Hungarian peasants. When he returned to it two years later, his point of view had been altered so much that—although in the perspective of forty-odd years the folk influence on the last movement is rather slight—at the time of its appearance it was viewed as unpalatable. Despite recognition of Bartók's importance as pianist, the public withheld approval of his own music, and he retreated gradually within himself, devoting his energies to teaching and to ethnological research, after 1912 writing only those works (with a few significant exceptions) that he was assured of bringing to performance.

We are therefore deprived of what might have been a considerable body of orchestral music. That loss would have been more deplorable had Bartók not diverted his creative forces into such forms as the string quartet, where he left an enduring monument unequalled by any of his contemporaries, and the solo concerto, in which his orchestral skills ripened to the full maturity of the Concerto for Orchestra.

Bartók's memorandum program for the *Kossuth* 'symphony' has recently been reproduced in facsimile.[1] It reads as follows:

In Hungarian history, 1848 is the one most celebrated year; it was then that the war for Hungarian liberty broke out: a life and death conflict whose final goal was freedom from the sovereignty of the Austrians and the Habsburg dynasty. The leader of the revolution was the patriot Lajos Kossuth. In 1849 the Austrians saw themselves faced by defeat at the hands of the Hungarian troops; they called for assistance to Russia, by whom the Hungarian army was completely vanquished. Thus the Hungarian state seemingly disappeared forever.

These events serve as a basis for the symphony's program. The work comprises ten closely related sections, with an explanatory inscription at the head of each.

I. ('Kossuth') This is intended to characterize Kossuth.

II. ('What grief weighs on thy soul, dear husband?') The faithful wife of Kossuth is anxious at seeing her husband sorrowful, his face wrinkled

with cares. Kossuth attempts to set her at ease, but finally he can no
longer suppress the ancient grief:

III. ('The country is in danger!') Soon he muses again on the glorious
past.

IV. ('The better time of days gone by . . .')

V. ('Soon to evil turns our fate . . .') The flute and piccolo, later the
bass clarinet, play a theme intended to characterize the tyranny of the
Austrians and the Habsburgs, and violence which acknowledges no law.
With these words

VI. ('On to battle') Kossuth is aroused from his musing; the taking up
of arms is at last determined on.

VII. ('Come forth, come, fine Magyar warriors, fair Magyar cham-
pions!') Kossuth rallies the youth of the Hungarian nation to his standard.
Immediately after this follows, little by little, the theme of the Hungarian
heroes. Kossuth repeats the summons to the assembled army, after which
it takes a holy oath to fight to the last breath. For a moment, very deep
silence, and then

VIII. the Austrian troops are heard slowly approaching. The theme is
the Austrian hymn (*Gott erhalte*), the first two measures distorted. The
combatants clash, the life-and-death struggle appears to be won; finally,
however, crude strength prevails. The great catastrophe occurs: the rem-
nants of the Hungarian army disperse.

IX. ('To all an end . . .') The country goes into deepest mourning.
But even that is forbidden, so therefore:

X. ('All is silence, silence.')

The score of *Kossuth* indicates that Bartók had learned a good deal
from Liszt, particularly in the matter of theme-transformation. The
structural principles shown here—a large form unified by means of
thematic manipulation, relying to a considerable extent upon developmental procedures, remained characteristic of Bartók throughout
his life. There are few works that are quite so prodigal with thematic
material, much of which resembles that of the Hungarian Rhapsodies. The double-dotted rhythms, ornamental gruppettas, and impassioned character link *Kossuth* to the popular art music of Hungary,
which is further represented in Bartók's catalogue by the Four Songs
of 1902. Augmented seconds are scrupulously avoided in the melodic
lines, but their harmonic flavor is everywhere present, and the basic
motive of the Rhapsody, opus 1, written late the following year, is
already to be found in essence in the Funeral March of this work:

44. *Rhapsody No. 1*

The other orchestral scores of the period are said to be a Scherzo and a Burlesque, opus 2, both withdrawn by the composer. A Scherzo for piano and orchestra, written in 1904-05, has now been published; but whether it is the same work as the Burlesque is not clear. It is closely related to the First Suite and the Rhapsody, with some of the grotesqueries of the Three Burlesques, the second Portrait, and the macabre *Mandarin*.

The First Suite, opus 3, is the first of Bartók's orchestral works available in score. In spite of the fact that it is dated 1905, the musico-ethnological work which had already begun to occupy him has left no imprint upon it; it is, on the other hand, conditioned throughout by German and neo-Hungarian influences. The themes themselves are such as Liszt might have considered autochthonously Hungarian. It is rather curious to find recent Hungarian writers [2] so considering them, and crediting their character to the simultaneous welling of Bartók's interest in the music of the Hungarian peasant. Certainly the desire was present in the Bartók of 1905 to arrive at an authentically Hungarian style in his original music, but it was several years before perceptible traces of such a style began to appear. There are few enough in the First Quartet of 1908; to find them in the First Suite is to mistake the intention for the deed.

Nevertheless the Suite is not without its significance. It shows the composer already well equipped technically to cope with composition in the large forms, provided with an adequate knowledge of the orchestral instruments in combination, and with some idea of structural relationship between separate movements, a problem that was increasingly to occupy his attention for most of his life. The five movements of the Suite are joined by a primitive sort of thematic interreference, not in the Franckian manner but somewhat less obviously and, it must be admitted, less efficiently. The principal thematic resemblance is a characteristic dip of a fourth, which returns to its original note and is followed by an ascending third. It is this motive which begins the work and forms a part of numerous themes which follow, in particular those of the Presto (third movement) and of the ensuing Moderato.

The forms of the Suite are lucid, depending largely upon repetition and development, with some variational procedures, chiefly ornamental, in the fourth movement. The Adagio is rather loosely organized, with a recurrent rubato theme which serves as point of reference. The Scherzo is a very fast waltz-like movement not too far in mood from the second of the Two Portraits; in the finale various materials from preceding movements are cited and combined.

The orchestration of the First Suite is hybrid. Much of it is rather thick, with many doublings; other parts are conceived in soloistic terms. The contrast in this regard between the two themes of the first movement is especially pronounced; the first theme is presented in strings, horns, clarinets, and bassoons, while the second is given to a solo oboe with very slight support. But the most striking thing about the scoring is the division of the strings, testifying to the lesson Bartók had learned from Strauss: in one long section of the Adagio there are as many as nineteen different string parts, the double-basses 'divisi a tre,' the other strings 'a quattro.'

Because of the interruption in the course of its composition, during which Bartók had intensified his long work of collecting and classifying the peasant music of Hungary, the Second Suite, opus 4, for orchestra, marks a turning point in his creative career, showing simultaneous old and new elements. There is in it a great deal that may be attributed to the influence of Strauss; passages here and there have a markedly Wagnerian sound; and, while there are in the first three movements folklike elements, they are elements in whose treatment Bartók leaned heavily upon his nineteenth-century predecessors in 'national' music, among them Smetana and Dvořák as well as Liszt.

When he resumed work on the Suite after a two-year lapse, Bartók was faced with the problem of integrating the style of the movements already completed with the new style which incorporated the essence of Magyar peasant music. To the casual ear there is little difference in the two at this point, since even in the fourth movement the guiding hand is still that of Strauss. It was only later that Bartók was able to shake off the yoke of Strauss and formulate an individual idiom from the elements of the peasant music. Nevertheless there was enough difference to Hungarian ears to prevent public acceptance of the Second Suite. The unpopularity of the work was intensified by its serious, introspective tone: the philosophical and the contemplative apparently had little place in the concert halls of Budapest at the period. To the listener in mid-century the Second Suite sounds rather old-fashioned and derivative through much of its length, and it is only here and there that one can see the more significant Bartók about to materialize.

Yet there are aspects of the working-out, the manipulation of materials, that predict the methods which became characteristic of Bartók in later years. One of the most striking of these is the motivic treatment which shows up in many places: Bartók's themes are, even as early as this, chosen for their motivic richness and the possibilities of fragmentation and recombination. In spite of the late-romantic sound of this music, the methods are clearly Beethovenian. There is as yet little interval modification, and almost no inversion, both procedures which became so prominent in Bartók's later work, but the basic technique is already here. The central section of the Andante, in which two short motives from the first section provide most of the material, is an admirable illustration.

The forms of the Suite demonstrate some of the structural ingenuity that characterizes the productions of Bartók's maturity. Both the first and the third movements are monothematic, the first falling into an A-A-B-A form in which B is the development of a rather unpromising motive from A, and in which A itself is continually varied; and the third constituting a ternary form in which the motives of the second part, as indicated above, derive from the first. The second movement and the fourth have some resemblance to sonata-form designs, but they by no means fall into predictable patterns.

One other element which becomes increasingly strengthened in the course of Bartók's creative development is the contrapuntal, exemplified here by the fugue in the second movement, and to a certain though lesser extent by the imitative work elsewhere.

In 1943 Bartók revised the Second Suite, the revision largely taking the form of structural tightening. Sections of the third and fourth movements were excised, some of the material simply omitted, some rewritten in a more compact and pertinent form. The first available recording was of the original version, facilitating comparison, but later recordings agree with the revised score generally accessible.

The preluding of the harp, which occurs throughout the first and last movements, gives a bardic, improvisational flavor to the work. This is borne out especially in the first movement, with its many complete closes and its resumption of activity through the offices of the harps. What may be considered the 'theme' of the movement is a succession of short motivic passages in which a solo cello plays a prominent part, with interruptions by the other strings, much divided. The section, having begun in B♭ major, closes in D; the harps begin again in B♭ and the theme is repeated and expanded, closing this time in G major. From this point on a brusque motive which had first appeared in the sixteenth measure becomes the germinating force: while other motives are present, this is the most important element of the B section. A shortened restatement of the original theme is followed by several codas, the first of which has an 'orientalized' version of the theme in the oboe and other woodwinds, its augmented seconds affording a surprise after the euphony of the diatonic major.

The Allegro scherzando, in which one analyst found 'no less than ten themes,' [3] is structurally not nearly so complex as the statement implies; the 'ten themes' are simply motives of a far smaller number of thematic complexes which can be assigned to the more or less classical sonata-allegro pattern. This does not mean that the form of the movement is conventional: there are individual qualities about it that prevent its becoming a mere formula.

Of the multitude of motives which make up the first part of the movement, a few recur with some regularity. Among these are the rocking octaves that introduce the movement and are present, at least in spirit, through much of its length, serving a function not unlike that of the harp chords in the first movement. They accompany, from the third measure, a motive in thirds, its acciaccaturas recalling the gipsy song in *Carmen*. From here on Bartók is concerned with a succession of motives, each with its own individuality and with great possibilities for development. These possibilities remain curiously dormant, since they are scarcely drawn upon save for restatement in the latter part of the movement.

It is a subsidiary thematic complex[4] which provides the entire material for the development section, two of its motives combining to form the subject of a rather extended fugue. It has been observed that one feature of Bartók's fugues which they do not share with those of Bach is the extreme plasticity of their subjects under contrapuntal manipulation: the shape of the subject, under pressure from this side and that, does not remain constant. Even in as early a work as the Second Suite, the tendency to alter the subject is already present; at one point an eighth-note is clipped from the head motive and the subject is wedged into a 5/8 meter, while at another the head motive is rhythmically altered and sequentially prolonged.

The recapitulatory process is concerned with the motives of the first section, repeated in their original order but all somewhat remolded, while those of the second group, having supplied the development material, are scarcely touched upon until the coda, where they are reworked in a ritenuto passage that has the color of the cimbalom.[5] Later the fugue subject is given to a solo violin; whereas before it was vigorous and forthright, it appears here with a rubato and glissando which can only be considered gipsy in inspiration.[6] The exaggeration is written in, possibly indicating that it is done for purposes of mockery. After the gipsy fiddler has picked up the 'presto volante' of his theme, its fragments are tossed to the woodwind and tumble down into the very cellar of that department, where they are shredded to grotesque bits by bassoon and contrabassoon. A few fortissimo measures bring the movement to a close.

The long rubato of the unaccompanied bass clarinet that opens the Andante is closer to the Magyar in its melos. The intervallic structure is stronger in fourths; there is a modal feeling that was not present in the preceding movements, and a slightly pentatonic flavor in the melodic turns. But the source is by no means autochthonous: besides the use of an unaccompanied woodwind there are actual melodic coincidences between this and the English horn passages in the third act of *Tristan und Isolde*, particularly the octave leaps just before the entry of the strings.

The movement is much more individual than the first two. Structurally it may be considered in three sections: theme, development,

and variation, with a short coda. Two motives of the theme are of
especial importance: one at the beginning, the other, a descending
arpeggio in the shape of a seventh chord, making its appearance
in the seventeenth measure. The two sections of the development
are predicated upon these two motives, with the latter assuming the
greater significance, eventually disintegrating in an imitative passage
in muted strings, a passage that is somewhat condensed in the revised version and in consequence does not so strongly emphasize the
separation from the reprise. This restatement, in which the central
portion of the theme is excised, gives the theme to the lower woodwinds in unison, their sombre, somewhat nasal quality contrasting
strongly with the shimmering background of trills, tremolos, and glissandos. The seventh-chord motive provides the coda, and in the last
chord it is verticalized in the same way that the intervallic relationships which generate the second movement of the Concerto for
Orchestra ultimately combine into a single cadence-chord.

The finale was the subject of Bartók's most drastic revision, with
the original prolixity rewritten, compressed, or eliminated altogether.
The shape of the movement as it now stands is not really very close
to the original form; it is much more compact, with better balance,
now that much of the 'padding' has been discarded. There are only
two themes, each of which has two characteristic parts. The first
appears in the bassoon, a folklike tune in a marching pace, answered
by a second phrase in the clarinets, whose two-line treatment, in
thirds, fifths, and sixths, recalls primitive wind instruments. Both
these phrases, which are repeated and somewhat modified, show both
intervallic and rhythmic characteristics of Hungarian peasant song,
though still in a very mild form.

The second thematic group has been rewritten and greatly compressed; it first opened with an extended passage for flutes, agile and
effective but not really pertinent. The actual second theme, which
now consists of two motives only, was previously verbose, and interrupted with extraneous material. As it now stands it is perhaps too
terse, since the expansive romantic treatment of its second motive
in the recapitulation may leave the listener wondering about its
origin. The development, fairly brief, is concerned only with the
first phrase of the movement, which is, in consequence, almost absent
from the recapitulation, stretches of which are almost blatantly
Straussian, while a few bars of the coda, in horns and low strings,

strongly recall the Valhalla motive from the *Ring des Nibelungen*. Four measures from the end there is an implied bitonality in the crowning of an E♭ triad in horns and bassoons with the essentials of B♭ major in the strings, even though the latter do not provide a complete triad at any point. The cadence has a modal touch in the horn's A♭ resolving upward into the B♭ triad.

Though he withdrew the First Violin Concerto before performance, Bartók incorporated its first movement into the Two Portraits for orchestra (1907-08), modifying it only slightly, and combining it with an orchestral version of the fourteenth of the Bagatelles, opus 6.

The Portraits represent two aspects of one subject: the first an ideal rendering, the second an ironic distortion. Both make use of the 'leitmotiv' D-F♯-A-C♯,* the first in a tender, evocative mood, the second in a fast, brittle waltz, pointed up by the shrillness of the E♭ clarinets and the piccolo. The solo violin has the statement of the first-movement theme entirely without support; then the violins of the orchestra are drawn in, a desk at a time, the woodwinds and lower strings are added, and the horns, achieving the first of the two climaxes of the movement. The trumpets, trombones, and tuba are used in only four measures at the major culmination point, and the two harps are not introduced until the wave has reached its crest, broken, and subsided.

The movement conveys an impression of serenity from beginning to end, even though its polyphony is occasionally involved, as in the somewhat fugal presentation of its materials. The solo violin soars in the upper reaches of the E-string much of the time; the division of the violins and violas attenuates the sonority, and the pace (marked Andante but actually Adagio in its effect) is one of extreme placidity. The sectional structure gives the movement an air of variation without interrupting its continuity; the materials are continually renewed without losing their identity.

Harmonically the first of the Portraits is not far removed from the Second Suite. The hand of Strauss is perceptible here and there, the wraith of Wagner hovers in the background. But in some of the unexpected modulations, the melodic turnings, the contrapuntal combinations, glimpses of individuality emerge.

* See note 9, p. 316.

Of the second Portrait, little needs to be added to the brief description in the chapter on Bartók's piano music. In the scoring, purely pianistic passages have been recast in orchestral terms, ornamental additions have been made, the last few bars filled in harmonically; but there is only one significant change: at no. 12 the accompanimental pattern has been omitted from the first bar and moved into the next, effecting a change of harmony and interrupting the inexorable plunging of the original—for a comparison of the two versions makes it clear that the one for piano must have come first. It was this movement that inspired Amy Lowell's astonishing poem, *After Hearing a Waltz by Bartók* (1914):

> But why did I kill him? Why? Why?
>   In the small, gilded room, near the stair?
> My ears rack and throb with his cry,
>   And his eyes goggle under his hair,
>   As my fingers sink into the fair
> White skin of his throat. It was I! . . .

The Two Pictures (Images), opus 10, lack the unification that is effected in the Portraits by an interchange of materials. The Pictures, however, have descriptive subtitles: *Virágzás*,[7] which means simply 'Bloom,' and A *falu tánca*, 'The Village Dance.' The first is a highly perfumed Adagio in which Bartók demonstrates his preoccupation with French impressionism, with its pedals and ostinatos, its consecutive perfect intervals, and especially its whole-tone scales. It is not surprising to find these manifestations here, since Bartók had become acquainted with the music of Debussy only three years earlier, and it was not until the following year, with the founding of the short-lived UMZE,[8] that the new French music was heard in Budapest, largely through Bartók's own performance.

In the decades that have elapsed since the production of the Two Pictures, the devices of impressionism have become threadbare, and in consequence the first Picture, which marks Bartók's most intensive cultivation of the Gallic vineyards, is dated, old-fashioned. That does not mean that nothing of interest remains in it: no work of the mature Bartók is entirely devoid of interest, and this is a sensitive, even moving, aquarelle. But it is an aquarelle, as opposed to the richly pigmented oils of the Village Dance, and as such the panels of the diptych lack congruence. The second, being stronger in both rhythmic and tonal considerations, makes the first appear even paler, and obscures its very real merits.

The Village Dance itself makes prominent use of segments of the whole-tone scale, but seldom more than four successive notes comprising the Lydian tetrachord, and this has a peculiarly Bartókian sound, its tritone emphasis remaining characteristic throughout the composer's life. The dance is one of those chain-like series which are found in the Second Quartet, the First Violin Sonata, the Dance Suite, and many other works. This one assumes the garb of a rondo through the repetition of its first dance-theme, though the materials are also subjected to a considerable amount of development.

Of Bartók's purely orchestral works, the Pictures are one of the most immoderate in instrumentation. For Bartók the normal orchestra required only pairs of woodwinds, four horns, two trumpets, three trombones, one tuba, percussion, two harps (except in the concertos), and strings. Here three of each woodwind are called for, with four trumpets and a celesta. After the First Suite, opus 3, only the Four Pieces, opus 12, and the Concerto for Orchestra require so many instruments.[9] The Concerto for Orchestra, of course, was written for a specific orchestra, the Boston Symphony, and it is altogether natural that Bartók should have made the fullest use of the available instrumentation in that work. But one is justified in wondering whether the more modest demands of the others were dictated by purely musical reasons or by performance practicality.

Between the Pictures and Bartók's next orchestral work, the Four Pieces, opus 12, lies the opera *Duke Bluebeard's Castle*. Between them also lies what amounts to an almost complete change of viewpoint, a change that threatened his whole future development. Had he persisted in the direction represented by the Four Pieces, it must have led to a morass of stagnation; these pieces mark not merely a renunciation—fortunately only temporary—of the structural methods which had already served him so well, but also of the folk-conditioned style which had begun to emerge, and which was so fertile a culture for the germs of his entire later production.

It is necessary, therefore, to examine these pieces, not for their intrinsic merits but for their indication of the disaster which might have overtaken their composer.

Although Bartók frequently transcribed for orchestra pieces originally written for piano—the Rhapsody, opus 1, the Sonatina, and others—the orchestral versions of these works seldom betray their keyboard origin. So it is all the more surprising that the Four Pieces

are so obviously conceived in keyboard terms and simply transferred
to the orchestral palette. The spacings throughout are conditioned
by the mechanism of the pianist's hand; many passages can be reduced for performance by a single player, and lie idiomatically under
his fingers, while those too complex for one performer can easily be
done by two. Yet these pieces exist, in published form at least, only
in an orchestral version; there is no indication that they were conceived in any other form. On the other hand, the score of *Duke
Bluebeard's Castle*, practically contemporary with them, is almost
entirely free from the considerations of the keyboard.

The result, in the Four Pieces, is that the texture tends to verti-
cality, with little polyphony and that seldom essential, while the
harmonies run to ninth-, eleventh-, and thirteenth-chords, parallel
progressions, chromatic side-slipping, and heterophony. Even the
melodies suffer: most of them are little more than horizontalized
harmonies. There is almost none of the closely knit motivic work
typical of the works that surround this one.

Consequently these pieces, like the first of the Two Pictures, with
their loose structure and their preoccupation with color, come closer
to the impressionist ideal than any other sizable work of Bartók.
The Preludio, with its dependence upon cluster-chords and glissandos, trills, tremolos, and all the glittering arsenal of harps, celesta,
piano, triangle, pianissimo cymbals, and tam-tam, strikes a mood
fortunately absent from his other writing—a mood whose place is
taken in the later scores by the infinitely more subtle 'night music.'
Its harmonic procedures are typified by the chord with which it begins and ends: a tonic seventh in E major, to which the C♯ has been
added. The Scherzo, in a moderately fast 3/4, is somewhat static,
with regular motives mechanically repeated; only occasionally (as in
the trumpet and trombone theme with five notes in some bars) is
there a suggestion of the Bartók who was so soon to write the Allegro
molto capriccioso of the Second String Quartet.

The most notable feature of the Intermezzo is the division of the
strings, especially the violins and violas, to provide the most translu-
cent of backgrounds; in only one ten-bar section does the dynamic
level ever exceed mezzo forte, and the strings are partially muted
throughout much of the movement. The waltz-like pace is interrupted
once by an agitated stringendo passage, but resumes to close.

The *Marcia funebre*, like that in the *Kossuth* symphony, has the conventional characteristics of most funeral marches: the rushing gruppettas to long notes, the string tremolos, the kettledrum rolls, the sobbing chromatics; but unlike the earlier piece, it shows almost no Hungarian characteristics. Whereas the *Kossuth* march could have passed for the lassú of a Hungarian rhapsody, this one is so international in its style—as are the other three movements—that it makes hardly the slightest of bows to the country of its origin.

So the Four Pieces may be considered an interruption of the direct line of Bartók's evolution; their lack of economy, their dependence upon color-devices, their tendency to harmonic succulence, and especially the absence of any marked relation to the peasant music of Hungary, with which Bartók had been working for more than six years, stamp them as atavistic. They are more closely related to the Second Suite, opus 4, than to any of the scores of their own period.

After these Four Pieces, Bartók produced no exclusively orchestral composition for eleven years, though *The Wooden Prince* and *The Wonderful Mandarin*, both dramatic works, date from the period. Within that decade he had established his position and determined to a great extent, though he was as yet unaware of it, the direction of his future development. The style had moved farther and farther from the conventional standards of tonality, but as it progressed, Bartók became increasingly concerned with the technical integration of his music through motivic variation and development. The Second Quartet and the two Sonatas for violin and piano were landmarks along the way.

Then, in 1923, came the occasion for a new orchestral piece. To celebrate the fiftieth anniversary of the merging of Pest, Buda, and Óbuda into the city of Budapest, the leading Hungarian composers were asked for music for a festival concert. Kodály wrote the *Psalmus hungaricus*, Dohnányi his Festival Overture, opus 31, and Bartók the Dance Suite. The pronounced folk character of the five dances that make up the Suite shows how far he had come since the Four Pieces; all are original themes, but might well have been derived from peasant sources. In the skilful combination of these into a continuous work, and especially in the summing-up which is the finale, it becomes apparent that Bartók has now reached the fullest mastery over his materials.

The Dance Suite is not only economical but spontaneous. The

dances are of the most varied character, linked by a recurrent interlude or ritornel. Emphasizing some of the differences between his
work and that of Kodály, who based his style upon Magyar peasant
music only, Bartók pointed out [10] that the Dance Suite demonstrates
the wider range of his own folkloric interests; the first and fourth
dances resemble Arabic music in certain respects, the second, the
third, and the ritornel are Magyar in spirit, and the fifth has a
'peculiarly primitive' Romanian cast, while the finale synthesizes all
these disparate characteristics.

The opening is dark and tentative, the bassoons having a perversely phrased chromatic theme which for many bars never exceeds
a tritone in its span. With many changes of pace it reaches a climactic section, Vivo, in which a single motive is shredded above a
percussive understructure, and returns to the original darkness in
the bassoons. Then over a pedal G four muted violins introduce the
ritornel. This is a gay tune in four seven-syllable lines, in the Aeolian
mode, repeated once and then prolonged to introduce the second
dance, vigorous and rustic, with a strong resemblance to the second
movement of the Second Quartet. The ritornel is varied in clarinet
and muted violins, very calmly; the third dance is introduced by a
pentatonic bagpipe-tune first presented over a drone but soon becoming more active, both harmonically and rhythmically, with some
measure-extensions where the motives burst the bounds of the original 2/4. The second part of this dance is frenetic, with a Lydian
flavor; the skirling becomes wilder, brass and percussion stamp the
offbeats; then with three glittering measures of trills, arpeggios, and
glissandos (flute, celesta, harp, and piano), the first bagpipe-dance
returns. The piano part (four hands) provides a four-voice canon,
each entry at the space of one quarter-note, but the result is heter-
ophonic since the scoring does not permit the lines to be heard separately. Two more themes appear in this dance, which comes to an
energetic close with the first one.

After a general pause the very tranquil fourth dance is introduced
by the flutes, horns, piano, and divided strings, which establish an
almost motionless atmosphere for the languid woodwind theme, with
each succeeding phrase of which another instrument is added; the
English horn and bass clarinet have the first, and successively enter
the oboe, the clarinet, the bassoons, and finally the flutes; then they

are withdrawn in reverse order. The pattern is one of alternation throughout: the melody always appears alone, phrase by phrase, interspersed with proportionate bits of atmospheric background. It is almost as if this were music heard in the stillness of the desert night, so vividly has Bartók employed the fruits of his study of Arabic music.

Afterward the ritornel is merely suggested; then, quietly but urgently, the fifth dance begins, building up in superimposed fourths until at the beginning of the finale nine of the twelve chromatic notes are sounding simultaneously. The cumulative processes of the Suite are summarized in the last thirty pages of the score, where all the dance-themes except the fourth, together with the ritornel, are interwoven into a masterly climax and crowned with two codas. Through these final pages the tonalities rise with the excitement; the consequent suspense is almost overpowering. At the very end, an impetuous descent of the strings and woodwinds eventuates in a pseudo-tonality of C (including the notes F and G as well); the close seems complete, but there is a general pause, and in a single bar a final and satisfying cadence is reached on G, the original key.

One of the most interesting features of the Dance Suite to the analyst is the way in which Bartók manages to combine without evident disparity quite divergent tonal treatments. He follows diatonic passages with chromatic, modal with pure major, pentatonic with polytonal; and yet—and in spite of the sectional division of the form itself, and the diverse national implications of its materials— the work makes its impression as a whole. Of course the ritornel serves as a point of reference, and the finale summarizes convincingly, binding together in retrospect most of the varied elements of the piece. But because of this summing-up, and because of the insistence of the rhythms throughout, the Dance Suite is heard less as a suite than as a continuous, uninterrupted work.

The Music for String Instruments, Percussion, and Celesta is the only one of Bartók's orchestral works to display the integrative processes that characterize the Fourth and Fifth Quartets and other scores of the period. It is one of the most intensively organized of all his compositions; the subject of its opening fugue generates the entire work, and yet it is at the same time so spontaneous and so communicative that only the rare listener is likely to be aware of its complexities.

Bartók chose for this work, written for Paul Sacher and the Basle Chamber Orchestra on the tenth anniversary of that organization, a quite remarkable medium: double string orchestra with celesta, harp, piano, xylophone, kettledrums, and a miscellaneous collection of percussion under the control of one player. The sonorous possibilities of such an ensemble are obviously broad. Bartók makes the most of them; the strings are used in combination and antiphonally, both with and without the percussion instruments, and the latter are called upon for their least traditional sounds. The placement on the stage, painstakingly specified by the composer, has the two string orchestras separated by the other instruments, and the directional sense is an important factor in the sound combinations. This work, perhaps more than any other nondramatic score of Bartók, is essentially three-dimensional, requiring actual performance or stereophonic reproduction for the full realization of its spatial relations.

The subject of the slow, sinuous fugue which forms the first movement is chromatic, comprising the eight semitones between A and E, and gathering gradual momentum through the extended repetition of the head motive:

45. *Music for Strings, Percussion, and Celesta*

The four motivic divisions of the subject assume functional importance in the third movement; in the first, however, it is treated as a whole, opening out in alternate higher and lower fifths from the initial A to E♭, where the movement attains its culmination point. From here to the close it reverses the procedure, the subject itself being inverted and, from the entry of the celesta, mirrored, to close on a unison A.

The remarkable economy of the movement is demonstrated in the total absence of any materials outside the subject. There is no countersubject; there are no episodes; there are no 'free' contrapuntal lines. The entire fabric is woven with a single thread. There are intervallic changes, and the other modifications which Bartók's fugue subjects normally undergo, the foreshortenings and prolongations; but every note may be directly traced to the subject itself.

The result is a movement of almost unparalleled concentration; its six and a half minutes represent a single crescendo to a climax and a subsequent falling away to silence. It displays a unanimity which is equalled in the work of no other composer, and which Bartók himself otherwise achieved only in the Fourth String Quartet.

The remainder of the Music for Strings is devoted to exploring the implications of the fugue subject, which is subjected to all kinds of transformations. The second movement, ostensibly a sonata-form structure, derives much of its material from the motives of the generating theme, as these excerpts demonstrate:

46. *Music for Strings, Percussion, and Celesta*

These do not by any means constitute the entire material of the movement; there are other themes apparently unrelated to them, but they are of secondary importance.

The movement is exuberant and dancelike, but it encloses a quite traditional plan: exposition, development (including a fugato on the last of the excerpts above), and complete recapitulation. It does not, of course, present a single face as did the first movement; it is full of contrast, swept on by the momentum of its rhythms.

The Adagio, on the other hand, is a study in sonorities, containing some of Bartók's most subtile 'night music.' Sectional in structure, it is also roughly archlike, though not bilateral: while the first and sixth sections correspond, the fifth section is a variant of the second but in the manner of the third—one block thus serving the function of two. The fourth section thus becomes the keystone, and its purpose is emphasized by the retrograde motion which begins with the forty-ninth bar, the ensuing measures representing those just preceding, but played backwards. The successive motives of the fugue subject serve as mortar between the stones of the arch, the head motive introducing the second section, the others the third, fifth, and sixth.

But in addition to this, all the materials of the movement are directly derived from the fugue subject, whether the melismatic *tárogató* melody of the opening or the percussive octaves of the central part. There is not the compactness of the first movement, since the various sections have been designed to show differing aspects of the materials; but nevertheless it impresses one as a perfectly balanced unit.

With the arrival of the finale, the kinks of the fugue subject have been straightened, and it takes the form of a Lydian scale in a Bulgarian rhythmic pattern:

47. *Music for Strings, Percussion, and Celesta*

The architecture of the movement is rondo-like, with each recurrence greatly varied. In this respect, but this only, it resembles the finale of the Piano Sonata. Bartók here presents his rondo theme as a ternary form, the central portion of which (bars 26-43) reverts to the chromatic shape of the generating theme, prolonged at the beginning with repeated notes, martellato. The digressions (sections A, C, E)

bear little resemblance to the fugue subject, but with section F that subject summarizes what has gone before in a new version with expanded intervals and a relatively diatonic cast:

48. *Music for Strings, Percussion, and Celesta*

From here on it is a matter of closing function, of a threefold coda which presents the Bulgarian version of the theme in still different lights, one—just before the end, 'meno mosso'—the most innocent of all. The cadence is jarring but final.

The Divertimento, like the Music for Strings the result of a commission from the Basle Chamber Orchestra, bears out the contention that external events have little effect upon the character of a composer's music. Almost Mozartean in its buoyancy, it is the most spontaneous and carefree work of Bartók since the Dance Suite, and without question the least problematical. The idiom is straightforward, the harmonies are simple and preponderantly triadic, the contrapuntal outlines clear, the structural patterns free from complexity. Only the central movement has introspective overtones; surrounded as it is by movements of childlike gaiety, and with the whole work written in fifteen days, its dark melancholy can hardly be credited to Bartók's concern for European civilization, which was at the brink of destruction in his last European summer.

For the medium of the Divertimento, a 'diversion' in a very real sense, Bartók looked back to the concerted works of the eighteenth century, the concerto grosso in particular, with its concertino of solo instruments and its ripieno consisting usually of an orchestra of strings. But he did not attempt to adapt to his use the characteristic forms of the concerto grosso. Instead, he found it more appropriate for the style of the work to employ the structural ideas developed in his own preceding scores. Thus the first movement falls into the sonata-form category, the finale is rondo-like (third rondo with a long terminal development), while the Adagio is in four sections of which the first and last correspond.

The metrical plan of the first movement provokes reflection upon the intrinsic characteristics of meter in the music of Bartók. It is predominantly in 9/8 and 6/8—signatures relatively rare in Bartók's music, and almost always devoted to music of a 'soft' character, seldom to that of pronounced motivic strength or developmental capabilities. More of the 6/8-9/8 movements are slow than fast, more are relaxed than energetic. The first scherzo of the Fourth Quartet is a notable exception in tempo, but it too is 'soft' dynamically; and while the first movements of the Music for Strings and the Second Quartet are motivically rich enough, they are both fairly slow. The Sonata for Two Pianos and Percussion has a really vigorous 9/8 movement, but there the 9/8-ness of the bar is seldom perceptible through the syncopation. Only in the Divertimento and the Sixth Quartet which followed it closely is the 6/8-9/8 both forthright and strong.

Strangely enough, there are several energetic 3/8 movements in Bartók, from the second of the Two Portraits to the Concerto for Orchestra and the Third Piano Concerto. But the prevalent rhythms of Hungarian music are duple, and it was more natural for Bartók to think in 2/4 and 4/4, especially in moods that suggested a dance derivation. The more dancelike the implication, the stronger the probability of its conforming to the 2/4 pattern. In this classification lie such forceful moods as in the second movements of the Second and Third Quartets, the finale of the First Violin Sonata, much of the Dance Suite, the Piano Sonata and the First Piano Concerto, the second and fourth movements of the Music for Strings, the 'Giuoco delle coppie' of the Concerto for Orchestra.

But exceptionally, while the finale of the Divertimento is notated in 2/4 meter, it is not really a 2/4 movement at all, since the bars group themselves irregularly in metrical units of two and three; the total impression is not one of excessive speed as the signature seems to indicate, since the half-note then becomes the basic unit of bars that might have been notated as 2/2 and 3/2, at a metronome speed of 100. The tempo indication, 'allegro assai,' is therefore a misnomer.

The main theme of the first movement is presented in the simplest fashion possible: as a single melody in the violins over a steady pulse of eighth-note chords. Its basic tonality is F, with a strong suggestion of the Lydian mode (B♮) in the supporting harmonies. There are occasional chromatic ambiguities, which cloud without totally obscuring the key feeling. A second thematic member is given to the concertino and ripieno in alternating bars; this is in A major and the meter becomes slightly irregular through the excision of an eighth-note or two from an occasional measure. The real subsidiary group is less identifiable as to tonality; although it is introduced by repeated octave F's, it departs immediately into other realms. A closing group has bitonal implications, a persistent B♭ clashing with successive sharp-key harmonies until at the beginning of the development it levels off into the key of B♭.

The working-out is largely imitative, with some five-part canons in its course, each part a fifth away from the preceding one. A few bars before the recapitulation there is a crescendo which opens out from a unison through clusters of minor seconds, turning itself inside out like the passage in the last movement of the Fifth Quartet. Immediately after, a free canon in the tritone is thickened with major seconds in each part—yet neither of these passages makes its impression by the harshness of its dissonance. No stylistic disparity exists between these and the purely diatonic passages, so logically are they conceived.

The recapitulation is disguised as further development, compressed in some of its parts and extended in others, the key relationships entirely changed and the principal tonality reappearing only with the coda.

The sombre Adagio makes little use of the solo quartet; its sonorities are too rich to permit scoring for single instruments. The opening bars impose upon an undulating eighth-note bass (doubled in three octaves) a despairing theme constructed from a tiny but pregnant motive of three notes only: E♯-G-F♯. This pattern, with varying intervals but always representing motion by a wider interval and turning back by a narrower, may be considered one of Bartók's *Urmotiven*. Here it is found in its lowest terms, spanning only two semitones. Repeated a tone higher, it is prolonged to complete a phrase, which itself is immediately repeated as a canon in the upper fourth,

then temporarily abandoned while other materials come to the fore.
A second section, marked by a dramatic outcry from the violas:

49. *Divertimento*

is closely related to the equally intense cello theme which is the core
of the Marcia in the Sixth Quartet. Since both were written within
a few weeks of each other, it is hardly surprising that intervallic successions should have carried over.[11]

The third section, built upon a dirge-like ostinato in which the
three-note motive is harmonized in fourths and fifths, has a medieval
quality. Above the steady, relentless tread the trills of the violins rise
to a shriek, then die away. Here at last the solo quartet is heard, its
solacing tones twice interrupted by orchestral agitation before it leads
to the closing section. Again the first theme, but the accompanying
undulations are evanescent, and with one more piercing outcry—the
same piangendo motive which also appears in the Fifth Quartet and
the Viola Concerto—the movement closes.

The most interesting feature of the finale, which is as joyous as
anything Bartók ever wrote, is the double fugato which forms its
central section.[12] The subject is stated in unison by all the strings,
then answered in the cellos with a second subject in the violas.
Second and first violins follow, the second subject appearing with
each statement. The exposition completed (except for the double-
basses), there is a momentary pause, then a unison inversion of the
subject, which is thereupon treated as before through two more statements. At this point the solo cello enters, but decides that he will
not join the fun: he improvises a few rhapsodic bars on the subject
as the tempo becomes progressively slower. In the same spirit the solo
violin, distorting the fugue subject entirely, takes the center of
the stage with gipsy melismas and a cadenza, thus showing his kinship with that earlier fugue-despising fiddler in the Second Suite.
With the resumption of activity by the orchestra, the themes of the

first half of the movement are inverted, and there is a long reworking at the close, in the course of which a part of the first theme becomes a mawkish polka [13] in the best café tradition—the violas, like the strings in *Der Rosenkavalier,* playing *stets in dem süsslichen Wiener glissando,* while the cellos and double-basses provide a pizzicato foundation. This is one more example of Bartók's violent humor, rather more appropriate in a 'diversion' than in a more profound work. As in those other scores in which he indulged this propensity, he brings the listener out with a shock—thirteen bars of rolling triplets which pile up into clusters and a vivacissimo coda.

It is difficult to understand why the Divertimento, so readily accessible, has not become one of Bartók's most popular compositions. It offers no barriers to comprehension, and yet it has a lasting appeal; repeated hearings do not dull its freshness. There are tunes which can be whistled upon occasion and, on the other hand, there are profundities as well. Despite this it has seldom been played in America, even in the Bartók revival since his death. The only reason that suggests itself for this neglect is the reluctance of conductors to perform music that requires less than a full symphonic instrumentation. But magnitude has never been a valid esthetic criterion, and once that is discovered by those responsible for performance there will be hope for a true scale of values.

Bartók's concern for the structural conviction of his music led him, as has been seen, to provide the separate movements of many of his larger works with thematic, or at least motivic, interrelationships. Simple recapitulation, or the principle of return after digression per se, was never a part of his esthetics; but one needs only to cite the numerous 'arch-form' works of his to demonstrate how carefully and consciously they are organized.

In other works, among them the First and Second Quartets, there is a tendency to achieve structural unity through the variation and expansion of almost microscopic motives, frequently of but two or three notes; while the Sixth Quartet alone has a 'signature' theme that introduces each of the first three movements and provides the principal material of the fourth.

In the light of these procedures, it is rather curious to discover in Bartók's last four large works [14] so little of these kinds of thematic interreference. Only in the Concerto for Orchestra, in which the introductory section furnishes the motives that are developed in the third movement, and a single fleeting reference to first-movement motives in the Adagio of the Viola Concerto, is there evidence of this type of calculation. The remaining three movements of the Concerto for Orchestra, as well as the other three works, make no further use of these architectural devices, yet it cannot be said that they are in consequence any less logically consistent.

The Concerto for Orchestra was written between 15 August and 8 October 1943, as the result of a commission from the Koussevitzky Foundation. Bartók had been spending the summer at Saranac Lake, where his health showed a marked if temporary improvement. For the first performance, in Boston on 1 December 1944, he provided these notes for the program:

The general mood of the work represents, apart from the jesting second movement, a gradual transition from the sternness of the first movement and the lugubrious death-song of the third, to the life-assertion of the last one. . . The title of this symphony-like orchestral work is explained by its tendency to treat the single orchestral instruments in a *concertant* or soloistic manner. The 'virtuoso' treatment appears, for instance, in the fugato sections of the development of the first movement (brass instruments), or in the *perpetuum mobile*-like passage of the principal theme in the last movement (strings), and especially in the second movement, in which pairs of instruments consecutively appear with brilliant passages. . .[15]

Both the harmonic and the melodic elements of the Concerto represent a distillation of Bartók's maturest style: the tendency toward more strongly affirmed tonality, lucid textures, plastic rhythms, is here intensified. But at the same time earlier characteristics become prominent. The 'parlando rubato' of the introductory section, as well as the intervallic structure of its melodies, is firmly rooted in Hungarian peasant music. The forms are strongly classic in function and intention, even when, as in the second and third movements, they seem chain-like.

In the hands of a lesser composer, such a concerto might have degenerated into a mere pretext for virtuoso performance. Bartók forestalled that danger by investing the work with a thematic substance of unusual richness, of which the first theme of the Allegro vivace is a good example:

50. *Concerto for Orchestra*

It is a theme that bears Bartók's imprint upon every note. The five-note scale spanning the tritone is characteristic, as is the fourth-second-fourth progression of the group following. The immediate inversion of the whole pattern, slightly modified in the fifth and sixth measures, is also typical; and the motivic prolongation to the cadence in the sixteenth measure is as compact as a lifetime of devotion to structural economy can make it. From the second motive comes the subject of the brass fugato in the development-group, one of its fourths filled in with passing-notes:

51. *Concerto for Orchestra*

while the second exposition of the fugato inverts the same subject.

Contrapuntal possibilities are motivating forces in Bartók's choice of materials; it is sometimes surprising to find a theme which has apparently been conceived as an entity combining with itself in canon of all kinds, both rectus and inversus, and elaborate stretto, and to realize that this thematic adaptability is never adventitious. On the other hand the subsidiary theme of the first movement, with its almost complete lack of melodic motion, precludes any such possibility and yet it is by no means inconsistent with the rest.

The second movement, entitled 'Giuoco delle coppie' (game of pairs), is one of Bartók's gayest inspirations. Its chain structure brings forth the wind instruments, two by two, in short sections of dance character: the bassoons in sixths, the oboes in thirds, the clarinets in sevenths, the flutes in fifths, and finally the muted trumpets in major seconds. The simple chorale for brass instruments and side drum without snares affords a pleasant contrast, and the entire first part is recapitulated: the bassoons are joined by a third bassoon in an independent, florid counterpoint; the oboes combine forces with the clarinets, most of the time in mirror; the clarinets and flutes join in interlocking sevenths which thus become superimposed fourths; the flutes draw all the woodwinds into their part of the game; and the trumpets, still muted, are accompanied by harp glissandi and tone-cluster trills in the divided strings. The final cadence combines the instrument-pairs, still in their original interval relationships, building up a D-F♯-A-C seventh-chord.

The Elegia is made up of several themes of folklike contour, derived from the introductory materials of the first movement. In the composer's words these 'constitute the core of the movement, which is enframed by a misty texture of rudimentary motifs'—'night music' again. The more important themes are all of 'parlando rubato' character, one of them (violas, bar 62) in an eight-syllable, four-line form which, except for its chromaticism, could almost pass for an authentic peasant tune.

Folklike also is the 'Intermezzo interrotto,' in a modified song-form: A-B-A-Interruption-B-A. The A and B melodies have the plasticity of Bulgarian rhythms; the 'interruption' has no plasticity whatever. According to the composer's son, Péter Bartók,[16] while the Concerto for Orchestra was in progress Bartók heard a broadcast of the Seventh Symphony of Shostakovich; he found the so-called 'crescendo theme' so ludicrous that he decided to burlesque it in his own work. The latter part of the Shostakovich theme appears in all its vapidity. Bartók's opinion of it may be judged by the disrespectful sounds made by the brass and woodwinds after the first appearance of the 'interruption,' and by the rather vulgar quickstep version that follows. But the serene themes of the Intermezzo return and quickly erase the impression.

The finale reverts to the dance rhythms that appear in so many of Bartók's larger works. Here the two principal ideas are a sort of 'perpetual motion' in the violins, out of whose ebullition numerous motives take form, and a broad fugue subject whose manipulations are extremely complex, embodying augmentation and diminution in several ratios, the expected inversion, and quadruple stretti. Aside from the astonishing fugue which opens the Music for String Instruments, Percussion, and Celesta, this is Bartók's most intricate fugal writing. Yet it never seems 'thought out'; it is spontaneous and free-flowing throughout.

For the listener unsympathetic to contemporary music, the Concerto for Orchestra offers an admirable introduction. Its tonalities are never obscure, even when clouded and 'misty' as in the Elegia. Most of its melodies are immediately attractive, and many are easy to sing or whistle. Its particular forms are—and in consequence its over-all form is—straightforward. These attributes do not mark a weakening of Bartók's style, or an esthetic regression. On the contrary, the Concerto for Orchestra is a strong, vital work, contemporary in the best possible sense, since in it are amalgamated into a homogeneous fabric all the diverse elements which touched Bartók from his earliest creative years to the end of his life. Within it may be discovered procedures that owe their presence to his early acquaintance with Brahms, Liszt, and Strauss; others that to the discerning eye and ear indicate relationships, however remote, with Debussy, Stravinsky, Schoenberg, with Bach and his predecessors; and, inextricably interwoven, the essence of Magyar peasant music which colors all the melodies, the harmonies, the rhythms.

But beyond all this, and above it, is the superlative integration of every aspect of the composition into a pertinent and personal whole. If it is eclectic to combine oils, pigments, and canvas from recognized sources into an original and personal work of art, then this is an eclectic work and Bartók an eclectic composer. For the traces of this or that 'influence,' this or that melodic turning or rhythmic pattern, may be analyzed chemically, as may pigments and oils, and their sources discovered.

But identification of the raw materials of a work of art neither condemns nor exalts it. Its content and its significance depend upon more fundamental considerations. If the creator has something trenchant to say, and says it with the greatest sincerity of which he is capable, microscopic dissection is pointless. Bartók's Concerto for Orchestra is a great work, one of the greatest produced in this century, not because of the startling originality of its materials or the novelty of their treatment, but because the problems it poses are broad and vital ones, solved with the utmost logic and conviction.

These are qualities that make the *Symphony of Psalms* Stravinsky's masterpiece, qualities that characterize such otherwise unlike works as the Brandenburg Concertos and the St. Matthew Passion, the 'Jupiter' Symphony and the last Beethoven quartets, *Die Meistersinger*, the Four Serious Songs, *Wozzeck*. Whether or not their composers—Bach, Mozart, Beethoven, Wagner, Brahms, Berg—left the art of music much different from the state in which they found it, the importance of these works is not in technical experimentation or academic speculation, but in the complete appropriateness of the language to the vitality of the idea. They are inevitable works—works which convey such impact that it is impossible to think of their having been written in any other way. Bartók achieved this inevitability for the first time in the Fourth String Quartet, and for the last in the Concerto for Orchestra.

THE DRAMATIC MUSIC

IN THE nationalist ferment of the 1840's, the Hungarian public was ready to greet with acclaim any art-work that embodied the political philosophies of the time. Ferenc Erkel took advantage of the Hungarian state of mind to produce in the early years of that decade his operas *Báthori Mária* and *Hunyadi László*, which laid the foundations for a national lyric theater. Their immediate success was somewhat clouded by the dark years following the collapse of the 1848 revolution and the exile of Kossuth, but *Hunyadi László* in particular retained a place in the repertory. Erkel's later operas, *Bánk Bán* and others, though still performed, never attained a comparable success.

Italianate in style, these works derive melodically from the *verbunkos-palotás-csárdás* style. Later Hungarian operas leaned in the Wagnerian direction, among them those of Ödön Mihálovich and Jenő Hubay, as well as Erkel's final work, *István király* (1885). But these could hardly be considered authentically Hungarian, and when Bartók completed his one opera, *Duke Bluebeard's Castle*, in 1911, its Hungarian elements were so unrecognizable that it was rejected as unperformable in a competition for a national opera.

The custom of translating the librettos of foreign operas for per-

formance in Hungary had led to imitation of their prosodic style by
such Hungarian composers as essayed the operatic form. Discrepancies in accentuation are almost unavoidable in the Magyarizing of
Italian and German texts; the Hungarian language, lacking the
anacrusis, can be made to fit the melodies of Western music only
by Procrustean methods. Nevertheless the Hungarian opera composers of the nineteenth century preserved in their own scores the un-
idiomatic musical dialect of the translated works, and it remained
for Bartók to show, through his sensitivity to the natural stresses of
the Hungarian tongue, the possibilities of a coupling of words and
music as subtle as that of Debussy—who had performed a similar
feat with the declamation of his own language.

Duke Bluebeard's Castle reaps the harvest of Bartók's investigation of the old peasant music of Hungary, with its 'parlando rubato'
tunes in which the rhythms are directly conditioned by the spoken
inflections, and with the variable 'tempo giusto' carrying over into
a more or less inflexible meter the irregular rhythmic groupings of
the 'parlando rubato.' Consequently the problem of performance is
reversed: the vocal lines are so strongly dependent upon Hungarian
inflections that they proscribe effective translation into the Indo-
European languages.

The vocal score is published with text in German and French, as
well as Hungarian. The stresses of the German language (similar to
those of English) make it necessary to effect the translation through
words accented on the first syllable:

> Dies ist also Blaubarts Feste!
> Nirgend Fenster? Nirgend Erker?
> Nimmer leuchtet hier Sonnenschein?
> Bleibt sie eisig, ewig finster?

and the text acquires thereby a monotony not present in the Hungarian. With English, the same necessity arises; in French, however,
the absence of strong accents makes it possible to translate without
doing too great violence to the prosody. Nevertheless, it is only in
Hungarian that the work can have its fullest realization, and for that
reason among others it is unlikely to achieve production outside
Hungary as more than an operatic curiosity.

The Bluebeard legend is an ancient one. Its origin has been traced
—though without historical confirmation—to the grisly career of

Gilles de Retz, marshal of France under Charles VII, who was with Joan at Orléans.[1] Bluebeard's place in literary history was assured by Charles Perrault's *Contes du temps passé, ou contes de ma Mère l'Oie* (1697), whose pages he shares with such familiar fairy-tale characters as Tom Thumb, Puss-in-Boots, and Little Red Riding-Hood. Perrault's story tells how Bluebeard's latest wife, having against the specific warnings of her husband opened the door behind which hang the heads of her predecessors, is saved from their fate by the timely arrival of her two brothers.

In the two-and-a-half centuries since Perrault, the legend has been retold in many forms, and with numerous modifications of both plot and psychology. It was not a stranger to the operatic stage when Bartók and Béla Balázs collaborated on their version; Grétry's *Raoul Barbe-Bleue* (1789), with Sedaine's text, Offenbach's *Barbe-Bleue* (1866), to a libretto by Halévy and Meilhac, and Paul Dukas's setting of Maeterlinck's *Ariane et Barbe-Bleue* (1907) preceded it, while a few years later Rezniček's *Ritter Blaubart* was produced in Darmstadt (1920), its libretto based upon a somewhat earlier dramatic piece by Herbert Eulenberg.

Although Maeterlinck's play furnished the initial inspiration for Balázs's libretto, there are fundamental differences in both treatment and point of view. *Ariane et Barbe-Bleue* is a full-scale symbolist tragedy, with Ariane attempting to liberate Bluebeard's five previous wives; but all refuse to leave Bluebeard, who has been wounded in an uprising of peasants, and Ariane departs after freeing him from his bonds. Dukas set the work in a style more orchestral than operatic, developing his themes symphonically, transforming them according to the cyclical concept, and even providing at the end a terminal development as coda, in which the themes of the whole work are summarized. The harmonic vocabulary relies heavily upon whole-tone scales and their derivative augmented triads, and the score makes up in the brilliance of its orchestration what it lacks in harmonic and thematic vigor.

Balázs shifts the emphasis from the last wife (whom he calls Judith) to the tragedy of Bluebeard himself, and compresses the drama into a single act. Both Perrault and Maeterlinck have Bluebeard entrust the keys of the seven doors to his wife, and discover upon his return that she has disobeyed him and opened them all; Balázs has Judith open the doors in Bluebeard's presence, persuading him to give up the keys one by one. The 'blood' element, strong in Perrault (the seventh key is stained with the blood of the previous wives, and will not come clean no matter how hard it is scrubbed), appears in Maeterlinck only in the blood-red rubies that cascade from the fifth door; but in the Balázs text it is omnipresent.

Duke Bluebeard's Castle is entirely lacking in dramatic action. Its protagonists are but two: Bluebeard and Judith, the three previous wives appearing only briefly in mute roles. Before the curtain, a bard introduces the tale, and at his behest the strings begin a somber pentatonic theme in unison as the curtain rises. The scene disclosed is a great round Gothic hall with a stairway going up to a little iron door. Beyond the stairway there are seven closed doors; there are neither windows nor ornaments, and the hall is like a great cavern hewn from rock. Into its obscurity the bard disappears.

Suddenly the little iron door opens and a square of light picks out the figures of Bluebeard and Judith, his last wife. Judith has left her parents, her brother, and her betrothed to follow Bluebeard, and refuses the opportunity he offers her to escape before he closes the door. She questions him about the castle, which the light never penetrates; she touches the walls and finds them damp—and the horns and oboes reveal, in the first appearance of the blood-motive, what it is that dampens them:

52. *Duke Bluebeard's Castle*

As Bluebeard shows Judith about the gloomy castle she is confronted by the seven closed doors, which he tells her may not be opened. She strikes the first door, and from behind it come sounds as of the wind sighing through ancient corridors. Judith demands the key from Bluebeard, determined to let the light into his castle and his life. As the door opens silently, a blood-red light is projected upon the floor of the hall, and the doorway becomes a crimson gash, like a wound: it is Bluebeard's torture chamber, and Judith discovers that the walls are weeping blood. She falls to her knees and plunges her cupped hands into the light; then she insists upon opening all the remaining doors. The second discloses an armory, blood gleaming red upon the weapons; the third a treasure chamber, the jewels bathed in blood; the fourth a garden of flowers, all ensanguined. Beyond the fifth door is a panorama of Bluebeard's broad domain, over which the clouds are bleeding.

When Judith asks for the last two keys, Bluebeard refuses, telling her that she has already accomplished what she intended: the castle glows in the light from the five opened doors. But Judith will not be content until she has unveiled the last mystery, and Bluebeard reluctantly gives her one more key. As she opens the door, a shadow passes over the hall and it grows darker. Beyond is a vast expanse of still white water: a Lake of Tears. Bluebeard takes Judith in his arms and tells her the seventh door must remain forever closed.

Her head upon his shoulder, Judith asks Bluebeard whether he has loved others before her; he evades an answer. She asks whether the others were more beautiful than she; again there is no reply. In desperation she tears herself away and demands that the last door be opened; Bluebeard remains silent. The blood-motive in the orchestra becomes increasingly urgent, and Judith thinks she understands at last what is hidden from her: the blood upon the weapons, the jewels, the flowers, upon Bluebeard's whole domain, prove to her that he has slain all his previous wives. Nevertheless she must be certain, and sadly Bluebeard gives her the last key.

As it turns in the lock, the fifth and sixth doors close and the hall becomes perceptibly darker. The seventh door emits only a pale moonlight, and Bluebeard says, 'See, there are all I loved before you.'

Judith is astounded to find the three wives alive; they file out slowly, pale, richly dressed and covered with jewels, crowns upon their heads, and before them Bluebeard falls to his knees. As if in a dream, he reveals that they live unforgotten; they brought him riches, broad domains—all he possesses came from them. The first came to him at dawn, rose-adorned, and remains eternally as then; the second in the golden flame of midday, the third in the shadowy dusk. Each disappears in succession, and as the fourth door slowly closes, Bluebeard turns at last to Judith, who came to him in the star-sewn night, takes from the threshold of the third door—which in its turn closes —mantle, diadem, and jewels, and despite her protests places the mantle around her shoulders, the crown upon her head, the jewels at her throat.

'You were the most beautiful of them all,' he tells her.

They stand a moment, looking silently at each other; then, bowed beneath the weight of her mantle and jewels, Judith follows the moonlit path to the seventh door. As it closes behind her, Bluebeard says softly, 'Now is it night forever. . .' In the darkness his form disappears.

The complex problems that faced Bartók in setting *Duke Bluebeard's Castle* was not entirely unforeseen. The libretto was apparently prepared for Kodály, and Bartók is said to have set it without the collaboration of the librettist. The opera has been criticized for the absence of dramatic elements, the static quality of its action, the lack of detailed character-drawing. The last of these objections may be countered by inquiring whether any opera can be cited as a model. As for the others, the third act of *Tristan* has long static stretches; but this, of course, is only a part of a much larger work, while Bartók's is devoid of activity throughout.

Whether it fulfills the definition of opera or not, *Duke Bluebeard's Castle* is a psychologico-symbolic piece not without strong impact upon the listener. In the well-remembered beauties of dawn, midday, and dusk, and the crowning beauty of night, Balázs has drawn an allegory: Bluebeard is Everyman, whose happiness is contingent upon those he loves, but who is powerless to hold them except in memory; the fulfillment he seeks is ever denied him. In her desire to open his inner life to the light, Judith finally awakens the memory of Bluebeard's earlier loves, and is thereby condemned to join them in eternal night. The tragedy is not hers, but Bluebeard's.

In consequence the working-out of libretto and music necessitated a progressive shift in emphasis. At the beginning, Judith's is the prominent part, with Bluebeard answering her in fragmentary, laconic phrases. As the work progresses, and more and more of his mystery is unveiled, Bluebeard assumes a greater significance, until at last his role overshadows hers, and in the final pages his restrained recitative becomes impassioned song. Melodically these lines are strongly dependent upon those of Hungarian folksong: a folksong by now assimilated and extracted of its essence, so that it is adaptable to a quite un-folklike use. Many phrases show the descending contour of

peasant songs, coupled with their modal elements and—necessarily—
their rhythmic characteristics, especially the large number of isorhythmic passages in 'tempo giusto' as well as the more obvious parlando elements of the recitatives.

Formally the opera provides opportunity for a symphonic logic
with digressions: its plan is archlike,[2] beginning in darkness, progressing gradually to light with the opening of the first five doors,
and then closing in to darkness again. Bartók takes advantage of the
dramatic form to recapitulate at the close the musical elements of
the first pages. There is a progressive amplification of the minor-
second blood-motive, from its first tentative appearance as Judith
discovers the dampness of the walls to the intense passage leading
up to the opening of the seventh door; and there is as well the musical revelation of what lies beyond each of the doors.

The torture chamber is characterized by a 46-measure trill (B-A♯)
in the violins with a graphic motive—a rapid scale-line, ascending a
tritone or a fifth and returning—in flute and piccolo, whose shrill,
almost shrieking sound is especially representational. Each of the
scenes as the doors open is treated in two (or three) sections: the
first always characterizes what meets Judith's view, the second (with
the blood-motive) her reaction to it. Here the blood-motive appears
in muted trumpets (G♯-A as before).[3] The armory is represented by
a fanfare in trumpets and horns; in the second section the horns have
the blood-motive.[4] The D-major triad in trumpets and tremolo strings
depicts the treasure room with its glittering gold and jewels; and the
blood-motive (in flute, oboe, and horns)moves up to A-B♭ and B-C,
showing, for the first time, signs of development.[5]

The garden of flowers is portrayed by a horn theme against gos-
samer string tremolos; the trumpets, muted, and flutes, supported by
minor-second trills, disclose that the stems bleed.[6] As the fifth door
swings open, Bluebeard's expansive domains call forth a great orchestral tutti with full organ, in a broad theme harmonized by consecutive major triads; three times it is heard, its melody notes appearing
successively as root, fifth, and third of their respective triads. The
blood-motive appears here in the violin tremolo G against the G♯ of
the climactic chord;[7] immediately the triads turn to minor in the
trombones. In the remainder of this scene the minor seconds take
on an additional function, underscoring in an agitated passage

Judith's fatal insistence that not one of the seven doors be forbidden her, while the vocal line also is colored with them:

53. *Duke Bluebeard's Castle*

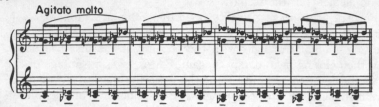

The minor seconds form an integral part of the representation of the Lake of Tears, appearing at the top of the arpeggio and in the sighing of the woodwinds,[8] since there is no further occasion for discovering the motive during the scene. But as Judith questions Bluebeard about his former wives, and finally accuses him of their deaths, the seconds pile up in a stretto above a constantly moving bass:

54. *Duke Bluebeard's Castle*

and the bass itself is presently converted into a succession of parallel seventh-chords:

55. *Duke Bluebeard's Castle*

while the culmination of the crescendo, just before Bluebeard surrenders the last key, brings the motive to its climax:

56. *Duke Bluebeard's Castle*

From this point on it is heard only a few times, when Judith tries to persuade Bluebeard to spare her the fate of the other wives; as she follows them through the seventh door, the orchestra begins the slow pentatonic theme of the opening bars, and the castle returns to darkness.

Balázs provided a story of quite another kind for the dance pantomime *The Wooden Prince* (or, more literally, *The Prince Carved from Wood*). It is the rather naive account of the love of a Prince for a Princess, who at first scorns him for a makeshift he has made from his staff but eventually turns from the plaything to the flesh-and-blood Prince. There is nothing unusual in this plot; but Balázs complicated it by writing in a Fairy who motivates the whole sequence, first by enchanting the trees and waves and setting them against the Prince as he tries to reach the castle of the Princess, and then, with an inexplicable change of heart, by providing him with the means of winning her.

The symbolism attempted here, in the introduction of the Fairy, is an extraneous, romanticized element at odds with the simplicity of the basic tale. When the wooden puppet brings in still a third element, that of grotesquerie, the direction of the work becomes confused, and a part of that confusion is perceptible in the music Bartók

wrote for it. Stravinsky, in *The Firebird*, found himself confronted
with a similar problem in the representation of natural and super-
natural elements; taking his cue from Rimsky-Korsakov's opera *The
Golden Cockerel*, in which the distinction is made on grounds of the
diatonic (for the human element) versus the chromatic (for the
magical), he used folksongs to characterize Ivan and the Princesses,
and motives based upon permutations of the tritone and the intervals
it contains to represent the Firebird and Kashchei.[9]

Bartók's solution does not entirely parallel Stravinsky's. The Prince
and the Princess are, like those in *The Firebird*, portrayed in folklike
terms, though not with actual folk themes; the Wooden Prince in
frenetic, fantastic colors not unrelated to those of Kashchei in the
Stravinsky ballet. But for the nature-music—the music that describes
the trees, the flowers, the waves—Bartók produces impressionist passages comparable to those that marked the opening of the doors in
Duke Bluebeard's Castle, as well as to the Four Orchestral Pieces,
opus 12, and the Two Pictures, opus 10.

The original production, with décor by Count Bánffy, left something to be desired from the standpoint of unification; the choreography was unsatisfactory, and for the 1935 revival, Gustáv Oláh and
Zoltán Fülop redesigned the sets and costumes in cubist terms, while
a new choreography was entrusted to Cieplinski. The discrepancies
of the work itself were further emphasized by the incompatibility of
the décor and the choreography; consequently in 1939 Oláh returned
to the original fairy-tale mood, and new dances were created, this
time by Gyula Harangozó. For the Bartók Festival in October 1948,
still further changes were made, especially in décor and staging, although the Harangozó choreography was retained.

From these numerous restagings and alterations (without taking
into consideration the performances outside of Budapest) it may
be observed that *The Wooden Prince* almost defies convincing production. Whether it is ever likely to be staged effectively is doubtful: there are so many disparate elements that it seems impossible
to co-ordinate them all. A Diaghilev might have approached a solution, but Diaghilev himself apparently thought little of Bartók as a
composer for the ballet, though he once made tentative plans for
the inclusion of a work of Bartók in an Austrian festival, in the 1923-4
season,[10] together with Schoenberg and various composers of the
eighteenth and nineteenth centuries.

The Wooden Prince begins with a long introduction largely based upon the C-major triad, as the prelude to *Das Rheingold* is based upon that of E♭ major. From the beginning to the curtain is somewhat over three minutes; the low sonorities of the first measures are gradually amplified as other instruments are drawn in, and by the time the scene is revealed and the action begins, the single chord has swollen to overwhelming proportions. Bartók's orchestra is very large here: woodwinds in fours with the addition of two saxophones, four horns, four trumpets, two cornets, three trombones, tuba, percussion (including glockenspiel and xylophone), celesta, two harps, and strings. The strings are usually divided, frequently into many groups; the celesta sometimes requires two players; and with the coloristic instrumentation used here (to a certain extent predicting the 'night music' of later works), the score glitters. The musical ideas are not always strong, and one is led to the conclusion that they are usually subservient to the orchestral sonorities.

As the curtain rises, a fairy-tale landscape is revealed. Two tiny castles are perched on hills at opposite sides of the stage. One of them, whose front wall is cut away to disclose a room with a spinning wheel and a chair, is surrounded by a stream with a bridge across it, and beyond that a forest—the trees and waves being represented by the *corps de ballet*. The Princess is playing in the wood; a Fairy works enchantment with strange, menacing gestures. The Princess is represented by a clarinet theme of gentle contour:

57. *The Wooden Prince*

As she dances, the gate of the second castle springs open, and the Prince appears on the threshold. The Fairy, with more gestures, brings the Princess back to her own castle as the Prince sets out on the way, to a marching theme of folklike character in the lower strings:

58. *The Wooden Prince*

Perceiving the Princess about to enter her door, the Prince is smitten and attempts to follow her. But the Fairy enchants the forest, the trees come to life and hinder his progress. The music for the Dance of the Trees rustles with divided string trills and tremolos, quivering scales, birdlike motives in the woodwind; all the strings have passages in whistling harmonics. The struggle of the Prince with the trees is depicted with the jagged rhythms of Magyar peasant dances.

Winning through, the Prince attempts to cross the bridge to the castle of the Princess, but the Fairy enchants the stream, and the waves lift the bridge high and prevent his crossing. The Dance of the Waves is accompanied with impressionist murmurs, scored for the harps, celesta four-hands, woodwinds, and greatly divided strings.

Despondent, the Prince falls back and considers his next move. Here Bartók characterizes the Prince's despair with a 'parlando rubato' line of pronounced Magyar feeling:

59. *The Wooden Prince*

With a flash of inspiration, the Prince takes his staff and fits it out so that it can support his cloak; this he holds up to catch the eye of the Princess, but she ignores it. The Prince places his crown at the top of the staff and again holds it up; the Princess notices it, but it makes no impression upon her. Then the Prince slashes off his golden locks and fastens them on the staff; at last the Princess is impressed and desires the plaything. She comes quickly down the stairs, but the Prince, stripped of his adornments, interposes himself. The Fairy enchants the staff, which comes to life and dances with the Princess, finally propelling her off the stage.

The music for the Wooden Prince is at first mechanical and grotesque, with clusters of adjacent notes:

60. *The Wooden Prince*

then it becomes more and more animated, its character related to the Scherzo of the Second Quartet, or to sections of the Dance Suite. Despite its barbaric abandon, it is still clearly founded on folk elements:

61. *The Wooden Prince*

(a)

(b)

(c)

Up to this point the logic of the libretto has been unexceptionable. The Fairy, as a sort of *dea ex machina*, has contrived through her control of the Princess as well as of the trees and the waves to keep the Prince from the object of his desire. She has acted thus as a guardian over the Princess in the best fairy-tale tradition. But now she reverses herself—a procedure unprecedented in fairy tales, where the good are consistently good, the bad unequivocally bad, and changes of heart never occur. The Fairy, having exercised her powers to put obstacles in the way of the Prince, now turns her efforts to eliminating them. Grief-stricken, the Prince has fallen asleep; the Fairy runs out of the wood and comforts him, bringing to life the flowers and other inanimate objects, which dance in homage before him. The Fairy restores the Prince's splendor, discovering golden curls in the calyx of a flower, a crown in another, a flowery mantle in a third. Thus adorned, he observes the Princess again, and the Wooden Prince, with whom everything has gone awry—cloak, crown, and peruke all hanging crooked.

The Princess now discovers that the real Prince is more desirable than the wooden makeshift, but the Prince, momentarily tempted, repulses her, and the forest rises against her. In her desperation she casts off her crown and mantle, and cuts off her own hair, then cowers in shame before the Prince. But he takes her in his arms, and as the trees and flowers return to their original forms the orchestra resumes its C-major triad and the curtain slowly falls.

In the light of its musical and theatrical disparities, it is rather strange that *The Wooden Prince* should have met with an enthusiastic reception when it was first performed, and that it has apparently retained interest for the Hungarian public, as witnessed by the number of mountings it has had. Musically it discloses, in addition to the influences shown by the works that preceded it—those of Hungarian and other peasant music, and of the composers who shaped Bartók's early style, among them Liszt, Wagner, Debussy, and Richard Strauss —new stylistic elements apparently derived from the ballets of Stravinsky. How much Bartók was indebted to the slightly younger Russian composer is not easily determined; in the Bagatelles (1908), for example, he showed a Stravinskian awareness of advanced stylistic possibilities before Stravinsky had been heard of, while in other early works he exhibited what Paul Bekker describes as *eine individuelle*

Begabung für das Burleske [11]—a gift which stands him in good stead for the grotesque dance of the Wooden Prince.

Structurally the pantomime is episodic, loosely linked, and with excessive emphasis upon the second and third dances—those of the trees and the waves. After these extended sections, which are more closely related to the older ballet style than to that of the post-Stravinskian period, the final sections are disproportionately compressed, so that the dénouement, such as it is, comes without preparation.

Nevertheless there are places in the score which, if they fall short of total success in their function, are still musically convincing and may stand beside Bartók's best productions of the period. In particular, the passages devoted to the Wooden Prince wear best; they contain fewer of the elements Bartók was soon to discard, and in a sense point the way to *The Wonderful Mandarin* and the later scores —though the stylistic resemblance between *The Wooden Prince* and the *Mandarin* is astonishingly slight. The bridge between the two stage works may be sought in the Second String Quartet, whose composition was begun while *The Wooden Prince* was under way, but completed a year afterward. The Scherzo of the Quartet shares the biting energy of the best parts of the ballet, while its immensely expressive outer movements avoid the shoals of glib impressionist glitter, on which the dances of the trees and waves run aground.

While *The Wooden Prince* attained performance soon after its completion, and the momentum of its success resulted in the staging of the neglected *Bluebeard*, Bartók's third and last dramatic work, *The Wonderful Mandarin*, was not given in Budapest until more than a quarter of a century after he finished it. That performance came only after Bartók's death. He had long since given up hope of its being done in Hungary; even at the time he wrote it he was not too confident as one of his letters indicates:

Who knows when my pantomime, *The Wonderful Mandarin*, will achieve performance? . . . Otherwise Galafrés should be willing to create it. [12]

The score, to a libretto by Menyhért Lengyel, was written between October 1918 and May 1919. [13] This was, of course, one of the most troubled periods of modern Hungarian history; under the circumstances it is surprising that Bartók found opportunity to write a major work during these difficult months. Yet *The Wonderful Mandarin* takes a place of importance in any listing of his music, marking as it does a further intensification of the elements already present in *Duke Bluebeard's Castle*, the Second Quartet, and *The Wooden Prince*.

Although it was staged in both Prague and Cologne (where the second performance was proscribed and the conductor, Jenő Szenkár, taken to task by the City Council), the *Mandarin* was not scheduled for Budapest until 1931, when it was intended to celebrate Bartók's fiftieth birthday—and then it was officially banned after the dress rehearsal. Another attempt to stage it, ten years later, met with a second official cancellation because of the objections of the clergy, even though the libretto had been expunged of some of its more questionable aspects. In an attempt to salvage some of the work for home consumption, Bartók had put together an orchestral suite from the ballet, which was played in Budapest by the Philharmonic Society in October 1928.

The story, lurid and fantastic, was originally set in a brothel room, to which a wanton entices men whom her accomplices beat and rob. In its various productions (and near-productions) the scene has been changed—to a dark, gas-lit street, to a ravine in a remote mountain fastness—but its locale is unimportant except as it affects the décor. After a brief but intense introduction the curtain reveals a girl and three men; the latter search everywhere for money and, finding none, order the girl to the window to attract men from the street. The first one who appears is a threadbare old cavalier who, despite his lack of money, becomes more and more insistent until the thugs leap upon him and throw him out. The girl goes back to the window and allures a timid young fellow whom the girl finds attractive but who, like his predecessor, is also penniless. He dances with her, shyly at first, then more and more passionately, until the ruffians seize him and throw him out also. The girl returns to her window and perceives to her horror the macabre figure of a mandarin, who comes up the stairs and stands motionless in the doorway. The girl struggles to quell her aversion, and dances for him; the dance runs a course from reluctance to sensuality, as the mandarin's burning eyes in his impassive face follow the dancer. She falls into his lap; he trembles with passion as he embraces her and, frightened, she tries to elude him. The chase becomes furious; the mandarin reaches the girl and they struggle.[14] The ruffians spring upon him and strip him of his jewels and money. Then, debating how to dispose of him, they try first to smother him under the pillows, but he will not die: his eyes look longingly at the girl. They stab him with a rusty sword, but he still stands, and tries to reach the girl. They hang him from a chandelier; it falls, and in the darkness the mandarin glows in a greenish light. Then the girl, overcome with compassion, embraces the mandarin; his longing fulfilled, his wounds at last begin to bleed, and he dies as the curtain falls.

The musical characterization in *The Wonderful Mandarin*, unlike Bartók's other dramatic works, is razor-sharp. While the characters in *The Wooden Prince* were painted in only the most general terms, and those of Bluebeard and Judith—even with benefit of text—hardly emerge 'in tondo,' there is no mistaking the participants in the *Mandarin* from the music assigned to them. The stylistic elements are no longer rhapsodic or improvisatory; the materials are organized with an intensity comparable to that of the Second Quartet. This is particularly true of the harmony, whose structure derives mainly from two elements: a three-note chord composed of superimposed tritone and perfect fourth (*a*), and an arbitrary scale which spans an augmented octave (*b*):

62.   (a)   (b)

As the illustration shows, the disjunct tetrachords of the scale are embraced respectively within the perfect fourth and tritone, while the outer notes of scale and chord provide the minor second (= minor ninth) and major seventh. The chromatic element exemplified by these latter intervals is subjected to expansion as the work progresses, but when the melodic lines become chromatic, the harmonic foundation is usually reduced to an ostinato of stamping chords related to, if not entirely constructed from, these few intervals.

Nevertheless, within the frame of these relationships, Bartók was able to devise a score in which characters and action are portrayed with distinctive strokes. The furious introduction, intended to represent the rush of metropolitan traffic outside the girl's room, is an exception: it is impersonal enough to permit a transfer of scene without serious anomaly. But as the girl ensnares the men, the successive clarinet cadenzas are the embodiment of erotic gesture; the elderly rake and the callow youth are painted in convincing colors; the mandarin himself betrays his ancestry in a pentatonic theme harmonized by two lines of tritones:

63. *The Wonderful Mandarin*

The seductive dance of the girl before the mandarin, in a languid waltzlike passage which recalls the first of the Ady songs,[15] grows more and more sensual; the feverish trembling of the mandarin, as depicted in the orchestra, is embarrassingly vivid; the chase, worked out fugally, is overwhelmingly violent. The unmitigated bareness of the plot placed upon Bartók the onus of maintaining emotional tension at a high level through his music; it is to him that credit is due for lifting the ballet far above the crassness of its libretto.

The Wonderful Mandarin's more vehement passages show a spiritual kinship to the *Allegro barbaro,* as well as to the earlier ballets of Stravinsky, in their almost primordial force. The music does not seek to shock through brute ferocity; its paroxysms are held within bounds, frequently by means of ostinatos. The rhythmic element is predominant, though somewhat less jagged than in *The Rite of Spring,* which must have had a direct influence upon it.

After its long neglect, *The Wonderful Mandarin* has since 1946 been played frequently in Budapest; [16] there have been performances in various countries of Europe, and in September 1951 it was finally given in New York, with choreography by Todd Bolender, who added some touches of obscure symbolism to the story. So far it has not been taken up by any of the major ballet companies, and, like *Duke Bluebeard's Castle,* it shows no sign of becoming a part of the standard repertory. The explicitness of its action militates against its acceptability even in a society not noted for its puritanism, and except for an adventurous production at rare intervals, the *Mandarin* is likely to be known only through the orchestral suite drawn from it.

After 1919, Bartók made no further attempt to conquer the dramatic field. The odds against him were too great: *Bluebeard* had taken seven years to reach the boards, and though *The Wooden Prince* was more fortunate in that respect, still both these works were for many years unperformed in Hungary because the librettist, Béla Balázs, was a political exile, and Bartók would not consent to have his name suppressed. *Bluebeard* had then had only eight performances, and it was more than fifteen years before it could again be heard in Budapest. *The Wooden Prince* in addition suffers from a preposterous libretto, a lack of proportion, and a certain stylistic discrepancy in the music. Although Bartók years later extracted a suite from the score, it has seldom been performed, and since it demands very large instrumental resources, it is unlikely that it will be taken up by many orchestras.

Had the theater shown more interest in Bartók, and had his three stage works not been pursued by misfortune, he might have greatly enriched the repertories of opera and ballet. Discouraged by the impediments placed in his way, he devoted himself to works he could be reasonably sure of bringing to performance—piano music and concertos he could play himself, chamber music, folksong transcriptions. From this time on he never undertook an orchestral work without a commission. The Dance Suite, the Music for Strings, Percussion, and Celesta, the Divertimento, and the Concerto for Orchestra, as well as the Concertos for violin and viola, were all commissioned; only the *Cantata profana*—of the scores requiring large resources— was written without specific performance in view. The theater's loss is the great gain of the concert hall.

B ÉLA BARTÓK'S ardent spirit enlightened every field to which he turned his attention.

Unsatisfied with his early compositions, he devoted his energies to becoming one of the finest pianists of his time, and shared that side of his nature for nearly thirty years with students who still carry on his ideas in their performance and their teaching. As a virtuoso he unselfishly lent his talents to the encouragement of his contemporaries by the performance of their music.

Almost by chance he discovered the vast reservoir of peasant song in his native country, previously unplumbed and on the brink of disappearance. Enlisting the services of a few other enthusiasts, he systematically collected and scientifically classified thousands of melodies from Hungary and other countries; his musico-ethnological publications, both books and periodical articles, have greatly enriched the store of knowledge concerning the Magyar, Romanian, Slovakian, and other peoples.

And from the elements of this folk music he achieved a personal compositional style both logical and expressive, of a significance equalled by very few in his time. The impact of his creative genius will long be felt, not only in Hungary where the younger composers have an Antaeus-like contact with its sources, but also in America and western Europe where its influence is already apparent.

The line of Bartók's creative development is more direct than that of most of his contemporaries. No new tendencies are to be observed in the four major works which he wrote in the United States, but only the confirmation and continuation of the creative directions demonstrated by the scores which preceded them. From the Fourth String Quartet on, his tonalities are more sharply defined, his melodies more folklike and frequently of a highly organized motivic structure, his harmonies tending toward greater lucidity or even toward extreme simplicity, his rhythms vital and varied. Polyphonic manipulation is intensified, with stress on canon, fugato, and free imitation. Thematic inversion is everywhere present, but the later works make little use of retrograde or cancrizans forms.

Formally, Bartók seldom strayed far from the fundamental principles of classical structure, but as time went on he found himself looking to earlier models than Haydn and Mozart: to Bach and the pre-Bach period for continuous or additive forms as opposed to the developmental and other closed forms of the Viennese composers. But in none of these did he feel confined or hampered; he adopted the basic principles, not the textbook patterns, and whether he wrote in a classical or a pre-classical 'form,' the structure took its ultimate shape from the logic inherent in its own materials.

Now that Bartók's work may be perceived in its entirety, its evolutionary line becomes its most striking aspect. In no other recent composer is there to be observed such an undeviating adherence to the same basic principles throughout an entire career. Schoenberg perhaps comes closer than many others, but his sharp break with tonality negates the tendencies of his early work. Hindemith began, like Bartók, with Brahms, but in the 1930's established a harmonic theory, ostensibly based upon acoustical experimentation, to which he adhered for the rest of his life. Stravinsky changed course many times after *The Firebird*—from Russian pictorial nationalism through the neo-classical and the neo-baroque to a post-Webernian dodecaphony. Honegger never succeeded in achieving a consistent idiom after experiments of many kinds; while Milhaud, despite his intensive cultivation of polytonality, produced few works of real distinction. With Bartók there were frequent additions to his creative equipment, but seldom subtractions; 'influences' were quickly assimilated, and no matter from what source, they became so personally a part of his style or his technique that their gravitation lost its pull and he continued undeviatingly in his own orbit.

In every age there have been great innovators; but every period of musical history has been crowned with the work of composers who brought the practices of their own time into a homogeneous and consistent flowering—the highest musical synthesis of the era. Impossible as it is to predict the ultimate verdict, it now seems likely that Bartók was such a composer. It is easy to lose sight of the direct line of his creative development: to take the manifestations of a given work or a given period as typical and to decide on that basis that Bartók was himself primarily an experimenter. But such an evaluation ignores the far more important synthetic aspect of his art. He himself said, 'I do not care to subscribe to any of the accepted contemporary musical tendencies. . . My ideal is a measured *balance* of these elements.' [1]

And that 'measured balance' is apparent in all of his later music, as it is in his own character and intellect. Constantin Brăiloiu's summary is succinct:

Like the poet, he followed his own road and held his head high. If art has lost in him a master, and science a luminary, this world of ethical conjecture in which we live has lost a man, in the fullest sense of the term: honest, without reproach, and—in a word—right.[2]

I. Biographical Study

1881-1905

1. Not Yugoslavia, as several writers indicate, apparently copying from Kodály's article in *La Revue musicale*, 1 March 1921.
2. Published in the second volume of Bartók's letters (see below), pp. 203-17.
3. 'Selbstbiographie,' in *Musikblätter des Anbruch* (Vienna), 1 March 1921, pp. 87-90.
4. II vols., ed. by János Demény. Budapest, 1948, 1951. These will hereinafter be abbreviated as *Lev.* I, *Lev.* II.
5. Letter to Wilhelmine Creel, 17 August 1943. *Lev.* II, pp. 178-9.
6. *Drei Lieder für eine Singstimme*. Facsimile of one of the songs in *Lev.* I, pp. 203-5.
7. *Lev.* II, p. 17.
8. *Lev.* I, p. 10.
9. Ibid. p. 11.
10. Born Emma Schlesinger; her family took the name Sándor.
11. *Budapesti Napló*, 22 October 1901.
12. *Lev.* II, p. 216.
13. 'Selbstbiographie' (1921).
14. Principal collections: Színi, Károly: A *magyar nép dalai és dallamai* (Pest, 1865); Bartalus, István: *Magyar népdalok, egyetemes gyüjtemény* (Budapest, 1873-96, VII vols.); Kiss, Áron: *Magyar gyermekjáték-gyüjtemény* (Budapest, 1891).
15. *Lev.* I, p. 22.
16. *Lev.* II, p. 217.
17. Ibid. pp. 37-8.
18. The latter was published, together with the Study for the Left Hand and two Fantasies, as Four Piano Pieces.
19. *Lev.* II, p. 51, letter of 29 October 1903.
20. Ibid. pp. 53-4, letter of 16 December 1903.
21. *Vossische Zeitung*, Dec. 1903, quoted in *Zenetudományi Tanulmányok*, II:409.
22. Volkmann (1815-83) was professor of composition at the Academy of Music in Budapest from 1878 until his death; Koessler succeeded him. Two sets of variations for piano are listed in *Robert Volkmann, sein Leben und seine Werke*, by Hans Volkmann (Leipzig: Hermann Seemann Nachfolger, 1903): one on the *Harmonious Blacksmith* theme by Handel (opus 26), the other on the *Rheinweinlied*. The former, dedicated to Hans von Bülow, is no doubt the one Bartók played.

23. Liszt, Ferenc: *The Gipsy in Music*. London: William Reeves, n.d., vol. II, pp. 290-95.

24. For a discussion of the parallel problem of Spanish folk music versus gipsy music, see Manuel de Falla's *El 'cante jondo'* (Granada: Editorial Urania, 1922), also J. B. Trend's *Manuel de Falla and Spanish Music* (New York: Alfred A. Knopf, 1934, pp. 20-35).

25. In 1950 Gyula Kertész and Zoltán Kodály undertook the recording of peasant music in the district around Mohács, discovering that many singers who had been recorded in the 1930's were still accessible. Comparison of the records of the two periods disclosed a pronounced deterioration of the peasant music, even in so short a time.

26. Magyar peasant music is preponderantly monodic, unaccompanied.

27. Bartók, Béla: *A magyar népdal*. Budapest: Rózsavölgyi, 1924. (In English: *Hungarian Folk Music*. London: Oxford University Press, 1931.) For quick reference this will hereinafter be abbreviated HFM.

28. HFM, p. 80. For Bartók's discussion of the interrelationships between Hungarian peasant music and that of neighboring countries, see *Népzenénk és a szomszéd népek népzenéje* (Budapest: Ed. Somló, 1934).

29. *Lev.* I, p. 56, letter of 15 August 1905, to Irmy Jurkovics.

30. Ibid. pp. 53-4.

31. Ibid. p. 61.

32. Ibid. p. 57.

33. Ibid. pp. 57-8.

34. Ibid. pp. 58-9.

35. Ibid. pp. 60-61.

36. *Lev.* II, pp. 70-81.

37. *Lev.* I, p. 68, letter of 10 September 1905.

1906-1921

1. *Lev.* II, p. 185, letter of 30 January 1944, to Joseph Szigeti.

2. *Lev.* I, p. 75, *Lev.* II, p. 59, letter of 11 April 1906.

3. See, for example, Bartók's review of *Das Lied der Völker*, vol. XII, in *Musical Quarterly*, April 1947 ('Gypsy Music or Hungarian Music?').

4. *Lev.* II, pp. 65-70.

5. Kienzl, Wilhelm. *Im Konzert: Von Tonwerken und nachschaffenden Tonkünstlern empfangene Eindrücke.* Berlin: Allgemeiner Verein für Deutsche Literatur, 1908, pp. 155-6.

6. *Lev.* I, pp. 80-81.

7. Ibid. pp. 81-2 (1907).

8. Randall Thompson, letter to the author, 26 July 1951.

9. Wilhelmine Creel Driver, letter to the author, 12 August 1950.

10. 'Selbstbiographie.' *Musikblätter des Anbruch*, 1 March 1921.

11. Vallas, Léon. *Claude Debussy, His Life and Works.* Translated from the French by Maire and Grace O'Brien. London: Oxford University Press, 1933, p. 61.

12. Eschman, Karl, *Changing Forms in Modern Music.* Boston: E. C. Schirmer Music Co., 1945. Chapter III: 'The Musical Sentence and Its Harmonic Punctuation.'

13. See Example 2, p. 122.

14. *Lev.* II, p. 83, letter to Etelka Freund, 28 June 1908.

15. Ibid. p. 84, letter to Etelka Freund, 31 July 1908.

16. The lassú of the Rhapsody, opus 1, had of course been published in 1908.
17. *Lev.* II, p. 86, letter of autumn 1908.
18. Ibid.
19. *Lev.* II, p. 87, letter of 3 January 1909, to István Thomán.
20. Ibid. p. 87, letter of 3 January 1909, to Etelka Freund.
21. Letter of Imre Waldbauer to the author, 31 August 1950.
22. His letter of 26 December 1909 (*Lev.* II, pp. 90-91), is written partially in the first person plural.
23. *Lev.* II, p. 91, *f.n.*, letter dated 17 December 1909.
24. Ibid. p. 91, letter to Etelka Freund, 5 January 1910.
25. Thomson, Virgil. *Music Right and Left.* New York: Henry Holt & Co., 1951, p. 127.
26. Vallas, Léon, op. cit. p. 223.
27. *Új Magyar Zeneegyesület* [New Hungarian Musical Society].
28. On 24 November 1911, Bartók wrote from Szabadka (*Lev.* II, p. 92): 'I am here not because of folksongs but because of the Szabadka Philh. Society. Unfortunately in this problematical affair I haven't a free hand, and must depend upon the decision in B. Well, there's already so much trouble with this UMZE that I wish it were in the depths of bottomless hell.'
29. The journal of the Hungarian Ethnographical Society.
30. 'A magyar zenéről' (*Válogatott zenei írásai*, pp. 10-11. For quick reference this will hereinafter be abbreviated VZI).
31. 'Mi a népzene?' *Új Idők*, 1931 (VZI, pp. 19-21).
32. See Bartók's article, 'Race Purity in Music,' in *Modern Music* (New York), vol. XIX, no. 3, March-April 1942.
33. Bartók, Béla. 'Hungarian Music.' *American Hungarian Observer* (New York), 4 June 1944, pp. 3, 7.
34. *Lev.* II, pp. 95.
35. Ibid. pp. 95-6.
36. 'A Biskra-vidéki arabok népzenéje,' *Szimfónia* (Budapest), 1917.
37. *Lev.* I, pp. 85-6, letter of 2 August 1915.
38. Ibid.
39. Ibid. pp. 88-9, letter of 21 March 1917.
40. Ibid.
41. Ibid.
42. Oláh, Gustáv. 'Bartók and the Theatre.' In *Béla Bartók, A Memorial Review.* New York: Boosey and Hawkes, 1950, pp. 54-60.
43. It was this recording (Polydor 66425-8) that introduced the author to Bartók's music in 1928.
44. 'A bécsi nagyszakállú'—in reference to the beard worn by the publisher out of admiration for Brahms, whom he fancied he resembled.
45. *Lev.* I, pp. 90-92, letter of 9 June 1919.
46. The communist government introduced the 'white money' for internal use, sending all the old currency abroad to buy munitions, with which Béla Kún's Red Army invaded Slovakia. But the peasants would not sell their produce for the new currency, and the city-dwellers were threatened with famine.
47. *Lev.* I, pp. 89-90, letter of Márta Bartók to her mother-in-law, Whitmonday 1919.
48. *Lev.* I, p. 92.
49. Ibid. pp. 93-4.
50. Ibid.

51. Ibid. pp. 94-5, letter of 28 November 1919.
52. Ibid.
53. *Erdélyi magyarság népdalok* (with Kodály), 1923; *Die Volksmusik der Rumänen von Maramureş*, 1923; *A magyar népdal*, 1924; *Népzenénk és a szomszéd népek népzenéje*, 1934; *Die Melodien der rumänischen Colinde*, 1935. For editions in other languages, see the bibliography.
54. Bartók, Béla. 'Selbstbiographie.'

1921-1945

1. *Lev.* I, p. 106, letter of 5 April 1923.
2. Ibid.
3. 14 March 1922.
4. For further discussion of the Violin Sonatas, see pp. 205-11.
5. Bekker, Paul. *Klang und Eros*. Stuttgart & Berlin: Deutsche Verlags-Anstalt, 1922, pp. 77-82.
6. *Lev.* II, pp. 105-6, letter of 22 July 1923.
7. *Lev.* I, pp. 107-9, letter of 13 August 1923.
8. Ibid. p. 109, letter of 10 September 1923.
9. Haraszti, Emil. *Béla Bartók, His Life and Works*, p. 27.
10. Letter to the author, 10 October 1950.
11. Pages 243-5, 426-7, 460-61.
12. Pages 214-24. The other members of the committee were Arnold Bax, Sir Hugh Allen, Edward J. Dent, Eugene Goossens, A. Eaglefield-Hull, Donald Tovey, and Ralph Vaughan Williams.
13. Péter Bartók, son of Bartók's second wife, Ditta Pásztory, was born in 1924.
14. Lambert, Constant. *Music Ho! A Study of Music in Decline*. London, Faber and Faber, 1934; rev. ed. 1937, pp. 122-3.
15. Bartók, Béla. 'Der Einfluss der Volksmusik auf die heutige Kunstmusik.' *Melos* (Berlin), 1920.
16. A sort of bread-pudding.
17. *Lev.* I, p. 113, letter of 22 July 1927. Frank Whitaker ('A visit to Béla Bartók,' in *Musical Times*, 1926) quotes Bartók's criticism of Poulenc and his confrères: 'They started by being simple and they have ended by being simpletons.'
18. Becker, Harry Cassin. 'Béla Bartók and His Credo.' *Musical America* (New York), 17 December 1927.
19. *The New York Times*, 23 December 1927, p. 16.
20. Bartók, Béla. 'The Folksongs of Hungary.' *Pro Musica* (New York), 1928. (VZI, pp. 14-17).
21. Bruno David Ussher, in Los Angeles *Express*, 12 January 1928.
22. *Sic*. The only really significant choral work, the *Cantata profana*, was still to be written.
23. *Lev.* I, p. 115, letter of 9 January 1928.
24. *ügyvéd*. The Spanish word *abogado* means advocate, but *avocado* is a corruption of the Spanish *aguacate*.
25. *Lev.* I, pp. 116-17, letter of 18 January 1928.
26. Halperson, Maurice. 'Béla Bartók Explains Himself.' *Musical America* (New York), 21 January 1928.
27. The second prize of $4000 was divided between H. Waldo Warner and one Carlo Jachino; Warner also received the third prize of $2000—thus exceeding by a thousand dollars the awards of the first prize winners.

28. *Lev.* II, pp. 108-9, letter of 29 October 1928.
29. Sacher, Paul. 'Béla Bartók zum Gedächtnis.' *Mitteilungen des BKO* (Basle), 17 November 1945.
30. By the decree of 17 September 1930.
31. *Lev.* I, pp. 122-6, dated Mondsee, 13 July 1931.
32. Ibid.
33. *Lev.* II, p. 110, fragment of a letter to Paula Bartók, dated 15 August 1931.
34. *Anbruch* (Vienna), February-March 1932, p. 60.
35. Quoted in *Anbruch* (Vienna), September 1934.
36. *Népzenénk és a szomszéd népek népzenéje.*
37. *Melodien der rumänischen Colinde (Weihnachtslieder).*
38. See his letters to Imre Deák, in *Lev.* II, pp. 114-15.
39. Letter to the author, 25 March 1952.
40. He also used ivory ear-plugs to deaden extraneous sounds while he composed (cf. *Lev.* I, p. 119, letter of 26 August 1930).
41. According to his letter to Imre Deák, dated 5 March 1935 (*Lev.* II, p. 114). Other sources give the date as 1935; and Bartók's address on assuming the new chair ('Liszt-problémák') is dated 1936 in vzi, pp. 70-76.
42. Unidentified. The information on which this section is based is drawn from Bartók's article, 'Népdalgyüjtés Törökországban' (*Nyugat*, 1937), and Saygun's article, 'Bartók in Turkey' (*Musical Quarterly*, 1951).
43. Szigeti, Joseph. *With Strings Attached.* New York: Alfred A. Knopf, 1947, p. 271.
44. *Lev.* II, pp. 121-2, letter to Mrs. Oscar Müller-Widmann, dated Brussels, 3 February 1937.
45. Ibid.
46. Letter to Zoltán Székely, dated Budapest, 12 January 1937.
47. *Lev.* II, pp. 122-4; letter to Mrs. Müller-Widmann, dated 24 May 1937.
48. Sacher, Paul. 'Béla Bartók zum Gedächtnis.'
49. Letter of 31 January 1938, original in English; published in Hungarian in *Lev.* II, pp. 127-8.
50. *Lev.* II, pp. 130-33; letter of 13 April 1938, to Mrs. Müller-Widmann.
51. Ibid.
52. Ibid.
53. Hawkes, Ralph. 'Béla Bartók, A Recollection by His Publisher.' *Tempo* (London), 1949.
54. *Lev.* II, p. 136, letter to Mrs. Müller-Widmann, dated London, 22 June 1938.
55. In the United States, everything he published before 1912, when reciprocal copyright arrangements with Hungary were effected, is in the public domain.
56. Dated 31 December 1938, however, since Székely asked for a more brilliant ending.
57. 24 October 1938. Excerpt: 'It is a shame que nous n'avons pas immédiatement répondu après avoir reçu les nouvelles és hogy nem kiáltottunk levélben: evviva il Francesco Jacopo, vive le petit François Jacobe, éljen a kis Ferencjákob sokáig mindenkinek örömére és szüleimek boldogságára, hurrah! živio! så traiască! Yasasîn küçüh oğlunuz! . . . I am afraid you will not quite understand my very genuine Hungarian expressions but I can't help it: in writing to you my mind poures out the most colorful words— Et puis je n'ai pas voulu faire usage de questa maladetta lingua dei nostri vicini, que j'abhorre plus que jamais.'

58. Letter of 10 January 1939 (original English).
59. *Lev.* I, pp. 130-32.
60. Letter to Mrs. Székely, dated Basle, 9 March 1939 (original English).
61. Sacher, Paul. 'Béla Bartók zum Gedächtnis.'
62. *Lev.* I, pp. 132-3.
63. In *Lev.* II, pp. 203-17.
64. *Lev.* II, p. 147, letter of 2 October 1939, to Imre Kún. See also: Szigeti, J. *With Strings Attached*, p. 325.
65. *Lev.* II, pp. 149-50; letter of 2 April 1940, to Mrs. Müller-Widmann.
66. Howard Taubman (14 April 1940).
67. *Lev.* II, p. 151, letter of 17 May 1940.
68. Ibid. pp. 151-3, letter of 6 September 1940, to Mrs. Müller-Widmann.
69. Ibid. p. 153 (dated 4 October 1940).
70. Ibid. pp. 153-4; letter to Mrs. Müller-Widmann, dated Geneva, 14 October 1940.
71. Ibid.
72. *Lev.* I, pp. 137-40; letter to Béla and Péter Bartók, dated Forest Hills, 24 December 1940.
73. *The New York Times*, 26 November 1940.
74. *Lev.* I, pp. 137-40; letter of 24 December 1940.
75. Letter of 8 December 1941, in possession of Victor Bátor.
76. Bartók, Béla, and Lord, Albert B. *Serbo-Croatian Folk Songs*. With a fore-word by George Herzog. New York: Columbia University Press, 1951.
77. According to Dr. Herzog these are not publishable as a unit, but will be incorporated with other materials on which work is still progressing at Harvard University.
78. 17 October 1941 (original English); published in *Lev.* II, pp. 165-6.
79. Ibid.
80. *Lev.* II, pp. 162-3, letter dated Riverton, Vermont, 26 August 1941.
81. 1 March 1942 (original English); published in Hungarian in *Lev.* II, pp. 169-70.
82. 31 December 1942 (original English); published in Hungarian in *Lev.* II, pp. 173-5.
83. Ibid.
84. Ibid.
85. Olin Downes, in *The New York Times*, 22 January 1943.
86. American Society of Composers, Authors, and Publishers. Although Bartók was not a member, he did belong to the British Performing Right Society affiliated with ASCAP.
87. Letter of 28 June 1943, to Mrs. Creel (original English); published in Hungarian in *Lev.* II, pp. 176-8.
88. Ibid.
89. Letter to Mrs. Creel, dated 17 August 1943 (original English); published in Hungarian in *Lev.* II, pp. 178-9.
90. Letter to Mrs. Creel, dated Asheville, 17 December 1943 (original English); published in Hungarian in *Lev.* II, pp. 180-82.
91. Ibid.
92. The sequence is untranslatable: *Hizom. Elhizom, Széthizom*. The prefix *el-* is intensive; *szét-* implies motion asunder.
93. *Lev.* II, pp. 183-5; letter to Joseph Szigeti, 30 January 1944.
94. Ibid.

95. Letter to Mrs. Creel, 17 December 1943 (original English); published in Hungarian (with significant omissions) in *Lev.* II, pp. 180-82.
96. Letter to Mrs. Creel, 17 December 1944 (original English); published in Hungarian in *Lev.* II, pp. 192-5.
97. They had lived for some time in the Bronx, at 3242 Cambridge Avenue, after leaving Forest Hills.
98. *The New York Times*, 27 November 1944.
99. Letter to Mrs. Creel, 17 December 1944.
100. Ibid.
101. Letter of 25 December 1944, published in Hungarian in *Lev.* II, pp. 195-6.
102. Letter to the author, 16 May 1950.
103. Letter of 6 June 1945, retranslated from the Hungarian of *Lev.* II, p. 197.
104. *Lev.* II, pp. 199-200; letter of 21 July 1945, to Mr. and Mrs. Pál Kecskeméti.
105. Letter to Mrs. Creel, dated 13 July 1945. The paragraph quoted was —understandably—omitted from the published version of the letter, in *Lev.* II, p. 199.
106. So spelled in his letter of 21 July 1945. An etymologist might find a relationship between the word *chipmunk* (of American Indian derivation) and the Hungarian *csíkos mókus* ('striped squirrel').
107. *Lev.* II, pp. 199-200; letter of 21 July 1945, to Mr. and Mrs. Kecskeméti.
108. *Lev.* I, pp. 150-51; letter to Eugene Zádor, 1 July 1945.
109. *Lev.* II, p. 201; letter of 4 August 1945, to Pál Kecskeméti.
110. Serly, Tibor, 'Story of a Concerto, Bartók's Last Work.' *The New York Times*, 11 December 1949.

II. The Music of Bartók

The Piano Music

1. This seventh-chord is, of course, the only one possible within the pentatonic scale, and it is undoubtedly because of Bartók's peasant music research that it comes into later prominence.
2. Literally 'Twisting Brook'—curiously appropriate for the origin of these melismatic tunes.
3. The translation as it appears in the Boosey and Hawkes edition is unfortunate, since 'popular' and 'folk' are by no means synonymous in present usage. Three Folksongs from the Csík District is a more accurate rendering.
4. Nüll, E. von der, *Béla Bartók, ein Beitrag zur Morphologie der neuen Musik*, p. 75; also *Lev.* I, p. 117.
5. Haraszti, E., *Béla Bartók, His Life and Works*, p. 35.
6. Milhaud quotes a few bars of this Bagatelle in his article, 'Polytonalité et atonalité,' *La Revue musicale*, 1 February 1923, analyzing it as in C♯ minor in the upper part, F minor in the lower, but ignoring the feeling of finality which establishes the mode. Through a curious typographical error the staves are marked *violon* and *violoncelle*, and Marion Bauer refers to the violin and violoncello parts of the Bagatelle in her *Twentieth Century Music* (1933), p. 231, overlooking the fact that the instrumental indications belong with an excerpt from Ravel's Sonata for violin and violoncello at the top of the next page.

7. His concern with exactness of notation is apparent throughout his life, and it extended to every field, not merely music. In one of his early letters (1902) he uses the sign ?! and writes, 'This is the so-called combined question-and-exclamation mark.' Another time he writes ? with the comment, 'I recommend this to your attention, this question-mark-with-comma, which I just invented. Take it up in your curriculum, to make your students acquainted with this device' (*Lev.* I, p. 20).

8. Demény, J., *Bartók élete és művei*, p. 66.

9. Bartók called it 'your own Leitmotiv' in a letter to the violinist Stefi Geyer (1907) [*Lev.* II, p. 80]. It also appears in the thirteenth Bagatelle, transposed to Db, at the point where 'she dies . . .' (*meghalt*).

10. Originally published as *Gyermekeknek*, II vols., and *Pro děti*, II vols., 85 pieces in all. The 1945 revision includes only 79 pieces; it is to this version that the discussion relates.

11. Bartók, B., 'The Relation of Folksong to the Development of the Art Music of Our Time,' *The Sackbut*, 1921.

12. The first Elegy is dated February 1908, the second 1909.

13. As in the Sonata for Solo Violin, IV:100.

14. As in *Contrasts*, III:34.

15. The first is dated Nov. 1908, the second May 1911, the third 1910.

16. In this connection see also the fugue subject in the Music for String Instruments, Percussion, and Celesta, and the viola theme in the Concerto for Orchestra, III:62-72.

17. Dedicated, like the first of the Burlesques, 'to Márta.'

18. Dedicated 'to Emma and Zoltán, August 1910.'

19. See also the discussion of Bartók's tonality in the chapter on his string quartets.

20. Although this melody appears in single notes in the revised (1950) edition, Bartók himself played it with the lower octave added through the first four bars.

21. Halperson, M., 'Béla Bartók Explains Himself,' *Musical America*, 21 January 1928; see also Bartók, 'Die Volksmusik der Araber von Biskra und Umgebung,' *Zeitschrift für Musikwissenschaft*, June 1920.

22. The instrumentation includes 2 flutes (1 piccolo), 2 clarinets, 2 bassoons, 2 horns, and strings. There are few essential changes, though No. 1 has a four-bar introduction, and there is occasional disagreement in metronome indications and expression marks.

23. The piano score has only six divisions; No. 7 begins at the 'più allegro' after the second double-bar. The titles of the movements are: *Joc cu bătă* (Stick Dance), *Brâul* (Sash Dance), *Pe loc* (In One Spot), *Buciumeana* (Horn Dance), *Poargă românească* (Romanian Polka), *Mărunţel* (Fast Dance), *Mărunţel*.

24. Universal-Edition, 1935. Most of the tunes were collected by Bartók himself, but some of those recorded in Maros-Torda in 1914 were collected by Márta Ziegler Bartók and notated from the phonograph by Bartók. Of these only one (Second Series, No. 1) is used in the Romanian Christmas Songs.

25. See also the Third String Quartet, *Seconda parte*, bars 15ff., for a similar canon. The Second Quartet has a rhythmic situation (1:54ff.) which results in the non-coincidence of bars, but the passage is not canonic; the same is true of the Second Rhapsody for violin and orchestra.

26. See Bartók, 'Az úgynevezett bolgár ritmus,' *Énekszó* (Budapest), 1938.

27. Bartók, *Hungarian Folk Music* (1931), No. 34a, prints 23 stanzas of this song.

28. The other composers represented in the collection are Arthur Benjamin, Mario Castelnuovo-Tedesco, Theodore Chanler, Eugene Goossens, Richard Hammond, Felix Labunski, Bohuslav Martinů, Darius Milhaud, Joaquin Nin-Culmell, Karol Rathaus, Vittorio Rieti, Ernest Schelling, Sigismond Stojowski, Jaromir Weinberger, and Emerson Whithorne. As in the *Tombeau de Debussy*, Bartók's contribution is almost alone in making no stylistic concessions in honor of the occasion.

29. But as late as 1937, he wrote to Mrs. Oscar Müller-Widmann, 'I too should hear with pleasure *Pierrot Lunaire*, but there is still no opportunity here; with us the performance of such works is completely impossible.' (*Lev.* II, p. 124.)

30. Bartók, 'A parasztzene hatása az újabb műzenére,' *Új Idők* (Budapest), 1931.

31. Bartók, 'A népzene jelentőségéről,' *Új Idők*, 1931.

32. The originals of Nos. 1, 3, 4, 6, and 8 may be found in Bartók's *Hungarian Folk Music* (1931), Nos. 37, 40, 244, 64, and 46 respectively.

33. 'Wait, thou raven, carry greetings to my father, my mother, and my bride. If she asks how I am, tell her I fain would rest in the churchyard at Győr.'

34. Supplement to No. 2 of *La Revue musicale*, 1 December 1920.

35. 'In the winter it's not good to plow: it's hard to hold the plow; better to remain in bed, to frolic with a bride.'

36. As Chopin, leaving Warsaw for Paris, wrote two concertos as vehicles for his anticipated concert performances.

37. In this movement Bartók writes for the extended bass compass of certain European pianos. With the usual 88-note keyboard it becomes necessary to transpose up an octave the left-hand sixths in bars 49-51.

38. It was in 1926, the year in which he wrote the Sonata, that Bartók made arrangements for Cowell to perform in Budapest.

39. Becker, H. C., 'Béla Bartók and His Credo,' *Musical America*, 17 December 1927.

40. Stravinsky's procedure in repeating the first variation in the second movement of the Octet is similar in intent.

41. The corresponding numbers of the Duos are as follows: 28, 32, 38, 43, 16, 36. Some of the titles vary in the two versions; thus *Slow Melody = Sadness; Walachian Dance = Dancing Song; Whirling Dance = Romanian Whirling Dance; Quasi pizzicato = Pizzicato; Ukrainian Song = Burlesque. Bagpipe* remains the same in both versions.

42. White, E. W., *Stravinsky*, New York, Philosophical Library, 1948, p. 90.

The Vocal Music

1. *Lev.* I, pp. 203-5; one page also reproduced in *Melos*, May/June 1949, p. 132.

2. In the collection *Der junge Bartók*, edited by Denijs Dille.

3. The title page and the third song are reproduced in *Lev.* I, pp. 206-7. The title, A *kicsi 'tót'-nak*, is a pun, *tót* meaning *Slovak*, while the songs were apparently written for Béla *Tóth*, Bartók's nephew, on his first Christmas.

4. *Lev.* II, p. 219. Demény gives two dates for the loss of the manuscript: 1945 (*Lev.* I, p. 38, f.n.) and 1943 (*Lev.* II, p. 46, f.n.).

5. *Lev.* II, p. 46.
6. Haraszti, however, considers it the 'most accessible' of the set.
7. Postscript to the revised edition (1938).
8. No. 6 is Dorian, No. 7 Phrygian, No. 3 Aeolian with a strong pentatonic cast, and No. 8 either Aeolian or Dorian, the identifying sixth scale-step being absent from the melody.
9. Nos. 1, 2, 4, and 5 are pentatonic on E, No. 6 Dorian on E. The finals of Nos. 3, 7, and 8 are Eb, F, and D respectively.
10. Haraszti, p. 42; Nathan, in *A History of Song* (ed. by Denis Stevens), p. 279.
11. For example, no. 4 of Four Hungarian Folksongs for mixed chorus (1930).
12. Hugo Leichtentritt ['Bartók and the Hungarian Folksong,' *Modern Music* (New York), March-April 1933] feels that some of the Twenty Hungarian Folksongs fall short of establishing a 'true proportion' between the primitive quality of the tunes and the complexity of the accompaniments. But compare Bartók's own point of view, in 'The Influence of Peasant Music on Modern Music,' that 'the simpler the melody the more complex and strange may be the harmonization and accompaniment that go well with it.'
13. The rhythmic notation of the 'parlando rubato' tunes varies as it might in actual peasant performance.
14. *Lev.* II, pls. XIV-XV.
15. By coincidence, before he knew this setting the author transcribed the same tune for viola and piano, using a canon in the same relationship. Since the phrases are in groups of 3, 2, and 3 quarter-notes, it was curious to discover that it had been done in exactly the same way many years before.
16. The latter has been reprinted (1950) by Boosey and Hawkes; the former had not been reprinted at the time of writing.
17. According to G. Láng, these date from 1914; all other sources consulted put the two sets in the same year, 1917.
18. In *Népzenénk és a szomszéd népek népzenéje* Bartók discusses the reasons for the lack of homogeneity in Slovak folk music. He finds the most pronounced 'Slovakian' character in the ancient Mixolydian parlando songs called *valanská* and *detvanská*, all from Zólyom; these are not represented in the settings under consideration.
19. The sources of the songs are as follows: (1) HFM 33a, collected in Somogy in 1906 by Bartók; (2) HFM 188, collected in Csík in 1907 by Bartók; (3) HFM 252, collected in Komárom in 1910 by Bartók; (4a) tune HFM 54b, collected in Tolna in 1907 by Bartók, text from HFM 45, 44, 54a; (4b) HFM 36, collected in Csík in 1911 by Antal Molnár.
20. Cf. also no. 6 of the Székely Songs (1932).
21. Universal-Edition; not reprinted by Boosey and Hawkes at the time of writing.
22. *Lev.* II, p. 123: letter to Mrs. Müller-Widmann, 24 May 1937.
23. *Lev.* I, p. 146: letter to his son Béla, 20 June 1941.
24. Demény, J., *Bartók élete és művei*, p. 101.
25. Veress accepts the long-held thesis that the Reading Rota dates from the middle of the 13th century; but cf. Bukofzer, 'Sumer Is Icumen In': A Revision (1944), placing it somewhat later.
26. Moreux (p. 81) translates the last line of the text as '*Désormais nous boirons aux sources claires de la liberté,*' and deduces that the *Cantata profana* was a protest against the restrictions of the Regent of Hungary, Miklós Horthy. But the Hungarian text, '*csak tiszta forrásból,*' says nothing whatever about 'the clear springs of freedom.'

27. Ottó, F., *Bartók Béla a* Cantata profana *tükrében* (Béla Bartók in the mirror of the *Cantata profana*), Budapest, 1936, p. 23ff.
28. *The Times* (London), 26 May 1934.

The Chamber Music: I

1. Nothing more has been discovered regarding this work than the bare listing in Kodály's article on Bartók in *La Revue musicale* (Paris), 1 March 1921.
2. Hawkes, Ralph, 'Béla Bartók, a Recollection by His Publisher,' *Tempo* (London), no. 13, Autumn 1949, p. 13.
3. Becker, Harry Cassin, 'Béla Bartók and His Credo,' *Musical America* (New York), 17 December 1927.
4. Rothe, Friede F., 'The Language of the Composer,' *The Etude* (Philadelphia), February 1941.
5. Miniature score, p. 8, 2nd and 3rd measures before no. 1.
6. For example René Leibowitz, 'Béla Bartók, ou la possibilité de compromis dans la musique contemporaine,' *Les Temps modernes* (Paris), October 1947.
7. Becker, op. cit.
8. Min. sc., p. 10, no. 6.
9. Min. sc., p. 32, 3rd measure, to p. 33, 4th system, 2nd measure.
10. Min. sc., p. 27, no. 17.
11. Rothe, op. cit.
12. Min. sc., p. 17, 2nd system.
13. Min. sc., p. 4, 3rd system.
14. Babbitt, Milton, 'The String Quartets of Bartók,' *Musical Quarterly* (New York), July 1949.
15. Min. sc., p. 6, 2nd measure.
16. Min. sc., p. 9, 3rd system.
17. Min. sc., p. 25, rehearsal no. 14, to p. 28, no. 18.
18. Min. sc., p. 26, after rehearsal no. 15.
19. Min. sc., p. 48.
20. It has been suggested that the principles of *Bogenform* may have come to Bartók's notice in the *Geheimnis der Form bei Richard Wagner* of Alfred Lorenz (1924). See Gerald Abraham, 'The Bartók of the Quartets,' *Music and Letters*, 1945.
21. Min. sc., p. 7, 4th system, to bottom of p. 8.
22. Min. sc., p. 4, no. 4. For a discussion of 'night music' in Bartók, see *Out of Doors* (1926), pp. 135-7.
23. Min. sc., p. 4, no. 4.
24. Min. sc., p. 7, no. 11.
25. Min. sc., p. 9, 1st and 2nd systems.
26. Min. sc., p. 20, no. 31.
27. Min. sc., p. 21, no. 34.
28. Min. sc., p. 23, no. 36.
29. Min. sc., p. 37, no. 10.
30. It most closely resembles in its contour the diatonic expansion of the basic motive, as seen in the preceding example.
31. Min. sc., p. 21.
32. Min. sc., p. 11, at *E*.
33. Min. sc., p. 11, *G* (second theme); p. 17, *H* (transitional theme); p. 18, *I* (first theme).

34. Min. sc., p. 68, E.
35. Min. sc., p. 75, G.
36. Min. sc., p. 79, H.
37. Min. sc., p. 88, M, 'Allegretto con indifferenza.'
38. Bartók discusses these rhythms in 'Az úgynevezett bolgár ritmus,' Énekszó (1938).
39. Lev. I, pp. 132-3.
40. Letter from R. Kolisch to the author, 28 May 1950.

The Chamber Music: II

1. For a discussion of the Rhapsodies, see the chapter on the Concertos.
2. For example, first 10 measures in the piano (cimbalom); p. 14, no. 20 (gamelan), et cetera.
3. For example: p. 21, 2nd system, last 3 measures with preceding anacrusis—only Ab duplicated.
4. Bartók, Hungarian Folk Music (1931), pp. 50-51.
5. Second Sonata, p. 9, third system; cf. Study, op. 18, no. 1, for piano.
6. The Husband's Grief, reproduced in facsimile in Lev. II, pls. XIV-XV.
7. They have also been recorded, by Victor Aitay and Michael Kuttner (Period SPLP 506), who begin and end with some of the more difficult pieces, scattering the easier ones through the middle of the group.
8. Ernő Lendvai devotes 86 pages to an analysis of the work (Bartók stilusa, 1955); see also his article in the Bartók issue of Zenei Szemle, Dec. 1948.
9. Cf. his comment on Molnár s analysis of the Violin Concerto, p. 247.
10. Serly, Tibor, 'Story of a Concerto, Bartók's Last Work,' The New York Times, 11 December 1949.
11. Since many players nowadays do not use the A clarinet, there is an alternative part for the Bb instrument throughout. Naturally this version does not lie so well for the player.
12. Measures 4, 8, 14-16, et cetera.

The Concertos

1. In La Revue musicale, 1 March 1921.
2. Lijst der werken, published in pamphlet form. Bartók's copy (receipt of which he acknowledged in a letter to Dille, 19 May 1939—Lev. II, p. 144) is in the possession of Dr. George Herzog.
3. See p. 265.
4. Nüll, E. von der, Béla Bartók, ein Beitrag zur Morphologie der neuen Musik, p. 108; also Lev. I, p. 118.
5. Henrietta Straus, in The Nation, 7 March 1928.
6. Bartók, in American Hungarian Observer, 1944.
7. Letter to the author, August 1950. According to Bartók, however, the cello version was a transcription. (Lev. III, p. 392)
8. Bartók here uses a signature of two sharps on F and G, to avoid the accidental before the C. Hindemith, in the Sonata, opus 11, no. 4, for viola and piano, employs the same signature, to avoid the writing of a few C♮'s on one page; in order to make his intention clear, he resorts to a footnote and ten precautionary accidentals at the beginning of the passage. While the piano score of the Bartók Rhapsody notates both parts with the same signa-

ture, adding sharps where necessary, the orchestral score has three sharps (or equivalent in the transposing instruments) for all but the solo line.

9. Quoted by Bagar and Biancolli, *The Concert Companion*, p. 22. New York: McGraw-Hill Book Co., Inc., 1947.
10. The only subsequent work which verges on the variation is the *Melodia* of the Sonata for Solo Violin (1944), *q.v.*
11. *Lev.* ii, p. 183; letter to Joseph Szigeti, 30 January 1944.
12. It is far from the author's intention to insist upon the Hungarian derivation of all such melodies. Fourths and fifths, seconds and sevenths, are a part of the universal vocabulary; they are particularly prevalent in the melodies of Hindemith—one of whose themes [Quartet in E♭ (1943), ii:27-30] might almost be a variant of one of these. But in general, the melodies of German composers abound in thirds and sixths, with less emphasis upon the other intervals.
13. Molnár, Antal, 'Bartók Béla hegedűversenye,' *A Zene* (Budapest), 15 November 1939.
14. *Lev.* ii, pp. 148-9.
15. Measures 105 and 107 do not appear in the manuscript score. Extension was suggested by Székely, and Bartók authorized him to add at this point for the first performance; later Bartók incorporated the extension into the final version. Many other corrections and revisions are shown by the manuscript.
16. Serly, Tibor, 'Story of a Concerto, Bartók's Last Work,' *The New York Times*, 11 December 1949. See also Serly's preface to the published score.
17. Letter to the author, 16 May 1950.
18. Second Piano Concerto, 1:32-57; Violin Concerto, 1:56-72.
19. ii:50-53, for example.
20. iv, Section c (Min. score, p. 53).

The Orchestral Music

1. *Egyetemi Nyomda Diáriuma*, March 1948; *Zenei Szemle*, December 1948. The memorandum is also printed in *Lev.* ii, pages 54-5.
2. For example, György Láng, János Demény, and others.
3. Haraszti, E., *Béla Bartók, His Life and Works*, p. 59.
4. Miniature score, p. 31, rehearsal no. 5; the fugue itself begins at no. 10 on p. 39.
5. Min. sc., p. 68, no. 33.
6. Min. sc., p. 71, no. 34.
7. It is unfortunate that the English and American publishers translate so many of Bartók's titles from the French rather than from the Hungarian. *Image* has somewhat different connotations in the two languages; *virágzás* has been translated as 'In Full Flower'; the confusion between *populaire* and *popular* has already been mentioned.
8. *Új Magyar Zeneegyesület* (New Hungarian Music Society).
9. The Four Pieces have the largest instrumentation, with woodwinds in fours and four trombones.
10. In the *American Hungarian Observer*, 4 June 1944.
11. Note also the resemblance between the main theme of the Marcia and the opening theme of *Contrasts*, written the year before.
12. Bars 184-236.
13. Bars 513-31.

14. Concerto for Orchestra (1943), Sonata for Solo Violin (1944), Third Piano Concerto (1945), Viola Concerto (1945).
15. Boston Symphony Orchestra program, 1 December 1944.
16. In a radio interview, CBS, 19 September 1948. In a letter to the author, Péter Bartók points out that the part of the theme Bartók used was not original with Shostakovich: 'But in any case I could mention that the famous theme was played much before the Seventh Symphony was written, in the form of Viennese cabaret songs. . . [In the Concerto for Orchestra] the first half of the theme is missing. That half did not originate in Vienna.'

The Dramatic Music

1. Gilles de Retz plays an important role in Joris-Karl Huysmans' *Là-bas* (1891); see also *The Soul of Marshal Gilles de Raiz* (1952), by D. B. Wyndham Lewis.
2. The term is employed here without reference to Bartók's use of arch-form in the instrumental compositions of the 1920's and 1930's.
3. Piano-vocal score, p. 24, no. 34.
4. Ibid. p. 30, no. 45.
5. Ibid. p. 36, no. 58.
6. Ibid. p. 41, no. 71.
7. Ibid. p. 44, no. 78.
8. Ibid. pp. 51ff.
9. Evans, Edwin, *Stravinsky—The Firebird and Petrushka*, London, Oxford University Press, 1933.
10. Lifar, Serge, *Serge Diaghilev, His Life, His Work, His Legend*, New York, G. P. Putnam's Sons, 1940, p. 231.
11. Bekker, Paul, *Klang und Eros*, Stuttgart & Berlin, Deutsche Verlags-Anstalt vereinigt mit Schuster & Loeffler, 1922, p. 81.
12. Letter of 9 June 1919, in *Lev.* I, p. 92.
13. Kodály, in *A Dictionary of Modern Music and Musicians* (1924), p. 30, refers to the *Mandarin* as 'not yet completed.'
14. Most of the music up to this point is contained in the orchestral suite.
15. *Three Autumn Tears*, opus 16, no. 1.
16. Choreography by Gyula Harangozó, décor by Gustáv Oláh.

Epilogue

1. Quoted by Harry Cassin Becker, in *Musical America*, 17 December 1927.
2. Brăiloiu, C., *'Béla Bartók folkloriste'* (Address at the third plenary session of the Commission Internationale des Arts et Traditions Populaires, Paris, October 1947).

CHRONOLOGICAL LIST OF WORKS

IN his later scores Bartók meticulously notated the dates of beginning work and of completion; the earlier ones, however, do not carry such notations and it is possible that in the list which follows there are occasional slight inaccuracies in the order of listing. Bartók's own correction and amplification of the list published by Denijs Dille in 1939 has been available for comparison. Information about first performances is conflicting in various sources, and has therefore been included only where it is possible to establish the date with reasonable assurance of accuracy.

(1) Juvenilia (188-?). Unpublished, not performed.
- a. *A Budapesti torna verseny* (Gymnastics Contest in Budapest [!])
- b. *Gyorspolka* (Fast Polka)
- c. *'Béla' Polka*
- d. *'Katinka' Gyorspolka*
- e. *'Jolán' Polka*
- f. *Nefelejts* (Forget-me-not)

(2) THE DANUBE RIVER (*A Duna folyása*), for piano (Nagyszőllős, 1890?). Unpublished. First performance, Nagyszőllős, 1 May 1892, by the composer.

(3) INTRODUCTION AND ALLEGRO (189-?), for piano. Unpublished.

(4) SCHERZO (189-?), for piano. Unpublished. Dedicated to Gabriella Lator.

(5) THREE PIANO PIECES (1897). Unpublished. Dedicated to Gabriella Lator.
1. Spring Song (*Tavaszi dal*)
2. Valse (*Valcer*)
3. In Wallachian Style (*Oláhos*) [?]

(6) THREE PIANO PIECES (Pozsony, 1897). Unpublished. Dedicated to Gabriella Lator.
1. Adagio-Presto
2. (Without title or tempo indication)
3. Adagio, sehr düster

(7) SONATA (1897), for piano. Unpublished.

(8) PIANO QUARTET (1898). Unpublished. First performance, Pozsony, 1898.

(9) THREE SONGS (*Drei Lieder*), for voice and piano (Pozsony, August 1898). Dedicated to Countess Matilde von Wenckheim. Unpublished; facsimile of No. 1 in *Lev.* I, pp. 203-5.
  1. Im wunderschönen Monat Mai (Heinrich Heine)
  2. Nacht am Rheine (Karl Siebel)
  3. Ein Lied

(10) STRING QUARTET (Pozsony, 1899). Unpublished.

(11) QUINTET (Budapest, 1899). Unpublished, probably incomplete.

(12) LOVE SONGS (*Liebeslieder*) for voice and piano, with texts by Friedrich Rückert (Budapest, 1900).
  1. Diese Rose pflück ich hier (I pluck this rose)
  2. Ich fühle deinen Odem (I feel your breath)

(13) MINUET (*Menüett*), for piano (1901). Unpublished.

(14) FOUR SONGS (*Négy dal*), for voice and piano, with texts by Lajos Pósa (1902).
  1. Autumn breeze (*Őszi szellő*)
  2. The girls of Szeged scorn me (*Még azt vetik a szememre*)
  3. There is no such sorrow (*Nincs olyan bú*)
  4. Well, well! (*Ejnye! Ejnye!*)

(15) SYMPHONY (1902). Unpublished; only piano reduction. Two movements, orchestrated by Denijs Dille, first performed in Budapest, 28 Sept. 1961, Orchestra of Hungarian Radio, conducted by György Lehel.

(16) SCHERZO for orchestra (1902). A part of the preceding; unpublished. First performance, Budapest, 29 February 1904, Budapest Opera Orchestra, conducted by István Kerner.

(17) EVENING (*Est*), for voice and piano (April? 1903). Text by Kálmán Harsányi.

(17a) EVENING (*Est*), for four-part male chorus (April 1903). Text identical to 17, but the music is entirely different. Published in Dille: *Documenta Bartókiana*, I (1964).

(18) FOUR SONGS (*Négy dal*), for voice and piano (June? 1903). Unpublished; manuscript lost.

(19) SONATA for violin and piano (1903). Published in Dille: *Documenta Bartókiana*, (1964-5). First performance (3rd movement only), Budapest, 8 June 1903, Sándor Kőszegi and composer; (entire work) Budapest, 25 January 1904, Jenő Hubay and composer.

(20) KOSSUTH, symphonic poem in ten tableaux (2 April-18 August 1903). First performance, Budapest, 13 January 1904, Philharmonic Society, conducted by István Kerner.

(21) FOUR PIANO PIECES (*Négy zongoradarab*).
  1. Study for the left hand (*Tanulmány balkézre*) (Budapest, January 1903); dedicated to István Thomán. First performance, Nagyszent-

miklós, 13 April 1903, by the composer.
2. Fantasy I. (*I. Ábránd*) (Budapest, 8 February 1903); dedicated to Emma Gruber. First performance, Budapest, 27 March 1903, by the composer.
3. Fantasy II (*II. Ábránd*) (Berlin, 12 October 1903); dedicated to Emsy and Irmy Jurkovics.
4. Scherzo (Budapest-Gmunden, June-September 1903); dedicated to Ernő Dohnányi. First performance, Budapest, 25 November 1903, by the composer.

(22) PIANO QUINTET (1904). Unpublished. First performance, Vienna, 21 November 1904, composer and Prill Quartet.

(23) THREE SONGS (*Három népies műdal*) for voice and piano (1904?). Published in Ö. Geszler: *Énekiskola*, I: 56 and 74, II: 36.
1. Evening song (*Esti dal*), text by Sándor Peres.
2. The benefactors (*A jótevők*), text by István Havas.
3. Bell sound (*Harangszó*), text by Béla Sztankó

(24) TWO SONGS for mixed chorus (1904?). Unpublished.
1. My hen is lost (*Elveszett a tyúkom*)
2. If I go in (*Ha bemegyek*)

(25) RHAPSODY, opus 1, for piano; also for piano and orchestra, and for two pianos (November 1904). Dedicated to Emma [Gruber]. First performance, solo version, Pozsony, 4 November 1906, by the composer; orchestral version, Budapest, 15 November 1909, Orchestra of the Academy of Music, conducted by Jenő Hubay.

(26) SCHERZO [opus 2], for piano and orchestra (1904). First performance, Budapest, 28 September 1961, E. Tusa, Orchestra of Hungarian Radio, conducted by György Lehel. (A *Burlesque* of the same year is mentioned by various writers, but is probably identical to the *Scherzo*.)

(27) SZÉKELY FOLKSONG (*Székely népdal*), for voice and piano (1905). Published in Supplement to *Magyar Lant*, 1905.

(28) HUNGARIAN FOLKSONGS (*Magyar népdalok*) for voice and piano. (1st series, 1905; 2nd series, 1906). The first series included four songs, the fourth fragmentary; only the first is published:
1. They have mown the meadow (*Lekaszálták már a rétet*)
From the second series, four songs have been published:
4. If I go to the inn (*Ha bemegyek a csárdába*)
6. I drank the red wine from the glass (*Megittam a piros bort*)
7. Maiden stringing pearls (*Ez a kislány gyöngyöt fűz*)
8. Hey, when they take me for a soldier (*Sej, mikor engem katonának visznek*)
(Not all these songs are authentic folksongs.)

(29) SUITE No. 1, opus 3, for large orchestra (Vienna, 1905). First performance (three movements only), Vienna, 29 November 1905, Ferdinand Loewe, Gesellschaftskonzerte.

(30) TO THE LITTLE 'SLOVAK' (*A kicsi 'tót'-nak*), five songs for a child (Vienna, 20 December 1905). Unpublished; No. 3 reproduced in facsimile in *Lev.* I, p. 207.

(31) TWENTY HUNGARIAN FOLKSONGS (*Magyar népdalok*), for voice and piano (December 1906; revised 1938). [Only the first ten were set by Bartók, the remainder by Kodály.]
1. I set out for my fair homeland (*Elindultam szép hazámbul*)
2. I would cross the Tisza in a boat (*Általmennék én a Tiszán ladikon*)
3. László Fehér stole a horse (*Fehér László lovat lopott*)
4. In the Gyula garden (*A gyulai kert alatt*)
5. I walked in the Kertmeg garden (*A kertmegi kert alatt sétáltam*)
6. In my window shone the moonlight (*Ablakomba, ablakomba be-sütött a holdvilág*)
7. From the withered branch no rose blooms (*Száraz ágtól messze virít a rózsa*)
8. I walked to the end of the great street in Tárkánya (*Végig mentem a tárkányi sej, haj, nagy uccán*)
9. Not far from here is Kismargitta (*Nem messze van ide kis Margitta*)
10. My sweetheart is plowing, jingle, clatter (*Szánt a babám csireg, csörög*)

(31a) THE STREET IS ON FIRE (*Ucca, ucca, ég az ucca*), for voice and piano (1906). Originally published as one of the TWENTY HUNGARIAN FOLKSONGS; deleted, as not an authentic folksong, from the 1938 revision.

(31b) ON MY MOTHER'S ROSEBUSH (*Édesanyám rózsafája*), for voice and piano (1906?). Intended as one of the TWENTY HUNGARIAN FOLK-SONGS, but deleted when no room could be found for it. One other transcription for the same group survives.

(32) SUITE No. 2, opus 4, for small orchestra (I-III, Vienna, November 1905; IV, Rákospalota, 1 September 1907; revised 1920 and 1943). First per-formance, Scherzo only, Berlin, 2 January 1909, conducted by the com-poser; complete, Budapest, 22 November 1909, Philharmonic Society, con-ducted by István Kerner. Arranged for two pianos by the composer, 1943.

(33) THREE HUNGARIAN FOLKSONGS FROM THE CSÍK DISTRICT (*Három csíkmegyei népdal*), for piano (1907). Also arranged for flute and piano by János Szebenyi; for clarinet and piano by György Balassa.

(34) VIOLIN CONCERTO [No. 1] (Jászberény, 1 July 1907-Budapest, 5 Feb-ruary 1908). Dedicated to Stefi Geyer. First performance, Basle, 30 May 1958, Hans-Heinz Schneeberger, Basle Chamber Orchestra, conducted by Paul Sacher. First movement incorporated into the TWO PORTRAITS, opus 5.

(35) TWO PORTRAITS (*Két portré*), opus 5, for orchestra (1907-8). First per-formance, Budapest, 1909, Imre Waldbauer, violinist, László Kún conduct-ing the Budapest Symphony. The second movement also forms the finale of the BAGATELLES, opus 6, where it is titled *Ma Mie qui danse*.

(36) FOURTEEN BAGATELLES (*Tizennégy bagatell*), opus 6, for piano (Budapest, May 1908). Only the last two have titles: (13) *Elle est morte*; (14) *Ma Mie qui danse*. First performance, Berlin, 29 June 1908 [for Bu-soni's piano class].

(37) TEN EASY PIECES (*Tíz könnyű zongoradarab*), for piano (June 1908). Numbers 5 and 10 transcribed for orchestra in 1931 as the first two move-

ments of HUNGARIAN SKETCHES; no. 5 transcribed for wind orchestra by József Pécsi, 1949.
Dedication (*Ajánlás*)
1. Peasant song (*Parasztdal*)
2. Frustration (*Lassú vergődés*)
3. Slovakian boys' dance (*Tót legénytánc*)
4. Sostenuto
5. Evening with the Széklers (*Az este a Székelyeknel*)
6. Hungarian folksong (*Magyar népdal*)
7. Dawn (*Hajnal*)
8. Folksong (*Azt mondják, nem adnak*)
9. Five-finger exercise (*Gyakorlat*)
10. Bear dance (*Medvetánc*)

(38) STRING QUARTET No. 1, opus 7 (27 January 1909). First performance, Budapest, 19 March 1910, by the Waldbauer-Kerpely Quartet.

(39) TWO ELEGIES (*Két elégia*), opus 8b, for piano (I, February 1908; II, December 1909). First performance, Budapest, 21 April 1919, by the composer.

(40) FOR CHILDREN (A *gyermekeknek; Pro děti*), for piano (1908-9). Original version, 85 pieces in four volumes; revised version (January 1945), 79 pieces in two volumes, vol. 1 based upon Hungarian folk tunes, vol. 11 on Slovakian folk tunes. The Swineherd's Dance (*Kanásztánc*, 1:40) was transscribed for orchestra in 1931 as the finale of HUNGARIAN SKETCHES. Other pieces have been transcribed for violin and piano by Joseph Szigeti (Hungarian Folktunes, 1927), Tivadar Országh (*Magyar népdalok*, 1934), and Ede Zathureczky (For Children, 1947), and for mixed chorus by Endre Székely (1947). 10 pieces transcribed for orchestra by Leó Weiner (*Tíz darab a Gyermekekéből*, 1952).

(41) SEVEN SKETCHES (*Vázlatok*), opus 9 [originally intended as 9b], for piano (1908-10; revised 19 January 1945).
1. Portrait of a girl (*Leányi arckép*); dedicated to Márta [Bartók]
2. See-saw, dickory-daw (*Hinta palinta. . .*)
3. Lento; dedicated to Emma and Zoltán [Kodály]
4. Non troppo lento
5. Romanian folksong (*Román népdal*)
6. In Walachian style (*Oláhos*)
7. Poco lento

(42) TWO ROMANIAN DANCES (*Két román tánc*), opus 8a, for piano (1909-10). First performance, Paris, 12 March 1910, by the composer. Also transscribed for orchestra by Leó Weiner, 1939.

(43) FOUR DIRGES (*Négy siratóének, Quatre nénies*) [originally intended as opus 9a], for piano (Budapest, 1910). First performance (in part), Budapest, 17 October 1917, Ernő Dohnányi. Number 2 transcribed for orchestra as no. 3 of HUNGARIAN SKETCHES, 1931.

(44) TWO PICTURES (*Két kép, Deux images*), opus 10, for orchestra (Budapest, August 1910). Also published for piano. First performance, Budapest, 25 February 1913, Philharmonic Society, conducted by István Kerner.
1. In full flower (*Virágzás, En pleine fleur*).
2. Village dance (A *falu tánca, Danse campagnarde*).

(45) THREE BURLESQUES (*Három burleszk*), opus 8c, for piano (I, November 1908; II, May 1911; III, 1910). Number 2 transcribed for orchestra as no. 4 of HUNGARIAN SKETCHES, 1931. First performance, Budapest, 17 October 1917, Ernő Dohnányi (nos. I and II only).
    1. Quarrel (*Perpatvar*); dedicated to Márta [Bartók]
    2. A bit drunk (*Kicsit ázottan*)
    3. Molto vivo, capriccioso

(46) DUKE BLUEBEARD'S CASTLE (A *kékszakállú herceg vára*), opus 11 (Rákoskeresztúr, September 1911). Opera in one act, libretto by Béla Balázs. Dedicated to Márta [Bartók]. First performance, Budapest, 24 May 1918, Egisto Tango conducting; Olga Haselbeck [Judith], Oszkar Kálmán [Bluebeard].

(47) ALLEGRO BARBARO, for piano (1911). First performance, Budapest, 27 February 1921, by the composer. Transcribed for orchestra by Jenő Kenessey, 1946.

(48) FOUR PIECES (*Négy zenekari darab*), opus 12, for orchestra (1912, orchestrated 1921). First performance, Budapest, 9 January 1922, Philharmonic Society, Ernő Dohnányi conducting.
    1. Preludio
    2. Scherzo
    3. Intermezzo
    4. Marcia funebre

(49) FOUR OLD HUNGARIAN FOLKSONGS (*Négy régi magyar népdal*), for 4-part male chorus, a cappella (1912).
    1. Long ago I told you (*Rég megmondtam*)
    2. Oh God, why am I waiting? (*Jaj istenem! kire vátok*)
    3. In my sister-in-law's garden (*Ángyomasszony kertje*)
    4. Farmboy, load the cart well (*Béreslegény, jól megrakd a szekeret*)

(50) THE FIRST TERM AT THE PIANO (*Kezdők zongoramuzsikája*), for piano (1913). Eighteen elementary pieces for the piano method of Sándor Reschofsky.

(51) DANSE ORIENTALE, for piano (1913?). Published in the Christmas 1913 issue of the *Pressburger Zeitung*. First (?) performance, Bakersfield, California, 23 October 1954, Halsey Stevens.

(52) SONATINA, for piano (1915), based on Romanian folk tunes. Transcribed for orchestra as TRANSYLVANIAN DANCES (*Erdélyi táncok*), 1931; also for violin and piano by Endre Gertler, 1931; for clarinet and piano by György Balassa, 1955. The three movements are entitled Bagpipers (*Dudások*), Bear Dance (*Medvetánc*), and Finale.

(53) ROMANIAN FOLK DANCES FROM HUNGARY (*Magyarországi román népi táncok*), for piano (1915). Dedicated to Prof. Ion Buşiţia. Transcribed for small orchestra, 1917, as ROMANIAN FOLK DANCES (*Román népi táncok*); also for violin and piano by Zoltán Székely, for string orchestra by Arthur Willner, for salon orchestra by Wilke.
    1. Stick dance (*Joc cu bâta*)
    2. Sash dance (*Brâul*)
    3. In one spot (*Pe loc*)

4. Horn dance (*Buciumeana*)
5. Romanian polka (*Poargă românească*)
6. Fast dance (*Mărunțel*)
7. Fast dance (*Mărunțel*)

(54) ROMANIAN CHRISTMAS SONGS (COLINDE) (*Román karácsonyi dallamok* ('*kolindák*')), for piano (1915). Two series of ten each.

(55) TWO ROMANIAN FOLKSONGS (*Két román népdal*), for 4-part women's chorus (1915). Unpublished.

(56) NINE ROMANIAN SONGS (*Kilenc román népdal*) for voice and piano (1915). Unpublished.

(57) FOUR SLOVAKIAN FOLKSONGS (*Négy szlovák népdal*) for voice and piano (Nos. 1-3, 1907?; No. 4, 1916).
    1. Near the borders of Bistrita (*V tej bystrickej bráne*) [Another version appears in FOR CHILDREN, II:11.]
    2. Mourning song (*Pohřební písen*) [Another version appears in FOR CHILDREN, II:43.]
    3. Message (*Priletel pták*)
    4. Tono whirls the spindle (*Krutí Tono vretana*)

(58) THE WOODEN PRINCE (*A fából faragott királyfi*), ballet in one act (1914-16). Libretto by Béla Balázs. Dedicated to Egisto Tango. First performance, Hungarian State Opera House, Budapest, 12 May 1917, Egisto Tango conducting. An orchestral SUITE from the ballet, 1931; first performance, Budapest, 23 November 1931, Philharmonic Society, Ernő Dohnányi conducting.

(59) SUITE, opus 14, for piano (Rákoskeresztúr, February 1916). First performance, Budapest, 21 April 1919, by the composer. There was originally an Andante between the first and second movements, withdrawn by the composer.

(60) FIVE SONGS (*Öt dal*), opus 15, for voice and piano (1915-16). Author of texts unknown; nos. 4 and 5 said to be by Béla Balázs.
    1. My love (*Az én szerelmem*)
    2. Summer (*Nyár*)
    3. Night of desire (*A vágyak éjjele*)
    4. In vivid dreams (*Színes álomban*)
    5. In the valley (*Itt lent a völgyben*)

(61) FIVE SONGS (*Öt dal*), opus 16, for voice and piano (Rákoskeresztúr, February-April 1916). Texts by Endre Ady. Dedicated to Béla Reinitz. First performance, Budapest, 21 April 1919, Ilona Durigó and the composer.
    1. Three autumn tears (*Három őszi könnycsepp*)
    2. Sounds of autumn (*Az őszi lárma*)
    3. My bed calls me (*Az ágyam hívogat*)
    4. Alone with the sea (*Egyedül a tengerrel*)
    5. I cannot come to you (*Nem mehetek hozzád*)

(62) EIGHT HUNGARIAN FOLKSONGS (*Nyolc magyar népdal*), for voice and piano (1907-17).
    1. Black is the earth (*Fekete főd*)

2. My God, my God, make the river swell (*Istenem, istenem, árasd meg a vizet*)
3. Wives, let me be one of your company (*Asszonyok, asszonyok*)
4. So much sorrow lies on my heart (*Annyi bánat az szűvemen*)
5. If I climb yonder hill (*Ha kimegyek arr' a magos tetőre*)
6. They are mending the great forest highway (*Töltik a nagy erdő útját*)
7. Up to now my work was plowing in the springtime (*Eddig való dolgom a tavaszi szántás*)
8. The snow is melting (*Olvad a hó*)

(63) FIFTEEN HUNGARIAN PEASANT SONGS (*Tizenöt magyar parásztdal*), for piano (1914-17). Numbers 6-12, 14, 15 transcribed for orchestra as HUNGARIAN PEASANT SONGS, 1933. Numbers 7-15 transcribed for orchestra by Tibor Polgár, 1927, as *Régi magyar táncok* (Old Hungarian dances).

(64) THREE HUNGARIAN FOLK TUNES, for piano (1914-17). Published in collection *Homage to Paderewski*, 1942. Number 1, in an earlier version, was published in *Periscop* (Arad, Romania, June-July 1925). Number 3 transcribed for orchestra by Tibor Serly, as Prelude to Suite from MIKROKOSMOS.

(65) STRING QUARTET No. 2, opus 17 (Rákoskeresztúr, 1915-October 1917). Dedicated to the Waldbauer-Kerpely Quartet. First performance, Budapest, 3 March 1918, by the Waldbauer-Kerpely Quartet.

(66) FIVE SLOVAK FOLKSONGS (*Szlovák népdalok*), for 4-part male chorus (1917). First performance, Vienna, 15 December 1917.
1. Hey, my dear, kind comrades (*Ej, posluchajte málo*)
2. If I must go to the war (*Keď ja smutny pojdem*)
3. Let us go, comrades (*Kamarádi mojí*)
4. Hey, if soon I fall (*Ej, a keď mňa zabiju*)
5. To battle I went forth (*Keď som šiou na vojnu*)

(67) FOUR SLOVAK FOLKSONGS (*Szlovák népdalok*), for 4-part mixed chorus and piano (1917). Probable first performance, Budapest, 5 January 1917, Emil Lichtenberg conducting. Transcribed for orchestra by Endre Szervánszky, 1950.
1. Thus sent the mother (*Zadala mamka*)
2. In alpine pastures (*Na holi, na holi*)
3. Food and drink's your only pleasure (*Rada pila, rada jedla*)
4. Let the bagpipe sound (*Gajdujte, gajdence*)

(68) THREE STUDIES (*Három tanulmány*), opus 18, for piano (Rákoskeresztúr, 1918). First performance, Budapest, 21 April 1919, by the composer.

(69) THE WONDERFUL MANDARIN (*A csodálatos mandarin*), opus 19, pantomime in one act (Rákoskeresztúr, October 1918-May 1919). Libretto by Menyhért Lengyel. First performance, Cologne, 27 November 1926, Jenő Szenkár conducting. Orchestral suite from the pantomime first performed by Philharmonic Society, Budapest, 15 October 1928, Ernő Dohnányi conducting.

(70) EIGHT IMPROVISATIONS ON HUNGARIAN PEASANT SONGS (*Rögtönzések magyar parasztdalokra*), opus 20, for piano (1920). Number 7, dedicated to the memory of Claude Debussy, published in the *Tombeau de Claude Debussy*, 1920. First performance, Budapest, 27 February 1921, by the composer.

(71) SONATA No. 1, for violin and piano (Budapest, October-12 December 1921). Dedicated to Jelly d'Arányi. First performance, London, Jelly d'Arányi and the composer, 24 March 1922.

(72) SONATA No. 2, for violin and piano (Budapest, July-November 1922). Dedicated to Jelly d'Arányi. First performance, London, Jelly d'Arányi and the composer, 7 May 1923.

(73) DANCE SUITE (*Táncszvit*), for orchestra (Radvány, North Hungary, August 1923). Composed to celebrate the fiftieth anniversary of the merging of Pest, Buda, and Óbuda into the city of Budapest. First performance, 19 November 1923, Budapest Philharmonic Society, Ernő Dohnányi conducting. Also published in reduction for piano.

(74) FIVE VILLAGE SCENES (*Falun, népdalok*), for voice and piano (December 1924). Slovak folksongs from the Zólyom district. Dedicated to Ditta [Pásztory Bartók]. First performance, Budapest, 8 December 1926, Mária Basilides and the composer.

(74a) VILLAGE SCENES (*Falun*), for four or eight women's voices and chamber orchestra (Budapest, May 1926). Transcriptions of numbers 3, 4, and 5 of the preceding. First performance, New York, 1 February 1927, Serge Koussevitzky conducting.

(75) SONATA, for piano (Budapest, June 1926). Dedicated to Ditta [Pásztory Bartók]. First performance, Budapest, 8 December 1926, by the composer.

(76) OUT OF DOORS (*Szabadban*), for piano (Budapest, June-August 1926). First performance, Budapest, 8 December 1926, by the composer (Numbers 1 and 4 only).
   1. With drums and pipes (*Síppal, dobbal*)
   2. Barcarolla
   3. Musettes
   4. The night's music (*As éjszaka zenéje, Musiques nocturnes*); dedicated to Ditta [Bartók]
   5. The chase (*Hajsza*)

(77) NINE LITTLE PIANO PIECES (*Kilenc kis zongoradarab*), (31 October 1926). [Sketches for MIKROKOSMOS, OUT OF DOORS, and CONCERTO No. 1]. First performance, Budapest, 8 December 1926, by the composer (one Dialogue omitted).
   1-4. Dialogues
   5. Menuetto
   6. Air
   7. Marcia delle bestie
   8. Tambourine
   9. Preludio, all' ungherese

(78) CONCERTO No. 1, for piano and orchestra (Budapest, August-12 November 1926). First performance, Frankfurt, 1 July 1927, the composer as soloist, Wilhelm Furtwängler conducting.

(79) THREE RONDOS ON FOLK TUNES, for piano (I, 1916; II and III, 1927). Transcribed for orchestra by Pál Bodon, 1938.

(80) STRING QUARTET No. 3 (Budapest, September 1927). Dedicated to the Musical Fund Society of Philadelphia. First performance, London, 19 February 1929, Waldbauer-Kerpely Quartet.

(81) RHAPSODY No. 1, for violin and piano (1928). Dedicated to Joseph Szigeti. First performance, Budapest, 22 November 1929, Joseph Szigeti and the composer. Also versions for violoncello and piano; violin and orchestra.

(82) RHAPSODY No. 2, for violin and piano (1928). Dedicated to Zoltán Székely. First performance, Amsterdam, 19 November 1928, Zoltán Székely and Géza Frid. Also for violin and orchestra (revised 1944); first performance, Amsterdam, 24 January 1932, Zoltán Székely, Concertgebouw Orchestra, Pierre Monteux conducting.

(83) STRING QUARTET No. 4 (Budapest, July-September 1928). Dedicated to the Pro Arte Quartet. First performance, Budapest, 20 March 1929, Waldbauer-Kerpely Quartet.

(84) TWENTY HUNGARIAN FOLKSONGS (*Húsz magyar népdal*), for voice and piano (1929). First performance, Budapest, 30 January 1930, Mária Basilides and the composer. Five of the songs orchestrated in 1933.
   1. In prison (*A tömlöcben*)
   2. Ancient grief (*Régi keserves*)
   3. The fugitive (*Bujdosó-ének*)
   4. Herdsman's song (*Pásztornóta*)
   5. Székely 'lassú'
   6. Székely 'friss'
   7. Swineherd's dance (*Kanásztánc*)
   8. Six-florin dance ('*Hátforintos' nóta*)
   9. The shepherd (*Juhászcsúfoló*)
   10. Joking song (*Tréfás nóta*)
   11. Nuptial serenade (*Párosító* I)
   12. Humorous song (*Párosító* II)
   13. Dialogue song (*Pár-ének*)
   14. Complaint (*Panasz*)
   15. Drinking song (*Bordal*)
   16. Oh, my dear mother (*Hej, édes anyám*)
   17. Ripening cherries (*Érik a ropogos cseresznye*)
   18. Long ago at Doboz fell the snow (*Már Dobozon régen leesett a hó*)
   19. Yellow cornstalk (*Sárga kukoricaszál*)
   20. Wheat, wheat (*Buza, buza*)

(85) FOUR HUNGARIAN FOLKSONGS (*Magyar népdalok*), for mixed chorus, a cappella (Budapest, May 1930).
   1. The prisoner (*A rab*)
   2. The rover (*A bujdosó*)
   3. The marriageable girl (*As eladó lány*)
   4. Song (*Dal*)

(86) CANTATA PROFANA: THE NINE ENCHANTED STAGS (A *kilenc csodaszarvas*), for double mixed chorus, tenor and baritone soloists, and orchestra (Budapest, 8 September 1930). First performance, London, 25 May 1934, Trefor Jones, tenor, Frank Phillips, baritone, BBC Symphony and Wireless Chorus, Aylmer Buesst conducting.

(87) CONCERTO No. 2, for piano and orchestra (October 1930-September-October 1931). First performance, Frankfurt, 23 January 1933, by the composer with Frankfurt Radio Symphony, Hans Rosbaud conducting.

(88) FORTY-FOUR DUOS, for two violins (1931). First performance (in part), Budapest, 20 January 1932, Imre Waldbauer and György Hannover. Numbers 28, 32, 38, 43, 16, and 36 were transcribed for piano (1936) as PETITE SUITE.

(89) TRANSYLVANIAN DANCES (*Erdélyi táncok*), for orchestra (1931). Transcription of the SONATINA for piano (1915).

(90) HUNGARIAN SKETCHES (*Magyar képek*), for orchestra (Mondsee, 1931). Transcriptions of the following: nos. 5 and 10 of TEN EASY PIECES (1908); no. 2 of FOUR DIRGES (1909-10); no. 2 of THREE BURLESQUES (1911); no. 40 of FOR CHILDREN, vol. 1. First performance, Budapest, 26 November 1934, Philharmonic Society, Heinrich Laber conducting.

(91) SZEKELY SONGS (*Székely dalok*), for male chorus, a cappella (Budapest, November 1932).
    1. How often I've regretted (*Hej, de sokszor megbántottál*)
    2. My God, my life (*Istenem, életem*)
    3. Slender thread, hard seed (*Vékony cérna, kemény mag*)
    4. In Kilyénfalva girls are gathering (*Kilyénfalvi középtizbe*)
    5. = 3.
    6. Do a dance, priest (*Járjad pap a táncot*)

(92) HUNGARIAN PEASANT SONGS (*Magyar parasztdal*), for orchestra (1933). Transcriptions of nos. 6-12, 14, 15, of FIFTEEN HUNGARIAN PEASANT SONGS (1914-17). First performance, Szombathely, 18 March 1934, Gyula Baranyai conducting.

(93) HUNGARIAN FOLKSONGS (*Magyar népdalok*), for voice and orchestra (1933). Transcriptions of nos. 1, 2, 10, 11, 14, of TWENTY HUNGARIAN FOLKSONGS (1929). First performance, Budapest, 23 October 1933, Mária Basilides with Philharmonic Society, Ernő Dohnányi conducting.

(94) STRING QUARTET No. 5 (Budapest, 6 August-6 September 1934). Dedicated to Mrs. Elizabeth Sprague Coolidge. First public performance, Washington, 8 April 1935, Kolisch Quartet.

(95) TWENTY-SEVEN CHORUSES (27 *két- és háromszólamú kórus*), for 2- and 3-part children's or women's chorus (1935). First performance (nos. 1-17, 25), Budapest, 7 May 1937; conductors: Paula Radnai, Lázló Prcisinger (Perényi), Mme. Ferenc Barth, Benjamin Rajecky, Adrienne Stojanovics. Orchestral accompaniments were provided for nos. 1, 2, 7, 11, 12.
    1. Don't leave me (*Ne menj el*)
    2. Hussar (*Huszárnóta*)

3. Letter to those at home (*Levél az otthoniakhoz*)
4. Play song (*Játék*)
5. I've no one in the world (*Senkim a világon*)
6. Alas, alas (*Héjja, héjja*)
7. Breadbaking (*Cipósütés*)
8. I have a ring (*Van egy gyűrűm*)
9. Girls' teasing song (*Lánycsúfoló*)
10. Don't leave here (*Ne hagyj itt!*)
11. Loafers' song (*Resteknek nótája*)
12. Wandering (*Bolyongás*)
13. Courting (*Leánynéző*)
14. Enchanting song (*Jószág-igéző*)
15. Suitor (*Leánykérő*)
16. Spring (*Tavasz*)
17. Boys' teasing song (*Legénycsúfoló*)
18. Had I not seen you (*Ne láttalak volna*)
19. Grief (*Keserves*)
20. Regret (*Bánat*)
21. The bird flew away (*Elment a madárka*)
22. Bird song (*Madárdal*)
23. Jeering (*Csujogató*)
24. Pillow dance (*Párnás táncdal*)
25. Michaelmas congratulation (*Mihálynapi köszöntő*)
26. God be with you (*Isten veled!*)
27. Canon: I'm dying for Csurgó (*Kanon: Meghalok Csurgóért*)

(96) FROM OLDEN TIMES (*Elmult időkből*), after old Hungarian folk- and art-song texts, for 3-part male chorus, a cappella (1935). First performance, Budapest, 7 May 1937, Béla Endre Chamber Chorus, Béla Endre conducting.
1. No one's more unhappy than the peasant (*Nincs boldogtalanabb*)
2. One, two, three, four (*Egy, kettő, három, négy*)
3. No one is happier than the peasant (*Nincsen szerencsésebb*)

(97) PETITE SUITE, for piano (1936). Transcriptions of nos. 28, 32, 38, 43, 16, 36, of FORTY-FOUR DUOS for two violins (1931). Transcribed for band by Charles Cushing (1963).

(98) MUSIC FOR STRING INSTRUMENTS, PERCUSSION, AND CE-LESTA (Budapest, 7 September 1936). Commissioned for the tenth anniversary of the Basle Chamber Orchestra. First performance, Basle, 21 January 1937, by the Basle Chamber Orchestra, Paul Sacher conducting.

(99) SONATA FOR TWO PIANOS AND PERCUSSION (Budapest, July-August 1937). First performance, Basle, 16 January 1938, by Béla and Ditta Bartók, Fritz Schiesser, and Philipp Rühlig. Transcribed as CONCERTO FOR TWO PIANOS AND ORCHESTRA (December 1940); first performance, New York, 21 January 1943, Béla and Ditta Bartók, New York Philharmonic Symphony, Fritz Reiner conducting. Commissioned by Basle section of the International Society for Contemporary Music.

(100) CONTRASTS, for violin, clarinet, and piano (Budapest, 24 September 1938). Dedicated to Benny Goodman and Joseph Szigeti. First performance, New York, 9 January 1939, Joseph Szigeti, Benny Goodman, Endre Petri.

(101) VIOLIN CONCERTO [No. 2] (Budapest, August 1937-31 December 1938). Dedicated to Zoltán Székely. First performance, Amsterdam, 23 March 1939, by Zoltán Székely, Concertgebouw Orchestra, Willem Mengelberg conducting.

(102) MIKROKOSMOS, 153 progressive pieces for piano (1926-39). The first two volumes are dedicated to Péter Bartók; nos. 148-153 (SIX DANCES IN BULGARIAN RHYTHM) to Harriet Cohen. Bartók transcribed seven pieces from the series for two pianos (nos. 113, 69, 135, 123, 127, 145, 146). Tibor Serly transcribed for orchestra, as SUITE FROM 'MIKROKOSMOS,' seven pieces (nos. 139, 137, 117, 142, 102, 151, 153), with the third of the THREE HUNGARIAN FOLK TUNES (1914-17) as prelude. Serly also transcribed for string quartet FIVE PIECES FROM 'MIKROKOSMOS' (nos. 139, 102, 108, 116, 142).

(103) DIVERTIMENTO, for string orchestra (Saanen, 2-17 August 1939). Dedicated to the Basle Chamber Orchestra. First performance, Basle, 11 June 1940, Paul Sacher conducting the Basle Chamber Orchestra.

(104) STRING QUARTET No. 6 (Saanen-Budapest, August-November 1939). Dedicated to the Kolisch Quartet. First performance, New York, 20 January 1941, by the Kolisch Quartet.

(105) CONCERTO FOR ORCHESTRA (Saranac Lake, 15 August-8 October 1943). Written for the Koussevitzky Music Foundation in memory of Mrs. Natalie Koussevitzky. First performance, Boston, 1 December 1944, Boston Symphony Orchestra, Serge Koussevitzky conducting.

(106) SONATA FOR SOLO VIOLIN (Asheville, 14 March 1944). Dedicated to Yehudi Menuhin. First performance, New York, 26 November 1944, by Yehudi Menuhin.

(107) THE HUSBAND'S GRIEF (A ferj keserve), Ukrainian folksong, for voice and piano (February 1945). Dedicated to Pál Kecskeméti. Unpublished, but reproduced in facsimile in Lev. II, pls. XIV-XV.

(108) CONCERTO No. 3, for piano and orchestra (1945). Unfinished; last 17 measures completed by Tibor Serly. First performance, 8 February 1946, by György Sándor with the Philadelphia Orchestra, Eugene Ormandy conducting.

(109) VIOLA CONCERTO (1945). Unfinished; reconstructed and orchestrated by Tibor Serly. Written for William Primrose. First performance, Minneapolis, 2 December 1949, by William Primrose with the Minneapolis Symphony Orchestra, Antal Dórati conducting.

(110) CADENZAS FOR THE CONCERTO IN E-FLAT (K. 482) by Mozart.

BIBLIOGRAPHY

1—Books and Pamphlets by Bartók

Cântece poporale românești din comitatul Bihor (Ungaria) (Romanian folksongs from the Bihor district). Bucharest: Librăriile Socec & Comp. și C. Sfetea, 1913. 371 tunes.

Erdélyi magyarság népdalok (Transylvanian folksongs). Budapest: Népies Irodalmi Társaság, 1923. Editions in Hungarian, French, English. 150 tunes. [With Zoltán Kodály.]

Die Volksmusik der Rumänen von Maramureș (The folk music of the Romanians of Maramureș). *Sammelbände für vergleichende Musikwissenschaft*, vol. IV. Munich: Drei Masken Verlag, 1923. 339 tunes.
In Romanian: see *Scrieri mărunte*, below.

A magyar népdal (The Hungarian folksong). Budapest: Rózsavölgyi és Társa, 1924. 320 tunes.
In German: *Das ungarische Volkslied*. Berlin: Walter de Gruyter, 1925.
In English: *Hungarian folk music*. London: Oxford University Press, 1931.
[This is abbreviated HFM in the preceding pages.]

Népzenénk és a szomszéd népek népzenéje (Our folk music and the folk music of neighboring peoples). Budapest: Ed. Somló, 1934; Zeneműkiadó, 1952. 127 tunes.
In German: *Die Volksmusik der Magyaren und der benachbarten Völker*. Berlin: Walter de Gruyter, 1935.
In French: *La Musique populaire des Hongrois et des peuples voisins*. Budapest: Archivum Europae Centro Orientalis, II (1936), pp. 197-244; also published separately as No. 5 of *Études sur l'Europe Centre-Orientale*, 1937. The latter edition also contains Bartók's 'Réponse à une attaque roumaine' (see below, II).
In Romanian: see *Scrieri mărunte*, below.
In Slovakian: *Maďarská ľudová hudba ľudová susedných národov*. Bratislava: Slovenská Akadémie Vied, 1954.

Die Melodien der rumänischen Colinde (The melodies of the Romanian Colinde). Vienna: Universal-Edition A. G., 1935. 484 tunes.

Halk müziği hakkinda (Three lectures on folk music). Ankara: Receb Ulosoğlu, 1936.
In Hungarian: 'A népzene.' *Új Zenei Szemle* (Budapest), 1954.
(First two lectures complete, the third abridged). (4)

Scrieri mărunte despre muzica populara românească (Short articles on Romanian folk music). Translated by Constantin Brăiloiu. Bucharest, 1937.

Miért és hogyan gyüjtsünk népzenét (Why and how do we collect folk music?). Budapest: Ed. Somló, 1936.
In French: *Pourquoi et comment recueille-t-on la musique populaire?* Geneva: Imprimerie Albert Kundig, 1948.

337

Önéletrajz; írások a zenéről (Autobiography; writings on music). Introductory study by János Demény. Budapest: Magyar Könyvnap Egyetemi Nyomda, 1946.

Válogatott zenei irásai (Selected writings on music). Edited by András Szőllősy; introduction and notes by Bence Szabolcsi. Budapest: Magyar Kórus, 1948. [This is abbreviated vzi in the preceding pages.]
Revised and enlarged edition, as *Válogatott irásai* (without introduction and notes by Szabolcsi, but with notes and bibliography by the editor). Budapest: Művelt Nép, 1956. [Abbreviated vzi ii.]

Bartók Béla levelek, fényképek, kéziratok, kották (Letters, photographs, manuscripts, facsimiles). Edited by János Demény. Budapest: Magyar Művészeti Tanács, 1948. [This is abbreviated *Lev.* i in the preceding pages.]

Bartók Béla levelei (az utolsó két év gyüjtése) (Letters collected in the last two years). Edited by János Demény; preface by András Mihály. Budapest: Művelt Nép Könyvkiadó, 1951. [This is abbreviated *Lev.* ii in the preceding pages.]

Serbo-Croatian Folk Songs. Texts and transcriptions of 75 folksongs from the Milman Parry Collection, and a morphology of Serbo-Croatian folk melodies. Foreword by George Herzog. New York: Columbia University Press, 1951. [With Albert B. Lord.]

Corpus musicae popularis Hungaricae. i. *Gyermekjátékok* (Children's Games); ii. *Jeles napok* (Festal Days); iiia/b. *Lakodalom* (Wedding Songs); iv. *Párosítók* (Pairing Songs). Edited by Béla Bartók and Zoltán Kodály; prepared for the press by György Kerényi. Budapest: Akadémiai Kiadó, 1952-

Scritti sulla musica popolare (Writings on folk music). Edited by Diego Carpitella; preface by Zoltán Kodály. Torino: Edizioni Scientifiche Einaudi, 1955.

Bartók Béla levelei. Magyar, Román, Szlovák dokumentumok (Letters; Hungarian, Romanian, Slovakian documents). Edited by János Demény. Budapest: Zeneműkiadó Vállalat, 1955. [Abbreviated *Lev.* iii.]

Bartók breviárium. Levelek, írások, dokumentumok (Bartók breviary: letters, writings, documents). Edited by József Újfalussy. Budapest: Zeneműkiadó, 1958.

Slovenské ľudové piesne (Slovakian folksongs). i. Bratislava: Slovenskej Akadémie Vied, 1959.

Ausgewählte Briefe (Selected letters). Collected and edited by János Demény. Budapest: Corvina, 1960.

II—Articles by Bartók

[Numbers following entries indicate inclusion in various collections: (1) in *Önéletrajz; írások a zenéről*; (2) in *Válogatott zenei irásai*; (3) in *Scrieri mărunțe*; (4) in *Válogatott irásai*; (5) in *Scritti sulla musica popolare*; (6) in Reich: *Béla Bartók.*]

'Kossuth.' *Zeneközlöny* (Budapest), 1904.
'Strauss: Simfonia domestica (Op.53).' *Zeneközlöny* (Budapest), 1905.
'Székely népballadák' (Székler ballads). *Ethnographia* (Budapest), 1908.
'Dunántúlii balladák' (Transdanubian ballads). *Ethnographia* (Budapest), 1909.
'Függelék a "Wohltemperiertes Klavier" revideált kiadása i. füzetéhez' (Appendix to the revised edition of the *Wohltemperiertes Klavier*, Vol. i). Budapest: Károly Rozsnyai, c. 1910.
'Strauss Richard Elektrája' (Richard Strauss's 'Elektra'). *A Zene* (Budapest), 1910; *Szimfónia* (Budapest), 1917. (4)

'Rhapsodie für Klavier und Orchester (Op. 1).' *Die Musik* (Vienna), 1910; *Schweizerische Musikzeitung* (Zürich), 1910.
'A magyar zenéről' (About Hungarian music). *Aurora* (Budapest), 1911. (1, 2, 4, 5)
In French: 'De la musique hongroise.' *La Revue musicale* (Paris), 1955.
In German: 'Über ungarische Musik.' *Der Merker* (Vienna), 1916.
Liszt zenéje és a mai közönség' (The music of Liszt and today's public). *Népművelés* (Budapest), 1911; *Zeneközlöny* (Budapest), 1911. (1, 2)
In English: 'Liszt's music and our contemporary public.' *New Hungarian Quarterly* (Budapest), 1961.
'Delius-bemutató bécsben' (A Delius première in Vienna). *Zeneközlöny* (Budapest), 1911. (2, 4)
'A magyar nép hangszerei' (Hungarian folk instruments). *Ethnographia* (Budapest), 1911-12.
'A hangszeres zene folklóréja Magyarországon' (Instrumental music-folklore in Hungary). *Zeneközlöny* (Budapest), 1911-12.
'A clavecinre írt művek előadása' (The performance of works written for the clavecin). *Zeneközlöny* (Budapest), 1912. (4)
'Az összehasonlító zenefolklore' (Comparative music-folklore). *Új Élet* (Budapest), 1912. (2, 4, 5)
'A hunyadi román nép zenedialektusa' (The Romanian folk-music dialect of Hunyad). *Ethnographia* (Budapest), 1914. (3; Szegő: *Bartók Béla a népdalkutató*).
In German: 'Der Musikdialekt der Rumänen von Hunyad.' *Zeitschrift für Musikwissenschaft* (Leipzig), 1920.
In Romanian: *Muzică şi Poezie* (Bucharest), 1936.
'Observari despre muzică popolară românească' (Observations on Romanian folk music). *Convorbiri literare* (Bucharest), 1914. (3)
In Hungarian: 'Megjegyzések a román népzenéről.' In Szegő: *Bartók Béla a népdalkutató*.
'Primitiv népi hangszerek Magyarországon' (Primitive folk instruments of Hungary). *Zenei Szemle* (Budapest), 1917.
'A Biskra-vidéki arabok népzenéje' (The folk music of the Arabs of Biskra and environs). *Szimfónia* (Budapest), 1917.
In German: 'Die Volksmusik der Araber von Biskra und Umgebung.' *Zeitschrift für Musikwissenschaft* (Leipzig), 1920.
'A zeneszerző a darabjáról' (The composer on his work: first performance of *The Wooden Prince*). *Magyar Színpad* (Budapest), 1917. (4)
'Die Melodien der madjarischen Soldatenlieder' (The melodies of the Hungarian soldier songs). *Programmheft des historischen Konzertes* (Vienna), 12 January 1918.
'Selbstbiographie' (Autobiography). *Musikpädagogische Zeitschrift* (Vienna), 1918; *Musikblätter des Anbruch* (Vienna), 1921.
In Hungarian: Önéletrajzom.' *Magyar Irás* (Budapest), 1921. (1, 2, 4)
In English: 'The Life of Béla Bartók.' *Tempo* (London), 1949; see also *Béla Bartók: A Memorial Review* (below, III).
In Italian: 'Autobiografia.' (5)
'Szerzők a darabjukról' (Composers on their works: first performance of Duke Bluebeard's Castle). *Magyar Színpad* (Budapest), 1918.
'Musikfolklore' (Music folklore). *Musikblätter des Anbruch* (Vienna), 1919.
Reprinted in Stuckenschmidt: *Neue Musik*.
In Hungarian: 'Zenei folklor.' (4)

'A. Schönbergs Musik in Ungarn' (A. Schoenberg's music in Hungary). *Musikblätter des Anbruch* (Vienna), 1920.
    In Hungarian: 'Schönberg zenéje Magyarországon.' (4)
'Ungarische Musik' (Hungarian music). *Musikblätter des Anbruch* (Vienna), 1920.
'Das Problem der neuen musik' (The problem of the new music). *Melos* (Berlin), 1920. (6)
'Bartók válasza Hubay Jenőnek' (Bartók's answer to Jenő Hubay). *Szózat* (Budapest), 1920. (2, 5)
'Der Einfluss der Volksmusik auf die heutige Kunstmusik' (The influence of folk music on the art music of today). *Melos* (Berlin), 1920; *Mitteilungen der Oesterreichischen Musiklehrerschaft* (Vienna), 1932; *Melos* (Mainz), 1949. (6)
    In Danish: 'Folkemusikkens indflydelse pa den moderne musik.' *Dansk Musiktidsskrift* (Copenhagen), 1951.
    In English: 'The Relation of Folksong to the Development of the Art Music of Our Time.' *The Sackbut* (London), 1921. Also 'The Influence of Peasant Music on Modern Music.' *Tempo* (London), 1949-50; see also *Béla Bartók: A Memorial Review* (below, III).
    In Hungarian: 'A parasztzene hatása az újabb műzenére.' *Magyar Minerva* (Bratislava), 1931; *Új Idők* (Budapest), 1931. (2, 4)
    In Italian: 'L'influsso della musica contadina sulla musica colta moderna.' (5)
    In Polish: 'O wpływic muzyki wicjskiej na twórczosc artystyczna.' *Muzyka* (Warsaw), 1927.
    In Romanian: *Revista Fundaților Regale* (Bucharest), 1934.
    In Swedish: 'Folkmusikens inflytande på den moderna musiken.' *Musik Revy* (Stockholm), 1951.
'La musique populaire hongroise' (Hungarian folk music). *La Revue musicale* (Paris), 1920.
'Kodály's Trio.' *Musical Courier* (New York), 1920.
    In Hungarian: 'Kodály Triójáról és Gordonkaszonátájáról.' (4)
'Kodály Zoltán' (Zoltán Kodály). *Nyugat* (Budapest), 1921. (2, 4, 5)
'Aki nem tud arabusul' (He who knows no Arabic). *Szózat* (Budapest), 1921. (2, 4)
'Two unpublished Liszt letters to Mosonyi.' *Musical Quarterly* (New York), 1921.
'Della musica moderna in Ungheria' (Of modern music in Hungary). *Il Pianoforte* (Turin), 1921. (5)
    In Hungarian: 'Az új magyar zenéről.' (2, 4)
'Lettera di Budapest' (Budapest letter), I-II. *Il Pianoforte* (Turin), 1921. (4)
'La Musique populaire hongroise' (Hungarian folk music). *La Revue musicale* (Paris), 1921.
'The Development of Art Music in Hungary.' *Chesterian* (London), 1922.
'Hungarian Folk Music'; 'Hungarian Musical Instruments'; 'Hungarian Opera, Pantomime, and Ballet'; 'Romanian Folk Music'; 'Slovak Folk Music.' Articles in *A Dictionary of Modern Music and Musicians;* also brief notices of many Hungarian composers and musicians. London: J. M. Dent & Sons, Ltd., 1924.
    The article on Romanian folk music also appears:
    In German: *Das neue Musiklexikon,* 1926.
    In Romanian: *Scrieri mărunțe* (3).
'U zródel muzyki ludowej' (The origin of folk music). *Muzyka* (Warsaw), 1925.

'Rundfragebeantwortung zum Problem "Klavier"' (Answer to the inquiry on the problem of the piano). *Musikblätter des Anbruch* (Vienna), 1927.

'The Folksongs of Hungary.' *Pro Musica* (New York), 1928.

In Hungarian: 'Magyar népzene és új magyar zene.' *Zenei Szemle* (Budapest), 1928. (1, 2, 4, 5)

'Digging for Folk Music' (as told to Joan Foster). *Musical Digest* (New York), 1928.

'Zenefolklore-kutatások Magyarországon' (Music-folklore research in Hungary). *Zenei Szemle* (Budapest), 1929; *Ethnographia* (Budapest), 1929 [abridged]. (2, 3)

In French: 'Les Recherches sur le folklore musical en Hongrie.' *Art populaire* (Paris), 1931.

In Romanian: 'Cercetările de folklore muzical în Ungaria.' (*Muzica şi poezie* (Bucharest), 1936.

'The National Temperament in Music.' *Musical Times* (London), 1929.

'Magyar népi hangszerek.' 'Román népzene,' 'Szlovák népzene' (Hungarian folk instruments; Romanian folk music; Slovak folk music). Articles in *Zenei Lexikon* (Budapest), 1930-31 (3—the first only).

'Möller, Heinrich: Ungarische Volkslieder. Das Lied der Völker' (Möller: Hungarian folksongs; the song of the people). *Zeitschrift für Musikwissenschaft* (Leipzig), 1931.

'Cigányzene? Magyar zene?' (Gipsy music? Hungarian music?) *Ethnographia* (Budapest), 1931). (2, 4, 5)

In English: 'Gipsy Music or Hungarian Music?' *Musical Quarterly* (New York), 1947.

In German: 'Über die Herausgabe ungarischer Volkslieder.' *Ungarische Jahrbücher* (Berlin), 1931.

'Nochmals: Über die Herausgabe ungarischer Volkslieder.' (Again: On the publication of Hungarian folksongs). *Zeitschrift für Musikwissenschaft* (Leipzig), 1931.

'The Peasant Music of Hungary.' *Musical Courier* (New York), 1931.

'Mi a népzene?' (What is folk music?) *Új Idők* (Budapest), 1931. (2, 4, 5)

'A népzene jelentőségéről' (The significance of folk music). *Új Idők* (Budapest), 1931. (2, 4, 5)

In English: 'On the Significance of Folk Music.' *Tempo* (London), 1949-50; see also *Béla Bartók: A Memorial Review* (below, III).

'Zum Kongress für arabische Musik—Kairo' (For the Congress of Arab music, Cairo). *Zeitschrift für vergleichende Musikwissenschaft* (Berlin), 1932.

'Gegenantwort an Heinrich Möller' (Counter-reply to Heinrich Möller). *Ungarische Jahrbücher* (Berlin), 1932.

'Neue Ergebnisse der Volksliedforschung in Ungarn' (New results of folksong research in Hungary). *Anbruch* (Vienna), 1932.

'Ungarische Volksmusik' (Hungarian folk music). *Schweizerische Sängerzeitung* (Berne), 1933. (5)

In Hungarian: 'A régi magyar népzenéről.' In *Kodály Emlékkönyv* (Budapest), 1943. (2, 4)

'Rumänische Volksmusik' (Romanian folk music). *Schweizerische Sängerzeitung* (Berne), 1933. (3, 4)

In Romanian: *Muzică şi Poezie* (Bucharest), 1936.

'Hungarian Peasant Music.' *Musical Quarterly* (New York), 1933.

In Hungarian: 'Magyar parasztzene.' (4)

'Answer to Percy Grainger's "Melody versus rhythm." ' *Music News* (Chicago?), 1934.
    In Hungarian: *Lev.* III, p. 399-400.
Interview. *Vremea* (Bucharest), 1934. (3)
'Miért gyüjtsünk népzenét?' (Why do we collect folk music?) *Zeneművészeti Főiskolai Értekezet* (Budapest), 1935; *Válasz* (Budapest), 1935; *Magyar Dal* (Budapest), 1936; *Apollo* (Budapest), 1935. For completion, see *Miért és hogyan gyüjtsünk népzenét?* (above, 1).
'Magyar népzene'; 'Román népzene'; 'Szlovák népzene' (Hungarian folk music; Romanian folk music; Slovak folk music). Articles in *Révai Lexikon*, supplementary volume (Budapest), 1935. (2, 4, 5)
'Liszt-problemák' (Liszt problems). Individual reprint from the *Liszt a mienk* volume. Budapest: Hornyánszky, 1936. *Nyugat* (Budapest), 1936; *Akadémiai Értésitő* (Budapest), 1935, *Magyar Dal,* 1936. (2, 4; excerpt, 5)
    In Dutch: 'Liszt problemen.' *Mens en Melodie* (Utrecht), 1948.
    In English: 'Bartók on Liszt.' *Monthly Musical Record* (London), 1948.
    In French: 'A propos du jubilé Liszt.' *La Revue musicale* (Paris), 1936.
    In German: 'Liszt und Ungarn.' *Musica* (Cassel), 1953.
'Népzene és népdalok' (Folk music and folksongs). *Szép Szó* (Budapest), 1937.
'A népzenéről' (On folk music). *Népszava Naptár* (Budapest?), 1936.
    In French: 'Musique et chansons populaires.' *Acta musicologica* (Copenhagen), 1937.
'A gépzene' (Machine music). *Szép Szó* (Budapest), 1937. (2, 4, 5)
'Népdalgyüjtés Törökországban' (Folksong collecting in Turkey). *Nyugat* (Budapest), 1937. (2, 4, 5)
    In English: 'Collecting Folksongs in Anatolia.' *Hungarian Quarterly* (Budapest), 1937; *Tempo* (London), 1949 [abridged].
    In German: 'Auf Volksliedforschungsfahrt in der Türkei.' *Musik der Zeit* (Bonn), 1953.
'Népdalkutatás és nacionalizmus' (Folksong research and nationalism). *Tükör* (Budapest), 1937 (1, 2, 4, 5)
    In Czech: 'Badáni o lidových písních a nacionalismus.' *Rytmus* (Prague), 1937.
    In French: 'Du lied populaire au nationalisme.' *La Revue internationale de musique* (Brussels), 1938.
'Válasz Petranuek támadására' (Answer to Petranu's attack). *Szép Szó* (Budapest), 1937. (2, 4, 5)
    In French: 'Réponse à une attaque roumaine.' *Études sur l'Europe Centre-Orientale,* no. 5. Budapest, 1937. [See *Népzenénk és a szomszéd népek népzenéje* (above, 1).] Also *La Revue internationale de musique* (Brussels), 1938.
    In German: 'Antwort auf einen rumänischen Angriff.' *Ungarische Jahrbücher* (Berlin), 1937.
'Sur la Sonate pour deux pianos et percussion' (On the Sonata for two pianos and percussion). *National-Zeitung* (Basel), 1938.
'Az úgynevezett bolgár ritmus' (The so-called Bulgarian rhythm). *Énekszó* (Budapest), 1938. (2, 4, 5)
'Ravel.' *La Revue musicale* (Paris), 1938. (4)
'Opinion de M. Béla Bartók (Varsovie [sic]). Opinions sur l'orientation technique, esthétique et spirituelle de la musique contemporaine' (Opinions on the technical, esthetic, and spiritual orientation of contemporary music). *La Revue internationale de musique* (Brussels), 1938.

Foreword and notes to *Mikrokosmos*, 1939.
'Analyse du "Deuxième Concerto" pour piano et orchestre de Béla Bartók par son auteur' (Analysis of the Second Piano Concerto, by the composer). *La Radio* (Lausanne), 1939. (4)
'Parry Collection of Yugoslav Folk Music.' *The New York Times*, 1942.
In Hungarian: Szegő: *Bartók Béla a népdalkutató*.
'Diversity of material yielded up in European melting-pot.' *Musical America* (New York), 1943.
In Hungarian: *Zenetudományi tanulmányok* 1. (See IV, below.)
In Italian: 'Le Energie musicali.' *Il Contemporaneo* (Rome), 1955. (4, 5)
'Bartók Views Folk-music Wealth of Hungary.' *Musical America* (New York), 1943. (4, 5)
'Hungarian Music.' *American Hungarian Observer* (New York), 1944.
'Race Purity in Music.' *Modern Music* (New York), 1942; *Tempo* (London), 1944. (5, 6)
     In German: *Mitteilungen des Basler Kammerorchesters* (Basle), 1947; *Musica* (Kassel), 1947; *Oesterreichische Musikzeitschrift* (Vienna), 1955; *Alte und neue Musik* (See IV below).
     In Hungarian: 'Zene és faji tisztaság.' (2, 4)
'Some Linguistic Observations.' *Tempo* (London), 1946. (4)
     In German: 'Marginalien zu slawischen Musikernamen.' *Musik der Zeit* (Bonn), 1954.
'Música popular y culta en Hungria' (Folk and art music in Hungary). *Nuestra música* (Mexico), 1946. [Not available for identification.]
'Frans Liszt als Hongaar' (Ferenc Liszt as Hungarian). *Mens en Melodie* (Utrecht), 1948. [Not available for identification.]
'O muzyce ludowej' (On folk music). *Muzyka* (Warsaw), 1950. [Not available for identification.]
     N.B. The following, published over the joint signatures of Bartók and Kodály, were actually written by Kodály:
1. Preface to *Magyar népdalok*. Budapest: Rózsavölgyi és Társa, 1906.
2. 'Az Egyetemes Népdalgyüjtemény tervezete' (The Universal Folksong-Collection project). *Ethnographia* (Budapest), 1913.

III—Books and Pamphlets about Bartók

Alexandru, Tiberiu. *Béla Bartók despre folklorul romînesc* (Bartók on Romanian folklore). Bucharest: Editura Muzicala, 1958.
Balzer, Jürgen. *Béla Bartók; en portraetskitse* (A portrait sketch). Folkeuniversitets Bibliotek; Musik, 2. Copenhagen: Rhodos, 1962.
Bátor, Victor. *The Béla Bartók Archives. History and Catalogue*. New York: Bartók Archives, 1963.
Citron, Pierre. *Bartók*. Collection 'Solfège.' Paris: Les Editions du Seuil, 1963.
Csobádi, Péter. *Bartók*. Budapest: Országos Béketanács, 1955.
Demény, János. *Bartók*. Budapest: Egyetemi Nyomda, 1946.
——— *Bartók élete és művei* (Bartók's life and works). Budapest: Székesfővárosi Irodalmi és Művészeti Intézet, 1948.
Dille, Denijs. *Béla Bartók*. Antwerp: N. V. Standaard-Boekhandel, 1939.
——— *Béla Bartók*. Brussels: Nationaal Instituut voor Radio-Omroep, 1947.
——— editor. *Documenta Bartókiana*. Budapest: Akadémiai Kiadó; Mainz: B. Schott's Söhne, I. 1964; II. 1965.

Engelmann, Hans Ulrich. *Béla Bartóks Mikrokosmos. Versuch einer Typologie 'Neuer Musik'* (Essay in 'New Music' typology). Würzburg: Konrad Triltsch Verlag, 1953.

Fassett, Agatha. *The Naked Face of Genius. Béla Bartók's American Years.* Boston: Houghton Mifflin Company, 1958.

—— *Bartók amerikai évei.* Budapest: Zeneműkiadó, 1960.

Fricsay, Ferenc. *Ueber Mozart und Bartók* (About Mozart and Bartók). Foreword by Yehudi Menuhin; afterword by E. Werba. Copenhagen: W. Hansen, 1962.

Geraedts, Henri. *Béla Bartók.* (Componisten-serie, 19.) Haarlem-Antwerp: Gottmer, 1952.

Geraedts, Henri, and Jaap Geraedts. *Béla Bartók.* Haarlem: J. H. Gottmer, 1961.

Haraszti, Emil. *Bartók Béla.* Budapest: Kortársaink, 1930.

—— *Béla Bartók, His Life and Works.* Paris: Lyrebird Press, 1938.

Jemnitz, Alexander. *Béla Bartók, his life and music.* New York: Hungarian Reference Library, 1940.

Kiss, Béla. *Bartók Béla művészete* (The art of Bartók). Cluj: Ifjú Erdély, 1946.

Kristóf, Károly. *Beszélgetések Bartók Bélaval* (Conversations with Bartók). Budapest: Zeneműkiadó, 1957.

Kuckertz, J. *Gestaltvariation in den von Bartók gesammelten rumänischen Colinde.* Cologne: Kölner Beiträge zur Musikforschung, vol. 23, 1963.

Láng, György. *Bartók élete és művei* (Bartók's life and works). Budapest: Grill Károly Kiadás, 1947.

Lendvai, Ernő. *Bartók stilusa* (Bartók's style). Budapest: Zeneműkiadó, 1955.

Lesznaj, Lajos. *Béla Bartók. Sein Leben—seine Werke* (Bartók: his life and works). Leipzig: Deutscher Verlag für Musik, 1961.

Lopes Graça, Fernando. *Béla Bartók. Três apontamentos sobre a sua personalidade e a sua obra* (Three annotations on his personality and his music). Lisbon: Gazeta Musical, 1953.

Martynov, Ivan Ivanovich. *Béla Bartók. Ocherk zhizni i tvorchestva* (Sketch of his life and work). Moscow: Gos. muz. Izd., 1956.

Molnár, Antal. *Bartók művészete* (The art of Bartók). Budapest: Rózsavölgyi és Társa, 1948.

Moreux, Serge. *Béla Bartók.* Paris: Richard-Masse, 1955.

—— *Béla Bartók.* English translation by G. S. Fraser and Erik de Mauny. London: Harvill Press, 1953.

—— *Béla Bartók.* Japanese translation of the 1955 edition. Tokyo: David Co., Ltd., 1957.

—— *Béla Bartók, Leben, Werk, Stil.* Zürich: Atlantis Verlag, 1950.

—— *Béla Bartók, liv, vaerker, stil.* Danish translation by Sven Møller Kristensen. Copenhagen: J. H. Schultz Forlag, 1951.

—— *Béla Bartók, sa vie, ses oeuvres, son langage* (Béla Bartók, his life, his works, his language). Paris: Richard-Masse, 1949.

Nüll, Edwin von der. *Béla Bartók, ein Beitrag zur Morphologie der neuen Musik* (Béla Bartók, a contribution to the morphology of the new music). Halle: Mitteldeutsche Verlags A.G., 1930.

Ottó, Ferenc. *Bartók Béla a Cantata Profana tükrében* (Béla Bartók in the mirror of the *Cantata profana*). Budapest: Kéve Könyvkiadó Kiadása, 1936.

de Paoli, Domenico. *Los cuartetos de Béla Bartók* (The quartets of Bartók). Madrid: Real Conservatorio de Música, 1953.

Petzoldt, Richard. *Béla Bartók, sein Leben in Bildern* (His life in pictures). Leipzig: Verlag Enzyklopädie, 1958.

Reich, Willi. *Béla Bartók. Eigene Schriften und Erinnerungen der Freunde* (His own writings and reminiscences of his friends). Basel-Stuttgart: Benno Schwabe & Co., 1950.

Révész, András. *Bartók Béla utja* (The way of Béla Bartók). Budapest: Apollo Füzetek, 1936.

Rondi, Brunello. *Bartók.* (Essay with a preface by Fedele d'Amico.) Rome: Ed. Petrignani, 1950.

Seiber, Mátyás. *The String Quartets of Béla Bartók.* London: Boosey & Hawkes, 1945.

Stevens, Halsey. *The Life and Music of Béla Bartók.* Japanese translation by Naosuke Uyama. Tokyo: Kinokuniya Books, 1961.

Suchoff, Benjamin. *Guide to the Mikrokosmos of Béla Bartók.* Silver Spring, Md.; Music Services Corporation of America, 1956 (=1962?).

Szabolcsi, Bence. *Béla Bartók, Leben und Werk* (Life and work). Leipzig: Verlag Philipp Reclam Jun., 1961.

Szabolcsi, Bence, editor. *Bartók, sa vie et son œuvre* (Bartók, his life and work). Budapest: Corvina, 1957. [Biographical study by the editor; essays on Bartók; essays, articles, and letters by Bartók; bibliography of his compositions and musicological writings by András Szőllősy.]

——— *Bartók Weg und Werk; Schriften und Briefe.* Budapest: Corvina; Leipzig: Breitkopf & Haertel, 1957.

Szabolcsi, Bence, and Ferenc Bónis. *Bartók Béla élete. Bartók élete képekben* (The life of Bartók; Bartók's life in pictures). Budapest: Zeneműkiadó, 1956.

Szegő, Julia. *Bartók Béla a népdalkutató* (Bartók the folksong researcher). Bucharest: Állami Irodalmi és Művészeti Kiadó, 1956.

Székely, Julia. *Bartók tanár úr* (Bartók the professor). Pécs: Dunántúli Magvetö, 1957.

Szentkirály, Joseph, editor. *Béla Bartók.* New York: Hungarian Reference Library, 1940.

Traimer, Roswitha. *Béla Bartóks Kompositionstechnik, dargestellt an seinen sechs Streichquartetten* (Bartók's technique of composition, as shown by his six string quartets). Regensburg: Gustav Bosse Verlag, 1956.

Uhde, Jürgen. *Béla Bartók.* (Collection 'Köpfe d. xx. Jahrhunderts,' 11). Berlin: Colloquium Verlag, 1959.

——— *Bartók Mikrokosmos—Spielanweisung und Erläuterungen* (Playing instructions and explanations). Regensburg: Gustav Bosse Verlag, n.d. (1954?).

Verhaar, Ary. *Het leven van Béla Bartók, 1881-1945* (The life of Béla Bartók). (Musica-serie. Kleine boeken over grote mannen, 14.) The Hague: J. P. Kruseman (1951?).

Béla Bartók, A Memorial Review. (Articles on his life and works, reprinted from *Tempo,* 1949-50.) New York: Boosey & Hawkes, 1950.

IV—References to Bartók in Other Books

Alte und neue Musik. 25 Jahre Basler Kammerorchester. Zürich: Atlantis Verlag, 1952, pp. 70-78, 181-3, 185-7.

Apel, Willi. *Masters of the Keyboard. A Brief Survey of Pianoforte Music.* Cambridge: Harvard University Press, 1947, pp. 292-3.

Bekker, Paul. *Klang und Eros.* Zweiter Band der gesammelten Schriften. Stuttgart & Berlin: Deutsche Verlags-Anstalt, 1922, pp. 77-82.

Blom, Eric. *Stepchildren of Music.* New York: The Dial Press, 1926. Contents include: 'Béla Bartók as Quartet Writer,' pp. 239-46.

Brook, Donald. *Composers' Gallery*. Biographical sketches of contemporary composers. London: Rockliff, 1946, pp. 121-5.

Carner, Mosco. *Of men and music*. London: Joseph Williams, Ltd., 1944. Contents include chapter, 'Bartók's string quartets.'

Cobbett, Walter Willson, editor. *Cyclopedic Survey of Chamber Music*. London: Oxford University Press, 1929/30, vol. I, pp. 60-65.

Coeuroy, André. *Panorama de la musique contemporaine*. Paris: Editions Kra, 1928, pp. 45-51.

Cohen, Harriet. *Music's Handmaid*. London: Faber, 1936; rev. ed. 1950, pp. 153-63.

Collaer, Paul. *A History of Modern Music*. Translated by Sally Abeles. Cleveland & New York: World Publishing Co., 1961, pp. 343-53.

Copland, Aaron. *Copland on Music*. Garden City, N.Y.: Doubleday & Co., Inc., 1960, pp. 246-9.

—— *Our New Music*. New York: Whittlesey House, 1941, pp. 66-70.

Demuth, Norman. *Musical Trends in the 20th Century*. London: Rockliff, 1952, pp. 265-76.

Edwards, Arthur C. *The Art of Melody*. New York: Philosophical Library, Inc., 1956, pp. 225-7.

Ewen, David, editor. *The Book of Modern Composers*. New York: Alfred A. Knopf, 1942, pp. 211-26; 520-22.

—— *Twentieth-Century Composers*. New York: Thomas Y. Crowell Co., 1937, pp. 161-9.

Forte, Allen. *Contemporary Tone-Structures*. New York: Bureau of Publications, Teachers College, Columbia University, 1955, pp. 74-90, 139-43, 167-70.

Foss, Hubert J. *The Heritage of Music*, vol. III. London & New York: Oxford University Press, 1951, pp. 172-91.

—— *Music in My Time*. London: Rich and Cowen, 1933, pp. 144-52, 164, 178.

Garcia Morillo, Roberto. *Siete músicos europeos*. Buenos Aires: Ollantay, 1949. Contents include chapter on Bartók.

Gilman, Lawrence. *Orchestral Music: An Armchair Guide*. New York: Oxford University Press, 1951, pp. 32-6.

Gray, Cecil. *A Survey of Contemporary Music*. London: Oxford University Press, 1924, pp. 194-209.

Hackenbroich, Heinz. *Musiker von Heute*. Fulda: Verlag Parzeller & Co., 1949, pp. 27-39.

Hansen, Peter. *An Introduction to Twentieth Century Music*. Boston: Allyn and Bacon, Inc., 1961, pp. 223-8.

Hartog, Howard, editor. *European Music in the Twentieth Century*. London: Routledge & Kegan Paul, 1957. Contents include: 'The Music of Béla Bartók,' by Everett Helm, pp. 11-39.

Heinsheimer, Hans W. *Fanfare for Two Pigeons*. Garden City: Doubleday & Co., 1952, pp. 104-23.

Hill, Ralph, editor. *The Concerto*. London: Penguin Books, 1952. Contents include: 'Béla Bartók (1881-1945),' by Mosco Carner, pp. 327-56.

Hodeir, André. *La Musique étrangère contemporaine*. Paris: Presses Universitaires de France, 1954, pp. 70-80.

Jacobs, Arthur, editor. *Choral Music*. Harmondsworth and Baltimore: Penguin Books, 1963. Contents include chapter on 'Four Revolutionaries,' by Dika Newlin, discussing mainly the *Cantata Profana*.

Jakobik, Albert. *Zur Einheit der neuen Musik.* (Debussy, Bartók, Hindemith.) Würzburg: Konrad Triltsch Verlag, 1957.

Machlis, Joseph. *The Enjoyment of Music.* New York: W. W. Norton & Co., rev. ed., 1963, pp. 563-71.

——— *Introduction to Contemporary Music.* New York: W. W. Norton & Co., 1961, pp. 183-98.

Magidoff, Robert. *Yehudi Menuhin. The Story of the Man and the Musician.* Garden City: Doubleday & Co., Inc., 1955, pp. 203, 254-60, 289, 295-6.

Moldenhauer, Hans. *Duo-Pianism.* Chicago: Chicago Musical College Press, 1950, pp. 336-8 (Sonata for Two Pianos and Percussion); see also index.

Mooser, Robert Aloys. *Regards sur la musique contemporaine, 1921-1946.* Lausanne: Librairie F. Rouge & Cie., S. A., 1946, pp. 113-14, 263-4, 268-70, 280-82, 419-21, 433-8.

Musikerkenntnis und Musikerziehung. Festgabe für Hans Mersmann. Kassel & Bern: Bärenreiter Verlag, 1957. Contents include: 'Über Bartóks letzte Lebensjahre. Emigration und Charakter—Schicksal und Spätwerk,' by Erich Doflein, pp. 30-43; 'Zur Struktur und Thematik des Violinkonzerts von Béla Bartók,' by Wilhelm Twittenhoff, pp. 143-57.

Ostransky, Leroy, editor. *Perspectives on Music.* New York: Prentice-Hall, Inc., 1963. Contents include: 'Bartók in America,' by Halsey Stevens, pp. 387-400.

Pijper, Willem. *De quintencirkel; opstellen over muziek.* Amsterdam: NVE Querido's Uitgevers-Mij, 1929. Contents include: 'Bartók en het neobeethovenisme,' pp. 141-51.

Rajeczky, Benjamin, and Lajos Vargyas, editors. *Studia memoriae Belae Bartók sacra.* Budapest: Akadémiai Kiadó, 1956. Contents include: 'Musical Folklore Research in Rumania and Béla Bartók's Contribution to It,' by Sabin Drăgoi, pp. 9-25; 'Bartóks Sammlung slowachischer Volkslieder,' by Jozef Kresánek, pp. 51-68.

Reti, Rudolph. *The Thematic Process in Music.* New York: Macmillan Co., 1951, pp. 81-5.

——— *Tonality, Atonality, Pantonality. A Study of Some Trends in Twentieth Century Music.* London: Rockliff, 1958 (see index).

Roland-Manuel (Lévy, Roland Alexis Manuel), and Tagrine, Nadia. *Plaisir de la musique, vol.* III: 'De Beethoven à nos jours.' Paris: Editions du Seuil, 1951, pp. 245-53.

Rosenfeld, Paul. *Discoveries of a Music Critic.* New York: Harcourt, Brace & Co., 1936, pp. 197-204.

——— *Musical Chronicle (1917-1923).* New York: Harcourt, Brace & Co., 1923, pp. 285-92.

Salazar, Adolfo. *Music in Our Time.* New York: W. W. Norton & Co., Inc., 1946, pp. 297-304.

——— *Música y músicos de hoy; ensayos sobre la música actual.* Madrid: Editorial Mundo Latino, 1928, pp. 327-37.

Saminsky, Lazare. *Music of Our Day: Essentials and Prophecies.* New York: Thomas Y. Crowell Co., 1932. Contents include: 'An Austro-German [sic] Triad: Schoenberg, Bartók, Berg,' pp. 137-46.

Schuh, Willi. *Zeitgenössische Musik.* Zürich: Atlantis Verlag, 1947, pp. 42, 45-9.

Slonimsky, Nicolas. *Music Since 1900.* New York: W. W. Norton & Co., 1938 (see index).

Starkie, Walter. *Raggle-taggle.* New York: E. P. Dutton & Co., Inc., 1933, pp. 59, 77-81, 371.

Stevens, Denis, editor. *A History of Song*. New York: W. W. Norton & Co., 1961. Contents include: 'Béla Bartók,' by Hans Nathan, pp. 272-86.

Stuckenschmidt, Hans Heinz. *Neue Musik (Zwischen den beiden Kriegen)*. Berlin: Suhrkamp Verlag, 1951 (see index).

Szabolcsi, Bence, and Dénes Bartha, editors. *Erkel Ferenc és Bartók Béla emlékére*. [*Zenetudományi Tanulmányok*, ii.] Budapest: Akadémiai Kiadó, 1954. Contents include: 'Bartók Béla tanulóévei és romantikus korszaka,' by János Demény, pp. 323-487.

—— *Liszt Ferenc és Bartók Béla emlékére*. [*Zenetudományi Tanulmányok*, iii.] Budapest: Akadémiai Kiadó, 1955. Contents include: 'Apámról,' by Béla Bartók, jr., pp. 281-5; 'Bartók Béla művészi kibontakozásának évei (1906-1914), by János Demény, pp. 286-459; and other articles.

—— *Bartók Béla megjelenése az Európai zeneéletben (1914-1926); Liszt Ferenc hagyatéka*. [*Zenetudományi Tanulmányok*, vii.] Budapest: Akadémiai Kiadó, 1959. Contents include: 'Bartók Béla művészi kibontakozásának évei. ii. rész. (1914-1926),' by János Demény, pp. 5-425.

—— *Bartók Béla emlékére*. [*Zenetudományi Tanulmányok*, x.] Budapest: Akadémiai Kiadó, 1962. Contents include: 'Bartók Béla pályája delelőjén (1927-1940),' by János Demény, pp. 189-727; and other articles.

Szigeti, Joseph. *With Strings Attached*. New York: Alfred A. Knopf, 1947, pp. 33-4, 128-30, 268-72, etc.

Thompson, Oscar, editor. *The International Cyclopedia of Music and Musicians*. New York: Dodd, Mead & Co., 4th ed., 1946, pp. 129-31.

Thomson, Virgil. *The Art of Judging Music*. New York: Alfred A. Knopf, 1948, pp. 176-7.

Ulrich, Homer. *Chamber Music*. The growth and practice of an intimate art. New York: Columbia University Press, 1948, pp. 356-7, 370-71.

Veinus, Abraham. *Victor Book of Concertos*. New York: Simon & Schuster, 1948, pp. 31-4.

Woerner, Karl H. *Musik der Gegenwart; Geschichte der neuen Musik*. Mainz: B. Schott's Söhne, 1949, pp. 106-9.

Zoltano Kodály octogenario sacrum. Budapest: Akadémiai Kiadó, 1962. Contents include: 'Tradition und Neuertum in Bartóks Streichquartetten,' by W. Siegmund-Schultze, pp. 317-28.

V—References to Bartók in Periodicals

Abraham, Gerald. 'The Bartók of the Quartets.' *Music and Letters* (London), 1945.

—— 'Bartók: String Quartet No. 6.' *Music Review* (Cambridge), 1942.

van Ameringen, Sylvia. 'Teaching with Bartók's "Mikrokosmos."' *Tempo* (London), 1951.

Asztalos, Sándor. 'Bartók a mienk.' *Új Zenei Szemle* (Budapest), 1950.

Austin, William. 'Bartók's Concerto for Orchestra.' *Music Review* (Cambridge), 1957.

Babbitt, Milton. 'The String Quartets of Bartók.' *Musical Quarterly* (New York), 1949.

Bartha, Dénes. 'Die neue musikwissenschaftliche Forschung in Ungarn.' *Archiv für Musikforschung* (Leipzig), 1937.

Bartók, János. 'Bartók Béla útja.' *A Zene* (Budapest), 1941-2.

—— 'Bartók, pionnier de la musicologie.' *La Revue musicale* (Paris), 1955.

Bátor, Victor. 'Bartók's Executor Speaks.' *Musical Courier* (New York), 1951.

Becker, Harry Cassin. 'Béla Bartók and His Credo.' *Musical America* (New York), 1927.
Benary, Peter. 'Die zweistimmige Kontrapunkt in Bartóks "Mikrokosmos."' *Archiv für Musikwissenschaft* (Trossingen), 1958.
Berger, Gregor. 'Motivische Gestaltung des Quintraumes bei Bartók.' *Musik im Unterricht* (Mainz), 1954.
Bie, Oskar. 'Brief an Béla Bartók.' *Musikblätter des Anbruch* (Vienna), 1921.
Boys, Henry. 'Béla Bartók, 1881-1945.' *Musical Times* (London), 1945.
Brăiloiu, Constantin. 'Béla Bartók folkloriste.' *Schweizerische Musikzeitung* (Zürich), 1948.
Braschovanoff, Stojan. 'Béla Bartók.' *Slowo* (Sofia), 1935.
Brelet, Giselle. 'Béla Bartók: musique savante et musique populaire.' *Contrepoints* (Paris), 1946.
——— 'L'Esthétique de Béla Bartók.' *La Revue musicale* (Paris), 1955; also in Hungarian, *Új Zenei Szemle* (Budapest), 1955.
Browne, Arthur G. 'Béla Bartók.' *Music and Letters* (London), 1931.
Bull, Eyvind H. 'Béla Bartók Replies to Percy Grainger.' *Music News* (Chicago), 1934.
Bull, Storm. 'Bartók the Teacher.' *Musical Facts* (Chicago), 1941.
——— 'Bartók's Teaching Pieces.' *Repertoire* (Lansing), 1951.
——— 'The Piano Music of Béla Bartók.' *Repertoire* (Lansing), 1951-2.
Calvocoressi, Michael D. 'Béla Bartók, An Introduction.' *Monthly Musical Record* (London), 1922.
——— 'Bartok and Kodály.' *Monthly Musical Record* (London), 1922.
——— 'Hungarian Music of Today.' *Monthly Musical Record* (London), 1922.
Carner, Mosco. 'Bartók's Viola Concerto.' *Musical Times* (London), 1950.
——— 'Béla Bartók.' *The Listener* (London), 1945.
——— 'Problems of Modern Harmonic Evolution.' *Music and Letters* (London), 1941.
Casella, Alfredo. 'In memoriam di Béla Bartók.' *Janus Pannonius* (Rome), 1947.
Chapman, Ernest. 'Béla Bartók, An Estimate and Appreciation.' *Tempo* (London), 1945.
Chapman, Roger E. 'The Fifth Quartet of Béla Bartók.' *Music Review* (Cambridge), 1951.
Collins, Adrian. 'Bartók, Schoenberg, and Some Songs.' *Music and Letters* (London), 1929.
Crankshaw, Geoffrey. 'Bartók and the String Quartet.' *Musical Opinion* (London), 1951.
Demarquez, Suzanne. 'Souvenirs et réflexions.' *La Revue musicale* (Paris), 1955.
Demény, Dezső. 'A kékszakállú herceg vára.' *Zenei Szemle* (Budapest), 1918.
Demény, János. 'Bartók—Dokumentumok Csehszlovákiából.' *Új Zenei Szemle* (Budapest), 1953.
——— 'Bartók "Kossuth"-szimfóniájának programmvázlata.' *Zenei Szemle* (Budapest), 1948.
——— 'The Results and Problems of Bartók Research in Hungary.' *New Hungarian Quarterly* (Budapest), 1961.
Dent, Edward J. 'Béla Bartók.' *The Nation and the Athenaeum* (London), 1922.
——— 'A Hungarian Bluebeard.' *The Nation and the Athenaeum* (London), 1922.
Doflein, Erich. 'A propos des "44 Duos pour deux violons" de Bartók.' *La Revue musicale* (Paris), 1955.
——— 'Bartók und die Musikpädagogik.' *Musik der Zeit* (Bonn), 1952.

────── 'Béla Bartóks Kompositionen für die Musikpädagogik.' *Musik im Unter-
richt* (Mainz), 1955.
Eimert, Herbert. 'Das Violinkonzert von Bartók.' *Muzik der Zeit* (Bonn), 1954.
Engel, Iván. 'A "Mikrokosmos"-ról.' *Zenei Szemle* (Budapest), 1948.
────── 'Ritmus = és tempóváltoztatások egyes Bartók-művekben.' *Új Zenei
Szemle* (Budapest), 1955.
Engelmann, Hans Ulrich. 'Chromatische Ausstufung in Béla Bartóks "Mikrokos-
mos." ' *Melos* (Mainz), 1951.
Farkas, Ferenc. 'Bartók Mikrokosmosa.' *A Zene* (Budapest), 1940.
Foss, Hubert J. 'An Approach to Bartók.' *Musical Opinion* (London), 1944.
Frid, Géza. 'Pleidooi voor de piano composities van Bartók.' *Mens en Melodie*
(Utrecht), 1947.
────── 'Ter herdenking van Béla Bartók.' *Mens en Melodie* (Utrecht), 1946.
Gavazzeni, Gianandrea. 'Béla Bartók.' *La Rassegna musicale* (Rome), 1939.
Gergely, Jean. 'Les Choeurs à cappella de Béla Bartók.' *La Revue musicale*
(Paris), 1955.
Gilman, Lawrence. 'Béla Bartók.' *The Herald Tribune* (New York), 1927.
Goddard, Scott. 'Perspective about Béla Bartók.' *The Listener* (London), 1948.
Gombosi, Ottó. 'Béla Bartók.' *Ungarische Jahrbücher* (Berlin), 1931.
────── 'Béla Bartók, 1881-1945.' *Musical Quarterly* (New York), 1946.
Halperson, Maurice. 'Béla Bartók Explains Himself.' *Musical America* (New
York), 1928.
Haraszti, Emil. 'La Musique de chambre de Béla Bartók.' *La Revue musicale*
(Paris), 1930.
Hawkes, Ralph. 'Béla Bartók, A Recollection by His Publisher.' *Tempo* (Lon-
don), 1949.
Hawthorne, Robin. 'The Fugal Technique of Béla Bartók.' *Music Review* (Cam-
bridge), 1949.
Heinsheimer, Hans W. 'Erinnerungen an Béla Bartók.' *Zeitschrift für Musik*
(Regensburg), 1951.
Helman, Alicja. 'Struktura tonalno-harmoniczna "Bagatel" B. Bartóka.' *Muzyka*
(Warsaw), 1956.
Herbage, Julian. 'Bartók's Violin Concerto.' *Music Review* (Cambridge), 1945.
Hernádi, Lajos. 'Bartók Béla a zongoraművész, a pedagogus, az ember.' *Új Zenei
Szemle* (Budapest), 1953; also in French, *La Revue musicale* (Paris), 1955.
Heseltine, Philip. 'Modern Hungarian Composers.' *Musical Times* (London),
1922.
Heyworth, Peter. 'Bartók's Lost Concerto.' *The Observer* (London), 1960.
Hussey, Dynelcy. 'Béla Bartók and the Hungarian Folksong.' *The Listener* (Lon-
don), 1946.
Jemnitz, Alexander (Sándor). 'Asien und Europa (Bartók Studie).' *Melos*
(Mainz), 1931.
────── 'Bartóks *Cantata profana*: Erstaufführung in Budapest.' *Schweizerische
Musikzeitung* (Zürich), 1937.
────── 'Béla Bartók.' *Musical Quarterly* (New York), 1933.
────── 'Béla Bartók: V. Streichquartett.' *Musica Viva* (Zürich), 1936.
────── 'Der holzgeschnitzte Prinz.' *Signale für die musikalische Welt* (Berlin),
1917.
────── 'Vázlat Bartók Béla arcképéhez.' *A Zene* (Budapest), 1936.
────── 'Der wunderbare Mandarin.' *Melos* (Mainz), 1931.
Kárász, A. 'Béla Bartók et la musique hongroise.' *La Revue européenne* (Paris),
1930.

Katz, Erich. 'Béla Bartók.' *Musikblätter des Anbruch* (Vienna), 1927.
Kerényi, György. 'Bartók, a népdal-lejegyző.' *Ethnographia* (Budapest), 1948.
——— 'Bartók és a népdal.' *A Zene* (Budapest), 1940-41.
——— 'Bartók hangneme.' *Énekszó* (Budapest), 1941.
——— 'Bartók karéneke.' *A Zene* (Budapest), 1938.
Kerényi, Karl. 'Ueber Bartóks *Cantata profana*.' *Schweizerische Musikzeitung* (Zürich), 1946.
Kevei, András. 'Beszélgetések Bartók Béláról Serly Tiborral.' *Zenei Szemle* (Budapest), 1948.
Kisielewski, Stefan. 'Béla Bartók (1881-1945).' *Ruch Muzyczny* (Krakow), 1945.
Klein, Sigmund. 'Béla Bartók, A Portrait.' *Pro Musica* (New York), 1925.
Kodály, Zoltán. 'Bartók Béla az ember.' *Zenei Szemle* (Budapest), 1947.
——— 'Bartók Béla első operája.' *Nyugat* (Budapest), 1918. In German, in *Bartók Weg und Werk*, ed. Szabolcsi; in French, in *Bartók, sa vie et son œuvre*, ed. Szabolcsi.
——— 'Bartók Béla gyermekkarai.' *Énekszó* (Budapest), 1936.
——— 'Bartók Béla II. vonósnégyese—Bartók első operája.' *Nyugat* (Budapest), 1918.
——— 'Bartók és a magyar ifjúság.' *Zenei Szemle* (Budapest), 1948.
——— 'Bartóks Kinderstücke.' *Musikblätter des Anbruch* (Vienna), 1920.
——— 'Béla Bartók.' *La Revue musicale* (Paris), 1921.
——— 'A folklorista Bartók.' *Új Zenei Szemle* (Budapest), 1950. Also in French, in *La Revue musicale* (Paris), 1952.
——— 'New Music for Old.' *Modern Music* (New York), 1925.
——— 'Ungarische Jugend bei Bartók in Schuld.' *Musik der Zeit* (Bonn), 1952.
Kösemihal, M. Ragib. 'Béla Bartók ve esseri.' *Ülkü* (Ankara), 1936.
——— 'B. Bartók aramizda.' *Ülkü* (Ankara), 1937.
Krehl, Stefan. 'Die Dissonanz als musikalisches Ausdrucksmittel.' *Zeitschrift für Musikwissenschaft* (Leipzig), 1919.
Landormy, Paul. 'Schönberg, Bartók, und die französische Musik.' *Musikblätter des Anbruch* (Vienna), 1922.
Landry, Lionel. 'La Musique autogène.' *La Revue musicale* (Paris), 1929.
Láng, Paul Henry. 'Editorial.' *Musical Quarterly* (New York), 1946 [Jan.].
Leibowitz, René. 'Béla Bartók.' *L'Arche* (Paris), 1946-7.
——— 'Béla Bartók, ou la possibilité de compromis dans la musique contemporaine.' *Les Temps modernes* (Paris), 1947. Also in English, in *Transition* (Paris), 1948.
Leichtentritt, Hugo. 'Bartók and the Hungarian Folksong.' *Modern Music* (New York), 1933.
——— 'On the Art of Béla Bartók.' *Modern Music* (New York), 1929.
Lendvai, Ernő. 'Bartók: Az éjszaka zenéje.' *Zenei Szemle* (Budapest), 1947.
——— 'Bartók: "Improvisations" sorozatárol.' *Zenei Szemle* (Budapest), 1947.
——— 'Bartók: Szonáta két zongorára és ütőhangszerekre (1937).' *Zenei Szemle* (Budapest), 1948.
——— 'Der wunderbare Mandarin. (Werkstattgeheimnisse der Pantomime Béla Bartóks).' *Studia musicologica* (Budapest), 1961.
——— 'Duality and Synthesis in the Music of Béla Bartók.' *New Hungarian Quarterly* (Budapest), 1962.
Lesznaj, Lajos. 'Bartók Béla (1881-1945), életrajzi vázlat.' *Zenei Szemle* (Budapest), 1948. Also in German, somewhat abridged, in *Melos* (Mainz), 1949.
Löwenbach, Jan. 'Béla Bartók.' *Tempo* (Prague), 1946.

Maroti, János. 'Tvorcheskie problemy vengerskoy muzyki.' *Sovietskaya muzyka* (Moscow), 1955.
Martynov, Ivan Ivanovich. 'Béla Bartók.' *Sovietskaya muzyka* (Moscow), 1955.
Mason, Colin. 'Bartók Through His Quartets.' Monthly Musical Record (London), 1950.
-———— 'Bartók's Rhapsodies.' *Music and Letters* (London), 1949.
———— 'Béla Bartók and Folksong.' *Music Review* (Cambridge), 1950.
———— 'Bartók's Early Violin Concerto.' *Tempo* (London), 1958.
———— 'An Essay in Analysis, Tonality, Symmetry, and Latent Serialism in Bartók's Fourth Quartet.' *Music Review* (Cambridge), 1957.
de Menasce, Jacques. 'Berg and Bartók.' *Modern Music* (New York), 1944.
———— 'The Classicism of Béla Bartók.' *Modern Music* (New York), 1946.
Mila, Massimo. 'Béla Bartók, il musicista della libertà.' *L'Italia socialista* (Rome), 1948.
———— 'La natura e il mistero nell'arte di Béla Bartók.' *La Rassegna musicale* (Rome), 1951.
Molnár, Antal. 'Adalékok Bartók Béla életrajzához.' *Zenei Szemle* (Budapest), 1947.
———— 'Bartók: A kékszakállú herceg vára.' *Zenei Szemle* (Budapest), 1918.
———— 'Bartók zenekara.' *A Zene* (Budapest), 1940-41.
———— 'Bartók Béla hegedűversenye.' *A Zene* (Budapest), 1939.
———— 'Bartók Béla művészetéről.' *Magyar Zenei Szemle* (Budapest), 1941.
———— 'Bedeutung der *Cantata profana* von Béla Bartók.' *Pester Lloyd* (Budapest), 1936.
———— 'Béla Bartók: Concert für Klavier und Orchester.' *Analyse* (Vienna), 1929.
Moore, Douglas. 'Homage to Bartók.' *Modern Music* (New York), 1946. Also in Polish, in *Ruch Muzyczny* (Krakow), 1947.
Munclinger, Milan. 'Bartókovo "Concerto pro orchestr."' *Tempo* (Prague), 1947.
———— and Ledec, Jan. 'Ještě k Bartókovu "Concertu."' *Tempo* (Prague), 1947.
Nirschy, A. 'Varianten zu Bartóks Pantomime Der wunderbare Mandarin.' *Studia musicologica* (Budapest), 1962.
von der Nüll, Edwin. 'Bartók zenéjének tartalmi és stilusbeli sajátosságai.' *Új Zenei Szemle* (Budapest), 1955.
———— 'Béla Bartók.' *Musikblätter des Anbruch* (Vienna), 1929.
———— 'Béla Bartók: Geist und Stil.' *Melos* (Mainz), 1933.
———— 'Stilelemente in Bartóks Oper "Herzog Blaubarts Burg."' *Melos* (Mainz), 1929.
———— 'Zur Compositionstechnik Bartóks.' *Musikblätter des Anbruch* (Vienna), 1928.
Odriozola, Antonio. 'La bibliografia sobre Béla Bartók y el reciente libro de Halsey Stevens.' *Musica* (Madrid), 1953.
Oláh Gustáv. 'Bartók and the Theatre.' *Tempo* (London), 1949-50.
de Paoli, Domenico. 'Los cuartetos de Béla Bartók.' *Musica* (Madrid), 1953.
Pataki, László (=Pollatsek, Ladislaus). 'Bartók és a néptánc.' *A Zene* (Budapest), 1935.
Perle, George. 'Symmetrical Formations in the String Quartets of Béla Bartók.' *Music Review* (Cambridge), 1955.
Petranu, Coriolan. 'Béla Bartók et la musique roumaine.' *Revue de Transylvanie* (Bucharest), 1937.
———— 'D. Béla Bartók şi muzică românească.' *Gând Românesc* (Cluj), 1936.

———— 'Epilogue de la discussion avec M. Béla Bartók sur la musique roumaine. *Revue de Transylvanie* (Bucharest), 1939.

———— 'Observations en marge des réponses de M. Béla Bartók.' *Revue de Transylvanie* (Bucharest), 1937.

Petyrek, Felix. 'Béla Bartóks Klavierwerke.' *Musikblätter des Anbruch* (Vienna), 1921.

Pleasants, Henry, & Serly, Tibor. 'Bartók's Historic Contribution.' *Modern Music* (New York), 1940.

Pollatsek, Ladislaus. 'Béla Bartók.' *Allgemeine Musikzeitung* (Berlin), 1930.

———— 'Béla Bartók.' *Der Auftakt* (Prague), 1928.

———— 'Béla Bartók and His Work.' *Musical Times* (London), 1931.

———— 'Der Weg Béla Bartóks.' *Schweizerische Musikzeitung* (Zürich), 1929.

Prahács, Margit. 'Bartók Béla.' *Magyar Szemle* (Budapest), 1941.

———— 'Bartók Béláról idegen nyelvcken megjelent cikkek és tanulmányok jegyzéke.' *Zenei Szemle* (Budapest), 1948.

———— 'Bartók bemutató—Musik für Saiteninstrumente, Schlagzeug und Celesta.' *A Zene* (Budapest), 1937-8.

———— 'Bartók Keleteuropa zeneszerzője.' *A Zene* (Budapest), 1940-41.

———— 'Népzene és nemzet.' *Magyar Szemle* (Budapest), 1935.

Rands, Bernard. 'The Use of Canon in Bartók's Quartets.' *Music Review* (Cambridge), 1957.

Reich, Willi. 'In Memoriam Béla Bartók.' *Schweizerische Musikzeitung* (Zürich), 1945.

Révész, Mrs. Antal. 'Bartók zongoraszvitjének kiadatlan tétele.' *Új Zenei Szemle* (Budapest), 1955.

Roiha, Aino. 'Béla Bartók.' *Työväen Musikkikehti* (Helsinki), 1948.

Romero, Hector Manuel. 'La herencia musical de Bartók.' *Orientacion musical* (Mexico City), 1947.

Rostand, Claude. 'Béla Bartók: chemins et contrastes du musicien.' *Contrepoints* (Paris), 1946.

Rothe, Friede F. 'The Language of the Composer.' *Etude* (Philadelphia), 1941.

Sabin, Robert. 'Revolution and Tradition in the Music of Bartók.' *Musical America* (New York), 1949.

Sacher, Paul. 'Béla Bartók zum Gedächtnis.' *Schweizerische Musikzeitung* (Zürich), 1945.

Saminsky, Lazare. 'Bartók and the Graphic Current in Music.' *Musical Quarterly* (New York), 1924.

———— 'Schoenberg and Bartók, Pathbreakers.' *Modern Music* (New York), 1924.

Saygun, A. Adnan. 'Bartók in Turkey.' *Musical Quarterly* (New York), 1951.

Schloezer, Boris de. 'A propos de Béla Bartók.' *Fontaine* (Paris), 1947.

———— 'Béla Bartók: History vs. Esthetics.' *Transition* (Paris), 1948.

———— 'Béla Bartók i Manuel de Falla.' *Ruch Muzyczny* (Krakow), 1947.

———— 'Nota su Béla Bartók.' *La Rassegna musicale* (Rome), 1948.

Schuh, Willi. 'Bartóks Basler Auftragswerke: Musik für Saiteninstrumente; Klavier-Schlagzeug-Sonata.' *Musik der Zeit* (Bonn), 1954; also in Schuh: *Béla Bartók*.

Schulhoff, Erwin. 'Das neue Clavierspiel: Béla Bartók der bedeutendste der jungungarischen-rumänischen Richtung.' *Der Auftakt* (Prague), 1924.

Seefried, Irmgard. 'Meine Wege zu Hindemith und Bartók.' *Oesterreichische Musikzeitschrift* (Vienna), 1954.

Seiber, Mátyás. 'Béla Bartók.' *Monthly Musical Record* (London), 1945.

——— 'Béla Bartók's Chamber Music.' *Tempo* (London), 1949.
Steinberger, Gábor. 'Béla Bartók.' *Revista musical Chilena* (Santiago), 1946.
Stevens, Denis. 'A Note on Bartók's Viola Concerto.' *Musical Survey* (London), 1950.
Stevens, Halsey. 'A Bartók Bibliography.' *Tempo* (London), 1949-50.
——— 'Pótlás a Zenei Szemle 1948 decemberi számában megjelent Bartók-bibliográfiához.' *Énekszó* (Budapest), 1950.
Stuckenschmidt, Hans. 'Béla Bartók.' *Die Sendung* (Berlin), 1930.
——— 'Urbanität und Volksliedgeist. Ueber Béla Bartók.' *Der Monat* (Berlin-Dahlem), 1953.
Szabó, Ferenc. 'Bartók nem alkuszik.' *Új Zenei Szemle* (Budapest), 1950.
Szabolcsi, Bence. 'Bartók és a népzene.' *Új Zenei Szemle* (Budapest), 1950.
——— 'Béla Bartók.' *Corvina* (Budapest), 1946.
——— 'Eastern Relations of Early Hungarian Folk-music.' *Journal of the Royal Asiatic Society* (London), 1935.
——— 'Két arckép: Bartók Béla és Kodály Zoltán.' *Alkotás* (Budapest), 1947. Also in Swedish, in *Musik Världen*, 1948.
——— 'Liszt and Bartók.' *New Hungarian Quarterly* (Budapest), 1961.
——— 'Man and Nature in Bartók's World.' *New Hungarian Quarterly* (Budapest), 1961.
——— 'Le Mandarin miraculeux.' *Studia musicologica* (Budapest), 1961.
——— 'Nowe dziela Bartóka s Kodályego.' *Muzyka* (Warsaw), 1927.
Székely, Endre. 'Bartók Béla.' *Éneklő Munkás* (Budapest), 1947.
Szelényi, István. 'Bartók stiluskorszakai.' *Zenei Szemle* (Budapest), 1947.
——— 'Új könyv Bartókról.' *Új Zenei Szemle* (Budapest), 1954.
Szervánszky, Endre. 'Stílusáltozások Bartók zenéjében.' *Új Zenei Szemle* (Budapest), 1955.
Szigeti, Joseph. 'A Tribute to Bartók.' *Tempo* (London), 1948-9.
Thyne, Stuart. 'Bartók's "Improvisations": An Essay in Technical Analysis.' *Music and Letters* (London), 1950.
Tóth, Aladár. 'Bartók Béla.' *Zenei Szemle* (Budapest), 1927.
——— 'Bartók új vonósnégyesei.' *Zenei Szemle* (Budapest), 1929.
——— 'Das neue Klavierkonzert von Béla Bartók.' *Pult und Taktstock* (Vienna), 1928.
Tóth, Dénes. 'Bartók és az expresszionizmus.' *A Zene* (Budapest), 1940-41.
Treitler, Leo. 'Harmonic Procedure in the Fourth Quartet of Béla Bartók.' *Journal of Music Theory* (New Haven), 1959.
Tryon, Winthrop P. 'How Bartók Composes.' *Christian Science Monitor* (Boston), 1927.
Újfalussy, József. 'A Bartók Béla Szövetség pünkösdi dalosünnepségeinek mérlege.' *Zenei Szemle* (Budapest), 1949.
Unger, Hermann. 'Der wunderbare Mandarin in Köln.' *Der Auftakt* (Prague), 1925.
Vancea, Zeno. 'Influenţa melosului popular asupra creaţiei lui Béla Bartók.' *Muzica* (Bucharest), 1956.
Veress, Sándor. 'Bartók Béla hegedüversenye.' *Magyar Csillag* (Budapest), 1944.
——— 'Bluebeard's Castle.' *Tempo*, (London), 1949-50.
——— '-Indførelse i Béla Bartóks strygekvartetter.' *Dansk Musiktidsskrift* (Copenhagen), 1951.
Vinton, John. 'The Case of *The Miraculous Mandarin*.' *Musical Quarterly* (New York), 1964.

Volek, Jaroslav. 'Nad partiturou velkého dila. Béla Bartók: Koncert pro orchestr.' *Rytmus* (Prague), 1947.
——— 'Jěstě'k Bartókovu "Koncertu." ' *Rytmus* (Prague), 1947.
Wagenaar, Bernard. 'Bartók's Quartets.' *The New York Times* (New York), 1949.
Weissmann, John S. (János). 'Bartók: An Estimate.' *Music Review* (Cambridge), 1946.
——— 'Bartók and Folk Music.' *Monthly Musical Record* (London), 1957.
——— 'Bartók művészi fejlődése és a III. zongoraverseny.' *Zenei Szemle* (Budapest), 1948.
——— 'Bartóks Klaviermusik.' *Musik der Zeit* (Bonn), 1952; *Melos* (Mainz), 1953; in French, *Feuilles musicales* (Lausanne), 1950.
——— 'Bartók's Piano Music.' *Tempo* (London), 1949-50.
——— 'Béla Bartók and Folk Music.' *Keynote* (London), 1946. Also in German, in *Melos* (Mainz), 1949.
——— 'Notes Concerning Bartók's Solo Vocal Music.' *Tempo* (London), 1955-6.
Wellesz, Egon. 'Die Streichquartette von Béla Bartók.' *Musikblätter des Anbruch* (Vienna), 1920.
Westphal, Kurt. 'Béla Bartók und die moderne ungarische Musik.' *Die Musik* (Stuttgart-Berlin), 1927.
Whitaker, Frank. 'A Visit to Béla Bartók.' *Musical Times* (London), 1926.
Woerters, Jos. 'De contrapunttechnik van Béla Bartók.' *Mens en Melodie* (Utrecht), 1958.
Wolff, Hellmuth Christian. 'Béla Bartók und die Musik der Gegenwart.' *Melos* (Mainz), 1952.
——— 'Béla Bartóks "Holzgeschnitzter Prinz" und seine Beziehungen zu Igor Strawinsky.' *Musik der Zeit* (Bonn), 1952.
——— 'Der "Mikrokosmos" von Béla Bartók.' *Musica* (Cassel), 1951.
Zimmerreimer, Kurt. 'Der Stil Béla Bartóks.' *Musica* (Cassel), vol. 1.